BULBS

The Bulbous Plants of Europe
and their allies

BULBS

The Bulbous Plants of Europe
and their allies

Christopher Grey-Wilson
Brian Mathew

Illustrated by
Marjorie Blamey

Line drawings by
Christopher Grey-Wilson

COLLINS
ST JAMES'S PLACE, LONDON, S.W.I

William Collins Sons & Co Ltd
London · Glasgow · Sydney · Auckland
Toronto · Johannesburg

First published 1981
© C. Grey-Wilson, B. Mathew, M. Blamey, 1981
ISBN 0 00 219211 X
Filmset by Jolly & Barber Ltd, Rugby
Colour reproduction by Heraclio Fournier, Vitoria, Spain
Made and printed by William Collins Sons and Co Ltd, Glasgow

Contents

Daffodil Family *Amaryllidaceae* 129

Iris Family *Iridaceae* 152

Arum Family *Araceae* 191

Orchid Family *Orchidaceae* 199

Colour Plates

Acknowledgements

We are very grateful to the following for help and advice on
various aspects of this book – Phillip Cribb, Tony Hall, Brian
Halliwell, Desmond Meikle and Jeffrey Wood all from the
Royal Botanic Gardens, Kew, Chris Brickell, the Director of
the Royal Horticultural Society's Garden, Wisley, and Martyn
Rix. Special thanks to Philip Blamey for a great deal of help
on many aspects of this book. Finally special thanks must go
to Professor J. P. M. Brenan, the Director of the Royal
Botanic Gardens, Kew, for permission to use the facilities of
the Gardens, especially the Herbarium and Library, during
the preparation of this work.

INTRODUCTION

The idea of writing a guide to the bulbous flora of Europe took place slowly, perhaps over a period of two or three years. There were already numerous good guides to European plants which included the bulbous species, though often missing all but the commoner ones, and yet surprisingly there was no work dealing solely with this subject. At the same time we felt rather apprehensive about the project, for after all was it not just another way of presenting old information and how useful would such a guide really be?

Two things became clear. Firstly the guide could be more than just a field guide but could, at the same time, be a guide to both the gardener and the grower to whom many of these plants have a great deal of appeal. If one thinks of daffodils, tulips, crocuses and snowdrops then it is clear that this is so. Secondly with the completion of *Flora Europaea* there was a chance to produce a standardised work based unashamedly on that account, but far less technical in detail and with the addition of illustrations.

The first thing that the reader will ask is 'What is a bulbous plant?'. The gardener can be excused for including under such a vague title any plant with a bulb, corm or tuber and in the past, apart from typical examples like the daffodil and tulip, there was included a miscellany of unrelated species ranging from

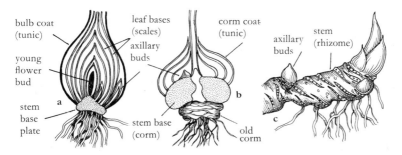

Differences between **(a)** a bulb, **(b)** a corm and **(c)** a rhizome can be easily observed. All are storage organs, the bulb consisting of overlapping fleshy leaf bases, the corm a swollen stem base and a rhizome a swollen fleshy horizontal stem

Anemones to Cyclamen and Corydalis. However, we decided on a much stricter approach and to include only what are technically referred to as the Petaloid Monocotyledons and their closest allies which all possess petals or petal-like structures. Hence all the European Monocotyledons are included with the exception of the Sedges and Rushes which would in any case require an additional volume. Although many of the species included are truly bulbous or tuberous, others have no swollen underground organs even though they are closely related. However they are included for the sake of completeness.

The area covered by the book includes the whole of Europe and European Russia together with the Azores and Iceland. In the Mediterranean the large islands of Sardinia, Corsica, Sicily, Crete, together with the Balearic Isles (Minorca and Majorca) and the many islands of the Aegean are included. The eastern boundary heads north-east from the Bosphorus across the Black Sea, following a line south of the Crimea to the north shore of the Caspian Sea, from where it turns north following the Ural Mountains along the 60°E longitude (see Map, p.13). The following broad divisions have been recognised for convenience. (1) N.W. Europe: Britain, Ireland, Iceland, Scandinavia, Denmark, Holland, Belgium and N. France. (2) N.E. Europe: Finland and the northern part of European Russia. (3) Central Europe: Germany, Poland, Czechoslovakia, Switzerland, Austria and Hungary. (4) E. Europe: Central and Southern European Russia including the Crimea. (5) S.W. Europe: Central and S. France, Spain, Portugal and the Balearic Isles. (6) S.E. Europe: Corsica, Sardinia, Sicily, Italy, Yugoslavia, Bulgaria, Roumania, Greece and the islands of the Aegean Sea. (7) S. Europe: S.W. and S.E. Europe as defined in 5 and 6 above. If the species is confined to the Mediterranean Region then this is stated instead of S. Europe.

Descriptions. Fairly full descriptions are given for most species, stressing important diagnostic features in *italics* where these help to distinguish a particular species from its closest allies. A minimum of measurements is given except to help distinguish a plant or to give it a scale. Each text description includes a certain amount of standardised information such as flowering time, habitat and distribution and these follow on after the description of the plant.

Family and generic descriptions are given throughout and in general this information is not repeated under the species description in order to avoid repetition. They should therefore be read carefully in conjunction with one another. Family and generic descriptions refer only to the species covered in the text and will not always apply to those found outside the boundaries of Europe.

Common names. Recognised and familiar common names are included in most cases though no attempt has been made to produce one if it does not already exist.

Scientific names in Latin follow, as far as possible, those of *Flora Europaea* which has done a good deal to standardise their use. At the same time important well known synonyms are presented in parentheses immediately after the correct name for each plant – for example *Narcissus requienii* (= *N. juncifolius*). *Flora Europaea* does not include variations below the rank of subspecies (subsp. in the text), but where varieties (var.) are considered significant these are also included.

Number. Where a genus consists of two or more species these are numbered in sequence – **1, 2, 3** and so on. Subspecies and varieties of a particular species are given the same number together with a small letter – **2a, 2b**. Closely related species come next to each other in the text and are often referred to each other to bring out their distinctions – for example '**5.** *Tulipa goulimyi* like (**4**) but . . .'. Besides these numbers, species illustrated are referred to by plate number, this occurring in brackets after the species name – for example *Lilium pyrenaicum* [3] is on plate 3.

Plant height. Following the pattern laid out by *The Wildflowers of Britain and Northern Europe* by R. & A. Fitter and M. Blamey, plant height unless otherwise stated is as follows:

low	0 – 10cm
short	10 – 30cm
medium	30 – 60cm
tall	60cm or over

The glossary at the end of the book (p.269) explains terms such as lanceolate, raceme, spike, spathe and scape which are descriptive terms used to denote certain characteristics of plants.

Flower shape is particularly important in identifying Monocotyledonous genera. Generally if the flowers open widely then their diameters are given, but if they are bell shaped or tubular then the length is stated instead. In most orchids the length of the lip is given rather than the diameter of the whole flower. It is also important to note whether or not the sepals and petals are free from one another or fused for part (as in the Hyacinth) or the whole of their length (as in Grape Hyacinths). When both sepals and petals are all alike then they are referred to as tepals.

Flower colour can be very uniform within a species or it may vary as it does in some crocuses. White flowered forms or albinos occur in many species which are normally coloured, but they are generally uncommon amongst the many normal ones.

Flowering time covers the species over its whole distribution. Thus in the northern part of its range a particular plant will normally be found in flower later than its counterpart in the south. At the same time typical mountain plants like the Spring Crocus of the Alps, *Crocus vernus*, will be found in flower earlier at lower altitudes than higher up the mountain in the same district. Late lying snow may also retard flowering for weeks.

Habitat is often an important clue to identification as some species are restricted to only a single type of habitat – for example several of the Tongue Orchids, *Serapias*, are found almost exclusively on coastal sandy areas of the Mediterranean region. In addition some plants prefer calcareous soils whilst others prefer neutral or acid ones. Many bulbous plants grow in areas which have a long dry summer, as is typical of much of southern Europe. Here, after flowering early in the year, the leaves die down during the summer and the plants remain dormant below ground throughout this unfavourable season until the autumnal rains commence. They then either flower in the autumn, or, as in the majority of species, wait until the following spring.

Distribution is presented in two ways. Firstly the general area covered by a particular species is given as outlined on p.10 – for example S.W. Europe. Then this is qualified by giving the countries in which it actually occurs by the use of large coded letters which follow, as far as it is possible, the internationally recognised country codes for the country concerned – CH for Switzerland, I for Italy and so on. This is aided by the use of a subsidiary code (in small lettering) to indicate occurrence in part of a country:

n – north	*e* – east	*c* – central
s – south	*w* – west	

A	Austria	H	Hungary
AEG	Aegean Islands	I	Italy
AL	Albania	IRL	Republic of Ireland
AZ	Azores	IS	Iceland
B	Belgium	K	Krym (Crimea)
BAL	Balearic Isles	M	Malta
BG	Bulgaria	N	Norway
CH	Switzerland	NL	Netherlands
CO	Corsica	P	Portugal
CR	Crete	PL	Poland
CS	Czechoslovakia	R	Roumania
D	Germany	RS	Russia
DK	Denmark	S	Sweden
E	Spain	SA	Sardinia
F	France	SC	Sicily
FA	Faroes	SF	Finland
GB	Great Britain	TR	Turkey (European)
GBG	Gibraltar	YU	Yugoslavia
GR	Greece – excluding the Aegean Islands (AEG)		

T indicates that the species occurs throughout the area covered by the book unless otherwise qualified.

Thus for example, A, CH, *s*D, *n*I, *nw*YU indicates that the species in question is

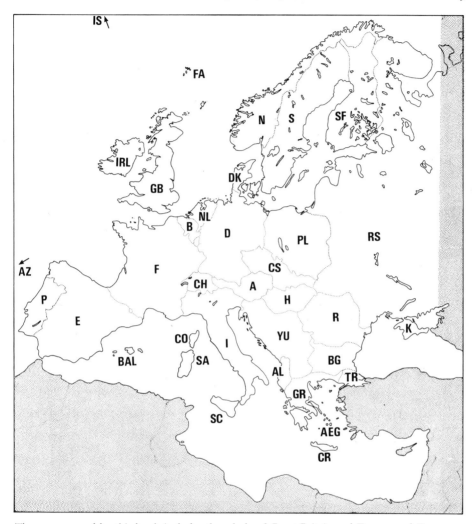

The area covered by this book includes the whole of Great Britain and Europe and European Russia including the Crimea. The Azores and Iceland are also included. The stippled zone on the map is not covered (North Africa, Turkey and the Middle East), however, if a particular species in the text overlaps into the stippled zone then its total distribution is referred to for sake of completeness. The distribution code (country symbols) are opposite.

found in Austria, Switzerland, southern Germany, northern Italy and north-west Yugoslavia; T – except GB, IRL indicates that the plant occurs throughout Europe except for Great Britain and Ireland.

Rarity is indicated by an asterisk * if the plant is considered to be very restricted.

Naturalised or introduced species are shown in parentheses and this may cover all or only a part of their range in Europe – for example E, P (F) indicates that the species is native to Spain and Portugal but introduced to France.

Altitude is indicated wherever possible, however, it should only be taken as an approximation. Thus '500–900m' indicates that the plant in question is usually found growing wild between 500 and 900m, whereas, 'to 900m' indicates that the plant can be found from sea level up to 900m altitude. Naturalised plants may often be found at uncharacteristic altitudes.

The illustrations have been drawn as far as possible from living specimens. Unless otherwise indicated all plants are painted life size. Over 400 are illustrated in colour and many others in black and white.

A * indicates that the species is widely cultivated and is readily obtainable in the horticultural trade. A ●, on the other hand, indicates that the plant is cultivated, in botanic gardens or private collections but is not generally obtainable.

Line drawings in the text generally include a scale, $\times 1$, $\times \frac{1}{2}$ for instance, to indicate their size in relation to the true size of the living plant. An fr. indicates fruit, otherwise drawings are of flowers.

Botanical keys. These are provided to help the identification of genera in all the major families in this book. Besides these, many important genera have keys to enable individual species to be recognised. The keys are mostly 'bracketed' so that each pair of contrasting characters has a number, these leading in turn to other brackets further down the key, or directly to the identification of a particular genus or species. e.g.

1.	Flowers yellow	2
	Flowers pink or red	4
2.	Leaves linear	*Sternbergia*, p.137
	Leaves heart-shaped	3
3.	Etc.	

Keys are not provided to identify species in orchid genera as they would be unnecessarily long and complicated. Instead each species has a line drawing of an individual flower next to its description in the text to aid identification.

A pictorial key is provided on p.22 to help those not acquainted with botanical keys. This works by simply comparing the drawings of flower or leaf shape with the live specimen. The drawings are supplemented by simple botanical phrases.

In addition there are some quick identification features to familiarise readers with the major families included in this book, p.23.

There are a number of botanical terms which refer especially to Monocotyledons, such as bulb, corm, fall, scape, speculum, standard, tepal and tunic. These are all explained in the Glossary at the end of the book. This begins on page 269.

What is a Monocotyledon?

The world of seed-bearing plants, or Spermatophytes, is divided into two broad groups, those in which the seeds are naked and those with seeds encased in a protective coat or coats. The first, relatively small group, known as the Gymno-sperms, contains those plants which we loosely refer to as the conifers such as Pine, Juniper, Fir, Spruce and Yew and numbers perhaps five hundred species.

The second group, the Angiosperms, or flowering plants, is much larger and the estimates of the number of species vary around 130,000. It is a part of this group which concerns us here. Fortunately it is possible to split this vast number of flowering plants into lesser groups and in the first instance there are again two clearly defined divisions known as Dicotyledons and Monocotyledons, the second of which is the smaller but which contains the most important family of plants on earth, the Grass family or Gramineae.

The embryo of any flowering plant, upon developing, produces cotyledons or seed-leaves before the young plant begins to take on its final form with properly developed leaves. The runner bean produces two seed-leaves and is therefore known as a 'dicotyledon' whereas the onion seed upon germinating produces only one thread-like cotyledon and is a 'monocotyledon'. Thus our major division is fairly simple but it is possible to add other features to 'strengthen' these differences. Monocotyledons on the whole have parallel veins in their leaves and their flower parts are in threes or multiples of three, whereas Dicotyledons usually have a network of veins (think of a tree leaf skeleton in winter) and their flower parts are usually in fives or less commonly fours. Although there are exceptions, the monocotyledon leaf is quite frequently narrow and grass-like, or strap-shaped or sword-shaped.

Within the Monocotyledons the groups of families are less well defined but it is possible to separate them for the purposes of a book such as this, and for horticulturalists, into those whose flowers are without petals to which grasses, sedges and rushes belong and those with petals which are often rather showy. This latter group of plants have become traditionally and rather affectionately known by their followers as the 'Petaloid Monocots' and it is the European representatives of these which we are describing in this book. The most well-known of the families in this group are the numerous and bizarre orchids belonging to the *Orchidaceae* family, the *Liliaceae* (Lily, Bluebell, Onion, Solomon's Seal etc.), *Iridaceae* (Iris, Crocus, Gladiolus etc.) and *Amaryllidaceae* (Narcissus, Snowdrop, Snowflake etc.). Besides these there are a few other less well-known families in Europe such as the *Alismataceae* which contains some attractive water plants like the Arrowhead and Water Plantains, *Butomaceae* to which the lovely Flowering Rush belongs and the *Hydrocharitaceae* which includes

Frogbit and that extraordinary plant the Water Soldier which is submerged or floating at different times of the year.

In addition we have applied the law of author's licence to include the *Araceae* or Arum family which contains the Cuckoo Pint or Lords and Ladies, which although not petaloid is a monocotyledon and does have a showy spathe or hood which surrounds and protects many flowers inside.

Other Plants. Readers may well be interested in a wider range of plants than those included in this book. Many of the habitats in which 'bulbous' plants are found also include an exciting range of other flowering plants. The following books, which are all well illustrated, will help in the identification of many of these:

Fitter, R., Fitter, A. & Blamey, M. (1974). *The Wild Flowers of Britain and Northern Europe*. Collins.

Grey-Wilson, C. & Blamey, M. (1979). *The Alpine Flowers of Britain and Europe*. Collins. A companion to the volume above.

Huxley, A. & Polunin, O. (1965). *Flowers of the Mediterranean*. Chatto & Windus.

Polunin, O. (1980). *Flowers of Greece and the Balkans*. Oxford University Press.

Polunin, O. & Smythies, B. E. (1973). *Flowers of South-west Europe*. Oxford University Press.

Cultivation of European Bulbs

On the whole the bulbous plants from Europe are fairly easy to grow providing a few simple rules are obeyed. It must be remembered that many monocotyledons and especially those with bulbs, corms or rhizomes have evolved this way in order to overcome a difficult period of drought during the summer. Thus they can go dormant during this period and survive through it in the form of a swollen storage organ and then spring to life again with the onset of rains in the autumn, or after the winter snows have receded. Quite a number of species of *Crocus* and *Colchicum* from the more southerly, milder parts of Europe have become autumn-flowering, their growth triggered into action by the cooler and damper atmosphere of autumn. In very mild areas where frosts and snow are rare these plants often have their leaves present with the flowers, but some species, mainly those from higher altitudes, flower without leaves. The leaves are then produced in the spring after the danger of frosts is past, and later still the capsules and seeds are formed.

The more conventional alternative to this is for the plant to stay dormant right through from the summer drought and cold winter until spring, and then produce flowers, leaves and seeds fairly quickly in spring before the onset of dry conditions once more.

Some monocotyledons such as snowdrops and bluebells inhabit shady or damp places and do not have hot sunny conditions to tolerate in the summer.

For their successful cultivation it is therefore of some importance to have a knowledge of the sort of conditions to which the various species are subjected in their wild state. From this we can decide whether or not they can be grown in a garden, far removed from their natural habitats and whether out-of-doors or with some form of protection.

It is of course quite impossible to give cultivation details for each species, for this will differ from country to country, region to region and even from one garden to another a few miles apart.

There are however, a few generalisations which can be made. For example, very tiny species, such as *Leucojum roseum*, are best grown in a pot where they can be seen and admired in close proximity rather than planted out and lost among other more robust plants. Species from low levels in the Mediterranean region are unlikely to be hardy in northern European and British gardens so should be given either an extremely sheltered place or protection in the form of a greenhouse or frame. High alpine species which inhabit cool mountain pastures are unlikely to thrive when brought to a sunbaked lowland garden and woodland plants such as snowdrops will tend to dwindle if planted in full sun on a light sandy soil. Positions must therefore be chosen where they will be protected from

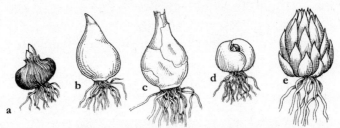

Some typical 'bulbs': **a**, Crocus corm; **b**, Tulip bulb; **c**, Daffodil bulb; **d**, Fritillary bulb; **e**, Lily bulb

any fierce heat and where the soil does not dry out excessively in the summer. On the other hand a great many bulbs inhabit open sunbaked hillsides in Mediterranean districts and these must be given a dry, warm rest period in summer when brought into our gardens. Thus, if our gardening is carried out in an area which has damp or cool summers then some provision must be made to cover the bulbs with glass or plastic in order to keep off the rain or to trap the sun's rays and raise the soil temperature. A frame devoted to bulbs is very satisfactory in this respect, for it can be covered with frame lights in the summer, then uncovered in autumn when it becomes necessary to start the bulbs into growth.

A cool greenhouse or alpine house probably provides the most satisfactory method of growing the more rare species as they can be kept in pots and treated according to their needs and regardless of outside weather conditions. If we have a particularly rare plant it is probably better to treat it in this way until there are a few spare bulbs to try in the garden.

So, to sum up, before attempting to cultivate a particular bulbous plant, especially if it is an uncommon one, find out where and under what conditions it grows in the wild and then attempt to reproduce these by artificial means.

The most effective way to distribute rare plants widely in cultivation is undoubtedly by seeds passed onto friends who are likely to succeed with them. If you do not already have a circle of correspondents it is probably best to send any surplus seeds to one of the specialist societies, such as the Alpine Garden Society and the Scottish Rock Garden Club, for their annual seed distributions. In this way the more uncommon species can be made available to a wider number of people and the risk of losing them from gardens will be lessened. Above all, please try to avoid being one of the fortunately small band of 'enthusiasts' who acquire rarities in order that they can boast sole possession of such and such a plant: this attitude can only lead to a plant's eventual loss to cultivation.

Finally let us make a plea. If you do collect any wild species of bulb, please make an attempt to propagate it, preferably by seed, and distribute it among friends. If all species were common in cultivation and readily available from nurserymen there would be little point in collecting any more from their natural habitats. This is very necessary if they are to survive the other pressures such as the ever increasing demand on their environment for building: by all means rescue those which are about to disappear under the tracks of a bulldozer but leave those in wild places which are in no danger of destruction or you will be the destroyer.

Conservation

Many of the plants referred to in this book have large and colourful flowers, and quite a few are good garden plants. For this reason there is a great temptation to dig them up in the wild and transport them back to one's garden. We do make a plea here – PLEASE DO NOT DIG UP ANY PLANT IN THE WILD, especially bulbous species. Leave them so that everyone can enjoy their beauty. By all means take a seed or two if they are available, otherwise leave well alone. Plants do not appreciate being dug up in full flower, instead why not capture them on film and then you will have a far longer lasting pleasure.

It should be borne in mind that most European countries now have laws which prevent the digging up of various wild plants, or indeed the uprooting of any wild plant. Many of the species described in this book come under these laws, especially the orchids. There are national parks and reserves to protect wild species of plants, as well as animals, in most countries. It may also be an offence to import or export wild live plants.

Left alone these beautiful plants will continue to flower and flourish. Uprooted and then planted in gardens their lives are often short.

Many of the finest European bulbous plants and their allies are available from the horticultural trade and there are numerous specialist nurseries in Europe selling many of the species. These cultivars and species have been cultivated and proven over the years and are the best to grow. For relatively little expenditure one can buy a whole host of exciting species, and know at the same time that one is not damaging wild populations. Many of these plants deserve wider cultivation, so make every effort to propagate them and distribute them among friends and fellow gardeners.

We have tried as far as possible in the text to identify species by their above ground characteristics. Using the descriptions provided in conjunction with the illustrations, details of habitat, distribution and flowering time, it is possible to name nearly all the species in this book accurately. It is rarely neccessary to resort to digging up a plant to examine characteristics of the rootstock or other features hidden beneath the soil surface.

Pictorial Identification of Genera

FLOWERS IN DENSE HEADS OR UMBELS

Onions p.73,
Nectaroscordium p.72,
Flowering Rush p.28

FLOWERS ARUM-LIKE

Arum Family p.191

FLOWERS CROCUS-LIKE

With 3 stamens
   Long flower-tube
   Short flower-tube

Crocus p.173
Sand Crocus p.170

With 6 stamens
   Yellow flowers, autumn flowering
   White, pink or purple flowers

Sternbergias p.137

   Tepals separate

Merendera p.66

   Tepals joined below into a tube
      Flowers with 1 style
      Flowers with 3 styles

Bulbocodium p.67
Colchicum p.56,
Androcymbium p.65

FLOWERS IRIS-LIKE

Leaves square, flowers green and black

Widow Iris p.166

Leaves linear, sword-shaped or channelled,
flowers white, blue, yellow or purple

Irises p.153,
Gynandriris p.165

FLOWERS ASYMETRIC, CURVED, BORNE IN   Gladiolus p.167
LONG SPIKES

 FLOWERS DAFFODIL-LIKE WITH A CENTRAL CUP OR
TRUMPET (CORONA)
 Stamens inside the corona   Daffodils and
Narcissi p.140
 Stamens on edge of corona   Sea Lilies p.139

 FLOWERS ERECT BELLS   Tulips p.40

FLOWERS TRUMPET-SHAPED
 Flowers yellow   Day Lily p.39
Flowers white
Stems leafy   Madonna Lily p.37

Stems leafless   St Bruno's Lily p.68
 Flowers orange or red, erect   Orange Lily p.37

 FLOWERS TURK'S CAP-SHAPED
Stems long and leafy   Lilies p.35
Stems short and leafless   Dog's Tooth
Violet p.40

 FLOWERS DROOPING, BELL OR LANTERN-SHAPED

Stems leafy

 Flowers broad bells or lanterns,
green, brownish or purple   Fritillaries p.48
Flowers narrow tubular bells, white   Solomon's Seals p.117

Stems scapose, without leaves
　　Flowers white or pale pink　　　　　　Snowdrops p.130,
　　　　　　　　　　　　　　　　　　Snowflakes p.133
　　Flowers green or brownish　　　　　　Dipcadi p.116,
　　　　　　　　　　　　　　　　　　Bellevalia p.111,
　　　　　　　　　　　　　Grape Hyacinths p.113

　　Flowers pink, blue, violet or blackish　　Bluebells p.107,
　　　　　　　　　　　　　　　Grape Hyacinths p.113,
　　　　　　　　　　　　　　　　　　Brimeura p.110,
　　　　　　　　　　　　　　　　　　Bellevalia p.111

FLOWERS STAR-SHAPED, WITH 6 TEPALS
(Herb Paris with 4, p.120)
　　Flowers blue or occasionally pink　　Blue-eyed Grass p.167,
　　　　　　　　　　　　　　　　　Aphyllanthes p.123,
　　　　　　　　　　　　　　Glory of the Snow p.101,
　　　　　　　　　　　　　　　　　　Scillas p.101,
　　　　　　　　　　　　　　　Italian Bluebell p.108
　　Flowers yellow or greenish-yellow　　Asphodels p.70,
　　　　　　　　　　　　　　　　Bog Asphodel p.122
　　　　　　　　　　　　　Eremurus spectabilis p.72,
　　　　　　　　　　　　　　　　　　Gageas p.97,
　　　　　　　　　　　　　　　　　　Tofieldia p.121
　　Flowers basically white　　　　　　Asphodels p.70, 71
　　　　　　　　　　　　　　　　　　Simethis p.69,
　　　　　　　　　　　　　　St Bernard's Lily p.69,
　　　　　　　　　　　　　　　　Ornithogalums p.91
　　Flowers green or blackish　　　　　　White and Black
　　　　　　　　　　　　　　False Helleborines p.118

FLOWERS WITH 3 SEPALS AND 3 PETALS　Waterplant families
　　　　　　　　　　　　　　　　　　　　pp.25–30

FLOWERS WITH A DISTINCT LIP,　　　　　　Orchids
USUALLY IN SPIKES　　　　　　　　　pp.199–267

LEAVES NEEDLE-SHAPED, OFTEN IN　　Asparagus p.124
SMALL BUNCHES

LEAVES HEART-SHAPED
Climbing plants

Black Bryony p.30,
Smilax p.128,
Yams p.30

Dwarf plants

Arums p.194,
May Lily p.123

LEAVES ARROW-SHAPED

Arums p.194,
Arrowhead p.27

LEAVES HAND-LIKE WITH 10 OR MORE LEAFLETS

Dracunculus p.197

Quick Identification of Major Families

Flowers with 3 distinct sepals and 3 petals, water plants

Butomaceae p.25
Hydrocharitaceae p.28
Alismataceae p.28

Flowers with a distinct lip and an inferior ovary

Orchidaceae p.199

Flowers with 6 tepals, 6 stamens and a superior ovary

Liliaceae p.31

Flowers with 6 tepals, 6 stamens and an inferior ovary

Amaryllidaceae p.129

Flowers with 6 tepals, 3 stamens and an inferior ovary

Iridaceae p.152

Flowers with a spathe and spadix, arum-like

Araceae p.191

Water Plantain Family ALISMATACEAE

Perennial aquatic or waterside plants, mostly rooting into the mud but some-times floating. Leaves submerged, floating or held above the water, mostly narrowly to broadly lanceolate but in some species arrow-shaped or elliptical. Flowers white or lilac-pink, usually with three conspicuous petals and three smaller sepals; sometimes the male and female flowers separate. Stamens usually six, but in *Sagittaria* more. Fruit consists of a cluster of nutlets or a group of small capsules.

An attractive family of water or water-margin plants. Species are often very variable because they can be amphibious; plants growing in water usually have long ribbon-like submerged leaves as well as the more characteristically shaped floating or aerial leaves, whilst land plants are generally dwarfer with thicker leaves.

BALDELLIA

1. Lesser Water Plantain *Baldellia ranunculoides* (*B. repens*) [1]   Short hairless perennial to 25cm tall, clump forming or sometimes creeping and rooting from the axils. Leaves basal, *narrowly lanceolate or narrowly elliptical*, tapered at the base, up to 12cm long, held well above water on long stalks. *Flowers bisexual, white or pale pink, about 10–15mm diameter*, usually carried on long stalks in terminal umbels but sometimes with another whorl lower down on the stem. *Fruits green, in globose heads.* Freshwater ponds and ditches, to 1500m. May–August. AZ, B, CH, CO, D, DK, E, F, GB, *w*GR, H, I, IRL, N, NL, P, PL, *w*RS, S, YU.●

A graceful little water plant, distinguished from the true water plantains by the globose head of fruitlets. In *Alisma* species the fruits are produced in a single ring or whorl.

2. Alpine Baldellia *Baldellia alpestris*.   Like (**1**) but smaller with shorter, ellip-tical, leaves, *rounded at both ends* and rather abruptly constricted into the leaf stalk. Shallow water in mountainous areas, 830–1500m. July–August. *nw*E, *n*P.

LURONIUM

Floating Water Plantain *Luronium natans* (= *Alisma natans, Elisma natans*) [1] Slender floating aquatic perennial, sometimes creeping along the water margins. Submerged leaves (if present) very narrow. *Floating leaves elliptical, up to 3cm long* and usually rounded at the base and apex. Flowers bisexual, *white with a yellow spot* at the base of each petal, 10–15mm diameter, produced on long stems from the leaf axils. Fruits, a ring of nutlets. In still or slow-moving water, to 1000m.

May–August. Much of W.&C. Europe – A, B, BG, CS, D, DK, E, F, GB*, GR, I, *s*N, NL, PL, R, *w*RS, S, YU.*

The small shiny green elliptical leaves and floating habit, combined with the comparatively large white flowers make this an attractive and easily recognised aquatic. Submerged plants can look quite different with their grassy leaves.

ALISMA

Short-stemmed perennials. Leaves *all basal*, aerial, floating or submerged, ribbed. Flowers in whorled racemes or panicles with both anthers and stigmas; stamens 6. Fruit with 11 or more nutlets.

1. Common Water Plantain *Alisma plantago-aquatica* [1]   Medium to tall robust perennial. *Leaves ovate or broadly lanceolate with a rounded or heart-shaped base*, carried well above water on long stalks, or floating. Flowers bisexual, white or very pale lilac, *8–10mm diameter, borne in many whorls* up the 30–65cm flower stem. Fruit, a ring of nutlets. Margins of freshwater, to 1000m. April–August. T – except AZ, BAL, FA, IS, SA, SC.*

The largest and most robust of the Water Plantains, and the commonest species in Europe. The leaves are much broader than in any of the other *Alisma* species.

2. Narrow-leaved Water Plantain *Alisma lanceolatum*.   Similar to *A. plantago-aquatica* but with smaller, narrower, more pointed leaves up to 25cm long, with a *tapering, not rounded, base. Flowers deeper pinkish-purple*. In fresh water, to 1000m. June–August. T – except FA, IS, N, *n*RS.*

This is rather rare in the northern part of its range. The easiest method of distinguishing it from the Common Water Plantain is to look for the tapering leaf base.

3. Ribbon-leaved Water Plantain *Alisma gramineum* [1]   Like *A. plantago-aquatica* but smaller, up to 20cm tall. Leaves shorter than the flower spike, *linear or very narrowly lanceolate*, up to 5cm wide, the submerged ones usually much narrower than the aerial ones. Flowers bisexual, usually pale lilac or whitish, *5–6mm diameter*, carried in one to three (rarely four) whorls on the stem. Edges of ponds and lakes, to 1000m. June–September. A, B, BG, CH, CS, D, DK, F, GB*, GR, H, I, NL, PL, R, *c,w*&*e*RS, S, TR, YU.*

This small Water Plantain is often submerged, except for the flowering spike, and has much more slender growth than the other Alismas.

4. Baltic Water Plantain *Alisma wahlenbergii* is very similar to the previous species and is sometimes treated as a subspecies. It is a very delicate little plant with very small white flowers only 3–5mm diameter and the inflorescences are *shorter than* the very slender leaves. *w*&*c*RS, S, SF.

DAMASONIUM

Star Fruit *Damasonium alisma* [1]   Small aquatic perennial, 5–40cm tall, with floating *oblong leaves often heart-shaped or rounded at the base*, up to 8cm long; sometimes grows in mud at the water's edge in which case the leaves are smaller and more lance-shaped. Flowers bisexual, *white with a yellow spot* on each of the three petals, 4–6mm diameter, carried in a loose umbel or in several well-spaced whorls. *Fruits up to 2cm across, spreading out like a star* with six points. Edge of ponds, lakes and slow-moving streams and rivers, to 1500m. June–September. E, F, *s*GB*, GR, I, P, *w*&*c*RS, SA, SC.●

This species is readily distinguished by its characteristic star-shaped fruits. Plants are very variable – robustness depending on the water depth. Occasionally dwarf plants will be found with narrower leaves growing on mudbanks by the water's edge.

SAGITTARIA

The Arrowheads are distinguished from the other genera in the family by their unisexual flowers, the males of which have 7 or more stamens. The fruit consists of many small nutlets forming a close head. Most species possess submerged ribbon-like leaves as well as the more characteristically shaped aerial ones.

1. Arrowhead *Sagittaria sagittifolia* [1]   Medium aquatic perennial of robust habit, 30–60cm tall. *Leaves held above water, strikingly arrow-shaped*; floating leaves occasionally present, lanceolate. *Flowers white with a purple blotch* at the base of each of the three petals, borne in racemes or panicles, 15–22mm diameter, the *male and female carried separately* from each other. Fruit globose, 1.5cm across, with many nutlets. In ponds, lakes, streams and rivers, to 1500m. July–August. T – except AL, BAL, CO, FA, IS, SC, but rare in the north and extreme south.*

A very striking plant with its large purple-blotched white flowers, worthy of cultivation in the larger water garden. The handsome leaves, with their two long basal lobes, leave no doubt about the identity of this plant. *Sagittaria* is the only European genus in the family to have unisexual flowers. In *S. sagittifolia* the female flowers are rather smaller than the male flowers and borne low down on the racemes or panicles.

2. *Sagittaria latifolia* Similar to (1) but flowers *plain white*, often larger, 20–32mm, anthers yellow. (CH, D, F, H, R) – native of North America.●

3. *Sagittaria natans* Medium perennial. Leaves mostly floating, linear to oblong, rounded at the base, or with two rounded lobes *directed downwards*. Flowers *plain white*, 14–16mm, in short racemes or umbels; stamens with yellow anthers and linear, hairless, filaments. Growing in still or slow moving, shallow water. July–August. *n*&*c*RS*, S*, SF*.

4. Canadian Arrowhead *Sagittaria rigida*   Medium/tall perennial. Leaves mostly aerial, linear to oval, sometimes with two short basal lobes. Flowers white, 12–22mm, in racemes, the male and female flowers on separate plants, the female short-stalked; stamens with yellow anthers and *dilated, hairy, filaments*. July–August. (*sw*GB) – native of North America.

5. *Sagittaria graminea*   Rather like (**4**) but the flowers pale pink or white; female flowers *long-stalked*, often on the same plant as the male flowers. (NL) – native of North America.

CALDESIA

Caldesia parnassifolia (= *Alisma parnassifolia*) [2]   Small aquatic perennial with *ovate floating or aerial leaves up to 5cm long, with a heart-shaped base*. Flowers bisexual, white, about 5–10mm diameter, carried in a few well-spaced whorls up the stem. Fruit, a ring of nutlets. Ponds, lakes and slow-moving water, to 1000m. June–September. (A), (BG), (CH), D, F, H, *n*&*c*I, PL, R, *w*&*c*RS, YU.●
   Distinguished from *Luronium* and *Alisma*, which also have their fruits in a single ring or whorl, by the heart-shaped base to the leaves.

Flowering Rush Family BUTOMACEAE

A family related to the *Alismataceae*, but unlike that family containing a single species only.

Flowering Rush *Butomus umbellatus* [2]   Tall hairless perennial forming tufts to 1.5m tall. Leaves all basal, long, linear, twisted, *three cornered*. Flowers bright pink or pinkish-white, 15–24mm, *in long-stalked, many flowered, umbels*; sepals and petals 3, the sepals shorter and greenish on the outside, stamens 9. Fruit egg-shaped, 6-parted, purple when ripe. Shallow fresh water, pond and lake margins, slow-moving rivers, June–August. T – except AL, BAL, CO, CR, FA, IS, SA, SC.✱
   This beautiful plant is widespread in Europe, though rather local and becoming increasingly scarce in Western Europe. It often grows along the banks of slow moving rivers amongst rushes and sedges. The distribution of the species extends into north and central Asia.

Frogbit Family HYDROCHARITACEAE

Floating or submerged aquatic plants. Leaves alternate or opposite, often with sheathing bases. Flowers solitary or several together enclosed by two common bracts, often one sex only; sepals and petals 3; stamens 2 to many. Fruit splitting into a star or irregularly.

STRATIOTES

Water Soldier *Stratiotes aloides* [2]   Submerged hairless perennial which floats to the surface at flowering time. Leaves in a dense rosette *like a pineapple top*, lanceolate, rather stiff and brittle, saw-edged. Flowers white, 26–40mm, the male and female flowers on separate plants. Still fresh water, particularly ponds. June–August. T – except AL, BAL, CO, CR, FA, GR, IS, K, P, SA, SC. Often rather local and rare in the south and west of its range.●

The Water Soldier is a fascinating plant, sometimes occurring in large numbers. As the plants come into flower they rise to the water surface allowing flying insects to pollinate them. As the flowers fade the plants sink below the surface once again, but can usually be seen resting on the bottom of clear water ponds and lakes.

HYDROCHARIS

Frogbit *Hydrocharis morsus-ranae* [2]   Small floating aquatic perennial, producing runners and plantlets but rarely rooting into the mud bottom. *Leaves kidney-shaped, up to 3cm across*, rather thick and deep brownish-green. Flowers unisexual, held above water, *white spotted with yellow* near the base of each of the three petals, 20–25mm diameter. Ponds, ditches and slow-moving water, to 1500m. July– August. Throughout Europe.●

A neat little plant, easily recognised by its small kidney-shaped deep green leaves.

VALLISNERIA

Tape Grass *Vallisneria spiralis*   Submerged aquatic perennial producing stolons and plantlets. *Leaves narrowly linear*, in grassy tufts to 60cm long. *Flowers very small, pale pink, only 2–3mm diameter*, on long slender stalks; the male ones break off and float away but the female ones are retained on the stem which coils after flowering. Slow or still water at low altitudes. June–September. BG, E, F, GR, I, R, *w*&eRS, TR. Naturalised in several other countries.*

Vallisneria is a popular water plant for aquaria. The male flowers have the curious habit of breaking away and floating to the surface where they pollinate the female flowers. The stems of the latter then coil and pull the fruits down below the surface. It is a difficult plant to observe in the wild.

Apart from the above members of the Hydrocharitaceae, *Flora Europaea* records several other water plants belonging to this family which are occasionally naturalised in Europe – most of them escapes from aquaria. They are as follows:

Blyxa japonica, naturalised in rice fields in I (native of S.E. Asia); *Egeria densa*, naturalised in D, GB, NL (native of S. America); *Elodea canadensis* (Canadian

Pondweed), naturalised throughout Europe (native of N. America); *E. ernistiae*, naturalised in CH, D, GB (native of S. America); *E. nuttallii*, naturalised in B, CH, D, GB, NL (native of N. America); *Halophila stipulacea*, naturalised in Mediterranean Sea (native of Red Sea and Indian Ocean); *Hydrilla verticillata*, recorded in D, GB, IRL, PL, RS (native of S.&E. Asia, Africa and Australia); *Lagarosiphon major*, naturalised in CH, GB, I (native of S. Africa); *Ottelia alismoides*, naturalised in rice fields in I (native of S.E. Asia, N.E. Africa, Australasia).

Yam Family DIOSCOREACEAE

A large family mainly centred on the tropics where there are a large number of 'YAMS' (*Dioscorea* species). In Europe the family is very poorly represented with only four species in three genera.

Tuberous rooted hairless perennials. Leaves usually heart-shaped. Flowers small greenish, in spikes or racemes, or in small clusters, in the axils of the leaves; the male and female flowers are borne on separate plants. The fruit is either a fleshy berry or a dry capsule.

TAMUS

Black Bryony *Tamus communis* [2]   Tall *climbing* and twining perennial, dying down in winter to a large underground tuber. *Leaves shiny green* on long stalks, alternating up the stem, *broadly ovate* usually 10–20cm long, *long-pointed* at the tip. *Flowers yellowish-green*, about 4–5mm diameter, *carried in long axillary spikes*; female with six narrow tepals and the male with six broader lobes. *Fruit a large shiny red berry*. Hedgerows and copses, to 1500m. May–August. A, AZ, B, BAL, BG, CH, CO, CR, D, E, F, GB, GR, H, I, K, P, R, SA, SC, TR, YU.

This is sometimes confused with the climbing White Bryony (*Bryonia cretica*, Cucurbitaceae), but is easily distinguished by the lack of tendrils, much smaller flowers and the hairless shiny leaves. The showy red berries are poisonous.

DIOSCOREA

Balkan Yam *Dioscorea balcanica*   Medium tuberous-rooted twining *climber* to 60cm tall. Leaves long-stalked, broadly heart-shaped, up to 8cm long, pointed at the tip. Flowers green, about 2mm diameter, in loose spikes, the male bell-shaped and the female with six lobes. *Fruit a capsule with three wings*, 20–25mm across. In scrub, to 1500m. June–July. *n*AL*, *sw*YU*.

The only European *Dioscorea*, which has a very limited distribution and is not often seen in the wild. The winged capsule makes it very distinct from Black Bryony which has fleshy berries.

BORDEREA

1. Pyrenean Yam *Borderea* (= *Dioscorea*) *pyrenaica* [2]   *Short upright non-climbing* tuberous rooted perennial to 15cm tall. Leaves broadly ovate with a heart-shaped base, *up to 2.5cm long*. Flowers green, very small, the male in several-flowered racemes up to 5cm long and the female in very few-flowered racemes. Fruit a dry capsule. In rocky places and screes, 1300–2500m. June–September. *n*E*, *s*F*; Pyrenees.●

A tiny little-known yam, unusual in being self-supporting. It is a difficult plant to find and should be preserved in its wild habitat at all costs. Fortunately it is a plant of curiosity rather than beauty.

2. *Borderea chouardii.*   Similar to the previous one, but with thin-textured, shiny leaves. Rocky places and screes, 1500–2500m. *n*E*.

This plant is very rare and is known only from a single valley in the central Pyrenees.

Lily Family LILIACEAE

This is one of the largest of the families of monocotyledons, excluding of course the grasses. There are approximately 250 genera and probably as many as 3700 species, spread throughout the world in all tropical and temperate regions. It is a very diverse family, ranging from small bulbous plants to shrubs, climbers and even trees. In Europe, the Lily family is mainly represented by bulbous plants, but nevertheless there is great variation. At one extreme there are the spectacular and beautiful Lilies, Tulips and Fritillaries, together with many well-known plants like the Bluebell, Scillas and Grape Hyacinths while at the other extreme there are seemingly unlikely plants such as Herb Paris, Butcher's Broom and Asparagus. The Onions and Leeks and their many relatives are also included, although they are sometimes put in a separate family, the Alliaceae, on account of their umbellate flower heads.

Herbaceous or evergreen, sometimes woody perennials; rootstock a bulb or rhizome or occasionally a tuber, or mass of fleshy roots without a well-developed bulb. The leaves are basal or carried on the stem (referred to as a scape when it is leafless), linear, oval or elliptical, sometimes thread-like and rarely heart-shaped (as in May Lily). Butcher's Broom provides a strange example in which there are no true leaves but instead the lateral stems are flattened and leaf-like and are known botanically as 'cladodes'. Asparagus also has these but they are narrow and produced in bunches like pine-needles. The flowers are usually regular and vary enormously in shape and size and may be solitary or in long spikes, racemes or umbels. The six tepals (3 inner and 3 outer, in two whorls) are either separate or joined into a short to long tube; they are usually equal in size; sometimes (as in the Grape Hyacinths) they are joined together for most of their length and the six lobes are reduced to small 'teeth'. There are six stamens which are often rather prominent. The ovary is superior, that is borne above all the other flower parts which join together immediately below it. The fruit is usually a dry 3-valved capsule or rarely a fleshy berry.

Key to genera of Liliaceae native to Europe

1. Flowers erect and Crocus-like, produced at
   ground level   2
   Flowers not as above   5

2. Style 1, with 3 short lobes at apex   *Bulbocodium*, p.67
   Styles 3, separate for their whole length   3

3. Leaves widened at the base and forming a collar,
   or 'involucre' immediately below the flowers   *Androcymbium*, p.65
   Leaves absent at flowering, or present and not
   forming an 'involucre'   4

4. Tepals joined into a distinct tube   *Colchicum*, p56
   Tepals free from each other   *Merendera*, p.66

5. Flowers produced in terminal umbels; plant
   usually smelling of onions   6
   Flowers not in terminal umbels; not smelling of
   onions   7

6. Tepals with 3–5 veins; flowers large pendulous
   bells on long stalks   *Nectaroscordum*, p72
   Tepals 1 – veined; flowers usually small and starry,
   cup-shaped or egg-shaped   *Allium*, p.73

7. Plant climbing with tendrils, spiny   *Smilax*, p.128
   Plant not climbing and spiny   8

8. Flowers produced on the mid-vein of a leaf-like
   cladode   *Ruscus*, p.127
   Flowers produced in spikes, racemes or panicles,
   sometimes axillary, rarely solitary   9

9. Stems with bunches of needle-like structures
   instead of true leaves   *Asparagus*, p.124
   Stems leafless or with normal leaves not in
   bunches   10

10. Tall, non-bulbous herbaceous perennial with
    broad pleated leaves   *Veratrum*, p.118
    Plant not as above   11

11. Plants evergreen and rush-like with erect starry
     blue flowers   *Aphyllanthes*, p.123
     Plants not rush-like and evergreen   12

12. Flowers erect and starry, yellow or greenish,
     1 – several in compact heads; plants dwarf   *Gagea*, p.97
     Not as above   13

13. Plants dwarf with thread-like leaves and 1 – few
     small white bell-shaped flowers, veined purple   14
     Plants not as above   15

14. Tepals with nectaries at base. (Mainly
     C.&N. Europe)   *Lloydia*, p.100
     Tepals with no nectaries. (S. Greece, Crete)   *Gagea graeca*, p.99

15. Leaves heart-shaped on long stalks; plant
     patch-forming   *Maianthemum*, p.123
     Leaves not as above   16

16. Flowers strongly scented, white and rounded
     bell-shaped, in a loose 1-sided raceme   *Convallaria*, p.123
     Flowers not as above   17

17. Leaves all strictly basal or in a more or less basal
     clump; flowering stem leafless or nearly so   18
     Leaves all, or at least most of them, carried on the
     flowering stem   41

18. Flowers funnel-shaped, yellow, 6cm or more long *Hemerocallis*, p.39
     Flowers less than 5cm long   19

19. Leaves mottled, paired; flowers large with
     sharply reflexed tepals   *Erythronium*, p.40
     Leaves not mottled; flowers not as above   20

20. Flowers usually white or greenish-white,
     sometimes with brown or green veins or stripes,
     or purple on the outside   21
     Flowers not coloured as above   29

21. Plants bulbous   22
     Plants rhizomatous or with fleshy or fibrous roots   24

22. Autumn-flowering; leaves produced later   *Urginea*, p.119
     Spring- or summer-flowering; leaves present or
     withered at flowering   23

23. Flowers pale greenish-white; tepals with a nectary
     at base   *Zigadenus*, p.120
     Flowers usually white, sometimes greenish, but
     with no nectary at base of tepals inside   *Ornithogalum*, p.91

24. Flowers funnel-shaped   *Paradisea*, p.68
Flowers starry when fully open   **25**

25. Plants dwarf with evergreen flat fans of leaves
and very small flowers in short dense spikes   *Tofieldia*, p.121
Plant at least 20cm tall, herbaceous with flowers
at least 5mm diameter   **26**

26. Stamens protruding well beyond the tepals.
(Crimea)   *Eremurus*, p.72
Stamens equal to, or shorter than, the tepals   **27**

27. Flowers stained purple outside   *Simethis*, p.69
Flowers sometimes veined but not stained purple   **28**

28. Tepals with 1 vein   *Asphodelus*, p.71
Tepals 3–5 veined   *Anthericum*, p.69

29. Flowers yellow or dirty brown-purple (sometimes
the upper sterile flowers are violet blue)
Flowers at least partly blue, violet, pinkish or   **30**
purplish   **33**

30. Plants non-bulbous with a flat fan of leaves;
flowers starry, yellow   *Narthecium*, p.122
Plants bulbous, flowers not starry   **31**

31. Flowers tubular or globose, much-constricted at
the mouth and with tiny teeth-like tepals   *Muscari*, p.113
Flowers bell-shaped or tubular, not constricted;
tepals free for at least ¼ their length   **32**

32. Outer 3 tepals distinctly recurved; inner 3 straight   *Dipcadi*, p.116
All tepals straight or slightly recurved   *Bellevalia*, p.111

33. Flowers globose or egg-shaped with a very
constricted mouth   *Muscari*, p.113
Flowers starry, tubular, funnel-shaped or
bell-shaped   **34**

34. Flowers starry, or at most cup-shaped when fully
open   **35**
Flowers tubular, funnel-shaped or bell-shaped   **38**

35. Tepals pink or greenish-pink with a dark mid-vein   *Urginea*, p.119
Tepals usually blue or lilac, or at least partly so   **36**

36. Tepals joined into a short tube. (Crete)   *Chionodoxa*, p.100
Tepals free or nearly so   **37**

37. Flower stalks with 1 bract at base   *Scilla*, p.101
Flower stalks with 2 bracts at base   *Hyacinthoides italicus*,
                                                                  p.108

Lilies LILIUM

A genus containing many beautiful species which are scattered across the Northern Hemisphere, including North America, but with the greatest density in S.E. Asia and Japan. Europe is represented by eight species.

The bulb consists of a large number of overlapping fleshy scales and the stems are leafy, particularly in the lower half. The flowers are showy, often large, with separate tepals; these may be either reflexed to form a typical 'turk's-cap' with prominent protruding stamens, or spreading to form a narrow or rather broad trumpet with the stamens inside.

Key to European Species of Lilium

1. Leaves in whorls 　　　　　　　　　　　　　　　　1. *L. martagon*
   Leaves alternate 　　　　　　　　　　　　　　　　2

2. Flowers erect; stems often with bulbils 　　　　　2. *L. bulbiferum*
   Flowers horizontal to nodding; stems without
   　bulbils 　　　　　　　　　　　　　　　　　　　3

3. Flowers trumpet-shaped, white 　　　　　　　　　3. *L. candidum*
   Flowers turk's-cap shaped, yellow, orange or red 　4

4. Flowers yellow 　　　　　　　　　　　　　　　　5
   Flowers orange or red 　　　　　　　　　　　　　7

5. Flowers large, lemon yellow, unspotted; tepals
   　8–12cm long 　　　　　　　　　　　　　　　7. *L. rhodopaeum*
   Flowers small, mid- or greenish-yellow, spotted
   　or unspotted; tepals 3–6.5cm long 　　　　　　　6

6. Leaves 3–9-veined, broad lanceolate, not
   　crowded; flowers usually unspotted 　　　　　6. *L. carniolicum*
   Leaves 3–5-veined, narrow lanceolate to linear,
   　crowded; flowers spotted 　　　　　　　　　4. *L. pyrenaicum*

7. Leaves 1–3-veined; flowers bright red, dotted and
   　lined with purple 　　　　　　　　　　　　8. *L. pomponium*
   Leaves 3–9-veined 　　　　　　　　　　　　　8

8. Leaves broad-lanceolate, 3–9-veined; flowers
   　orange or red, unspotted 　　　　　　　　　6. *L. carniolicum*
   Leaves narrow-lanceolate to linear, 3–5-veined 　9

9. Flowers bright red, unspotted 　　　　　　5. *L. chalcedonicum*
   Flowers orange, finely spotted 　　　　　　　4. *L. pyrenaicum*

1. Martagon Lily *Lilium martagon* [3]　　Tall slender-stemmed plant to 1.5m tall; stem usually pink or red spotted. Leaves mostly in whorls, elliptical, broadest above the middle, each 7–9-veined. Flowers in racemes of five or more on arching stems, small turk's-caps, pink or purplish usually, with darker spots, or rarely white, rather unpleasant smelling; anthers orange-yellow or purplish on slender pink stalks. Wooded slopes and scrub, occasionally grassy banks or meadows, usually on calcareous soils, to 2800m. June–July. T – except AL, B, (GB), IRL, IS, S, SF and the Mediterranean Islands.*

1a. *L.m.* var. *cattaniae* (=var. *dalmaticum*) [3] is taller with deep wine-purple or maroon unspotted flowers. YU.*

The Martagon Lily is the most widespread European species whose distribution extends eastwards to the Caucasus, Siberia and Mongolia. It is an elegant plant

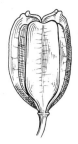

Martagon Lily fruit capsules, × 1

which is widely cultivated, the dark maroon and white flowered forms being particularly sought after. In some areas of England it has become naturalised, especially in wooded places. The flower odour is strong and unpleasant to most people.

2. Orange Lily *Lilium bulbiferum* [3]   Medium rather stout-stemmed plant to 60cm tall, rarely more; stems green, with purplish bulbils at the leaf bases. Leaves spirally arranged, lanceolate, hairy edged, 3–7-veined. Flowers solitary or 2–3 together, orange-red, spotted black, *upright open* trumpets; anthers orange or reddish-brown on orange stalks. Mountain pastures, woods and rocky places to 2400m. June–July. A, CO, CH, CS, D, E, F, H, I, N, NL, PL, R, SF, *sw*RS.*

2a. *L.b.* var. *croceum* is generally taller and without stem bulbils. *e*F, CH, *n*I.●

A large flowered lily easy to recognise on account of its upright flowers and stems which often bear small bulbils in the leaf axils.

3. Madonna Lily *Lilium candidum* [3]   Tall rather stout, green-stemmed hairless plants to 1.2m tall. Leaves alternate, lanceolate, shiny-green, 3–5-veined. Flowers *white trumpets* in loose clusters of 5–6 usually, sweetly and strongly scented; anthers yellow on white stalks. Seed rarely set. Rocky places in the mountains, widely naturalised. May–July. (AL, BAL, BG, CH, CO, CR, CS, D, E, F, GR, H, I, P, R).*

3a. *L.c.* var. *salonikae* is sometimes distinguished on its ready ability to set seed. *n*GR.●

The Madonna Lily has been cultivated for many centuries. It was grown on Knossos by the Cretan civilisations and was much featured in Renaissance paintings, besides being closely associated in Mediterranean countries with churches and graveyards. No one is quite sure where this lovely plant really comes from though it is probably indigenous to parts of the Balkan Peninsula and the Eastern Mediterranean.

In Britain it has long been cultivated and is often to be seen in old established cottage gardens where they have remained undisturbed for years.

4. Pyrenean or Yellow Turk's-cap Lily *Lilium pyrenaicum* [3]   Medium to
tall, green-stemmed plant to 1m tall. Leaves alternate, narrow-lanceolate, hairy
edged. Flowers in clusters of up to 8 usually, rarely solitary, small turk's-caps,
yellow or greenish-yellow or occasionally orange, finely spotted and lined with
purple, foxy-scented; anthers reddish-brown on pale green stalks. Meadows,
woodland clearings, rocky places, in the mountains to 2200m. June–July. *n*E, *s*F,
IRL, (*sw*GB).*

A small flowered elegant lily which takes kindly to cultivation given the right
conditions, and where it may often multiply. The orange-flowered form from
northern Spain is sometimes distinguished as var. *rubrum*. In the wild *L.
pyrenaicum* is often local and rather rare.

5. *Lilium chalcedonicum* (= *L. heldreichii*) [4]   Medium tall green-stemmed plant
up to 1.2m tall, though usually less. Leaves alternate, lanceolate to oval, hairy
beneath and on the edges, 3–5-veined, *with a strong contrast* with the lower
spreading outwards and the upper erect and pressed closely to the stem. Bracts
often present. Flowers in loose clusters of up to 7 usually, rarely solitary, small,
orange-red or bright red, unspotted turk's-cap; anthers red on pale yellow stalks.
Open woods and rocky places in the mountains. AL, GR.*

A beautiful and rather red turk's-cap which is rarely seen in cultivation. On
the pine wooded slopes of Mt Olympus in Macedonia it is one of the most
beautiful sights of the early summer.

6. *Lilium carniolicum* (= *L. albanicum*) [4]   Variable plant from 25–80cm tall,
rather thin-stemmed. Leaves alternate, lanceolate, hairy beneath and on the
edges usually, 3–9-veined, the lower spreading and gradually merging into the
upper which are more or less erect and pressed closely to the stem. Bracts absent.
Flowers in loose clusters of up to 6, sometimes solitary, small red, orange or
yellow turk's-caps, sometimes with brownish-purple spots inside, tepals 3–
6.5cm long; anthers orange or red on yellowish stalks. Meadows, scrub, rocky
places and screes, often on limestone, to 2300m. June–July. *se*A, AL, BG, *n*GR, H, I,
R, YU.*

A variable and lovely plant whose distribution extends from the south-eastern
Alps down to Greece and eastwards as far as the mountains of Bulgaria and
Roumania. The typical plant has bright red flowers and various other colour
forms have been distinguished in the past; var. *albanicum* with pale orange-yellow
flowers from S. Yugoslavia, Albania and the neighbouring areas of Greece and
var. *jankae* with bright lemon-yellow, purple spotted, flowers from a similar
area, but it is difficult to uphold these as anything other than minor variants.

It is readily confused with the previous species *L. chalcedonicum* but can be
separated on account of its leaves which merge gradually from the lower
spreading ones into the upper erect ones. In the latter the contrast is much more
abrupt and the lower leaves are often broadest above the middle, besides which
they usually have fewer veins.

7. *L. rhodopaeum* [4] is a taller plant than (**5**) with longer narrower leaves and larger flowers. Flowers generally in clusters of 3–5, bright lemon-yellow, unspotted, *large* turk's-caps; tepals 8–12cm long. BG*.●

8. Red Lily *Lilium pomponium* [4]   Medium thin-stemmed plant to 75cm tall, stems often purplish. Leaves alternate, linear, 1–3-veined, hairless beneath but with a hairy edge. Flowers in clusters of up to 6, sometimes solitary, small turk's-caps, glistening bright red, lined and spotted with dark purple inside; anthers red on pale green stalks. Rocky places in the mountains, but rarely much above 1000m. May–July. *ne*E*, *se*F*, *nw*I*.●

This splendid little lily is easily identified by its narrow grassy leaves and brilliant red flowers. In the wild it is local and rare, its main stations being in the Maritime and Provence Alps and the Ligurian Apennines. Rarely met with in cultivation and then often only short lived.

Two further Lilies have become naturalised in central and eastern Europe. The Tiger Lily, *L. tigrinum*, which comes from China and Japan is distinguished by its large orange turk's-caps, the size of *L. rhodopaeum*, which are spotted with dark purple inside. The narrow lanceolate leaves are all spreading and bear bulbils at their bases (A, BG, H, R, SF). The well known Regal Lily, *L. regale*, from southern China is distinct with its large highly fragrant, white trumpet flowers which are flushed with rose-purple and green on the outside and yellow inside at the base. The leaves are only 1-veined (BG, H, R).

HEMEROCALLIS

A very well-known genus in gardens, the majority of species of which occur in eastern Asia. Europe has only one native representative. There are many colourful garden hybrids which make admirable herbaceous border plants. They are non-bulbous clump-forming plants with heads of trumpet-like flowers.

Day Lily *Hemerocallis lilioasphodelus* (= *H. flava*)   *Tall herbaceous perennial* plant, 50–90cm tall; roots rather fleshy, often with swollen tubers near the tips. Leaves

Day lily, × ½

many, basal, linear with a strong keel, 0.5–1.5cm wide. *Flowers 4–8, yellow, funnel-shaped*, about 4–6cm diameter at the mouth and 8–10cm long; tepals six, joined into a slender 1.5–2.5cm long tube and recurved at their tips; stamens six. Fruit a capsule with 3 valves, containing a few large black seeds. Woods, shady rocky places and damp meadows, 500–1500m. June–July (–August). *ne*I, *n*YU.* Also naturalised in several other countries.

In addition to this species, the commonly cultivated *H. fulva*, which has orange flowers, is sometimes seen as an escape from gardens.

ERYTHRONIUM

The genus *Erythronium* with its small turk's-cap flowers borne on leafless stems is distributed mainly in N. America and Asia with a single species native in Europe. All the species have dainty pendulous flowers with recurved tepals and prominent anthers.

Dog's Tooth Violet *Erythronium dens-canis* [4]   Low bulbous-rooted perennial, hairless. *Leaves two*, basal and opposite, elliptical to lance-shaped, stalked, deep blue-green marbled with reddish-brown or white. Flowers solitary on slender scapes, nodding, the tepals *reflexed*, pale to deep pink or pinkish-mauve, with orange marks at the base inside; anthers bluish, projecting. Meadows, woods, and rocky slopes in the mountains, 500–2000m. March–May. A, AND, CH, CS, *n*&*c*E, P, PL, *sw*RS.*

The graceful early flowering Dog's Tooth Violet is often to be found growing wild in large numbers. The flowers have characteristic reflexed tepals, like an open turk's-cap flower, set off amongst the attractive, often marbled foliage. It takes kindly to cultivation and a number of fine forms are available on the market. It gets its common name from the oblong whitish bulb which supposedly resembles a dog's tooth.

Dog's Tooth Violet fruit capsule, × 1½

Tulips TULIPA

The Tulip, like the Narcissus, is undoubtedly one of the widest known and best loved of bulbous plants, being widely planted and grown throughout much of Europe. There are relatively few species in Europe itself, these being confined mainly to the south and south-east. It is from further east, from Turkey, Iran, Afghanistan and the southern USSR that the majority of species have their

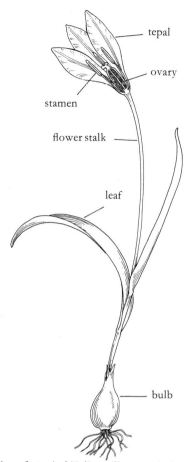

tepal

ovary

stamen

flower stalk

leaf

bulb

Cross-section of a typical Tulip to illustrate the botanical details

homes. From these latter have developed numerous sports and hybrids which have given rise to the 'garden tulips' as we know them today.

Indeed, the craze for new tulips reached a zenith in Holland in the sixteenth century and the resulting 'tulipomania' caused vastly inflated prices for the bulbs of new hybrids.

Several of the 'oriental' species, *T. praecox, T. agenensis* and *T. gesnerana* in particular, have become widely naturalised in south-eastern France and northern and central Italy and although their exact wild counterparts have never been precisely located their origins undoubtedly belong in the Middle East. The simple answer is that naturalisation from man-picked forms has resulted in a large number of apparently distinct clones, a process vastly accelerated by the ability of many of these to reproduce by underground stolons rather than by seed. Nineteenth-century botanists were perplexed by this proliferation and assigned many with specific names, quite erroneously in most cases. Today the general view is more conservative and most of the plants are placed in only one or two species.

Bulbous perennials, often with creeping underground stolons, the inside of the bulb tunic lined with a felt of wool of hairs, or with a few straight hairs. Leaves few, alternate on the lower part of the stem, usually solitary and basal in non-flowering specimens, rather fleshy. Flowers solitary or two-four together, generally large and showy, bowl-shaped or starry with 6 shiny petal-like tepals; stamens 6, the stalks (filaments) with or without a tuft of hairs at the base. Fruit a 3-valved capsule, erect, containing many rather flat seeds.

Key to European Species of Tulipa

1. Stamen stalks (filaments) hairy at the base; flowers
   noticeable waisted near the base   2
   Stamen stalks hairless at the base; flowers not
   waisted   6

2. Flowers orange, orange-brown or yellow; leaves
   long-linear, channelled   3
   Flowers white, pink, lilac or purple; leaves usually
   broad and rather flat, if narrow then rather short   4

3. Flowers yellow, often greenish or pink stained on
   the outside   1. *T. sylvestris*
   Flowers orange or orange-brown, often greenish
   stained on the outside   4. *T. orphanidea*
                                                                  (Balkans and Crete
                                                                     excluding the
                                                                     Peloponnese)
                                                                  5. *T. goulimyi*
                                                                  (S. Peloponnese only)

4. Leaves short, narrow and channelled, dull
   greyish-green; flowers white with a yellow centre   6. *T. biflora*
   Leaves broad, shiny green   5

5. Anthers up to 3mm long; flowers small, white
   with a yellow centre, sometimes lilac tinged   3. *T. cretica*
   Anthers 5mm long or more; flowers large pale
   pink, lilac or purple with a yellow centre   2. *T. saxatilis*

6. Flowers white flushed pink-crimson on the
   outside; leaves linear, channelled   7. *T. clusiana*
   Flowers yellow, orange or red   7

7. Leaves with conspicuous undulating margins;
   tepals all long-pointed, scarlet   8. *T. undulatifolia*
                                                                     (Balkans)
   Leaves with straight, rarely slightly wavy margins   8

8. Tepals all about the same length   9
Tepals unequal, the inner about three-quarters the
length of the outer   11

9. Plants small, to 25cm tall   12. *T. schrenkii* (USSR) and
11. *T. urumoffii* (Bulgaria)

Plants large, 30–55cm tall   10

10. Flowers yellow   10. *T. hungarica*
(Roumania)

Flowers usually orange or red, rarely yellow   9. *T. gesnerana*
(S.W. Europe)

11. Leaves grey-green; tepals twice as long as broad
with a conspicuous yellowish-green median
stripe   13. *T. praecox*
Leaves green; tepals three times as long as broad,
without a conspicuous median stripe   14. *T. agenensis*

1. Wild Tulip *Tulipa sylvestris* [5]   Short/medium plant often forming tufts;
stem slender, flexuous. Leaves 2–3, rather straggling, strap-shaped, channelled.
Flowers solitary, rarely 2 together, often fragrant, *drooping in bud*; tepals 3.3–7cm

Wild Tulip fruit capsule, × 1½

long, elliptical to oblong, pointed, *clear yellow* occasionally pale yellow or
whitish, the outer 3 flushed yellowish-green, rarely reddish on the back; anthers
yellow, 9–14mm long. Fields, scrub, banks and cultivated areas, usually at low
altitudes. April–May. AL, BG, CH, E, F, GR, I, P, R, SA, SC, YU, (A, B, DK, GB, H, N,
PL, S, SF).*

1a. *T.s.* subsp. *australis* (= *T. australis, T. biebersteiniana*) [5] is a smaller, more
slender plant; tepals 2–3.5cm long, the outer 3 *tinged with pink or crimson*; anthers
2.5–4mm long. Mountain meadows and stony places to 2000m. April–June. A,
AL, BG, CH, CS, E, ʃ&eF, GR, H, n&cI, K, P, R, c,w&eRS, YU.*

The delicate Wild Tulip is the most widespread in Europe and is often sold in
bunches in the markets of Spain and Italy in the late spring. The lowland form,

T.s. subsp. *sylvestris*, is a larger plant which has become naturalised in many areas including parts of Great Britain. The plant is a triploid and probably arose as a natural sport of the upland subsp. *australis*. In the south of Spain and extending into North Africa there is a late flowering form with leaves that coil on the ground that is sometimes distinguished as a separate species, *T. celsiana*, but it is probably best regarded as a variety of subsp. *australis*.

2. Rock Tulip *Tulipa saxatilis* [5]   Short hairless plant often forming patches by underground stolons. Leaves 2–3, broad lance-shaped, *shiny-green*. Flowers solitary or 2–4 together; tepals 3.8–5.4cm long, pale pink or lilac to purple-magenta with a large egg-yellow basal zone inside, opening widely in sunshine; anthers 5–7mm long, yellow or purplish-brown, filaments hairy at base. Rarely setting seed. Rocky slopes and crevices, fields, to 1500m. March–April. CR, (SI).*

An attractive tulip sometimes seen in cultivation and readily recognised by its rather large, pale pink or purplish flowers. Like *T. cretica* this species is endemic to the island of Crete being locally common there in the late spring. The dark flowered form, which tends to have a rather smaller flower, is sometimes distinguished as *T. bakeri*, though there seems to be no real reason for this. However, botanists are not generally agreed on the best way of treating this plant and its variants.

3. Cretan Tulip *Tulipa cretica* [5]   Low plant with hairless stems and leaves, to 11cm tall. Leaves narrow lance-shaped, usually lying flat on the ground, shiny green above, red-edged. *Flowers small*, solitary or 2–3 together; tepals 1.5–3.2cm long, *white*, often tinged with pink or purple and greenish on the outside, with a dull yellow basal zone inside; anthers yellowish, 1.5–3mm long, filaments hairy at base. Rocky slopes and screes, mainly in the mountains, 500–2200m, rarely lower. April–May. CR.●

The second of the Cretan endemic species, *T. cretica*, is like a small pale version of *T. saxatilis*. The flowers are basically white with a yellow central zone inside and various shadings of pink, purplish or greenish on the outside.

4. Orange Wild Tulip *Tulipa orphanidea* (=*T. hageri*) [5]   Short/medium plant; stem slender, flexuous, hairy or hairless. Leaves 2–5, rarely 6, narrow strap-shaped, channelled, deep green with a reddish or purplish edge. Flowers solitary, sometimes 2 together, starry or bowl-shaped when fully open; tepals 2.5–5.7cm long, *orange-red, coppery-brown or buff-orange* with a darker zone at the base inside, the outer 3 flushed with green and purple hues on the back; anthers greenish-yellow or orange-brown, filaments hairy at base. Damp meadows and grassy mountain slopes, 450–1000m. March–May. *e*BG, CR, *n*&*c*GR, TR.*

The orange tulip of the Greek mountains and neighbouring regions is very like an orange flowered form of the Wild Tulip, *T. sylvestris*. In all probability the two species hybridise in the wild where they grow close together and this would account for some of the yellow-orange forms sometimes seen. *Tulipa orphanidea* extends eastwards into Asia Minor where it is known under the name of *T. whittalii*. A number of forms are widely cultivated, some of the dwarfer ones being particularly attractive.

5. *Tulipa goulimyi*.   Like (**4**) but with 5–7 *wavy-edged* leaves. Sandy fields and stony ground. March. sGR* – Kythira Island.●

A rare and little known tulip discovered only fairly recently in 1954 on the island of Kythira by Dr C. N. Goulimis. *T. goulimyi* closely resembles (**4**) but there are a larger number of leaves which have a distinct wavy edge. The flowers vary in colour from bright orange to brownish-red. The bulbs of the two species are very different, those of *T. goulimyi* with a thick felt of hairs inside the bulb coat or tunic, whereas those of *T. orphanidea* have a tuft of straight hairs only at the top of the bulb coat. However, it is *not necessary* to dig up plants to ascertain the species for they do not grow in the same vicinity.

6. *Tulipa biflora* (= *T. callieri, T. mariannae*) [5]   Low to short plant up to 18cm tall though generally less. Leaves *usually 2 at ground level*, narrow lanceolate or linear, slightly channelled, grey-green, hairless. Flowers *small*, solitary or 2–4 together, starry when opened; tepals 1–2.7cm long, white with a dull yellow basal zone inside, the outer 3 flushed with green and a little crimson on the back; anther yellow tipped purple, 2–3mm long, the filaments hairy at the base. Dry sandy places and rocky slopes. March–April. K, seRS, sYU*.*

A dainty species which has its centre of distribution in Turkestan and the neighbouring area of Iran, but reaching westwards into European Russia and with an isolated locality in southern Yugoslavia. In Europe it is a rather uniform plant, dwarf with small white flowers which on opening reveal a yellow 'egg yolk' centre. In the Middle East it is very much more variable and consequently is known under a variety of names including *T. polychroma* and *T. turkestanica*, plants often being grown under these names in gardens, and featuring commonly in bulb catalogues. Most of these forms are well worth cultivating.

7. Lady Tulip *Tulipa clusiana* [5]   Short to medium plant; stem slender, hairless. Leaves 3–5, narrow lanceolate to linear, channelled. Flowers solitary, erect in bud; tepals 2.5–6cm long, *white with a purplish basal zone inside*, the outer 3 flushed with pinkish-crimson. In and around cultivated land to 250m. March–April. (E, sF, GR, I, P).*

The Lady Tulip has been known for many centuries, indeed since the time of Clusius when it was considered a good garden plant. In Europe as a naturalised plant and as a garden plant it rarely sets seed but spreads instead by the production of underground stolons. Like the other species naturalised in Europe the Lady Tulip is a triploid plant, finding its allies and probable origins in diploid Asiatic species. Wild *T. clusiana* is found in Afghanistan, Pakistan and Kashmir.

8. *Tulipa undulatifolia* (= *T. boeotica*) [5]   Short to medium plant up to 40cm tall, though generally less; stem usually hairy. Leaves 3–4, grey-green, the lower two broad lanceolate, *wavy edged*, the upper narrower. Flowers solitary, scarlet; tepals 3–7cm long, *long-pointed*, with a basal black blotch inside edged with yellow. Fields, rocky and stony places, often rather local, to 500m. March–April. GR, TR, SYU*.●

The scarlet tulip of Greek wheat fields is readily distinguished from the other European red tulips by its finely pointed tepals and its wavy edged leaves. The species is rather common in Asia Minor and is frequently associated with cultivated fields where the bulbs grow deep and are able to survive the plough, although the modern methods of deep ploughing have eliminated it in some areas.

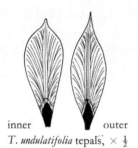

inner   outer
T. undulatifolia tepals, × ½

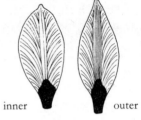

inner   outer
T. gesnerana tepals, × ½

9. *Tulipa gesnerana* (= *T. didieri*, *T. suaveolens*) [6] A very variable medium, often rather coarse plant, to 60cm tall; stem hairy or hairless. Leaves 2–7, the lowermost broad, oblong or lanceolate, the upper smaller and narrower. Flowers large, scarlet, orange, yellow or purplish, sometimes variegated ('broken'); tepals 3.8–8.2cm long, the inner and outer *more or less* equal in length, with or without a basal blotch inside, blunt or shortly pointed. Naturalised mainly in and around cultivated land in S.W. Europe. March–May. (w&sCH, E, s&eF, nGR, n&cI).* – some forms only.

The orange and yellow tulips of Tuscany and the neighbouring areas of Italy and France have probably been there since the Renaissance, no doubt brought back by merchants returning from missions in the Middle East. In the markets there they are still sold in bunches in the late spring, and there are many forms and colours with so called 'broken' ones which have mottled or variegated colouring. All these have provided an enormous variation which has been valuable in the development over the centuries of some of the garden tulips which we admire today. Botanists were long perplexed by the range of variation and describe numerous new species from the south of France and northern Italy in particular – over thirty in fact. However, it is generally agreed today that these are all clones or sports of the same species, *T. gesnerana* which Linnaeus described in his Species Plantarum of 1753. The wild origins of *T. gesnerana* are, however, more questionable. Undoubtedly its ancestors hail from the Middle East or more likely Turkestan, although no exact counterpart exists there today. Just as the modern strains of say tomatoes or roses look very different from their wild ancestral parents so the tulips of the *T. gesnerana* complex have become similarly modified.

10. *Tulipa hungarica* [6]   A robust plant like (**9**) with broad, rather grey-green, lower leaves. Flowers large, *yellow*; tepals 5–10.5cm long, *without* a basal blotch inside. Limestone rocks in the Gorge of the River Danube. April–May. *sw*RM*, *ne*YU*.●

The endemic tulip of the Danube Gorge above the Iron Gates was described as *T. hungarica* in the days when this region belonged to the Hungarian Empire. This tulip is rather rare today and apparently shy of flowering, however, it is a fine plant with its large, rather flat, leaves and clear yellow flowers which closely resemble some forms of *T. gesnerana*.

11. *Tulipa urumoffii* (= *T. rhodopea*)   A short plant to 30cm tall, sometimes as little as 15cm; stem hairless. Leaves, usually glabrous, the lower oblong or lanceolate, upper linear-lanceolate. Flowers medium sized, yellow or red; tepals 3.5–6cm long, with or without a dark basal blotch. Mountain slopes and rocky places. March–April. *s*BG*, *s*YU*.● A little known species confined mainly to the central and eastern Rhodope Mountains.

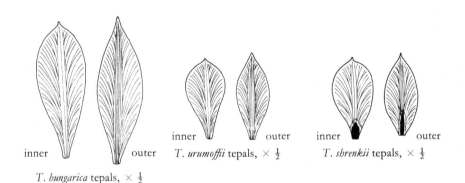

inner   outer   *T. hungarica* tepals, × ½

inner   outer   *T. urumoffii* tepals, × ½

inner   outer   *T. shrenkii* tepals, × ½

12. *Tulipa shrenkii* like (**11**) but dwarfer, only 7–16cm tall, rarely more; stem finely hairy or hairless. Leaves 3–4 finely hairy or hairless. Flowers smaller, crimson, yellow or white; tepals 2.5–5.5cm long, usually with a dark basal blotch. Steppes and semi-desert places. April–May. *se*RS.

Another little known species whose distribution extends eastwards into Asiatic Russia.

13. *Tulipa praecox*   Short to medium rather stout plant to 65cm tall; stem hairless or slightly hairy. *Leaves bluish-green*, 3–4, the lower ones large, lanceolate, upper linear-lanceolate, all hairless. Flowers orange flushed with green on the outside; tepals 3.6–8.2cm long, ovate or obovate, each with a basal brownish-green blotch which is bordered with yellow; inner three tepals shorter than the outer and *with a pronounced median yellowish stripe*. Fruit capsules rarely formed. Cultivated land and waste places. April–May. (CO, F, GR, I, TR). *

A large flowered species which probably has its ancestry in species from south-west or south-central Asia. It is locally naturalised in southern Europe but rarely sets seed, multiplying instead by means of underground stolons. It is sometimes sold as a cut flower in Italian markets.

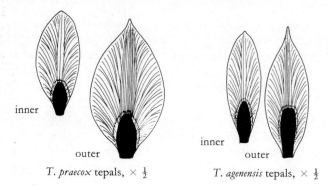

T. praecox tepals, × ½   T. agenensis tepals, × ½

14. *Tulipa agenensis* (= *T. oculis-solis*)   Rather like (**14**) but *leaves green*. Flowers reddish-orange, the tepals 4.8–8.5 cm long, elliptic to oblong-elliptic, pointed, the inner three shorter than the outer. In and around cultivated land. April–May. (SF, I). *

An attractive large flowered species probably originating in south-west Asia. It is sometimes found as a casual in parts of south-east Europe. *T. agenensis* is often confused with *T. praecox* but the latter is readily distinguished by its bluish-green and orange flowers in which the inner three tepals have a characteristic, yellowish stripe down the centre.

FRITILLARIA

Beautiful bulbous plants which are immediately recognisable by their pendulous, bell- or cone-shaped, flowers on leafy stems, usually in shades or mixtures of green, brown, purple or yellow.

It is a large genus, distributed throughout the temperate zone of the Northern Hemisphere from western Europe across Asia to Japan, and North America. The most important region is western Asia, especially Turkey and Iran where there are many species of very diverse appearance from miniature single-flowered plants to the tall many-flowered Crown Imperial. In Europe the species are not so varied in their features, but nevertheless there are some very distinct ones in Greece which differ markedly from those in other parts of Europe. The best known is undoubtedly the Snakeshead Lily, *F. meleagris* since it is the most wide-spread in the wild, and is very easy to cultivate in gardens.

Low to medium bulbous perennials, the bulb usually with two large rather fleshy scales. Stems leafy, the leaves opposite, alternate or sometimes whorled, narrowly linear to lanceolate leaves, usually rather loosely arranged, green or covered with a waxy greyish 'bloom'. Flowers bell-shaped or conical, either produced singly at the apex of the stem or in a few-flowered raceme; tepals six, free from each other, each with a glistening nectary near the base inside; stamens six, attached at the base of the tepals; style entire or 3-branched at the apex. Fruit an upright capsule, sometimes with narrow wings along the six angles; seeds many, flat.

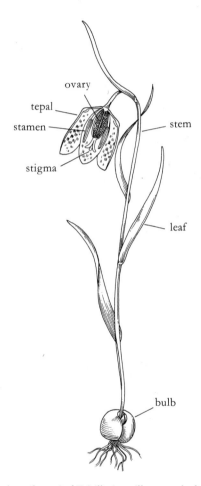

Cross-section of a typical Fritillaria to illustrate the botanical details

Key to European Species of Fritillaria

1. Flowers wholly clear yellow, rather small   2
   Flowers either not yellow or large and chequered
      on a yellow ground   3

2. Leaves grey-green. (Euboea)   21. *F. euboeica*
   Leaves green. (S. Peloponnese)   20. *F. conica*

3. Flowers widely and rather squarely bell-shaped,
   about as long as wide, usually 2.5–5cm diameter   4
   Flowers conical or narrowly tubular-bell shaped,
   usually 1.5–2.5cm diameter   23

4. Upper three leaves in a whorl around the flower   5
   Upper leaves not whorled   12

5. Upper leaves tendril-like and coiled   14. *F. ruthenica*
   Upper leaves not tendril-like   6

6. Flowers chequered outside, sometimes only
   faintly   7
   Flowers not chequered on the outside   11

7. Plant less than 15cm tall. (Albania,
   S.W. Yugoslavia)   3. *F. macedonica*
   Plant more than 15cm tall   8

8. Lowest pair of leaves usually 0.3–1cm wide   9
   Lowest pair of leaves usually 1.1–2.5cm wide   7a. *F. graeca thessala*

9. Flowers usually pale green, slightly chequered
   brown. (Maritime Alps)   11. *F. involucrata*
   Flowers dark green or brown, with darker
   chequering   10

10. Nectaries lance-shaped, 6–10mm long, flowers
    slightly chequered   5. *F. messanensis*
    Nectaries linear, 10–15mm long; flowers strongly
    chequered   15. *F. orientalis*

11. Flowers deep brown-purple; stem to 10cm tall   9. *F. epirotica*
    Flowers green, often stained pale brown; stem
    15–45cm tall   10. *F. pontica*

12. Flower bicoloured, purple with yellow tips.
    (Hydra Is.)   23. *F. rhodokanakis*
    Flower not coloured as above   13

13. Flower deep brown-purple, not chequered
    outside; stem 5–10cm. (N.W. Greece)   9. *F. epirotica*
    Plants not as above   14

14. Flowers green and brown, not chequered; leaves
    very broad, grey and sheathing stem   12. *F. gussichae*
    Plants not as above   15

15. Tepals usually with a green stripe along the centre   16
    Tepals usually with no green stripe   18

16. Lowest leaves more than 1cm wide	7. *F. graeca*
Lowest leaves less than 1cm wide	**17**
17. Flowers brownish, scarcely chequered. (S.&W. Yugoslavia)	5a. *F. messanensis gracilis*
Flowers green to brown, usually noticeably chequered. (Spain, Portugal)	6. *F. lusitanica*
18. Flowers purple, pinkish, white or yellow	**19**
Flowers pale to very dark blackish-brown or green	**20**
19. Leaves narrowly lance-shaped; flowers purple and glaucous on the outside, or yellow. (S.W. Alps)	2. *F. delphinensis*
Leaves linear; flowers purple, pinkish or white	1. *F. meleagris*
20. Lowest leaves broad, 1.5–3cm wide. (S. Peloponnese)	8. *F. davisii*
Lowest leaves narrow, usually less than 1cm wide	**21**
21. Lowest leaves usually opposite, shiny green. (S.&W. Yugoslavia)	5a. *F. messanensis gracilis*
Lowest leaves alternate	**22**
22. Tepals markedly flared outwards at the mouth. (Pyrenees)	4. *F. pyrenaica*
Tepals not markedly flared outwards. (Russia, Bulgaria)	16. *F. meleagroides*
23. Flowers narrowly tubular-bell shaped, striped green and metallic purple. (Turkey, Bulgaria)	22. *F. stribrnyi*
Flowers conical, or nearly so, deep purple-brown or blackish	**24**
24. Style 3-lobed at the apex	**25**
Style undivided. (Euboea, Cyclades)	19. *F. ehrhartii*
25. Flowers purple-brown or reddish-brown. (N. Greece, Bulgaria)	13. *F. drenovskii*
Flowers blackish, glaucous on the outside. (S. Greece)	**26**
26. Plant 20–35cm tall; flowers up to 5. (Kythnos)	17. *F. tuntasia*
Plant 10–20cm tall; flowers 1–2. (Attica)	18. *F. obliqua*

1. Snakes' Head Fritillary *Fritillaria meleagris* [7]   Low to medium plant, 10–30cm tall. Leaves alternate, grey-green, narrowly linear. Flowers solitary, *pale to deep pinkish-purple or white, chequered darker*, widely lantern-shaped, about

Snake's Head Fritillary fruit capsule, × 1½

2.5–4cm diameter and 3–5cm long; style 3-lobed. Damp meadows, to 1000m. April–May. A, B, CH, CS, D, F, GB, H, I, NL, PL, R, c&swRS, YU.* Also naturalised in several other countries.

This is a beautiful and satisfactory garden plant for growing in rock gardens, borders and in grass where it will naturalise if allowed to seed before mowing takes place.

1a. *F.m.* subsp. *burnatii* is like (**1**) but it has *shorter leaves*, less than 8cm long. Flowers purple. Alpine meadows. wCH, eF, nwI. This plant occurs in the south and south-west part of the Alps only.●

2. *Fritillaria delphinensis* (=*F. tubiformis*) [7]   Low to short plant, 10–25cm tall. Leaves alternate, grey-green, linear-lanceolate. Flowers solitary, *purple, chequered and covered with a grey 'bloom' on the exterior*, widely lantern-shaped, about 2.5–4 (–5)cm diameter and 3–5cm long; style 3-lobed. Grassy hillsides and rocky alpine meadows, 1500–2000m. June–August. sF, nwI.*

This species occurs mainly in the Maritime Alps and is rather similar to *F. meleagris*. The leaves however, are narrowly lance-shaped, not linear, and the flowers glaucous on the outside.

2a. *F.d.* subsp. *moggridgei* similar to (**2**) but *flowers yellowish* chequered with brown. Habitat and distribution as above.*

3. *Fritillaria macedonica*   Rather like *F. delphinensis* but the *lower two leaves are opposite* and the upper three are in a whorl. Alpine meadows, 1200–2500m. May–June. eAL*, swYU*.

4. Pyrenean Fritillary *Fritillaria pyrenaica* [7]   Short to medium plant, 15–40cm tall. Leaves grey-green, alternate narrowly lance-shaped. Flowers solitary, *purplish-brown or reddish-chocolate, sometimes yellowish chequered*, widely bell-shaped *with a flared mouth*, about 2.5–3.5cm diameter and 2.5–3.5cm long; style 3-lobed. Alpine meadows, stony slopes and mixed woodland, 1000–2000m. May–July. nwE, swF.*

A rather robust species restricted to the Pyrenees, easily cultivated but having a rather unpleasant smell. Occasionally a rare plain yellowish-green flowered form can be found growing amongst the normal coloured ones in the wild.

5. *Fritillaria messanensis* [7]   Short to medium plant, 20–35cm tall. Leaves grey-green, linear, the *lowest two opposite*, the *upper three usually whorled* and the intermediate ones alternate. Flowers solitary, *green or brownish, chequered*, sometimes with a green band along the centre of each tepal, widely bell-shaped or urn-shaped with a flared mouth, 2.5–3cm diameter, 2–3.5cm long; style 3–lobed. In scrub, grassy hillsides, or light woodland, 100–1500m. February–April (–May). AL, CR, GR, *s*I, SC.●

A rather beautiful but variable species. The forms with elegant urn-shaped flowers are the most attractive.

5a. *F.m.* subsp. *gracilis* (=*F. gracilis, F. neglecta*)   Like (**5**) but the leaves are *glossy green* and the upper ones are not in a whorl of three. Flowers scarcely chequered and not flared at the mouth. Light woodland and grassy places, 300–2200m. April–June. *n*AL, *s&w*YU.●

6. *Fritillaria lusitanica* (=*F. hispanica*) [7]   Short to medium plant, 20–50cm tall. Leaves grey-green, alternate, *narrowly lance-shaped*. Flowers solitary or sometimes 2–3 in a raceme, *green or brownish-red, often chequered* and with a *green or yellowish band along the centre* of each tepal, widely bell-shaped, usually flared at the mouth, 2–3cm diameter, about 2–4cm long; style 3–lobed. Light woodland or rocky places, 200–2500m. March–May. *c,s&e*E, *c&s*P.*

An extremely variable species in flower colour, ranging from pale green to deep reddish-brown, usually with some chequering, though this can be very slight or absent.

7. Greek Fritillary *Fritillaria graeca* (=*F. guicciardii*) [7]   Low to short plant, 5–25cm tall. Leaves grey-green, lance-shaped, the *lowest two opposite* and the rest alternate. Flower usually solitary, *deep purple-brown, chequered*, usually with a green stripe along each tepal, widely bell-shaped, 2–3cm diameter and 2–3cm long; style 3–lobed. Scrub, light woodland, on ledges or in scree, 300–2200m. May–June. CR, *c&s*GR.●

7a. *F.g.* subsp. *thessala* (=*F. ionica, F. thessalica*)   Like (**7**) but the leaves are broader and the upper three are in a whorl, overtopping the flower. Flower green, slightly chequered with pale brown, 2.5–3.5cm diameter and 3–4cm long. Scrub or light woodland, 200–2200m. *s*AL, *nw*GR, *s*YU.●

Fritillaria graeca also resembles *F. pontica* (**10**) which does not however, have any trace of chequering on the flower.

8. *Fritillaria davisii* [7]   Similar to *F. graeca* but the leaves are *shiny green*, not greyish, and the flowers *do not have a green stripe* along the tepals. Fields, olive groves and open rocky hillsides, to 200m. February–March. *s*GR.*

This species occurs only on the Mani peninsular of the Greek Peloponnese. Although very like *F. graeca*, the brown, chequered flowers without green stripes and the shiny green leaves make it fairly easy to distinguish.

9. *Fritillaria epirotica*   Like *F. graeca*, but the upper three leaves are sometimes whorled. Flowers widely bell-shaped, *deep brown-purple, chequered inside but not* on the *outside*, about 2.5–3cm diameter, 2–2.5cm long. (The nectary at the base of each tepal is about 10mm long, whereas in *F. graeca* it is only about 5mm long.) Open rocky mountain slopes, about 2500–2700m. June. *nw*GR.●

A dwarf alpine plant, usually with much darker flowers than *F. graeca* and they are unstriped.

10. *Fritillaria pontica* [7]   Low to medium plant, 15–45cm tall. Leaves usually grey-green, lance-shaped, the lowest two opposite or nearly so, the *upper three in a whorl* and the intermediate ones opposite or alternate. *Flowers 1–3, green*, often with some brownish staining, or with brown tips to the tepals, *not chequered*, broadly lantern-shaped and usually not flared at the mouth, about 2.5–3cm diameter, 2.5–4.5cm long; style 3-lobed, woods or scrub, sea level to 2300m. May–June. *e*AL, *s*BG, *n*GR, TR, YU.*

A common species in the wild and easily recognised by the non-chequered greenish flowers and the whorl of grey leaves near the top of the stem. It is an easily grown attractive species which will tolerate outdoor conditions even in northern gardens.

11. *Fritillaria involucrata* [7]   Rather like *F. pontica* but with *linear or very narrowly lance-shaped leaves*. Flowers *pale green*, slightly but distinctly chequered with purplish-brown, rarely heavily marked and appearing almost mahogany coloured. Clearings in light woodland, in scrub, or rocky places, 500–1500m. April–June. *se*F, *nw*I.*

Although superficially resembling *F. pontica* this species can be separated instantly by the very pale green flowers with their darker chequering. The capsule is rounded with no wings, whereas that of *F. pontica* has six distinct wings on the angles.

12. *Fritillaria gussichae* [8]   Short to medium plant, 20–35cm tall. Leaves grey-green, *broadly lance-shaped*, alternate, *clasping the stem* at their base. *Flowers 1–3, green*, glaucous on the outside, usually with a little pale brown suffusion on the tepals, *not chequered*, broadly bell-shaped, about 2.5–3cm diameter, 3cm long; style 3-lobed. Scrub and deciduous woodland, 500–1500m. April–May. *w*BG, *n*GR, *s*YU.●

Although related to *F. pontica* and *F. graeca* this is an easily recognised species with its broad alternate, very grey leaves.

13. *Fritillaria drenovskii* [8]   Short plant, 15–30cm tall. Leaves grey-green, alternate, narrowly lance-shaped. *Flowers 1–4, deep wine* or purple-brown, not chequered and not flared at the mouth, *narrowly bell-shaped* or *rather conical*, about 1.5–2cm diameter, 1.5–2.5cm long; style 3-lobed. Light woodland and scrub, 1000–1500m. May. *sw*BG, *ne*GR.*

There are other species which have dark smallish non-chequered flowers but

F. drenovskii can be separated from them by having a divided style and rather few (up to 8) narrow leaves.

14. *Fritillaria ruthenica* (=*F. minor*) [8]   Short to medium plant, 20–50cm tall. Leaves grey-green, opposite or whorled, the upper three always whorled and *tendril-like*. Flowers 1–5, *deep blackish-brown, chequered*, widely bell-shaped, not flared at the mouth, about 2–3cm diameter, 2–3cm long; style 3-lobed. Capsule with wings on the angles. In scrub, to 1000m. April–May. *c,sw*&*se*RS.*

Easily recognised by its coiled upper leaves which are capable of clinging to other plants to give support to the slender stems.

15. *Fritillaria orientalis* (=*F. tenella, F. montana*)   Like (**14**), but the lowest leaves are opposite or whorled, the intermediate ones alternate and the whorled upper three are *not tendril-like*. Flowers generally *paler, strongly* chequered with deep brown. Capsule not winged. April–June. AL, BG, F, GR, I, R, *sw*RS, YU.●

16. *Fritillaria meleagroides*   Similar to *F. ruthenica* but the leaves *all alternate*. Flower solitary. Capsule not winged. Damp meadows, to 1000m. April–June. *sw*BG, *c,sw*&*se*RS.

17. *Fritillaria tuntasia* [8]   Short to medium plant, 20–35cm tall. Leaves many (up to 20) grey-green, lance-shaped, alternate, rather twisted and densely clothing the stem. *Flowers 1–5, blackish* with a grey 'bloom' on the outside, *somewhat conical in shape*, about 2–2.5cm diameter and 2–3cm long, style 3-lobed. Scrub and rocky places, to 230m. *s*GR.●

This is endemic to Kythnos Island in the Cyclades and is a very distinctive plant with its many twisted leaves and very dark flowers.

18. *Fritillaria obliqua*   Very similar to (**17**) but generally only 10–20cm tall and with *fewer leaves and flowers*. Rocky hillsides, 200–700m. March–April. *s*GR.●

Unlike *F. tuntasia* this occurs only on the Greek mainland in Attica.

19. *Fritillaria ehrhartii* [8]   Like a small form of *F. tuntasia*, but the lowest two leaves are opposite, the rest alternate. Flowers solitary, *deep purple-brown*, tipped with yellow, glaucous on the outside, *mid-way between conical and bell-shaped*, about 1.5–2cm diameter, 1.5–2cm long; style undivided. Rocks and scrub, usually not on limestone, 150–350m. February–May. *s*GR.●

This species is confined to Euboea and the Cyclades. The undivided style distinguishes it from the other European small-flowered dark purple fritillaries.

20. *Fritillaria conica* [8]   Low to short plant, 10–20cm tall. *Leaves shiny green*, not glaucous, alternate with the lowest two more or less opposite, lance-shaped. *Flowers, 1–2, clear yellowish-green, conical*, about 2cm diameter, 1–2cm long; style 3-lobed. Limestone hills, in scrub and cultivated land, 100–500m. February–March. *s*GR.●

A small yellow fritillary from the south-western Peloponnese. It is an easily grown and attractive little plant for alpine house cultivation.

21. *Fritillaria euboeica* Like *F. conica* but only 5–10cm tall, with *grey-green leaves*. Flowers narrowly bell-shaped rather than conical. Limestone screes, about 500m. *s*GR.●

This is an endemic of Euboea and the only small yellow-flowered fritillary in Europe with greyish-green leaves.

22. *Fritillaria stribrnyi* [8] Low to medium plant, 10–50cm tall. Leaves grey-green, alternate, narrowly linear, the upper three in a whorl. Flowers 1–3, *green with a rather metallic purple suffusion* and greyish 'bloom' on the outside, not chequered, *narrowly tubular* or narrowly bell-shaped, 1.5–2cm diameter, 2–3cm long; style undivided. Scrub and grassy places, to 500m. March–April. *s*BG, TR.●

A rather rare plant in the wild and easily overlooked for it grows in scrub where the slender stems and leaves and dull coloured flowers do not show up.

23. *Fritillaria rhodokanakis* [8] Low plant, 5–15cm tall. Leaves green, mostly alternate but the lowest two opposite, lance-shaped. Flowers solitary, *deep purplish-brown with the tips of the tepals yellow and flared outwards*, widely bell-shaped, about 2–2.5cm diameter, 1.5–2.5cm long; style 3-lobed. Rocky hillsides, 200–600m. March–April. *s*GR.●

A beautiful plant that occurs only on the island of Hydra (Idhra). It is easy to recognise with its short bicoloured bells, widely flared at the mouth, though occasionally the colour is plain green.

COLCHICUM

A moderately large genus occurring from Portugal and North Africa eastwards through Europe and Asia as far as the Himalayas. In Europe it is mainly Mediterranean in its distribution, although the well-known 'Autumn Crocus' *C. autumnale* is a very widespread plant reaching as far north as Britain. There are both autumn- and spring-flowering species, the autumnal ones usually having no leaves visible at flowering time. These appear some time later and remain green until late spring by which time the seed capsules are mature as well. The spring species produce their leaves together with the flowers and in general the foliage of these is much smaller than that of the autumn species. A few species break this general rule and have leaves at flowering time in autumn.

Colchicums usually have rather goblet shaped flowers which might be confused with those of a *Crocus*. The quick and easy method of distinguishing between them is to count the stamens – three in *Crocus* and six in *Colchicum*. In addition, the leaves of *Colchicum* are never white-striped on the upper surface like those of a *Crocus* and, in most species, are much wider. There are no yellow-flowered *Colchicum* species in Europe so that any yellow flower of this shape will be a *Crocus* or *Sternbergia* (Amaryllidaceae).

Colchicums contain colchicine, a substance long known for its ability of artificially inducing polyploidy in other plants. The corms and leaves are poisonous to animals and man.

Low perennial cormous plants, the corm rather elongate vertically and with a 'foot' projecting downwards on one side of the base; in one or two species the corm is more slender and lies horizontally in the soil so that it moves sideways in a stolon-like manner. Leaves either appearing with the flowers or later, varying from narrowly linear and channelled to broadly elliptic and pleated, or flat. Flowers pink, purplish, or white sometimes chequered, goblet-shaped, funnel-

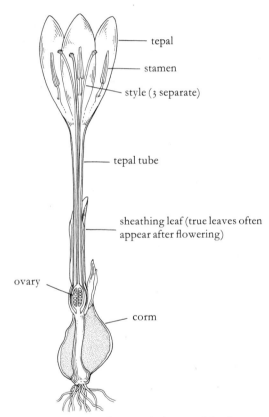

tepal

stamen

style (3 separate)

tepal tube

sheathing leaf (true leaves often appear after flowering)

ovary

corm

Cross-section of a typical Colchicum to illustrate the botanical details

shaped or flattish with the six segments joined into a long tube which arises below ground; ovary below ground at flowering time but as they mature and become seed capsules they are pushed above ground with the developing leaves; stamens six, joined to the base of the tepals the anthers yellow, purplish, brown or blackish before they burst to reveal yellow pollen; styles three, free from each other. Fruit a capsule splitting lengthways when mature.

When identifying colchicums it is necessary to note the colour of the anthers before they burst, or dehisce, whether or not the flowers are checked in appearance, the tepals size and if possible the details of corm and leaves. Always choose specimens which are typical of the population as a whole rather than strikingly different ones. Also, remember that plants in cultivation often behave quite differently to those in the wild and may have a different flowering time and un-typical measurements.

Key to European Species of Colchicum

1. Flowers normally produced between January and
   May 2
   Flowers normally produced between August and
   December 4

2. Leaves usually 2 .... 23. *C. hungaricum*
   Leaves usually 3 3

3. Leaves hairy on the margin. (Gelibolu peninsular
   only, Turkey) .... 20. *C. burttii*
   Leaves rough, but not hairy on the margin ...... 19. *C. triphyllum*

4. Leaves visible at flowering time 5
   Leaves absent at flowering time 7

5. Leaves usually 3 or more .... 22. *C. pusillum*
   Leaves usually 2 6

6. Corm with stolons. (S. Peloponnese only) ...... 18. *C. psaridis*
   Corm without stolons .... 21. *C. cupanii*

7. Flowers chequered, sometimes only slightly so 8
   Flowers plain, with no chequering 14

8. Anthers purplish or brownish 9
   Anthers yellow 12

9. Leaves extremely large, bright green and pleated,
   10–15cm wide. (Crete) .... 6. *C. macrophyllum*
   Leaves less than 6cm wide. (Widespread but not
   in Crete) 10

10. Flowers flattish or rather widely funnel-shaped ...... 6. *C. variegatum*
    Flowers goblet-shaped 11

11. Tepals strongly chequered .... 7. *C. bivonae*
    Tepals obscurely chequered .... 4. *C. lusitanum*

12. Flowers deep reddish-purple .... 17. *C. chalcedonicum*
    Flowers pinkish-lilac 13

13. Tepals usually more than 4cm long. (Spain,
    Portugal, N. Italy)   4. *C. lusitanum*
    Tepals usually less than 4cm long. (Albania,
    Greece)   12. *C. lingulatum*

14. Anthers blackish. (Bulgaria)   8. *C. callicymbium*
    Anthers yellow, purplish or brownish   **15**

15. Corm with horizontal stolons. (S. Greece)   9. *C. boissieri*
    Corm upright   **16**

16. Flowers deep reddish-purple   16. *C. turcicum*
    Flowers pinkish-lilac to white   **17**

17. Leaves usually 5 or more, 2–4mm wide.
    (Peloponnese)   10. *C. parlatoris*
    Leaves either less than 5 per corm or more than
    5mm wide   **18**

18. Tepals usually 4.5cm or more long; leaves up to
    35cm long and 6 cm wide   1. *C. autumnale*
    Tepals usually less than 4.5cm long; leaves smaller   **19**

19. Flowers small and very pale pink or white. (Russia
    and Turkey)   **20**
    Flowers darker pinkish-lilac to purple-pink   **21**

20. Tepals incurved at the apex; leaves 1.5cm or more
    wide. (Crimea)   15. *C. umbrosum*
    Tepals not incurved, flowers starry; leaves 1cm
    or less wide. (Turkey)   13. *C. micranthum*

21. Leaves normally 2; flowers small and
    purplish-pink with tepals 3cm or less long.
    (Alpine meadows)   3. *C. alpinum*
    Leaves normally 3 or more; flowers paler
    pinkish-lilac or relatively larger   **22**

22. Stigmas at the tips of the styles only. (Sandy
    places. E. Yugoslavia eastwards)   11. *C. arenarium*
    Stigmas produced laterally on the styles. (Rocky
    places and in scrub and meadows. W. Yugoslavia
    westwards)   **23**

23. Tepals normally less than 3cm long. (S. Corsica)   14. *C. corsicum*
    Tepals normally more than 3cm long   **24**

24. Leaves usually less than 15cm long, wavy and flat
    on the ground. (Albania and Greece)   12. *C. lingulatum*
    Leaves usually more than 15cm long, erect.
    (C.&W. Mediterranean)   2. *C. neapolitanum*

1. Meadow Saffron *Colchicum autumnale* [9]   Short to medium plant, 8–15cm tall in flower, up to 35cm in leaf. *Leaves normally 4–5*, absent at flowering time, glossy green, usually up to 6cm wide. Flowers one to several, pinkish-lilac, *not chequered*, about 2.5–3.5cm diameter when fully open; *tepals usually 4.5–6cm long and 1–1.5cm wide*; anthers yellow. Meadows and damp grassland, to 1000m.

Meadow Saffron in leaf and fruit, $\times \frac{1}{3}$

August–September. A, B, BG, CH, CS, D, E, F, GB, ?GR, H, I, NL, P, PL, R, *nw,c&sw*RS, YU, and naturalised in a few other countries.*

C. autumnale is one of the most widespread and well-known of the species and is very commonly cultivated for its showy autumnal flowers. It has the disadvantage as a garden plant that in spring the very large leaves tend to swamp other smaller plants nearby. It can, however, be very useful for naturalising in grass or beneath shrubs where the foliage does no harm.

C. rhodopaeum is considered to be closely related, if not the same, as *C. autumnale*. *s*BG.

C. pieperianum is probably very similar to *C. autumnale* but is little known. *n*AL.

2. *Colchicum neapolitanum* (=*C. kochii, C. longifolium*)   This is like *C. autumnale* but generally smaller with 3–4 leaves usually up to 25cm long and 1–2cm wide. Flowers with *tepals normally 3–4.5cm* long and about 1cm wide. Meadows and grassy hillsides, to 500m. CO, E, *s*F, *w*GR, I, P, SA, *w*YU.●

3. Alpine Colchicum *Colchicum alpinum* [9]   Rather similar to *C. autumnale* but much smaller. Leaves absent at flowering time, *usually 2*, strap-like, only 10–15cm long when mature and normally less than 1cm wide. Flowers often solitary, purplish-pink, about 1.5–2.5cm diameter when fully open; *tepals usually 1.5–3cm* long and about 5mm wide (occasionally more). Alpine meadows, 800–1800m. August–September. ?A, CH, CO, SF, I, SA, SC.●

This is the tiny autumn Colchicum of alpine pastures, occasionally growing near *C. autumnale* and apparently rarely hybridising with it.

C. macedonicum is probably rather like *C. alpinum* but is a little-known species. It is said to flower in June. Alpine meadows, about 2000m. SYU.

4. Colchicum lusitanum [9]   Similar to *C. autumnale* but the flowers are usually *rosy-pink and faintly chequered*, and the anthers are often purple or pinkish. Dryish hillsides, to 500m. September–November. E, NI, P.●

The flowers are much less strongly chequered than in the more easterly-occurring *C. bivonae*.

5. Colchicum variegatum [9]   Low plant, to 10cm tall. Leaves 3–4, absent at flowering time, often greyish-green, usually spreading on the ground and undulate at the margins, 10–15cm long and 1–2cm wide. *Flowers flattish*, about 5–6cm diameter, one to three, pinkish-purple or reddish, *strongly chequered*; tepals pointed, 4.5–7cm long and 1–1.5cm wide at the base; anthers deep purple. Rocky hillsides, in scrub or beneath pines, to 1200m. September–December. AEG, SGR – mainly in the Cyclades and Aegean Islands but also common in S.W. Turkey.*

This is one of the most beautiful Colchicum species with its flattish heavily chequered flowers and relatively small undulate leaves.

C. agrippinum is a frequently cultivated plant resembling *C. variegatum*. It has less undulate, more upright leaves and the flowers are less strongly chequered. It is unknown in the wild and may be a hybrid between *C. autumnale* and *C. variegatum*.

6. Colchicum macrophyllum [9]   Similar to *C. variegatum* when in flower, although the flowers are generally larger with broader tepals, slightly more funnel-shaped and usually paler; they are distinctly *chequered, pinkish-lilac on a whitish ground*. *Leaves elliptical, bright green*, up to 40cm long and 10–15cm wide, strongly pleated looking very like the leaves of a *Veratrum*. Rocky places, to 600m. September–October. CR.● Also occurring in Rhodes and S.W. Turkey.

Although in flower this resembles *C. variegatum*, the two species are very distinct. The flowers are not so flat and starry as those of *C. variegatum* and are paler. The enormous leaves are not unattractive with their rather strikingly pleated appearance.

7. Colchicum bivonae (=*C. sibthorpii, C. bowlesianum, C. visianii*) [9]   Low to short plant, up to 15cm in flower and up to 25cm in leaf. Leaves usually 5–9, absent at flowering time, glossy green and more or less erect, 15–23cm long and 1–1.5cm wide. *Flowers goblet-shaped*, 4–6cm diameter, one to five, varying from pale pinkish-lilac to deep rosy-purple, *strongly chequered*; tepals generally 5–6cm long and 1–2cm wide; *anthers purple or brownish*. Rocky places or dryish grassy hillsides, often in scrub, to 1500m. August–October. *s*BG, GR, *s*I, SA, SC, TR, YU.*

This is an extremely variable species over its entire range. It can be distinguished from *C. variegatum* and *C. macrophyllum*, which are also chequered, by having goblet shaped flowers. *C. lusitanum* and *C. turcicum* are also chequered, but much more obscurely so.

It is an attractive species and easily cultivated so that it is a good garden plant. It is one of the parents of a number of vigorous garden hybrids.

8. *Colchicum callicymbium.*   Short to medium plant up to 40cm tall in leaf. Leaves usually 3–5, absent at flowering time, green, linear, about 25–40cm long and 1–5cm wide. Flowers about 2–2.5cm diameter, two to four, *lilac-purple, not chequered*; tepals 3–3.5cm long and 1–1.5cm wide; *anthers blackish*. *sw*BG, ?*ne*GR.

This species is known only from plants cultivated in gardens from corms said to have come from Bulgaria. It has not been recollected there.

9. *Colchicum boissieri* [10]   Low to short plant to 20cm tall in leaf. *Corm producing horizontal stolons.* Leaves usually 2, green, absent or the tips just appearing, at flowering time, linear, normally 10–20cm long and 0.5–1cm wide. Flowers 2.5–4cm diameter, generally solitary, *pinkish-lilac, not chequered*; tepals 2–4cm long and 0.5–1cm wide; *anthers yellow*. Stony hillsides in scrub or beneath pines, to 1300m. September–December. *s*GR.●

A slender species, very distinct in having stoloniferous corms. In cultivation it increases very rapidly by this method but is unfortunately not very showy. The only other species in Europe with stolons is *C. psaridis*, but this species has smaller flowers with narrow tepals and has the leaves developed at flowering time.

C. pinatziorum from Euboea is considered to be a synonym, although it is little-known at present.

10. *Colchicum parlatoris*   Low plant, to 5cm tall. *Leaves many, usually 6–10*, absent at flowering time, spreading, green, linear, 5–10cm long and *only 0.2–0.4cm wide*. Flowers 1.5–2.5cm diameter, normally solitary, pinkish-lilac, not chequered; tepals about 2–3cm long and 0.5–1cm wide; anthers yellow. Edge of fields, on stony hillsides or in scrub, to 500m. August–November. *s*GR – occurs only in the Peloponnese.●

This small-flowered species is rather distinctive with its many narrow leaves.

11. *Colchicum arenarium* [10]   Low to small plant, up to 20cm tall in leaf. Leaves usually 3–5, absent at flowering time, green, *strap-like*, 10–20cm long and 0.5–1.5cm wide. *Flowers about 2–3cm diameter*, one to four, pinkish-lilac, *not chequered*; tepals normally 2.5–4cm long and 0.5–1cm wide; anthers yellow. Grassy places, usually in sandy soil, to 500m. September–October. CS, H, YU.●

A small Colchicum, not unlike *C. alpinum* but having more than two leaves and generally larger flowers.

12. *Colchicum lingulatum* [10]   Low plant, up to 15cm tall. Leaves usually 4–6, absent at flowering time, slightly greyish-green, *held flat on the ground, strap-like,* 10–15cm long and 1–2cm wide, *often undulate* at the margins. Flowers 2.5–4cm diameter, usually two to six, pinkish-lilac, sometimes with faint chequering; tepals normally 3–4cm long and 0.5–1cm wide; anthers yellow or perhaps rarely brownish. Stony or grassy hillsides and in pinewoods, or scrub, 500–2300m. September–October. AL, GR.●

A local species in the wild, related to the widespread *C. autumnale*. The spreading strap-shaped leaves are, however, very different to those of the latter species.

C. parnassicum is a poorly known species, apparently rather like *C. lingulatum*. It has longer leaves, arching over rather than prostrate. Flowers one to three, larger, with tepals to 5cm long. *c&s*GR.

13. *Colchicum micranthum* [10]   Low plant to 15cm tall in leaf. Leaves 2–3, absent at flowering time, green, linear about 10–15cm long and 0.5–1cm wide. Flowers 1.5–2.5cm diameter, one or two, very pale pink or white, not chequered; tepals 1.5–2.5cm long and 0.3–0.6cm wide; anthers yellow. Stony places, to 500m. September–October. TR.●

This species has small pale flowers, and occurs in the Istanbul region of Turkey.

C. borisii may be the same as *C. micranthum* but is poorly known. It is said to have slightly larger flowers and wider greyish-green leaves. *s*BG.

14. *Colchicum corsicum*   Low plant to 10cm tall in leaf; leaves 3–4, absent at flowering time, green, narrowly lance-shaped, up to 10cm long and 0.5–1cm wide. Flowers about 1.5–3cm diameter, one or two, pinkish-lilac, not chequered; tepals usually 2–3cm long and only 0.4–0.7cm wide; anthers yellow. Rocky hillsides, to 500m. September. *s*CO.●

This species is restricted to the southern part of Corsica, although it may also occur in Sardinia.

15. *Colchicum umbrosum*   Low plant to 15cm tall in leaf. Leaves 3–5, absent at flowering time, green, linear or narrowly lance-shaped, about 8–15cm long and 1.5–2cm wide. Flowers 1.5–2.5cm diameter, usually one to three, *very pale* pink or whitish, not chequered; tepals 1.5–3cm long and 0.3–0.5cm wide, *generally incurved at the apex*; anthers yellow. Woods and scrub, to 1000m. August–September. K, *sw*RS.●

This species occurs mainly in the Caucasus and Asiatic Turkey.

C. laetum is similar to *C. umbrosum* but is larger flowered. It is a poorly known species. *se*RS.

16. *Colchicum turcicum* [10]   Low plant to 15cm tall. Leaves 5–9, grey-green, absent at flowering time, narrowly lance-shaped, 10–15cm long and 0.5–2.5cm wide, often undulate. Flowers 1.5–3cm diameter, three to eight, generally *deep reddish-purple*, not chequered; tepals 3–4cm long and about 0.5–1.5cm wide; anthers normally yellow. Grassy or stony places, to 500m. August–October. sBG, neGR, ?eR, TR.●

The deep coloured flower with their rather narrow tepals assist in the recognition of this plant, and the wavy leaves are also distinctive.

17. *Colchicum chalcedonicum*   Very similar to *C. turcicum* but usually with solitary flowers which are the same deep colour but *slightly chequered*. Possibly occurs in nwTR.●

18. *Colchicum psaridis* [10]   Low plant to 5cm tall. *Corm producing horizontal stolons.* Leaves usually 2, bright green, *well-developed at flowering time*, 3–10cm long and 0.3–0.5cm wide, expanding somewhat in the fruiting stage. Flowers small 1.5–2cm diameter, one to five, pinkish-lilac, not chequered; tepals about 1–2.5cm long, 0.3–0.6cm wide, anthers brownish. Olive groves and stony ground, to 300m. September–December. sGR.●

This tiny species occurs in the southern Peloponnese. It most closely resembles *C. cupanii* which, however, does not have a corm with stolons.

19. *Colchicum triphyllum* (=*C. catacuzenium*) [10]   Low plant to 8cm tall. *Leaves usually 3*, dull green, *present at flowering* time but rather short, normally 3–5cm long, and 4–6mm wide, later expanding to 15cm long and 1cm wide. Flowers about 2–3cm diameter, one to four, pinkish-lilac, not chequered; tepals 1.5–3cm long, 0.5–1cm wide; anthers blackish or purplish. Stony places, to 1500m. Usually February–March. BG, E, GR, K, R, swRS, TR.●

An attractive little spring Colchicum with goblet-shaped flowers, rather widespread in distribution, but never common. It is not unlike *C. hungaricum* (**23**) but does not have the two leaves characteristic of this species.

C. davidovii and *C. diampolis* are poorly known species related to *C. triplyllum*. Both are said to grow in eBG.

20. *Colchicum burttii*   Similar to *C. triphyllum* but thick leathery corm tunics (thinly papery in the latter) and leaves with hairy margins. Stony hillsides, to 300m. TR.●

This species occurs in the Gelibolu Peninsula and in the adjacent part of Asiatic Turkey.

21. *Colchicum cupanii* [11]   Low plant to 8cm tall. *Leaves usually 2*, bright or dull green, *present at flowering time*, but often short, linear or narrowly lance-shaped, very variable in size, up to 15cm long and 0.5–1.5cm wide. Flowers about 1–2cm diameter, one to five (rarely more), pinkish-purple or pale pink; tepals 1–2.5cm long and 0.3–0.6cm wide; anthers deep brownish-purple. Rocky places, to 1300m. *September–December.* CR, F, GR, I, SA, SC.●

C. cupanii is a delightful little species, very common in southern Greece but rather local elsewhere. It is extremely variable from small, narrow-leaved plants with few flowers to many-flowered broad-leaved ones. The leaves can be bright shiny green or dull dark green and they vary a great deal in their degree of development at flowering time.

C. cousturieri is very similar to *C. cupanii*. It has flowers in which the tepals are purple-striped. It occurs on two islands off the south coast of Crete.

22. *Colchicum pusillum* (=*C. cretense, C. andrium*) [11] Low plant to 5cm tall. *Leaves 3–5*, green, normally present at flowering time but sometimes only the tips visible; thread-like or narrowly linear, up to 4cm long and 0.1–0.2cm wide, expanding later to about 6–8cm long and 2–3cm wide. Flowers 1–2cm diameter, one to four, pale mauve-pink or white; *tepals 1–2cm long* and 0.2–0.3cm wide; anthers yellow, brownish or purplish. Rocky or sandy places, to 2100m. October–November. CR, *s*GR.●

The amount of leaf visible at flowering time varies considerably and in some cases the leaves are dormant until just after the flowers have faded. Plants from the Peloponnese usually have purplish anthers and those from the Cyclades brown.

C. peloponnesiacum is similar but has slightly larger flowers to 2.5cm diameter, with tepals to 3cm long and 1cm wide. Rocky places, to 100m. *s*GR – only in the southern Peloponnese.

23. *Colchicum hungaricum* (=*C. doerfleri*) [11] Low plant, to 10cm tall. *Leaves usually 2*, dull green with *silvery hairs* on the margins and sometimes all over the lower surface as well, developed at flowering time and about 3–8cm long, 0.3–0.5cm wide, expanding later to 20cm long and 1–2cm wide. Flowers 1.5–2.5cm diameter, usually two to six, *pinkish-lilac or white*; tepals 2–3cm long and 0.5–0.7cm wide; anthers dark brown or purplish-brown. Stony places, to 1500m. Usually January–April. AL, BG, *n*GR, H, *s&w*YU.●

An attractive small spring-flowering species with goblet-shaped flowers. It is variable in colour and stature, and in the hairiness of the leaves. In northern Greece and southern Yugoslavia a robust form occurs with deep pink flowers and strong erect leaves, whereas the more normal forms have pale pink or white flowers and arching leaves.

ANDROCYMBIUM

A rather small little-known genus, mainly distributed in east tropical Africa and South Africa but with a few species in Mediterranean regions. They are related to the much more common and well-known colchicums but differ in having their tepals free from each other, not joined into a tube. Furthermore, they have a cluster of conspicuous bract-like leaves, an 'involucre' surrounding the flowers and in this respect they differ also from the other allies, *Merendera* and *Bulbocodium*. The tepals of *Androcymbium* have conspicuous swollen yellow glands near the base of the blade.

1. *Androcymbium europaeum* [11]   Low plant, to 5cm tall in flower. Corm elongate with a tough blackish tunic. *Stem very short, the leaves thus appearing as a rosette at ground* level. Leaves 6–10, linear-lanceolate, glossy green, about 1cm wide in the lower portion which forms the involucre, *long*-tapering to an acute apex, up to 10cm long when fully mature. Flowers 1–several, *pinkish or white*, striped with mauve and sometimes faintly darker speckled, 2–2.5cm diameter; tepals six, about 2–2.5cm long and 0.3–0.5cm wide with a narrow claw at the base and *long-pointed at the apex*; stamens six joined to the base of the blade of the tepals; styles 3, free from each other. Fruit a 3-valved capsule, splitting open at its base. Open sandy or rocky places, or in sparse grass, to 300m. December–February. *se*E*.

A rare plant, known only from Cabo de Gata in Spain. It has been confused with the North African *A. gramineum* which does not occur in Europe.

2. *Androcymbium rechingeri*   Similar to *A. europaeum* but with *shortly-pointed tepals*. The capsule does not split open but eventually rots and breaks up irregularly. Rocky places near the sea. *w*CR* – only on Elaphonisi Island.

MERENDERA

A small genus of dwarf *Colchicum*-like plants, distributed from Europe eastwards to Afghanistan and extending southwards as far as Ethiopia. In Europe there are both autumn and spring-flowering species. They differ from *Colchicum* in having their tepals free from each other, and in having three separate styles, thus distinguishing them from the 1-styled *Bulbocodium*.

Low cormous perennials, the corm elongated, usually with a thick brown tunic, rarely with stolons. Leaves basal, linear or narrowly lance-shaped, produced with the flowers or later when the flowers have finished. Flowers stemless, funnel-shaped or flattish; tepals six, free from each other; stamens six, attached at the base of the widened part of the tepals; styles three, separate. Fruit a capsule with three valves, splitting from the apex downwards.

1. *Merendera bulbocodium* (=*M. montana*) [11]   Low plant, to 5cm tall in flower. Leaves 3–4, narrowly linear, *appearing after flowering time* or sometimes with the tips just visible, later becoming 10–20cm long and usually about 0.5–0.9cm wide. *Flowers one or two, rosy-purple or violet*, about 3–5cm diameter with blunt tepals normally 3–5cm long and 0.4–0.7cm wide; anthers yellow. Grassy hillsides and alpine pastures, 900–2500m. July–October. E, *sw*F, P.*

This is the most well-known species, with large bright purple-pink flowers opening out nearly flat in sunshine. It is an attractive plant for cultivation in an alpine house or on a rock garden.

2. *Merendera filifolia* Similar to *M. bulbocodium* but the leaves are 5–10 in number and *only 1–3mm wide*. Flowers generally slightly smaller. Dry sandy and stony places in scrub and beneath pines, to 200m. August–November. BAL, s&seE, sF.●

3. *Merendera attica* (=*M. rhodopaea*) [11] Low plant, to 5cm tall in flower. *Leaves 3–4, linear, appearing at flowering time* and rather short, but expanding later to 8–15cm long and 0.3–0.6cm wide. Flowers usually 2–several, *white or pale pinkish-purple*, 2–3cm diameter with narrow tepals about 1.5–3cm long and only 0.3–0.4cm wide; anthers dark brown or deep violet. Open stony places and in sparse grass or scrub, to 1000m. October–December (rarely to March). sBG, ?sE, sGR.●

This species is easily recognised by having normally several pale flowers, produced in succession. The tepals are so narrow as to give the flower a spidery appearance lacking the substantial form of those of *M. bulbocodium*. It is very common in western Asiatic Turkey where it tends to be spring-flowering.

In southern Spain, in Ronda, there is a similar plant to *M. attica* which is spring-flowering. The anthers appear to be attached to the filaments at the base whereas in the typical plant they are attached at the middle of the anther. This is probably just a local variant of *M. attica*.

4. *Merendera sobolifera* Low plant, to 5cm tall in flower. *Corm producing horizontal stolons.* Leaves 3, narrowly lance-shaped, visible at flowering time and expanding later to 10–15cm long and 0.4–0.7cm wide. Flowers one or two, white or pinkish-purple, 2–3.5cm diameter with tepals 2–4cm long and about 0.3–0.5cm wide; at the base of each of the tepals are *two hair-like structures hanging downwards*; anthers dark brown or violet. Moist sandy, grassy places, to 1000m. February–April. BG, R, TR, YU.●

This species is most like *M. attica* in having pale flowers with dark stamens, but it has a rather curious stoloniferous corm and hair-like appendages on the lower part of the blade of the tepals. Neither of these features are present in *M. attica*. It is a widespread species as far eastwards as Iran, but it is never very common.

BULBOCODIUM

A small genus of two species only, both confined to Europe; they are related to *Colchicum* species but the tepals are free from each other, not joined into a tube as in *Colchicum*. Also closely allied is *Merendera* which has free tepals, but *Bulbocodium* differs from this in having only one style instead of three.

1. *Bulbocodium vernum* [11] Low plant, to 5cm tall in flower and to 15cm tall in leaf. Corm elongate, with a brown tunic. Leaves 3, basal, linear or narrowly lanceolate, very short at flowering time but when mature up to 15cm long and 0.8–1.8cm wide. *Flowers 1–3, purple, rarely white, stemless,* 2.5–4.5cm diameter when fully open; *tepals narrowly strap-shaped, 3–6cm long, free from each other* but hooked together by small teeth near the base of the widened part of the blade; stamens 6, joined to the base of the blade of the tepals; style 3-lobed at the apex. Fruit a capsule carried at ground level, with three valves, splitting open at the apex. Grassy hillsides and mountain pastures, 500–2000m. March–May. *s*A, CH, *ne*E, *sw*F, *n*I.*

Bulbocodium vernum is well known to bulb enthusiasts, for its a useful early spring-flowering plant of easy culture, although it is best grown in the protection of an alpine house.

2. *Bulbocodium versicolor* (=*B. ruthenicum*) Like *B. vernum* but with smaller flowers with rounded lobes instead of teeth at the base of the blade of the tepals. Grassy places, to 500m. March–April. *e*H, *c*I, *c*R, *c,sw*&*se*RS, *ne*YU.

PARADISEA

A beautiful genus resembling *Anthericum* but having trumpet-shaped rather than flat flowers.

Medium hairless herbaceous perennials with a short underground rhizome and fleshy roots. The leaves are borne in a basal tuft and are long and linear. The flowers are borne in a loose graceful one-sided raceme, each with 6 equal tepals, shortly joined at the base; the style and stamens are curved upwards. Fruit a capsule containing several black seeds in each of the three chambers.

1. St Bruno's Lily *Paradisea liliastrum* [12] Short to medium plant to 50cm tall. Leaves 4–7, up to 6mm wide, shorter or as long as the flower stem. Flowers glistening white, each tepal tipped with green, *trumpet shaped*, 3.5–5cm long, 3–10 to a raceme. Style and stamens curved. Alpine meadows and rocky slopes, 1000–2300m. June–July. A*, CH, *ne*F, *s*F, *s*F, *n*I, *n*YU*.*

This graceful plant resembles a small white-flowered trumpet-lily and is sometimes seen in large colonies in the wild. A very useful herbaceous border plant, it is hardy and easily grown and surprisingly uncommon in gardens.

2. *Paradisea lusitanica* is a similar species but generally taller with more numerous and smaller flowers. P.

St Bruno's Lily fruit capsule, × 1½

St Bernard's Lily fruit capsule, × 2

ANTHERICUM

A similar genus to *Paradisea* but with flatter flowers carried in a raceme or panicle. The style may be straight or curved but the stamens are always straight. The genus contains only 3 European species, though it is widely distributed in other areas, particularly Africa. The St Bernard's Lily is particularly popular in cultivation.

1. St Bernard's Lily *Anthericum liliago* [12]   Short to medium hairless herbaceous perennial to 60cm tall. Leaves grey-green, in a basal tuft about half the length of the flower stem, each 3–8mm wide. Flowers white, flattish and starry when open, 2–4cm, 5–30 carried semi-erect in a *loose raceme*; tepals 3-veined and the style curved. Grassy and stony places and open woodland, 300–2500m. June–July. A, AL, B, BG, CH, CO, CS, D, DK, E, F, GR, H, I, P, PL, R, wRS, SF, YU.*

The commonest and most attractive European species. With its fairly large glistening white flowers it makes a useful herbaceous border plant for early summer. It is easily grown.

2. *Anthericum ramosum*   Similar to the previous but with smaller flowers, about 1.5cm, which have rather reflexed tepals when fully open, carried in a *several-branched panicle*; style straight. Dry grassy places and scrub, or open woodland, 200–1500m. June–August. A, AL, B, BG, CH, CS, D, E, F, H, I, PL, R, swRS, SF, TR, YU.

A less attractive species than St Bernard's Lily and easily recognised by its branched flower stem.

3. *Anthericum baeticum*   Similar to (1) but with *very slender leaves*, 1–2mm wide and smaller flowers, 1.5–2.5cm. Damp grassy and stony places, to 2700m. June–July. *se*E – Sierra Nevada.

SIMETHIS

A genus related to *Anthericum* but the flowers are stained purple on the outside and the stamens have hairy stalks or filaments. The solitary species is not a well known plant since it is not very showy and can be easily overlooked.

Kerry Lily *Simethis planifolia* [12]   Short to medium rather delicate herbaceous perennial, to 50cm tall, often less. Leaves hairless, linear, in a basal tuft, 2–8mm wide. Flowers white flushed with purple on the outside, starry, 1–2cm, 10–40 in a *loose panicle*; tepals free from one another; stamens yellow with *white hairy filaments*. Fruit a rounded capsule containing 3–6 black seeds. Dryish grassy or rocky places, or scrub, to 1000m. April–June. CH, CO, F, sGB*, I, swIRL*, P, SA.●

A widespread plant in south-western Europe which is easily recognised by its

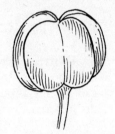

Kerry Lily fruit capsule, × 3

branched flower stem and the colour of the flowers. In Britain it is confined to the Bournemouth area and in Ireland to Kerry.

ASPHODELINE

An attractive genus with three European representatives commonly seen in south-eastern Europe, especially Greece. They can be easily distinguished from *Paradisea* and *Anthericum* by having their leaves carried on the stem instead of in a basal tuft. Asphodelines are medium hairless perennials which have a short rhizome and fleshy yellow roots. There are many leaves packed tightly together on the stem. The flowers are borne in a dense raceme, the flowers open fully usually in the evening; tepals 6 joined into a short tube, each tepal with 3 veins.

1. Yellow Asphodel *Asphodeline lutea* [12]   Medium to tall plant 40–120cm tall. Leaves linear, 2–3mm wide, carried on *the whole length of the stem*. Flowers yellow, each tepal with a median green stripe, 3–4cm, in a *dense raceme*. Rocky places, generally in hilly or mountainous areas, to 2000m. March–May. AL, BG, CR, GR, I, R, SC, TR, YU.●
     The most well known species which is sometimes grown in our gardens, though it is not a spectacular plant. The yellow flowers separate it immediately from the otherwise somewhat similar *Asphodelus albus* (p.73).

2. *Asphodeline liburnica*   Similar to the previous but a more slender plant with leaves borne *only on the lower two thirds of the stem*. Flowers yellow, in a loose raceme. Dry rocky hills or scrub, to 1000m. June–July. AL, BG, CR, GR, I, TR, YU.●

3. *Asphodeline taurica*   Medium to tall plant, to 100cm tall. Leaves linear, crowded together on the lower two thirds of the stem. *Flowers white*, 3–4cm, each tepal with a dark median stripe, enclosed by *large silvery bracts*, borne in a very dense raceme. Mountain screes and rocky hills, 1000–2200m. May–June. AL, BG, GR, R, ?TR, ?YU.

White Asphodel fruit capsule, × 2

Yellow Asphodel fruit capsule, × 2

ASPHODELUS

A genus of robust hairless herbaceous perennials. These rather coarse-looking plants are often seen in great numbers where over-grazing has taken place, for animals dislike the leaves. In general appearance they resemble the Anthericums which also have flat white flowers but the latter are smaller plants with slender flat leaves, whereas those of the *Asphodelus* are broad V-shaped or hollow-cylindrical in cross section.

The leaves of *Asphodelus* are borne in a basal tuft and the leafless stems support a raceme or panicle of starry flowers, each subtended by a papery bract. The fruit capsules contain several angular seeds.

1. White Asphodel *Asphodelus albus* [12] Medium to tall perennial with swollen roots, to 100cm tall. Leaves grey-green, up to 10, 1–2.5cm wide. Flowers white, 3–4cm, each tepal with a thin green stripe, carried in a dense *simple spike-like raceme*; bracts usually *dark brown*. Rocky ground, waste places, open woodland and meadows, to 2000m. March–June. AL, BAL, BG, CH, E, F, H, I, P, SA, SC, YU.●

The white 'spikes' of this species are often seen on mountain pastures in the Alps and Pyrenees, though it is widespread in other areas. The dense unbranched 'spike' of flowers serves to distinguish this from the other species.

2. Common Asphodel *Asphodelus microcarpus* (=*A. aestivus*) Similar to the previous species but with a *much-branched flower* stem and *whitish bracts*; the widely spreading branches are often almost as long as the central raceme. Flowers white, often pink-tinged. Fields and rocky hills, to 1050m. April–June. AL, BAL, CO, CR, E, F, GR, I, P, SA, SC, YU.

Probably the most frequently encountered species, the large pyramidal panicles of flowers immediately recognisable and rather striking.

3. *Asphodelus ramosus* (=*A. cerasiferus*) Similar to the previous species but the side branches of the stem are *short* and stubby compared to the central raceme.

This species has a similar distribution to *A. microcarpus*. In general character it seems to come midway between *A. albus* and *A. microcarpus* and some botanists consider it to be a hybrid between these two species.

4. Annual or **Hollow-stemmed Asphodel** *Asphodelus fistulosus* [12]   Short to medium *annual with fibrous roots*, to 60cm tall, though often less. Leaves linear, *hollow and cylindrical*, less than 5mm wide. Flowers white or pinkish, 1.6–2cm, each tepal with a brown or pink mid-vein, carried in branched or unbranched racemes. Dry rocky, grassy or waste places, to 2000m. April–June. AZ, BAL, CO, CR, E, F, GR, I, P, SA, SC, TR, YU.

The Annual Asphodel is a much more delicate-looking plant than the other species, often occurring as a weed in and around cornfields. It is now widespread in the world, probably having been transferred with cereal seeds.

Asphodelus tenuifolius is sometimes separated as a distinct species or subspecies, but it is very similar and doubtfully distinct. The leaves and flower stems are rough (scabrid) and the flowers rather smaller, but these features are very variable.

EREMURUS

A large genus of robust stately plants with long showy spike-like racemes of white, yellow, pink or brownish flowers. Most of the species occur in Asia, especially in Iran and Afghanistan and the adjacent areas of the USSR. Europe is poorly represented and has only two species, both of these confined to the Crimea. *Eremurus* make beautiful garden plants but require very well drained soils and a hot sunny position.

1. Foxtail Lily *Eremurus spectabilis* [12]   Tall hairless herbaceous perennial, 100–200cm tall. Leaves grey-green, linear, in a basal tuft, channelled and with a sharp keel. Flowers yellow, rather cup-shaped, 1.5–2cm, with separate tepals, 100 or more in a very dense raceme. Fruit a rounded capsule with several very angular seeds. Stony hillsides, 500–1500m. April–June. K*.*****

One of the most striking species with its masses of bright yellow flowers. It has a wide distribution in Asia.

2. *Eremurus tauricus*   Similar to the previous species but having white flowers, each tepal with a green mid-vein. Stony hillsides. K*.

NECTAROSCORDUM

A small genus of only 2 or 3 species closely related to *Allium* and possessing a similar onion or garlic smell when crushed or bruised. The very robust habit and umbels of large pendulous bell-like flowers make it very distinctive. The tepals have 3–5 veins along their centres, whereas the tepals of *Allium* species have only a single vein. *Nectaroscordums* make interesting garden plants and their large erect capsules dry excellently for winter flower arrangements.

Nectaroscordum siculum (=*Allium siculum*) [12]   Medium to tall hairless bulbous perennial 50–150cm tall. Leaves mostly basal, strongly keeled on the underside, to 5cm wide, partly withered at flowering time; inner leaf sheathing the flower stem for one third of its length. Flowers greenish-white or greenish-maroon, *bell-shaped*, 14–16mm long, in *a loose umbel*, each flower on long arching stalks

Nectaroscordum siculum flower, × 1½

which become erect in fruit. Woods or scrub, below 1000m. April–June. BG, CO, F, I, K, R, SA, SC, TR.*

A delightfully graceful plant widely cultivated in Europe and often producing large numbers of seedlings if left undisturbed. Inside each flower can be seen three glistening oval nectaries.

The whitish-green flowered form from Bulgaria, Turkey, Roumania and the Crimea is sometimes called *N. bulgaricum* but, apart from the slight differences in flower colour, the two forms appear to be inseparable.

ALLIUM

This is the very well-known and large group of plants which includes Onions, Leeks, Garlic and Shallots. Nearly all the species have the characteristic strong onion-like smell but many are not edible and some have a most unpleasant pungent odour. A few species are attractive enough to be useful garden plants and the flower heads are sometimes used for dried decorations in winter.

Low to tall bulbous perennials, the whole plant usually smelling of onions when crushed. Bulbs covered with papery or fibrous tunics, solitary or clustered, sometimes grouped together on a short rhizome. Leaves linear or elliptic, rarely ovate, basal or sheathing the flower stem for part of its length. Flowers starry, cup-shaped or bell-shaped, carried in an umbel of few to many. Tepals six, free or occasionally slightly joined at the base. Stamens six, attached to the base of the segments. Stigma entire or with three short lobes. Fruit consisting of a capsule with one or two, sometimes more, black seeds in each of the three valves.

In addition to the many wild species of allium in Europe there are several which are cultivated and may occasionally be found on rubbish dumps or in derelict gardens. They are *A. cepa*, the onion and its various forms, and *A. fistulosum*, Welsh Onion, both of which have inflated portions in the middle or lower part of the flowering stems; *A. sativum*, garlic, which has a bulb consisting of several separate bulblets ('cloves') and the Leek which is a form of the wild *A. ampeloprasum*, a description of which will be found below. There are also numerous non-European allium species cultivated in gardens for their decorative value, some being very useful for dried flower arrangements in winter. The only species which is likely to be encountered as an escape is *A. paradoxum*. It is a distinctive plant with solitary, occasionally more, large pendulous white bell-shaped flowers and green bulbils in the umbel. It is a native of Iran and the Caucasus.

European allium species number over one hundred. It would be impossible here to give a full description of each since in order to distinguish between many of them it is necessary to go into very minute details. The following list of species is as near complete as possible, and follows fairly closely the species as accepted by Dr W. T. Stearn for his revision of the genus in Europe. In an attempt to reduce the complications of identification in this guide, only the most widespread have been illustrated and given descriptions. These are arranged alphabetically. The many species which have a more restricted distribution are mentioned with a few comments, after that widespread species which they superficially most resemble.

One striking species from southeast European Russia is best mentioned here, since it is unrelated to any other species in Europe and cannot easily be compared. It is *A. caspium*, a plant most easily recognised by its enormous umbel, up to 10cm diameter in the fruiting stage, although the whole plant is only 10–25cm in height.

1. *Allium acutiflorum*   Short to medium plant, 15–50cm tall; bulb egg-shaped; leaves linear 3–6mm wide, sheathing the lower part of the stem, long-tapering at the apex. Umbel usually 2–4cm diameter, hemispherical, many-flowered; flowers purple, bell-shaped, with *sharply pointed tepals*. Sandy and rocky places in scrub, to 1000m. June–August. BAL, CO, F, E, I, SA.

The very acute tepals give the umbel of this species a very 'spiky' appearance.

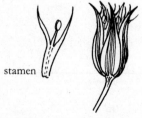

A. acutiflorum flower, × 2

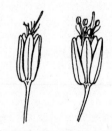

A. amethystinum flower, × 2

2. *Allium amethystinum*   Medium to tall plant, 30–120cm tall; bulb rounded or egg-shaped; leaves linear, 5–15mm wide, hollow, sheathing the lower part of the stem and shrivelled at flowering time. Umbel 3–5cm diameter, nearly spherical, many-flowered, the outer flowers often on pendulous pedicels and the inner, upright; flowers purple, rather tubular. Rocky places, often in or near cultivated land, to 1000m. May–July. AL, CR, GR, I, SC, YU.

The stamens of this species have long hair-like appendages to their filaments, which protrude from the flower.

3. Wild Leek *Allium ampeloprasum* [13]   Medium to tall plant, 30–150cm tall; bulb rounded or egg-shaped, producing many bulblets; leaves linear, 5–20mm wide, rough on the margin, sheathing the lower part of the stem and shrivelled by flowering time. Umbel 5–10cm diameter, spherical, very densely flowered but occasionally with bulbils and few flowers; flowers pink, reddish or white, cup- or bell-shaped, the tepals less than 5mm long and with small hair-like protruberances on the outside. Usually in or near cultivated land or in dry rocky or sandy places, to 1000m. May–July. AL, BAL, CR, E, F, GR, I, P, SA, SC, TR, YU (also naturalised in some other countries).●

Some variants of this have a lot of bulbils in the flower head, and var. *babingtonii* is particularly well-developed in this respect. The cultivated Leek is a selection of *A. ampeloprasum* known as var. *porrum* or sometimes just *Allium porrum*.

A. pardoi is similar to *A. ampeloprasum* but has a smaller umbel, up to 5cm diameter, with more cylindrical-shaped flowers without any protruberances on the outside of the tepals, which are greenish-white. *ne*E (and N. Africa).

A. bourgeaui is very similar to *A. ampeloprasum* but the bulb does not produce a lot of bulblets. The tepals are widest near the base (widest near the middle in *A. ampeloprasum*). AEG, CR.

A. pyrenaicum looks like *A. ampeloprasum* but has larger whitish flowers with tepals 8–9mm long. *e*E (Pyrenees).

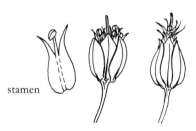

stamen

Wild Leek flowers, × 2

A. polyanthum is similar to *A. ampeloprasum* but has smooth-margined leaves and stamens included within the flower; not exserted or protruding as in the more widespread species. BAL, CO, E, F.

A. scaberrimum is similar to *A. ampeloprasum* but is less robust with a more hemispherical umbel 3–5 cm in diameter and white flowers which have tepals smooth on the outside. seF.

4. *Allium angulosum* [13]   Short to medium plant, 20–50 cm tall; bulbs slender and elongated, clustered on a rhizome to form clumps. Leaves basal, linear, usually 2–4 mm wide with a sharp keel on the underside. Umbel about 3–4 cm diameter, hemispherical, many-flowered; flowers pale purple, cup-shaped. Damp grassland, to 1400 m. June–August. AL, BG, CH, CS, D, F, H, I, PL, R, *c,e*&*w*RS, YU.●

A. suaveolens is rather like *A. angulosum* but its leaves sheath the stem for at least the lower quarter of the stem; flowers pink or whitish with a pink line along the centre of each tepal. Damp grassy places and heathland. A, AL, CH, D, E, F, H, I, YU.

Both *A. angulosum* and *A. suaveolens* closely resemble *A. senescens* and its relatives which are described below under that species. These two, however, can be distinguished from the rest by having keeled leaves. *A. senescens* and related species (p.87) with their pink or purple flowers, all have leaves that are flat or rounded on the underside. The other clump-forming alliums, *A. ericetorum* and its relatives, have whitish or yellowish flowers. They will be found under *A. ericetorum* (p.79).

A. angulosum flower, × 2   *A. atropurpureum* flower, × 2

5. *Allium atropurpureum* [13]   Medium to tall plant, 40–100 cm tall; bulb rounded; leaves all basal, linear, about 10–20 mm wide. Umbel 4–6 cm across, broadly shuttlecock-shaped with many flowers; *flowers deep red-purple*, flat and starry. Dryish places in grass or scrub, to 1500 m. May–June. A, BG, H, TR, YU.●

The rich deeply coloured flowers and basal leaves make this an easily identified, rather handsome, onion.

6. *Allium atroviolaceum* [13]   Medium to tall plant, 40–100 cm tall; bulb egg-shaped with clusters of small dark purple bulblets. Leaves linear, 3–8 mm wide, sheathing the lower part of the stem. Umbel 3–5 cm diameter, spherical, densely-flowered; flowers deep purple, cup-shaped. Dry grassy places, in fields or scrub, to 1000 m. May–July. BG, GR, H, K, R, *w*RS, TR, YU.●

A 'drumstick' allium with rather striking deep purple flowers. It is superficially similar to *A. rotundum* (p.85), but in *A. atroviolaceum* the stamens protrude out of the flower while in *A. rotundum* they are included within it.

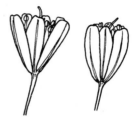

A. atroviolaceum flower, × 2   *A. callimischon* flowers, × 2

7. *Allium callimischon* [13]   Low to medium plant, usually 10–30cm tall; bulb egg-shaped. Leaves thread-like, about 1mm wide, sheathing the stem for most of its length. Umbel shuttlecock-shaped, about 2–3cm across, with about 10–25 flowers; *flowers papery white* with a brown-reddish mid vein on each tepal, cup- or funnel-shaped. Rocky places, to 1300m. September–December. *s*GR.●

This is unusual in flowering in the late autumn. The flowers have a very papery appearance.

7a. *A.c.* subsp. *haemastictum*   This is a similar but smaller plant only 4–10cm tall and with *reddish spots* on the tepals. Rocky places, to 1500m. September–December. CR.*

This is a popular little rock garden plant with dwarf habit and curious red-spotted, almost transparent flowers.

8. Keeled Garlic *Allium carinatum* [13]   Short to medium plant; usually 30–50cm tall; bulb rounded. Leaves linear, 1–3mm wide, hairless, sheathing the lower part of the stem. Umbel 2–5cm diameter, loose and often containing bulbils; flowers purple, cup-shaped, inner ones on upright stalks, outer curving downwards. Grassy places and scrub, to 1800m. June–August. A, AL, BG, CH, CS, D, E, F, GR, H, I, R, *w*RS, S, TR, YU (and naturalised in several other countries).*

Keeled Garlic flowers, × 2

A. tardans is like a small *A. carinatum* with stems less than 30cm and a more compact umbel only 1–2.5cm diameter, with pink flowers. CR.

A. pulchellum is a well-known late summer flowering plant much grown for its richly coloured purple flowers, with no bulbils in the umbel. It is probably only a form of *A. carinatum*.

A. hirtovaginum is similar to *A. carinatum* but is generally shorter, with pink flowers and hairy leaves and leaf sheaths. *n*GR (Lesvos).

A. podolicum is a beautiful species related to *A. carinatum* but with many, larger, shell pink flowers, the tepals about 6mm long. *e*H, R, *sw*RS.

9. *Allium chamaemoly* Low plant to 5cm tall; bulb rounded. Leaves linear, 2–8mm wide, *spreading out flat on the ground in a rosette*, hairy on the margins and long-tapering at the apex. Umbel almost stemless, about 2cm diameter, rather shuttlecock-shaped with up to 20 flowers; flowers white or greenish, flat and starry. Sandy and stony places, to 50m. November–February. BAL, CO, E, F, GR, I, SA, SC, YU.●

An unmistakable allium because of its rosette-like habit.

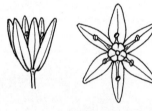
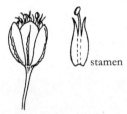
stamen

A. *chamaemoly* flowers, × 2   A. *commutatum*, × 2

10. *Allium commutatum* Medium to tall plant, 50–100cm tall; bulb large, rounded, with numerous bulblets. Leaves long and linear, 10–20mm wide, channelled on the upper side, sheathing the lower part of the stem. Umbel usually nearly spherical, generally about 4–6cm diameter, many-flowered; flowers pinkish, egg-shaped. Usually near the sea in dry grassy places, to 100m. May–June. CO, CR, GR, I, SA, SC, YU.

This species has a single long spathe with a beak, 20–30cm long, but it often falls off before the flowers are fully open.

11. *Allium cupanii* [13] Low to short plant usually 10–25cm tall; bulb egg-shaped with a fibrous tunic. Leaves thread-like, only 0.5mm wide, sheathing the lower part of the stem. Umbel shuttlecock-shaped, 2–4cm diameter, with up to 15 flowers; flowers pink or nearly white with a central darker vein along each of the acute tepals, rather tubular. Dry stone places, to 1200m. May–October. AL, BG, CR, GR, I, SC, YU. 9

A. parciflorum is similar but with a more papery bulb tunic. CO, SA.

A. rouyi is similar to *A. cupanii* but with yellowish flowers. *sw*E.

A. peroninianum is probably the same as *A. cupanii*. TR.

A. obtusiflorum is superficially similar to *A. cupanii* but the bulb tunic is papery and the umbel is more globose with the lower flowers on recurving pedicels. The flowers are smaller and have rounded tepals. s&eGR, sc.

A. cupanii flower, × 2   *A. ericetorum* flower, × 2

12. *Allium ericetorum* (=*A. ochroleucum*) [13] Low to medium plant, 10–40cm tall; bulbs very slender forming small clumps on a rhizome, covered with pale brown fibrous tunics, the fibres parallel. Leaves nearly all basal, only 3–4 per bulb, linear, about 1–2mm wide. Umbel usually 1.5–2cm diameter, hemispherical or nearly spherical, dense; flowers white or sometimes pinkish-tinted, cup-shaped, with long protruding stamens and style. Rocky places and heathland, 300–1600m. August–September. A, E, F, I, P, R, *sw*RS.

Similar to this are a number of species forming a complex group, which are difficult to distinguish. They are often mountain plants, forming clumps or patches.

A. albidum differs from *A. ericetorum* mainly in having the bulb tunics thinly papery, not fibrous, and the flower stalks minutely scabrid. BG, K, R, *c,e&w*RS.

A. horvatii differs from *A. ericetorum* in having rather tough, non-fibrous bulb tunics which split lengthways into strips. It is generally a smaller plant with very short flower-stalks in the umbel and yellowish-white flowers. Rocky places by the sea. *nw*YU.

A. obliquum is more robust than *A. ericetorum*, 60–100cm tall, with leaves up to 20mm wide sheathing the lower half of the stem; umbel 3–4cm diameter; flowers yellowish-green. The bulb tunics are brownish and membranous. *c*R, *se*RS.

A. marschallianum is rather similar to *A. ericetorum* but has bulbs with tough dark brown or blackish tunics which split into coarse strips. It has thread-like leaves. *n*I, K, R, *n*YU.

A. stellerianum is like *A. ericetorum* but has papery bulb tunics and rather fewer flowers in the umbel, but on longer stalks usually 1–1.5cm long. *c*RS–Urals.

13. Small Yellow Onion *Allium flavum* [13] Low to medium plant, 5–30cm tall, rarely more; bulb rounded. Leaves cylindrical, about 1–2mm wide, grey-green, sheathing the lower part of the stem. Umbel about 1.5–3cm diameter, loose, few to many flowered, the inner flowers on upright stalks and the outer curving downwards but becoming erect in the fruiting stage; *flowers pale to deep yellow, bell-shaped* with tepals more than 5mm long. Dryish grassy places, to 2900m. June–August. A, AL, BG, F, GR, H, I, K, R, *c,e* &*w*RS, SC, TR, YU.*

Allium flavum is a very variable species, especially in stature and shade of yellow. Dwarf mountain plants tend to retain their habit in cultivation and are useful rock plants. Some forms are delicately scented.

A. hymettium is similar but has flowers with tepals less than 5mm long and they are carried in a more compact umbel with the flower-stalks less than 1.5cm long. *s*GR.

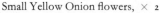

Small Yellow Onion flowers, × 2

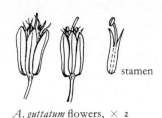

A. guttatum flowers, × 2

14. *Allium guttatum* (=*A. margaritaceum*) [13]   Short to medium plant, usually 15–50cm tall; bulb egg-shaped. *Leaves thread-like*, withered at flowering time, sheathing the lower part of the stem. Umbel usually 1.5–3cm diameter, nearly spherical, dense and many-flowered; flowers whitish with a green or pinkish line on each tepal, or with a purple blotch, or wholly pinkish or purple, rather tubular in shape. Dry grassy and stony places, to 1500m. A, BG, CR, GR, E, I, K, P, R, *w*RS, SC, TR, YU.●

A very variable species, especially in flower colour and it is sometimes divided into several subspecies based on colour.

A. staticiforme looks like *A. guttatum* but is generally shorter, not exceeding about 20cm tall. It has very slender leaves and usually a smaller more dense umbel of whitish or pinkish flowers with reddish, green or lilac veins on the tepals. AEG, CR.

A. sabulosum has an umbel of flowers rather like *A. guttatum* with many greenish or whitish globose flowers. The bulbs however, are long and bottle-shaped and the leaves linear, 1–3mm wide. *se*RS (mainly from C. Asia).

A. chamaespathum is rather like a stout *A. guttatum*, about 25–30cm tall with rather fleshy hollow leaves which completely sheath the stem. The long spathe often hangs on to the umbel for a long time before falling. The umbel is about 3.5–4cm diameter, spherical and very dense with white or greenish flowers. AL, CR, GR.

A. dilatatum is very similar to *A. guttatum* and is separated mainly by having the flowers always white with a green line on each tepal. The inner tepals are longer than the outer (subequal in *A. guttatum*). The umbel has about 15–35 flowers. *sw*CR.

A. caeruleum is superficially like *A. guttatum* but has a larger umbel, 3–4cm diameter, with many blue, darker-veined flowers. Salt marshes. *se*RS. A species found mainly in Siberia and C. Asia.

15. Yellow Onion *Allium moly* [13] Short plant, 15–30cm tall; bulb rounded. Leaves basal, usually 1 or 2, linear–lanceolate or lanceolate, 1.5–4cm wide, greyish-green. Umbel 3–6cm diameter, hemispherical, few to many-flowered, rarely with bulbils instead of flowers; *flowers deep yellow*, fading to whitish, starry and rather flat. Shady rocky places and in scrub, 1000–2000m. June–July. E, *sw*F. *

A very distinctive onion with its broad grey leaves and quite large yellow flowers. It is a popular garden plant.

A. scorzonerifolium is similar in having starry yellow flowers, but the leaves are only 3–7mm wide. *sw*E, P.

Yellow flower, × 2

A. moschatum flowers, × 2

16. *Allium moschatum* [13] Short plant, usually 15–25cm tall; bulb narrowly egg-shaped with a fibrous tunic, generally several clustered together. *Leaves thread-like*, 0.5mm wide, rough on the margins, sheathing the lower part of the stem. Umbel 1–3cm diameter, shuttlecock-shaped with only 3–15 flowers *on equal stalks* 1–1.5cm long; flowers bell-shaped pink or white with a darker brownish or pinkish mid-vein on each tepal; stamens not protruding beyond the tepals. Dry grassy places and in rock crevices, to 2000m. June–September. AL, BG, E, F, GR, I, K, R, *w*RS, TR, YU.

A. melanantherum is superficially rather similar but the bulb has a more papery tunic, the leaves are up to 2mm broad and the pedicels are up to 2.5cm long; the flowers are larger and more tubular. BG, *n*GR, *e*YU.

A. inequale is very similar to *A. moschatum* but carries the flowers on *very unequal* stalks. K, *w*,*c*&*e*RS.

A. bornmuelleri is like *A. moschatum* but has *ciliate leaf margins* and purple stamens. sYU.

A. rubellum is like *A. moschatum* but the bulb has tough, almost leathery non-fibrous tunics; the *anthers are yellow*. seRS.

A. meteoricum is like *A. moschatum* but the bulb has papery, non-fibrous tunics; *anthers orange*. AL, c&nGR, sYU.

A. delicatulum resembles *A. moschatum* but the bulb has papery tunics; anthers yellow. seRS.

A. frigidum is similar to *A. moschatum* but the bulb has papery tunics and the stamens are exserted from the flower. sGR—Peloponnese.

A. chrysonemum is like *A. moschatum* but has papery bulb tunics, an umbel about 4cm diameter and greenish-yellow flowers with green mid-veins on the tepals. seE—Jaen Prov.

A. grosii is similar to *A. moschatum* but has darker, purple, flowers. BAL—Ibiza.

17. *Allium narcissiflorum* [13]   Low to short plant, 15—30cm tall; bulbs narrowly bottle-shaped, clustered together to form a clump, covered in a thick mat of fibres. Leaves linear, about 2—4mm wide, not basal but sheathing the stem only in the very lowest part. Umbel pendent with about 5—10 flowers, becoming erect in the late flowering and fruiting stage; flowers purple, bell-shaped, about, 10—13mm long. Rocky slopes, 800—2300m. July—August. sF, nI, nwP.*

This is one of the most beautiful of the European onions with its pendulous, large purple flowers. It is a good rock garden plant.

A. insubricum is similar to *A. narcissiflorum* but has an almost naked bulb with few or no fibres covering it. The leaves up to 5mm wide and larger flowers about 15—20mm long. Rocky places on limestone, 800—2300m. August. nI.

A. inderiense also has large bell-shaped purplish flowers but they are usually less than 10mm long, carried in a hemispherical or shuttlecock-shaped umbel which is not nodding. The tepals are much narrower than in either of the above species. Grassy places. seRS.

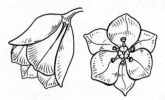

A. narcissiflorum flowers, × 2   Naples Garlic Flower, × 2

18. Naples Garlic *Allium neapolitanum* [13]   Short to medium plant, 20—45cm tall; bulb rounded. Leaves usually only 2—3, linear, about 1—2cm wide, sheathing the lower part of the stem. Umbels 5–9cm diameter, hemispherical or shuttle-cock-shaped, many-flowered; flowers large, each up to 20mm diameter, white, cup-shaped or starry. Dry grassy and stony places, to 500m. March–April. BAL, CO, CR, E, F, GR, I, P, SA, SC, TR, YU.*

The very large glistening white flowers make this an attractive onion. It is useful for cutting for decorative purposes and is often sold by florists.

19. *Allium nigrum* [14]   Medium to tall plant, 55–80cm tall; bulb egg-shaped. Leaves only 2–3, all basal, broadly linear, 2.5–4.5cm wide, long-tapering to a pointed apex. Umbel usually 6–8cm diameter, hemispherical or shuttlecock-shaped, many-flowered, or occasionally with some bulbils in the head; flowers white or pale pink with a green mid-vein on each tepal, flat and starry when fully open; tepals 1.5–3mm wide, not curving inwards at the apex; *ovary very dark green or blackish*. Usually in or near cultivated land, to 1000m. April–June. AL, BAL, BG, CO, CR, E, F, GR, I, P, SA, SC, TR, YU.●

A distinctive species with its rather wide basal leaves and starry white flowers with a blackish 'eye' (the ovary).

A. cyrilli is very similar but has the tepals only 1–1.5mm wide and curving inwards at the tips. *e*GR, SI.

A. decipiens is like *A. nigrum* but has leaves only 2–10mm wide. SRS.

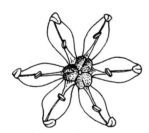

A. *nigrum* flower, × 2

Field Garlic flowers, × 2

20. Field Garlic *Allium oleraceum* [14]   Short to tall plant, 20–80cm tall; bulb egg-shaped or rounded. Leaves thread-like or narrowly linear, up to 3mm wide, sheathing the lower half of the stem. Umbel about 2–4cm diameter, loose, with a few flowers on long stalks to many-flowered and spherical, occasionally bulbils replace the flowers altogether; flowers whitish tinged with green, pink or brown, bell-shaped. Waste places and in scrub, or on rocky hillsides, to 2500m. July–September. A, B, BG, CH, CO, CS, D, DK, F, ?GB, H, I, N, NL, PL, RS, S, SC, YU.●

A rather common slender allium with a very untidy umbel, caused by some of the flowers being replaced by bulbils. The umbel has two spathes which distinguishes it from the one-spathed *A. scorodoprasum* and *A. vineale*, both of which sometimes have many bulbils in the umbel.

21. *Allium paniculatum* [14] Medium plant, 30–50cm tall; bulb egg-shaped. Leaves *narrowly linear*, about 1.5–3mm wide, sheathing the lower part of the stem. Umbel 3–5cm diameter, rather loose, hemispherical or egg-shaped, many-flowered, the pedicels 1–7cm long with the outer flowers drooping on longer stalks; flowers lilac, brownish, yellowish, greenish or whitish, bell-shaped; stamens about as long as the tepals. Dry grassy or stony places, sometimes on cultivated land, to 1000m. June–October. AL, BG, CO, CR, E, F, GR, H, I, K, R, *w,c &e*RS, SA, SC, TR, YU.●

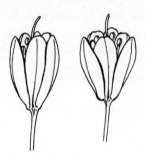

A. paniculatum flowers, × 2

A. pallens is similar to *A. paniculatum* but usually has thread-like leaves and a much smaller, often more compact, 1.5–3cm diameter hemispherical or shuttlecock-shaped umbel with flower stalks only 5–15mm long; flowers white or pink, narrowly bell-shaped, anthers yellow. Dry grassy or scrub, to 1800m. May–July. BAL, BG, CO, CR, GR, E, I, P, SA, SC, R, YU.

A. rupestre is like *A. pallens* but has violet anthers. K.

A. favosum is like *A. paniculatum* and differs mainly in having the cells on the leaf sheaths about as long as wide, whereas in the latter they are much longer than wide. *n*GR.

A. sipyleum is like a dwarf few-flowered *A. paniculatum* with the stamens shorter than the tepals. Rocky places. CR.

A. macedonicum is very similar to *A. paniculatum*. It has many flowered umbels of pink flowers which are more cup-shaped. *ne*GR–Mt Pangaion.

A. parnassicum is like a small *A. paniculatum*, only 10–25cm tall. It has a more compact shuttlecock-shaped umbel 2.5–3cm diameter and longer, funnel-shaped flowers. *s*GR.

A. luteolum is similar to *A. paniculatum* but is shorter, rarely more than 15cm, with thread-like leaves and a smaller umbel of yellowish flowers, very rarely pinkish. *s*GR–Cyclades.

A. pilosum is like *A. paniculatum* but is shorter, 10–15cm tall, and has lilac flowers with blunt tepals; in the latter they are acute. *s*GR–Cyclades.

22. Rose Garlic *Allium roseum* [14]   Short to medium plant, usually 15–55cm tall; bulb egg-shaped or rather rounded. Leaves linear, varying from almost thread-like to 15mm wide, sheathing the lower part of the stem. Umbel 4–7cm diameter, shuttlecock-shaped or hemispherical, with or without bulbils; *flowers large, pink or white*, broadly cup-shaped. Fields, vineyards, sandy and stony waste places, to 700m. April–June. AL, BAL, CO, CR, E, F, GR, I, P, SA, SC, TR, YU.*

The large rather attractive usually bright pink flowers are easy to recognise. Variants having bulbils in the umbel have been called var. *bulbiferum*. The species is sometimes cultivated.

A. massaessylum is similar but the flowers are white with a purple mid-vein along each tepal; there are two spathes, whereas *A. roseum* has only one spathe, divided at the apex into three or four lobes. P, *sw*E.

A. phthioticum is like *A. roseum* but the flowers are less cup-shaped and flatter, white with more pointed tepals. Mountain meadows. *sc*GR.

A. breviradium is similar to *A. roseum* but has white flowers in a shuttlecock-shaped umbel; flowers narrower and with pointed tepals. It differs from *A. phthioticum* in having flower stalks only 1–1.5cm long, whereas the latter has flower stalks 3–6.5cm long. *s*AL, *n*GR, *s*YU.

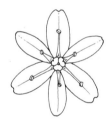

Rose Garlic flower, × 2

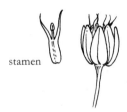

stamen

A. rotundum flowers, × 2

23. *Allium rotundum* [14]   Medium to tall plant, 30–80cm tall; bulb egg-shaped. Leaves linear, 2–8mm wide, sheathing the lower part of the stem. Umbel 2–4cm diameter, subspherical or hemispherical, very dense and many-flowered, without bulbils; flowers bicoloured, the outer tepals deep purple, the inner paler pinkish-purple with a darker stripe along the centre, egg-shaped. Dry grassy or waste places, to 1000m. June–July. A, BAL, BG, CH, CO, CR, CS, D, E, F, GR, H, I, K, R, *w*&*sw*RS, TR, YU.●

Easy to recognise with its very compact drumstick-like head of dark flower-heads with no bulbils.

A. waldsteinii is very similar but the flowers are wholly dark purple, not bicoloured. *ne*I, K, *e*R, RS, *n*YU.

A. jubatum is like *A. rotundum* but has the inner tepals strongly toothed. *c*BG.

A. baeticum has a similar dense umbel to *A. rotundum* but the flowers are whitish and the bulb has a very long fibrous neck at its apex. *s*E, P. The species also occurs in N. Africa.

A. rubrovittatum looks rather like *A. rotundum* but usually has a smaller umbel, less than 2cm diameter, with reddish-purple flowers which have pale margins to the tepals. CR, & Karpathos.

A. pervestitum is rather like *A. rotundum* but has whitish or yellowish, sometimes pink-tinged flowers with the stamens slightly protruding. Salt marshes. *sw*RS– S. Ukraine.

A. gomphrenoides looks like *A. rotundum* in having a very compact umbel but this is usually only 1–2cm diameter with pink to purple flowers; the leaves are thread-like, only 1–2mm wide. *s*GR – S. Peloponnese, Kythira.

24. Chives *Allium schoenoprasum* [14]   Short to medium plant, 10–45cm tall; bulbs narrowly bottle-shaped, grouped together to form tufts. Leaves cylindrical, 2–5mm wide, sheathing the lower part of the stem or more or less basal. Umbel usually 2–4cm diameter, hemispherical or egg-shaped, very compact; flowers lilac or pale purple, bell-shaped, up to 10mm long, on stalks up to 15mm long, often held more or less erect. Grassy alpine slopes or in rock crevices, 1000–2500m. May–August. A, BG, CG, CO, D, E, F, GB, GR, H, I, N, P, RS, S, YU.*

The well-known culinary chives is a very variable plant in the wild and does not always look the same as the familiar form which we grow in our gardens. A particularly vigorous robust form is called var. *sibiricum*.

A. schmitzii belongs to the same group as this but is a large plant with smaller flowers on stalks up to 25mm long. Rocky places near rivers. *c*P.

A. heldreichii is not related to chives but has an umbel which resembles it. It has a small solitary rounded bulb, quite unlike the slender clustered ones of *A. schoenoprasum*. Mountain rocks. *n*GR.

Chives flowers, × 2

stamen

Sand Leek flower, × 2

25. Sand Leek *Allium scorodoprasum* [14]   Medium to tall plant, 40–80cm tall; bulbs egg-shaped. Leaves linear, 5–15mm wide, sheathing the lower part of the stem. Umbel usually 2–4cm diameter, with few flowers and many purplish bulbils; flowers lilac to deep purple, egg-shaped. In scrub, waste places, hedges and grassy banks, to 1500m. May–June. A, BG, CH, CS, D, F, GB, H, K, N, NL, PL, R, RS, S, YU.●

This species is considered by W. T. Steam to be derived from *A. rotundum* presumably selected for its bulbil production for culinary purposes. It spreads very rapidly by means of these bulbils. *A. rotundum* although similar, never has bulbils in the umbel.

A. albiflorum is very similar to *A. scorodoprasum* but has whitish flowers. K.

26. Mountain Garlic *Allium senescens* [14]   Short to medium plant, 10–35cm tall; bulbs bottle-shaped, covered with pale brown papery tunics, grouped on a rhizome to form leafy clumps. Leaves basal, linear, usually 2–4mm wide, rounded on the underside with no strong keel. Umbel 2–5cm diameter, hemispherical, many-flowered; flowers lilac or pinkish-purple, cup-shaped, with protruding stamens. Mountain pastures or damp rocky places, 500–2300m. July–September. A, BG, CH, D, E, F, H, I, P, PL, R, *w*&*nw*RS, S, SC, YU.*
A pleasing rock garden plant, forming dense clumps and flowering in late summer. There are several other clump-forming pink or purple-flowered alliums in Europe and they are not always easy to distinguish from one another.

Mountain Garlic flower, × 2

A. angulosum and *A. suaveolens*, described on page 76 differ from *A. senescens* and its allies in having their leaves keeled on the underside. In the latter species and its relatives the leaves are flat or rounded below, and sometimes ribbed, but not keeled.
Species related to *A. senescens* are as follows:

A. lineare is similar but the bulb has netted-fibrous tunics and leaves which sheath the lower part of the stem. A, CH, CS, D, F, I, P, *c,w*&*e*RS.

A. rubens is like *A. senescens* but has the stamens shorter than the tepals and therefore not protruding; the leaves are only 1–2mm wide. *c*&*e*RS.

A. kermesinum is like *A. senescens* but has fibrous bulb tunics and a small umbel only 1.5–2cm diameter. YU – Slovenian Alps.

A. saxatile differs from *A. senescens* in having thread-like leaves only 0.5–1mm wide and tough dark brown or blackish bulb tunics. BG, I, K, R, *w*RS.

A. palentinum is like *A. senescens* but has glossy brown bulb tunics and leaves which sheath the lower part of the stem. *n*E – Leon Province.

A. hymenorhizum also belongs to this group but it is much larger, often reaching 80cm tall, and forms dense compact tufts rather than spreading clumps; the bulbs are very long and slender with shiny brown leathery tunics and the leaves sheath the lower half of the stem. Damp meadows. *w*RS.

27. Round-headed Leek *Allium sphaerocephalon* [14]   Medium to tall plant, 30–80cm tall; bulb egg-shaped. Leaves semi-cylindrical, 1–5mm wide, sheathing the lower part of the stem. Umbel about 2–4cm diameter, usually spherical, many-flowered, sometimes with bulbils; flowers pink to reddish-purple, rarely white, tubular or egg-shaped; stamens much-protruding. Sandy and rocky places in grass or scrub, to 1100m, rarely more. June–August. A, AL, B, BAL, BG, CH, CO, CS, D, E, F, GB, H, I, K, P, PL, R, *w*RS, SA, SC, TR, YU.*

A. arvense is very similar to this but has white flowers with a green mid-vein on each tepal. AL, GR, I, SC.

A. sardoum is also similar to *A. sphaerocephalon* but has white flowers in a more shuttlecock-shaped umbel. SA.

A. proponticum is like *A. sphaerocephalon* but very robust and taller with a hemispherical umbel about 6.5cm diameter. TR.

A. pruinatum is similar to *A. sphaerocephalon* but generally smaller, only 20–40cm tall, with leaves 3–5mm wide, the umbel 1–2cm diameter, hemispherical; stamens not protruding beyond the tepals. *c&s*P.

A. integerrimum resembles *A. sphaerocephalon* but is usually not more than 40cm tall, has thread-like leaves and a more compact umbel, 1–2.5cm diameter; flowers bell-shaped, pink. *e*GR – Olympus.

A. talijevii is like *A. sphaerocephalon* but the flowers are white and the leaves linear, 5–12mm wide; umbel hemispherical, 2.5–5cm diameter. *sw*RS – Donetsk.

A. regelianum is similar to *A. sphaerocephalon* but has only one spathe (two in the latter) and the rather tubular flowers have stamens that are only slightly protruding. *w&c*RS.

A. melananthum is like *A. sphaerocephalon* but has leaves 2mm wide and a 1–2cm diameter umbel of dark purple flowers. *s*E – Almeria.

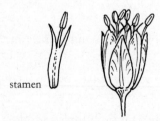

Round-headed Leek flower, × 2

A. stamineum flower, × 2

28. *Allium stamineum*   Short to medium plant, 10–35cm tall; bulb egg-shaped. Leaves thread-like, only 0.5–1mm wide, sheathing the lower part of the stem. Umbel 2.5–5cm diameter, many-flowered but rather loose, more or less spherical or shuttlecock-shaped; flowers pale pinkish-purple with darker mid-veins along the tepals, cup-shaped. Dry grassy or stony places, to 1600m. July–August. BG, CR, GR, TR.●

This species differs from the rather similar *A. paniculatum* (see page 21) in having the stamens protruding out of the flower. *A. carinatum* (page 85) is also like this but has darker purple flowers and often has some bulbils in the umbel.

29. *Allium subhirsutum* [14]   Short to medium plant, 10–30cm tall; bulb rounded. Leaves linear, usually 2–7mm wide, only sheathing the stem near the base, *distinctly hairy on the margins*. Umbel about 3–6cm diameter, loose and hemispherical or rather shuttlecock-shaped; flowers white, flat and starry. Dry stony and sandy places, to 1300m. April–June. AEG, BAL, CO, CR, F, GR, I, SA, SC, YU. *

A common allium, especially near the sea, and easily recognised by its hairy leaves and bright starry flowers. It is a useful garden plant for a warm situation.

A. permixtum is very similar but has non-hairy leaves. SC.

A. circinnatum is like a diminutive *A. subhirsutum* with coiled leaves and a very small, few-flowered shuttlecock-shaped umbel. CR, ?SGR.

A. subhirsutum flower, × 2

A. subvillosum flower, × 2

30. *Allium subvillosum*   Rather like *A. subhirsutum* but with more flowers in the umbel, which is 2.5–3.5cm wide; flowers white, shallowly cup-shaped. Sandy and grassy places, to 1500m. March–May. BAL, GR, E, P, SC. A common species in North Africa.●

A. longanum is not unlike *A. subvillosum* but its leaves are only 3–8mm wide and the more shuttlecock-shaped umbel bears pink-tinged, bell-shaped flowers. AEG – known only from two small islands in the Aegean.

31. *Allium trifoliatum* Short to medium plant, 15–45cm tall; bulb rounded. Leaves linear, about 5–10mm wide, sharply pointed, more or less basal, sparsely hairy. Umbel about 3–4cm diameter, shuttlecock-shaped, loosely flowered; flowers white or pinkish with a pink stripe along the centre of each tepal, starry. Grassy and rocky places, to 500m. April. CR, F, I, SC, SA.●

The leaves are usually still green at flowering time and are very long tapering to an acute apex.

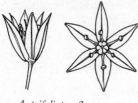

A. trifoliatum flower, × 2

Three-cornered Leek flowers, × 2

32. Three-cornered Leek *Allium triquetrum* [14]   Short to medium plant, 15–30cm tall; bulb rounded. Leaves linear with a sharp keel, about 5–13mm wide. *Scape 3-cornered.* Umbel about 2–4cm diameter, *one-sided*, loose with only 5–15 flowers; flowers white with a green stripe on each tepal, 9–15mm long, bell-shaped. Damp woods or in scrub near streams and in waste places, to 1000m. March–June. BAL, CO, E, F, (GB), I, (IRL), P, SA, SC.*

This most attractive allium is a useful garden plant for growing beneath shrubs or naturalising in grass. Its 1-sided umbel with large white flowers make it very easy to recognise.

A. pendulinum is similar in its leaves and flower colour but the flowers are rather starry at first, becoming bell-shaped later, and are not carried in a 1-sided umbel. Woods. CO, I, SA, SC.

33. Ramsons *Allium ursinum* [14]   Short to medium plant, 10–45cm tall; bulb narrowly bottle-shaped. Leaves elliptical to ovate, about 2–6cm wide at the widest point, all basal, with long stalks. Umbel usually 3–5cm diameter, rather loose with less than 25 flowers, shuttlecock-shaped, flowers white, flat and starry. Dampish woods, to 1600m. May–June. T, especially in the central and north. *

Easily recognised by its broad basal leaves, besides which it is the only allium like this occurring in woods. The plants have a powerful smell of garlic when crushed underfoot.

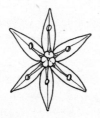

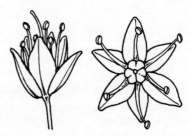

Ramsons flower, × 2

Alpine Leek flowers, × 2

34. Alpine Leek *Allium victorialis* [14]   Medium plant, 30–60cm tall; bulb narrowly bottle-shaped, clustered to form a clump. *Leaves leathery, lance-shaped to* *widely elliptical*, usually 2.5–6cm wide, sheathing the lower part of the stem. Umbel usually 2.5–4cm diameter, more or less spherical with many flowers; flowers whitish, flat and starry. Stony slopes or on rocks in the mountains, 1500–2500m. June–August. A, BG, CH, CS, D, E, F, H, I, P, PL, R, *w*&*sw*RS, YU. **✱**

One of the most distinctive European alliums with its broad leaves and clump-forming habit.

35. Crow Garlic *Allium vineale* [14] Medium to tall plant, 35–100cm tall; bulb egg-shaped. Leaves cylindrical, 2–4mm wide, sheathing the lower part of the stem. Umbel very dense, 2–4cm diameter, nearly spherical to hemispherical or egg-shaped, with or without bulbils; flowers pinkish, reddish or greenish, bell-shaped. Grassy places and waste ground, to 2300m. June–August. T – except AZ, CR, I, FA, *n*&*e*RS.**✱**

The forms which have a lot of bulbils in the umbel usually have only a few flowers. It differs from *A. scorodoprasum*, which may also have many bulbils in the umbel, in having hollow cylindrical leaves (flat in *A. scorodoprasum*).

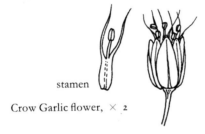

stamen

Crow Garlic flower, × 2

ORNITHOGALUM

A large genus of very common bulbous plants in Europe, especially in the Mediterranean region, including the Star of Bethlehem, *O. umbellatum*. They are always very easy to recognise as being ornithogalums although it is rather more difficult to distinguish between the species. Nearly all of them have white flowers, usually starry, and most have a green stripe on the outside of each tepal. A few are yellowish-green and in the Iberian Peninsula one or two species occur with plain white flowers.

Although most species are not very showy, they are attractive and easily grown plants and some are particularly useful in gardens for naturalising in grass or beneath shrubs.

In addition to the European species there are many in western Asia, tropical Africa, North Africa and South Africa, where yellow and orange-flowered species occur.

Low to tall bulbous plants. Leaves all basal, solitary to several in a rosette, or a cluster. Flowers white or yellowish-green, generally starry but sometimes bell-shaped, produced in racemes which are often dense and nearly flat-topped; tepals six, free, often green-striped on the outside; stamens six. Fruit a three-valved capsule containing many seeds.

1. Pyrenean Star of Bethlehem, Bath Asparagus *Ornithogalum pyrenaicum*

[15]   Medium to tall plant, 30–100cm. Leaves usually 5–8, linear, green, normally about 5–9mm wide, withered at flowering time. *Flowers pale greenish-yellow* usually 15–40 in a *long slender raceme,* each about 15mm diameter with tepals only 2–3mm wide and unrolled at the margins, giving the flowers a very starry appearance; flower stalks 1–2cm long, becoming erect in fruit. Scrub and woods, to 1500m. May–July. A, B, BG, CH, CO, E, F, GB, GR, I, K, P, R, *w*RS, SA, YU.*

The young shoots of this species are sometimes eaten like Asparagus.

Bath Asparagus fruit capsule, × 2

The following (species 2–4) are sometimes recognised as being separate species:

2. *O. sphaerocarpum* is very similar to *O. pyrenaicum* but the flowers are transparent or whitish. Grassland or scrub. A, AL, BG, CS, H, I, GR, R, SA, TR, YU.

3. *O. visianicum* is like *O. pyrenaicum* but the tepals are white on the outside. Rocky places. *w*YU – on the island of Palagruza only.

4. *O. creticum* is very similar to *O. pyrenaicum*. The tepals are greenish-yellow and the ovary is more or less spherical (egg-shaped or cylindrical in *O. pyrenaicum*). Rocky places. CR.

5. *Ornithogalum narbonense* [15]   Like *O. pyrenaicum* in general aspect but usually with 3–5 grey-green leaves which are not withered away at flowering time and are normally 10–15mm wide. *Flowers up to 50 in a long raceme,* white with a narrow green central stripe on each tepal, 15–25mm diameter; tepals 2–3mm wide, but not unrolled at the margins so that the flower has a more substantial appearance than that of *O. pyrenaicum*; flower stalks 1–3cm long, erect in the fruiting stage. Fields, rocky hillsides and waste places, to 1000m. April–July. AL, BAL, BG, CO, CR, E, F, GR, I, P, SA, SC, TR, YU.●

A very common species with long racemes of starry white flowers, very conspicuous on sunny hillsides when the flowers are wide open.

6. *O. ponticum* is similar to (**5**) but has a cylindrical, rather than ovoid, ovary. к.

7. *O. fischeranum* is like *O. narbonense* but has narrower leaves, usually 2–5mm wide; the ovary is tapered at the apex not blunt as in the latter. *sw*Rs.

8. *O. prasinantherum* is similar to *O. narbonense* but has narrower leaves, the ovary is cone-shaped at the apex and the anthers are greenish (yellow in *O. narbonense*). *s*GR – only recorded from the Peloponnese.

9. *O. pyramidale* is like *O. narbonense* but has a very short ovary, less than 2.5mm long and the style is less than 1.7mm long. In the latter the ovary is 3.5mm or more long and the style 3.5mm or more. A, CS, D, H, R, YU.

10. *Ornithogalum reverchonii* [15]   Medium to tall plant, 40–100cm. Leaves pale or greyish-green, usually 5–6, up to 45cm long and 15–25mm wide, trailing on the ground or hanging from the cliffs. *Flowers up to 15, white,* with or without a green stripe on the outside, *rather bell-shaped* and 20–30mm diameter with broad tepals giving a flower of substantial appearance; flower stalks nearly absent or up to 10mm long, exceeded by the large papery bracts. Rocky ledges and crevices, 800–1500m. May–June. *s*E*.*****

A very attractive ornithogalum and a good garden plant although at present it is rare, both in the wild and in cultivation.

11. *Ornithogalum oligophyllum* [15]   Low plant usually 7–15cm tall. *Leaves grey-green, usually 2,* not shrivelled at flowering time, 3–15mm wide, *becoming broader towards the apex* which is abruptly narrowed. Flowers 2–7, white with a broad green stripe on the outside of each tepal, produced in a short raceme; flower stalks erect in flower, reflexed in fruit. Rocky and grassy places in the mountains, sometimes in sparse woodland, 1000–2000m. April–June. AL, BG, GR, TR, YU.●

An easily recognised little alpine species with its two grey leaves that are widest at the tips.

12. *Ornithogalum montanum* [15]   Low to short plant, usually 6–20cm tall. Leaves 3–6, green, generally 10–20mm wide at the base and *long-tapering to the pointed apex,* produced in a basal rosette. Flowers about 5–15, white with a broad green stripe on the exterior of each tepal, about 20–30mm diameter, carried in a wide, often rather flat-topped raceme; flower stalks 3–8cm long, horizontal or semi-erect in fruiting stage. Grassy or rocky places, and on damp mountain meadows, 1000–1500m. April–June. BG, GR, I, SC, TR, YU.●

The dwarf habit, combined with rather wide green leaves in a rosette give this species a very distinctive appearance.

13. *O. atticum* is rather similar to *O. montanum* but has grey-green, often twisted, or undulate-edged, leaves. Rocky places. *s*GR.

14. *O. oreoides* is like *O. atticum* but the leaves are narrower, usually only 2–5mm wide. Dry grassy or stony hills. *n*BG, R, *sw*RS.

15. Hairy Star of Bethlehem *Ornithogalum fimbriatum* [15]   Low plant, usually 5–15cm tall. *Leaves greyish*, 2–5, longer than the flower stem but often coiled on the ground, about 3–5mm wide, *covered with silvery hairs* which are generally downward pointing. Flowers normally 3–10, white with a green stripe on the outside of each tepal, about 10–15 (–20m)mm diameter, carried in a wide flat-topped raceme; flower stalks semi-erect at flowering time, deflexed in the fruiting stage. Rocky or dry grassy places, to 1800m. April–May. BG, GR, K, R, *sw*RS, TR, ?YU.●

This is often very dwarf with the flowers carried almost at ground level amid the narrow hairy leaves.

16. Common Star of Bethlehem *Ornithogalum umbellatum* [15]   Short plant, 15–30cm tall. Bulb usually producing many offsets, each of which produces a single narrow leaf thus *forming leafy clumps at flowering time*. Leaves 2–5mm wide, dark green with a *white central stripe on the upper surface*. Flowers usually 5–20, white with a bright green band on the outside of each tepal, about 15–25mm in diameter, produced in a wide often flat-topped raceme; flower stalks horizontal

Common Star of Bethlehem fruit capsule, × 1½

at fruiting time. Fruit capsule with six equal lobes. Woods and grassy places, to 2000m. April–May. In most European countries, either native or naturalised.*

This is the most widespread and common *Ornithogalum* which has distinctive white-striped leaves and is commonly cultivated. There are several other species resembling this and the differences are often obscure.

17. *O. orthophyllum* (=*O. kochii*, '*O. tenuifolium*') is like *O. umbellatum* but lacks, or has a few only, leafy bulblets around the base of the parent bulb. The capsule is six-lobed, but the lobes are produced in *three groups of two* rather than being equally spaced. A, BG, CH, CS, ?D, E, H, I, P, PL, R, *sw*RS, YU.*

18. *O. gussonei* (=*O. collinum*) is similar to *O. umbellatum* but the bulb has no bulblets around it; flower stalks semi-erect or horizontal. It is often a more compact plant. The bulb is said to differ in having the scales free from each other, not fused together as in *O. umbellatum* but this is a very difficult feature to observe. AL, CO, CR, E, F, GR, I, SA, SC, TR, YU.●

19. *O. costatum* is like *O. gussonei* in most of its characters but differs in having almost *thread-like leaves* only 1–2mm wide and a three-lobed capsule. *s*GR – in the Peloponnese.

20. *O. woronowii* is similar to *O. gussonei* but has the flower stalks *curved downwards* in the fruiting stage so that the capsule rests on the ground. K, and in the Caucasus.

21. *O. amphibolum* is like *O. gussonei* but has thread-like leaves about 1–2mm wide, and cylindrical capsules with three rather rounded lobes. In these respects it resembles the Greek *O. costatum* but this is said to have the capsule lobes grooved near the apex. BG, R, *sw*RS.

22. *O. wiedemannii* is similar to *O. gussonei* but has the flower stalks horizontal or turned downwards in the fruiting stage. The young fruits and capsules have *six distinct wings* on the lobes. *ne*GR, TR and in Asiatic Turkey.

23. *O. armeniacum* is like *O. gussonei* but has *very narrow hairy leaves*, only 1–2mm wide; flower stalks horizontal or slightly down-turned in fruit. Mainly from Asiatic Turkey but thought to occur in *n*GR, *s*YU.

24. *Ornithogalum comosum* [15]   Short to medium plant, 15–35cm tall. Leaves about 5–7, *green with no white stripe* on the upper surface, *hairy on the margins*, about 3–7mm wide. Flowers usually 10–30, white with a rather narrow green band on the outside of each tepal, about 25–30mm diameter, produced in a cylindrical raceme; flowerstalks semi-erect in the fruiting stage. Grassy places, to 1000m. April–June. A, BG, *s*CS, GR, H, I, R, YU.●

The unstriped leaves with small hairs on the margins assist in the identification of this species. Although *O. fimbriatum* also has hairy leaves the two need not be confused for in *O. comosum* the raceme is not flat-topped and the flower stalks become erect in fruit, not deflexed as in *O. fimbriatum*. In the latter the leaves are much more silvery-hairy.

25. *Ornithogalum refractum* [15]   Low plant, usually 5–10cm tall, with the visible part of the flower stem below the first flower only 1cm or less long. Bulb with many dormant bulbs surrounding it (not leafy as in *O. umbellatum*). Leaves about 5–10, green with a white stripe on the upper surface, usually 2–5mm wide. *Flowers large with broad tepals*, white with a narrow green stripe on the outside of each tepal, 25–40mm diameter, produced in a rather wide, or rather flat-topped raceme; *flower stalks turned sharply downwards at fruiting time*. In dry grassy or stony places, or in disturbed land, to 1500m. April–June. BG, H, I, K, R, *sw*RS, TR, YU.●

Although somewhat similar to the common *O. umbellatum* the strongly reflexed flower stalks readily distinguish *O. refractum*.

26. *O. divergens* (=*O. pater-familias*) is very like *O. refractum*, but the visible part of the stem below the first flower is 5–10cm long. The flowers have a broader green stripe on the backs of the tepals, and the stalks do not reflex so sharply. BAL, BG, CO, CR, E, F, GR, H, I, R, SA, SC, YU.●

27. *O. exaratum* is like *O. divergens* and is said to differ in that its leaves do not appear until the spring, whereas in the latter they are clearly visible in the autumn. *e*GR – in Euboea only.

28. *O. exscapum* is like a dwarf, smaller-flowered *O. refractum* with a flat-topped raceme carried almost stemless amid the leaves. Unlike *O. refractum* the bulbs do not produce a lot of dormant bulblets around their base. Dry grassy places. AL, CO, E, I, SA, SC, YU.●

29. *O. sibthorpii* (=*O. nanum*) is very like (**28**), and is said to differ mainly in having the flower stalks grooved at the apex just below the flower, and not very rigid. In *O. exscapum* they are rigid and cylindrical, not grooved. BG, CR, GR, R, TR, YU.●

30. *Ornithogalum nutans* (including *O. boucheanum*) [15]   Short to medium plant, usually 15–35cm tall. Leaves about 5, green, linear, 10–15mm wide. Flowers generally 5–10, white or rather silvery with a broad green stripe on the exterior of each tepal, often nearly *bell-shaped* with tepals flaring outwards, carried on short stalks in a *dense raceme which is* usually more or less *1-sided*. In scrub, woods and damp fields, to 1000m. March–May. BG, CS, GR, H, TR, YU. Naturalised in many other countries.*
This is a very attractive species and is widely cultivated for ornamental purposes. It is especially useful for naturalising beneath shrubs. It frequently occurs in apparently wild situations but is almost certainly a relic or an escape from cultivation outside the countries given above.

31. *Ornithogalum arabicum* [16]   Medium to tall plant, usually 35–75cm tall. Leaves about 6–8 in a basal rosette, green, long-tapering at the apex from the 10–30mm wide base. *Flowers creamy-white* with a slightly greenish exterior, very *large and saucer-shaped, about 30–40mm diameter*, carried in a very dense flat-topped raceme. Ovary and young fruit blackish, giving the impression of a *dark eye to the flower*. Rocky places to 300m. April–May. BAL, CO, E, GR, I, P, SA, SC, YU. In some of these countries it might be naturalised rather than native.*
Probably one of the most striking of the European *Ornithogalum* species with its large heads of creamy, black-eyed, flowers. It is very useful as a cut flower as well as for display in a sunny border.

32. *Ornithogalum unifolium* [16]   Low plant, 3–10cm tall. *Leaf usually solitary*, about 4–6mm wide. Flowers 3–6, *white with no green stripe*, about 10mm diameter, each one nearly stemless and carried upright in a short dense raceme. In pine woods and rocky places, or heathy places, to 300m. March–June. *c*&*w*E, P.●

The compact spikes of erect unstriped white flowers and solitary leaf make this a very distinctive and attractive species.

33. *O. concinnum* (=*O. subcucullatum*) is rather like 32 but has 2–4 leaves, is taller, up to 30cm tall and has *more flowers on longer stalks.* P.●

GAGEA

A small group of diminutive bulbous plants normally with starry flowers. They are often very common where they do occur and can sometimes colour an alpine meadow in the early spring. Not all the species are alpine plants however, and some can be found near sea level in dry or stony situations.

Small bulbous perennials having one to several basal leaves and one or two stem leaves, the upper one adjacent to the base of the inflorescence. Flowers with six tepals, yellow, greenish or white, flat and starry or somewhat bell-shaped, carried in an umbel or very compacted raceme; stamens six, attached to the base of the tepals. Fruit a three-valved capsule containing many flat or rounded seeds.

A very confusing group of plants, all looking superficially rather similar except for *G. graeca* and *G. trinervia* which have white, more bell-shaped flowers.

When trying to identify a gagea it is necessary to know the number of basal leaves per bulb, usually one or two. It may be a variable character and it is best to look at several specimens in order to decide whether they more commonly have one or two leaves coming out of the bulb.

1. *Gagea pratensis* [16]   Low plant, usually 8–15cm tall; stem hairless. Basal leaf solitary, minutely hairy on the margin, linear, 4–5mm wide. Flowers usually 2–5, yellow with a greenish exterior, 20–30mm diameter, carried on hairless stalks. Grassy places, often in or near fields, to 1000m. April–May. A, BG, CH, CS, D, DK, E, F, GR, H, I, K, NL, R, *w*RS, S, SC, YU.●
A rather large-flowered gagea with a single fairly broad leaf.

2. *Gagea pusilla* [16]   Similar to *G. pratensis* but generally smaller, usually 3–8cm tall, with a solitary basal leaf, 1–2mm wide. Flowers usually about 10–20mm wide with narrower tepals, giving the whole flower a more starry appearance. Dry sandy and rocky places, to 500m. March–April. A, AL, BG, CS, GR, H, I, R, *sw*RS, YU.●
A rather smaller, more slender plant than *G. pratensis.*

3. Yellow Star of Bethlehem *Gagea lutea* [16]   Low to short plant, 10–20cm tall; stem hairless. Basal leaf solitary, linear, about 5–11mm wide. Flowers up to 10, yellow with a green exterior, 15–25mm diameter, carried on hairless or minutely hairy stalks. In light woodland or coppices, to 2000m. April–June. A, B, BG, CH, CO, CS, D, DK, E, F, GB, GR, H, I, N, NL, PL, R, *n,w* &*s*RS, S, SC, TR, YU.●
This is easily recognised by the rather wide strap-like leaf and robust habit.

4. *Gagea minima* Low plant, normally 8–15cm tall, often forming clumps with clusters of very narrow erect leaves; stem hairless. Basal leaf solitary, 1–2mm wide. Flowers yellow with a green exterior, about 10–15mm diameter, the tepals long-pointed giving the flower a very 'spidery' appearance. Woods and open grassy places, to 1000m. April–June. A, BG, CH, CS, D, DK, GR, H, I, K, N, PL, R, *n,w&s*RS, S, SF, YU.●

The very narrow tepals are distinctive, and these are often reflexed.

5. *Gagea reticulata* [16] Very low plant only 2–5cm tall (rarely to 10cm); bulb with an extended neck at its apex and covered with curled fibrous roots; stem minutely hairy. Basal leaf solitary, often curled and lying flat on the ground, 1–3mm wide, nearly cylindrical. Flowers yellowish with a green exterior, about 20–30mm diameter, on hairy stalks; tepals long-pointed and rather stiff. Dry stony or grassy hillsides, to 1000m. April–May. BG, CR, GR, R, *se*RS, ?YU.●

A rather distinctive little gagea with its quite large starry flowers on short stems and a fibrous-coated bulb.

6. *Gagea fibrosa* This is very like *G. reticulata* and is said to differ only in having a flattish rather than cylindrical leaf. AEG, GR.

7. *Gagea taurica* This is very similar to *G. reticulata* but the bulb has no extended neck at the apex. K.

8. *Gagea bulbifera* A low slender species less than 10cm tall with several thread-like leaves having bulbils in their axils. Flowers 1–3, yellow, less than 15mm diameter. Dryish hills. April. K, R, *w&se*RS.●

9. *Gagea spathacea* [16] Low to short plant, 10–15cm tall; stem hairless. Basal leaves two, hollow, about 2–3mm wide. Flowers yellowish with a green exterior, about 20mm diameter, on slightly hairy stalks. Dampish woods in scrub, to 1500m. April–June. B, CS, D, DK, F, H, I, NL, PL, R, *c&sw*RS, S, YU.

10. *Gagea fistulosa* (=*G. liotardii*) [16] Low to medium plant, 10–20cm tall; stem hairless. Basal leaves usually two (rarely one), hollow, about 3–4mm wide. Flowers yellow with a green exterior, 25–35mm diameter, with broad tepals giving a flower of substantial appearance. Mountain meadows and rocky places, 1000–2500m. May–June. A, BG, CH, CO, E, F, GR, I, K, R, *n,sw&se*RS, SC.●

The rather wide cylindrical, bright green, fleshy leaves are distinctive and almost rush-like and make this particular species easy to identify.

11. *Gagea arvensis* (=*G. villosa, G. dubia, G. granatellii*) [16] Low to medium plant, 5–15cm tall, stem minutely hairy. Basal leaves two, flat, linear, 3–4mm wide. Flowers often numerous, up to 20, yellow with a green exterior, about 15–20mm diameter, on hairy stalks; tepals usually silvery-hairy. Dryish stony places or dry fields, to 1000m. A, BG, CH, CO, CS, D, DK, E, F, GR, H, I, K, NL, PL, R, *se&sw*RS, S, SA, SC, TR, YU.●

The silvery hairs on the tepals and bracts often give the whole plant a rather grey appearance.

12. *Gagea peduncularis* [16]   Low plant, 2–10cm tall; stem minutely hairy. Basal leaves two, thread-like. Flowers usually only about 1–3, yellow with a green exterior, about 10–20mm diameter, on hairles stalks. In dry scrub or sparse grassy places, to 1000m. March–April. BG, CR, GR, TR, YU.
    This is rather similar to *G. bohemica* and its relatives (see page 00) but the flower stalks elongate as the flowers fade.

13. *Gagea nevadensis* (= *G. soleirolii*) is very similar to *G. peduncularis* but *has hairless stems* and the flowers about 10mm diameter. Alpine turf and rocks, 1500–3000m. June–August. BAL, CO, E, F, P, SA.●

14. *Gagea amblyopetala* (= *G. heldreichii*) is like *G. peduncularis* but has broader linear leaves, 1–2mm wide, and hairless stems. Flowers about 10mm diameter with less sharply pointed tepals. Grassy, rocky places and scrub, to 1750m. March– May. CR, GR, K, *sw*RS, TR, YU.

15. *Gagea foliosa* [16]   Low plant, usually 5–12cm tall; stem hairless. Basal leaves two, rarely one, narrowly lance-shaped, about 3–4mm wide. Flowers 1–4, yellow with a green exterior, 15–25mm diameter, on hairy stalks. In sparse woodland or scrub, to 2000m. April–July. CO, I, SA, SC.●
    This species has bulbils in the leaf axils.

16. *Gagea polymorpha* is similar to *G. foliosa* but does *not have bulbils* in the leaf axils. E, *e*P.

17. *Gagea bohemica* (= *G. saxatilis, G. szovitsii*) [16]   Very low plant, usually 2–6cm tall, stem hairy or hairless. Basal leaves two, thread-like, often curled and lying on the ground. Flowers 1–4, yellow with a greenish exterior, about 10–20mm diameter on hairy or hairless stalks. Dry rocky or grassy places, to 500m. A, BG, CH, CO, CR, CS, D, F, *w*GB*, GR, H, I, K, P, R, *sw*RS, SA, SC, YU.●
    This is always a very tiny plant with extremely narrow leaves.

18. *Gagea graeca* (= *Lloydia graeca*) [16]   Low plant 5–10cm tall; stem glabrous. Basal leaves two to four, narrowly linear. Flowers 1–5, *white with purple stripes* on the tepals, widely funnel-shaped or bell-shaped, about 7–10mm diameter. Stony slopes and rock crevices, to 1000m, April–May. AEG, CR, *s*GR.●
    A beautiful delicate little plant, easily distinguished from other gageas by the more bell-like white, purple-striped, flowers.

19. *Gagea trinervia*   Very like *G. graeca* but usually with only one (rarely 2–3) flowers. It has a longer style and pointed stamens (blunt in *G. graeca*). Scrub and rocks. SC. The distribution of this species extends into North Africa.

LLOYDIA

A small genus of tiny, graceful bulbous plants, related to Gagea but having only one or two bell-shaped white flowers with nectaries at the base of the tepals. In Europe there is only one species, which is very widespread from the arctic regions of Russia, south to Italy and Bulgaria. In the northern part of its range it can occur nearly at sea level, whereas in the Alps it is a high mountain plant.

Snowdon Lily *Lloydia serotina* [16]   Low to short slender plant to 20cm tall. Bulb sometimes producing stolons, covered with fibrous long-necked tunic. *Basal leaves 2, thread-like* about 1mm wide but up to 25cm long, stem leaves 2−5, slightly wider and becoming progressively shorter up the stem. Flowers usually solitary, *white with purple veins*, about 10−15mm diameter; bell-shaped, carried on

Snowdon Lily fruit capsule, × 2

slender stalks 20−25mm long; tepals about 10−15mm long, each with a pitted nectary near the base; stamens six. Fruit a rounded capsule with three valves, containing many seeds. Rocky slopes, crevices, mountain meadows and open peaty places, to 3000m. (May−) June−August. A, *sw*BG, CH, CS, D, F, *w*GB*, I, PL, R, *n*&*sw*RS, YU.●
    Although very rare in Britain and known only from N. Wales, it is relatively common in other parts of its extensive range.

CHIONODOXA

A delightful little genus of Scilla-like plants commonly known as Glory of the Snow because they often flower as soon as the snow melts. In Europe the genus is only found in Crete where there are three small-flowered species. The remaining species are of Turkish origin and include several much larger-flowered species including *C. lucilliae* commonly cultivated in our gardens, its blue and white flowers one of the loveliest sights of early spring.
    Chionodoxa are bulbous plants which have a pair of narrow basal leaves and a leafless flower stem. The flowers are solitary or a few in a loose raceme. The six

tepals are joined together near the base into a short tube whilst the flattened filaments form a 'cup' in the centre of the flower.

Although very similar to scillas, *Chionodoxa* can be immediately recognised by its flower tube and by the filament 'cup'. *Scilla* has free tepals and spreading stamens.

1. Cretan Glory of the Snow *Chionodoxa cretica* [17]   Low to short plant 7 to 30cm tall, though often less. Leaves 2, narrow, 3–12mm wide. Flowers *lilac-blue with a white centre*, solitary or rarely 2–3 together, 12–20mm, on slender stems; stamens prominent, creamy. Shady rocky places in scrub, often near melting snow, 1300–2000m. April–May (–July). CR*.●

Although very easy to cultivate this species is not showy enough to become widely popular.

2. *Chionodoxa nana*   Like the previous species but shorter, only 5–10cm tall, with leaves up to 5mm wide. *Flowers small*, 9–10mm. Near snow patches in the mountains. May–July. CR*.●

Some authorities consider this to be only a high altitude form of *C. cretica*.

3. White Glory of the Snow *Chionodoxa albescens*   Like (1) but with *small whitish flowers* held erect, each rather funnel-shaped with the tepals not widely spreading. Rocky places in the mountains. April–June. CR*.

SCILLA

A delightful widespread genus of small or medium-sized bulbous plants. Scillas or squills are generally associated with spring, when their bright starry flowers are much appreciated by gardeners. In the wild they can often be found growing in large numbers. There are a few species with white or pink flowers, but the predominant flower colour is blue or purple. Most species are spring flowering, though two occur in the late summer or autumn.

The genus is fairly large, being distributed through Europe and western Asia to India and China with a southward extension through Africa to the Cape. Some of the African species however, which have dark-spotted leaves, are considered by some botanists to belong to a separate genus, *Ledebouria*.

Scillas are small, mostly hairless, bulbous perennials with basal thread-like or strap-shaped leaves. The leafless flower stems carry a raceme of small starry or bell-like flowers which have separate and similar tepals and stamens spreading. A solitary bract subtends each flower, or the bract may be absent altogether. The fruit capsule is small and rounded and contains 3 or several blackish seeds.

The only other genera in Europe which might be confused with *Scilla* are *Hyacinthoides* (=*Endymion*) which contains the well known Bluebell, and *Chionodoxa*. However, the former has 2 bracts (an outer and an inner) subtending each flower and the latter has its tepals joined into a short tube and the stamens held close together.

Key to European Species of Scilla

1. Flowers appearing in late summer to autumn   2
   Flowers appearing in spring   3

2. Leaves 1–3mm wide, hairless   7. *S. autumnalis*
   Leaves more than 5mm wide, margins hairy   8. *S. intermedia*

3. Plant tall and slender, 30–100cm with 40 or more
   flowers in cylindrical racemes; bracts 1–1.5mm
   long   14. *S. hyacinthoides*
   Plant not as above   4

4. Leaf solitary   4. *S. monophyllos*
   Leaves 2 or more   5

5. Bracts 5mm long or more   6
   Bracts less than 2mm long or absent   10

6. Leaves 5–10 in number, wider towards apex then
   narrowing abruptly, 1–3cm wide   13. *S. liliohyacinthus*
   Leaves parallel-sided or lance-shaped but if
   wider towards apex then less than 5 in number   7

7. Flowers usually in a large broad conical or
   flat-topped raceme; leaves usually 1–6cm wide;
   bracts 2–4cm long   15. *S. peruviana*
   Flowers in a cylindrical or small dense flat-topped
   raceme; leaves less than 1cm wide; bracts
   0.8–1.7cm long   8

8. Leaves green, roughly parallel-sided to the tip,
   then narrowing abruptly   3. *S. verna*
   Leaves grey-green, narrowly lance-shaped,
   tapering gradually to the tip   9

9. Flowers scented, mid to deep purple-blue, bell-
   shaped   6. *S. odorata*
   Flowers unscented, pale to mid blue, flat   5. *S. ramburei*

10. Leaves usually 2; flowers erect in a 1-sided
    raceme, or pendent and bell-shaped   11
    Leaves 3–7; flowers not as above   12

11. Flowers erect and starry   1. *S. bifolia*
    Flowers drooping and rather bell-shaped   2. *S. sibirica*

12. Flowers 5–7mm diameter; lower pedicels usually
    more than 10mm long   12. *S. pratensis*
    Flowers 8–14mm diameter, lower pedicels usually
    less than 10mm long   13

13. Leaves 3–5; raceme rather dense (Bulgaria,
    Turkey)   9. *S. bithynica*
    Leaves 4–7; raceme rather loose (southern Greece)   10. *S. messeniaca*

1. Alpine Squill *Scilla bifolia* [17]   Low to short plant to 15cm tall. Leaves *usually* 2, linear or becoming wider towards the tip, 5–10mm wide. Flowers deep purple-blue, 10–15mm, starry, 1–7 in a rather loose *one-sided raceme*; lower pedicels 10–30mm long, slender; bracts absent. Short grass or light woodland, often near snow patches, to 2700m. January–May. A, AEG, AL, *s*B, BG, CH, CS, *e&s*D, E, *c&s*F, GR, H, I, PL, R, *sw*RS, SA, SC, TR, YU.*

Alpine Squill flower, × 1½

This is one of the most widespread of all scillas, often occurring in large numbers. It is usually one of the first spring bulbs to emerge after the winter. The flower colour and habit is quite variable. Some of the most vigorous forms occur on the Greek Islands (Cyclades) where they may reach 30cm tall with up to 5 leaves per bulb. These variants are recognised as separate species by some botanists, but the differences are very slight and they overlap.

The Alpine Squill is a popular garden plant, commonly grown in the rock garden. The distribution of the species extends into Asia Minor and the Middle East.

2. Siberian Squill *Scilla sibirica* [17]   Short plant to 15cm tall. Leaves usually 2, rarely 3, strap-shaped, *widest towards the tip*, 10–15mm wide, bright shiny green. Flowers vivid deep blue, *widely bell-shaped, pendent*, 16–20mm, solitary or several in a raceme, each on a short stalk 5–10mm long; bracts tiny, 1mm. Scrub or light woodland, 1000–2000m. March–April. *sw*RS*.*

The Siberian Squill is a beautiful species and quite hardy which makes it of great value in gardens for its intense blue flowers produced in the early spring. Although it is confined in Europe to Russia the species is common in Turkey and N. Iran.

3. Spring Squill *Scilla verna* [17]   Low to short plant to 20cm tall. Leaves 2–6, linear, deep green, 2–5mm wide, *parallel-sided* but *narrowing abruptly at the tip*. Flowers lilac-blue to violet, starry, 7–10mm, 2–12 occurring in a *dense, almost flat-topped raceme*; lower pedicels 5–13mm long; bracts 8–17mm long, finely pointed. Short turf or scrub, to 2000m. April–July. Western Europe – E, F, FA, *n&sw*GB, *e*IRL, N, P.*

An attractive little spring bulb, often found near the sea but not confined to these areas. It is locally quite common, though mainly in western Europe. In Britain it occurs in the southwest of England, in Scotland, Northumberland and Ireland.

4. One-leaved Squill *Scilla monophyllos* [17]   Low to short plant, 5–20cm tall. *Leaf solitary*, narrowly lance-shaped, tapering to a hooded apex, 10–20 (–30)mm wide. Flowers mid to deep blue, starry, 8–12mm, usually 6–20 to a raceme; lower pedicels 10–15mm long; bracts 4–7mm long. Scrub beneath pines, 200–1000m. February–May. *w*E, P.*

The solitary quite broad leaf makes this an easily recognised species.

5. *Scilla ramburei* [17]   Short to medium plant to 50cm tall. Leaves several, narrowly lance-shaped, 3–10mm wide, *tapering gradually to a sharp point, grey-green* on the upper surface. Flowers bluish, starry, 8–15mm, unscented, 6–30 carried in a loose raceme, tepals pointed; longest bracts 15–17mm long. Open grassy, or slightly shaded places, often near the sea, 100–1100m. *se*E, P.●

This species can be distinguished by its grey-green tapering leaves and pale blue flattish flowers.

6. Scented Squill *Scilla odorata*   Similar to the previous species but with *mid to deep purple-blue scented flowers* which are rather more bell- or cup-shaped with blunt tepals; bracts 7–14mm long. Grassy places and beneath pines, often in sandy soil, at low altitudes. March. *s*E*, *s*P*.

An attractive species, unfortunately little known in cultivation and apparently rather local and uncommon in the wild.

Scented Squill, × ½

7. Autumn Squill *Scilla autumnalis* [17]   Low to short plant, 2–25cm tall. Leaves 3–12, linear, *absent at flowering time* (rarely just showing), 0.5–3mm wide, hairless. Flowers pale to deep lilac, blue or pinkish-purple, rarely white, starry, 5–7mm, up to 35 in a spike-like raceme; *bracts absent*. Rocky, grassy or sandy places, often near the sea, to 2000m. August–October. AL, BG, CO, E, F, *se&sw*GB*, GR, H, I, K, P, R, *w*RS, SA, SC, TR, YU.*

A very widespread and often abundant plant and perhaps one of the most common European bulbs. Its autumn-flowering habit separates it from all other species except *Scilla intermedia* which is much more restricted in distribution. The Autumn Squill is not one of the more attractive species and is not often seen in cultivation, though its autumn-flowering habit gives it some appeal.

8. *Scilla intermedia*   Like the previous species but with 2–5 leaves which tend to spread out on the ground, each 5–17mm wide, linear or lance-shaped with a *minutely hairy margin*. Grass or scrub, at or near sea level. August–September. CO, SA, SC.

In flower, this species is indistinguishable from the previous, but the wider, spreading, leaves clearly distinguish it later on. It is clearly related to, or the same as, the North African *S. obtusifolia* whose leaves may reach 25mm wide.

9. Bithynian Squill *Scilla bithynica* [17]   Short plant to 15cm tall. Leaves 3–5, linear or slightly widened towards the top, 5–10mm wide. Flowers pale to mid-blue, 8–10mm, starry, slightly cupped, horizontal to nearly upright, 6–14 in a rather *dense raceme*; lower pedicels 5–10mm long; *bracts only 1–2mm long*. Shady damp places, to 1000m. April. BG, *nw*TR. *

A bright easily grown spring bulb which is surprisingly restricted in its distribution. It will naturalise itself readily in British gardens.

10. Messenian Squill *Scilla messeniaca*   Closely resembles the previous species, but with *up to 7 long leaves*, 6–15mm wide. Flowers pale blue in a *rather loose raceme*. Rocky or grassy places in light shade, below 500m. February–April. *s*GR – Kalamata region.●

Although similar to *Scilla bithynica*, this species has a few small differences which have been pointed out above, besides being separated geographically. It is known only from the south-west Greek Peloponnese.

11. Albanian Squill *Scilla albanica*   Similar to the previous species and possibly indistinct. The plants are however, less leafy-looking, with fewer, shorter leaves. Rocky places, to 2000m. February–April. AL*, ?*sw*YU.

12. Meadow Squill *Scilla pratensis* (=*S. amethystina*) [17]   Similar in general appearance to the preceding 3 species. Low to short plant 8–20 (–30)cm tall. Leaves 3–6, linear or lance-shaped, tapering very gradually to the pointed tip, 3–8mm wide. Flowers blue or sometimes violet-pink, rather starry, 5–7mm, 10–30 in a fairly dense raceme; pedicels 10–15mm long; bracts 1–1.5mm long. Grassy and stony, or rocky places, to 2000m. April–June. *w*YU.●

The smaller flowers and longer flower stalks distinguish this species from its closest relatives, *S. bithynica* and *S. messenaica*, besides their distinct distributions. *Scilla pratensis* is occasionally seen in cultivation.

13. Pyrenean Squill *Scilla liliohyacinthus* [18]　Low to short plant to 15cm tall. Leaves shiny-green, 5−10, strap-shaped, broadest above the middle with an abruptly narrowed tip, 10−30mm wide. Flowers blue, starry, 10−15mm, 5−15 in a loose raceme; bracts 10−20mm long, papery-white and long-tapering. Woods and meadow margin, 500−2000m. April−June. *n*&*c*E, *c*&*s*F.*

An easy species to recognise with its broad shiny leaves and long papery bracts. In the wild it often forms quite large colonies the flowers looking disproportionately small against the leaves. The bulb is curious in that it consists of a series of yellowish, lily-like, rather loose scales, and is quite unlike that of any other species of *Scilla*.

14. *Scilla hyacinthoides* [18]　Medium to tall plant, 30−100cm tall. Leaves 5−12, rather tough, shiny, more or less narrowly oblong, 13−30mm wide, minutely hairy on the margin and with a pointed apex. Flowers mid lilac-blue, starry, 8−12mm, *many, 50−150* carried in a long spike-like raceme, tepals narrow; *bracts 1−1.5mm* long. Rocky places and rather dry fields, to 500m. April−May. CR, E, F, GR, I, P, SA, SC, YU.*

The tallest European *Scilla*, quite unlike any other with its long 'spikes' of small flowers. It is quite hardy in cultivation, though not often seen.

15. *Scilla peruviana* [18]　Short to medium plant 15−50cm tall. Leaves 4−9, often spreading, lance-shaped, tapering to the apex, 10−35mm wide, sometimes with a hairy margin. Flowers deep violet-blue or whitish, starry, 10−20mm, up to 100 carried in a rather *flat topped or broadly-conical raceme*; lower pedicels 3.5−10cm long; bracts 2−4cm long, papery-white. Damp places and sandy places near the sea, at low altitudes. March−May. E, I, P, SA, SC.*

In spite of its name this is an entirely Mediterranean species, not at all connected with Peru from where it was first thought to have originated. It is one of the most striking species, widely cultivated, and well worth trying in a warm border.

Scilla peruviana is very variable plant and various names have been given to some of the more distinct forms. *Scilla elongata* has hairy leaves and bracts, whilst *S. hughii* is a robust plant with leaves up to 50mm wide. *Scilla cupanii* is a small variant with only 5−15 flowers on short scapes and leaves 7−15mm wide. *Scilla sicula* has pedicels and bracts almost equal in length, 4−6cm long.

Bluebells HYACINTHOIDES (= ENDYMION)

A very well-known genus since it contains the much loved common English Bluebell. All the species of *Hyacinthoides* were once included in the genus *Scilla* and indeed they are very similar and closely related. Probably the easiest way to distinguish them is by their bracts – *Scilla* species have only a solitary bract below each flower, whereas *Hyacinthoides* have two bracts, one on each side of the pedicel at its base, the lower and outer bract larger and partly concealing the other. There is, however, another important feature that can be seen in the bulbs, which is less easy to see without dissection. The *Hyacinthoides* bulb is almost solid and non-scaly, whereas *Scilla* has scaled bulbs like daffodils and onions. Apart from these differences the plants closely resemble scillas, especially the starry-flowered *H. italica*.

Most people will know the Bluebell under the Latin generic name of *Endymion*. Unfortunately, and regrettably, this is predated by *Hyacinthoides*.

1. Common or **English Bluebell** *Hyacinthoides* (= *Endymion*) *non-scripta* [18] Short to medium plant to 40cm tall. Leaves 3–6, bright green, strap-shaped, 5–20mm wide, equalling or shorter than the raceme. Flowers deep blue or occasionally pink or white, scented, narrow *tubular, bell-shaped*, drooping, 15–20mm long, 4–20 in a rather one-sided raceme nodding at the apex; anthers yellow. Woods, especially of beech and oak, and in scrub, to 1500m. April–May. Western Europe – B, E, F, GB, IRL, NL, P. *

The Bluebell is so well known that it scarcely needs describing. Its attractive, sweetly scented flowers often form large drifts in the spring and it is widely grown and naturalised. There is no mistaking it from the other members of the genus, for its narrow tubular flowers are quite unique.

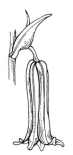

Common Bluebell flower, × 1½

Bluebell fruit capsule, × 1½

2. Spanish Bluebell *Hyacinthoides* (= *Endymion*) *hispanica* (= *Scilla campanulatus*) [18]   Habit similar to the previous species but the leaves more substantial and up to 25mm wide. Flowers pale to mid-blue, pink or white, unscented, *broadly bell-shaped*, 12–20mm long but just as broad, carried in a loose raceme which is *neither nodding or one-sided*; anthers blue. Meadows, in slight shade and in rocky scrub, 1000–1500m. April–May. E, P.*

The Spanish Bluebell is a common and easily cultivated garden plant which has naturalised itself in several European countries. Through selection it now exists in several colour forms such as deep blue, pink or white.

3. Italian Bluebell *Hyacinthoides* (=*Scilla*) *italica* [18]   Short plant to 30cm tall. Leaves 4–10, deep green, linear, 3–11mm wide. Flowers mid to deep lilac-blue or violet-blue, starry, 6–12mm, 3–30 in a *dense raceme*, sometimes rather flat-topped; anthers deep blue. Rocky or grassy places, often in scrubland or woods, to 1700m. March–May. E, F, I, P.*

Italian Bluebell flower and fruit, × 1½

This species is quite unlike the other two species, having starry flowers rather than bell-shaped ones. Indeed it is more like *Scilla verna* except for the two bracts per flower. It is also usually rather taller.

There are two closely related but little known species. *Hyacinthoides vicentina* from southern Portugal (Cape St Vincent) is very similar but has yellow pollen rather than blue and *H. reverchonii* from southern Spain (Jaen Province) has a looser, longer, raceme with more cup-shaped flower.

HYACINTHELLA

A small genus of blue-flowered bulbs from eastern Europe and western Asia, related to *Hyacinthus* and *Bellevalia*. They can be distinguished from both of these genera by their very small flowers in which the tepals remain attached to the flower stalk right through the fruiting stage. The leaves have several prominent veins, a feature not noticeable in either of the other genera. An interesting and very obvious feature of the bulb itself is the liberal coating of white crystals, appearing powder-like on the bulbcoats.

Hyacinthellas are small hairless bulbous perennials with 2–3 basal linear leaves which are broader towards their tips. The flower stem or scape is leafless and carries a raceme of small tubular flowers; tepals joined into a narrow bell-shaped tube with 6 small lobes, with the stamens attached near the top of the tube inside. The fruit is a small capsule with 3 chambers each containing 1 to several black seeds.

Key to European Species of Hyacinthella

1. Flowers 7–10mm long (S. Russia)   2. *H. pallasiana*
    Flowers 4–6mm long   **2**

2. Leaves horizontal or arching (Yugoslavia)   1. *H. dalmatica*
    Leaves erect   **3**

3. Flowers deep blue (C. Greece)   4. *H. atchleyi*
    Flowers pale blue or nearly white (E.&S.E. Europe,
      S. Russia)   3. *H. leucophaea*

1. Dalmatian Hyacinthella *Hyacinthella dalmatica* [18]   Low plant 3–10cm tall. Leaves 2 linear, 2–4mm wide, arching. *Flowers mid-blue, tubular, about 4mm long*, 6–20 in a dense spike-like raceme; tepal lobes one-third the length of the tube; pedicels 1mm long or less, but extending to 5mm in fruit. Among rocks and in open scrub, 300–400m. March–April. *w*YU.

This is the only species having arching rather than erect leaves. It is endemic to the Dalmatian Mountains and although an attractive little plant it is really too diminutive to become a popular garden plant.

2. *Hyacinthella pallasiana*   Like the previous species but with 2–3 erect leaves, 1–6mm wide. *Flowers pale blue, 7–10mm long*. Grassy places. March–April. *sw*RS.

This attractive plant can be easily distinguished from all other European species by its long flowers.

Hyacinthella pallasiana, × ½

3. Pale Hyacinthella *Hyacinthella leucophaea* (=*H. rumelica*) [18]   Low to short plant to 15cm tall. Leaves erect, 2–14mm wide. *Flowers pale blue or whitish,*

4–5mm long, up to 25 in a spike-like raceme; pedicels 1–3mm long. Rocky and grassy places in the open and in light woodland, 150–900m. March–May. BG, *n*GR, K, PL, *sw*&*c*RS, *se*YU.

4. *Hyacinthella atchleyi*   Low to short plant rather like the previous species, to 15cm tall. Leaves erect, 3–10mm wide. *Flowers deep blue, 4–6mm long*; pedicels 2–4mm long. Stony and grassy -places, to 150m. February–March. *c*GR – Halkis and Thebes areas.

This species is not unlike a deep blue flowered version of *H. leucophaea*, but with slightly larger individual flowers.

BRIMEURA

This is a small genus of only two species, confined to the Mediterranean region and probably better known as *Hyacinthus*, although they bear little resemblance to the cultivated hyacinth of our gardens. The main difference, apart from flower size, lies in the bracts which subtend each flower stalk: in *Brimeura* they are long and tapering while in the *Hyacinthus* they are minute and insignificant.

Small hairless bulbous perennials. Leaves narrow, linear, all basal. Flowers carried in short racemes, bell-shaped or tubular with six tepals joined in the lower part to form a short tube. Flower stalks much shorter than the narrow long-tapering bracts. Fruit a small 3-valved capsule.

1. *Brimeura* (*=Hyacinthus*) *amethystina* [19]   Short plant 10–25cm tall. Leaves bright green, narrowly linear. *Flowers bright blue* or rarely white, tubular, nodding, about 10mm long, 5–15 carried in a *loose one-sided raceme*, tepal lobes shorter than the tube, curved outwards at the tips. Grassy slopes and rocky places, up to 2000m. April–June. *s*F, *n*E, YU*.***

This attractive little plant resembles a miniature bluebell but is an even brighter blue. The fact that the tepals are joined into a tube makes it easy to distinguish since in bluebells they are free from each other. *Brimeura amethystina* has a curious distribution, in the Pyrenees and Croatia, but is rare in the latter locality. It is sometimes seen in gardens where under favourable conditions it may naturalise freely.

2. *Brimeura fastigiata* (*=Hyacinthus pauzolzii*) [19]   Low plant, usually only 5–7cm tall. Leaves narrowly linear, dark green. *Flowers white* or *pale pinkish-lilac*, 5–7mm long, bell-shaped, horizontal or slightly erect, 1–10 borne in a *short dense raceme, not one-sided*; tepal lobes longer than the tube and flared outwards so that the flower appears rather starry. Peaty pockets in scrub or in rocks, up to 1000m. April–June. BAL, CO, SA.

A rather insignificant little plant resembling a pale *Scilla*, but they all have their tepals free from each other.

BELLEVALIA

Short to medium bulbous perennials with basal strap-shaped or lanceolate leaves and leafless flower stems. Flowers tubular or bell-shaped, usually numerous, in spike-like racemes which are dense at first, elongating in fruit and becoming more loose; pedicels usually also elongating in fruit; tepals fused for a half to two-thirds of their length into a cylindrical tube; stamens often bluish, attached near the mouth of the flower. Fruit a 3-valved capsule containing blue-black spherical seeds.

Bellevalias are, on the whole, dull plants with brownish, greenish or dirty-white flowers. They are related to the Grape Hyacinths (*Muscari*), but the mouth of the flower is not constricted.

Key to European Species of Bellevalia

1. Flowers whitish, becoming green or brown with age   2
   Flowers not whitish at first   3

2. Flower-stalks (pedicels) only 1mm long (Crete)   8. *B. brevipedicellata*
   Flower-stalks (pedicels) 20mm long   2. *B. romana*

3. Flower-stalks 4–10cm long (Russia)   7. *B. sarmatica*
   Flower-stalks up to 4cm long   4

4. Flowers blue or bright violet at first   1. *B. dubia*
   Flowers dull purplish at first   5

5. Flowers 10mm or more long   6
   Flowers 5–6mm long   7

6. Flower-stalks 3–4cm long   6. *B. ciliata*
   Flower-stalks under 1cm long   3. *B. trifoliata*

7. Leaf margins rough with tiny teeth (Crimea)   4. *B. lipskyi*
   Leaf margins smooth (Italy)   5. *B. webbiana*

1. *Bellevalia dubia* [19] Medium plant 30–40cm tall. Leaves 3–5, long and narrowly lance-shaped with a long-tapering tip. *Flowers brilliant steely-blue or violet* in bud, changing soon to a dingy brown, 5–7mm long, *tubular*, about 20–30 carried in a *cylindrical raceme* with the flower-stalks 5–7mm long and held at right angles to the flower stem. Grassy places, often in cultivated land such as olive groves, below 1000m. March–May. AL, CR, GR, I, *sw*YU, SC, *sp*.●

The Portuguese plants are sometimes referred to as *B. hackelii*, but are scarcely any different from the rest.

Bellevalia dubia is one of the most striking species in a rather dull genus. The very bright young flowers are quite showy but they rapidly change to a greenish or brownish colour.

2. *Bellevalia romana* [19]   Short to medium plant 15–35cm tall. Leaves 3–6, long and linear. *Flowers dirty-white*, becoming brown later, 7–10mm long, *bell-shaped* with the lobes flared outwards, 20–30 carried in a cylindrical raceme on semi-erect flower-stalks which are usually 10mm, rarely to 20mm, long. Cultivated and grassy places, below 1000m. April–May. CO, F, GR, I, SC, YU.

This is one of the more widespread and common species, easily recognised by its white flowers with flared tepals, borne on relatively long stalks.

3. *Bellevalia trifoliata*   Similar to the previous species but with *tubular dull violet or purplish flowers*, 12–15mm long, lobes not flared and flower-stalks less than 10mm long. Grassy places, often on sandy soil, to 100m. March–April. CR, F, GR, IT, TR.

The very long tubular flowers on short stalks make this a rather distinctive species.

4. Lipsky's Bellevalia *Bellevalia lipskyi*   Similar to *B. romana* but *flowers deep dull purple*, becoming yellowish-brown with age, 5–6mm long, on flower-stalks about 5mm long. Cultivated land. April–May. K.

5. Webb's Bellevalia *Bellevalia webbiana*   Similar to *B. romana* but *flowers deep dull purplish, becoming brown* with age, each about 5–6mm long and borne on flower-stalks 5–7mm long. Grassy places. April–May. ɴI.

Although rather like *B. lipskyi* in general appearance, this has smooth leaf-margins and is geographically separate. The leaves of *B. lipskyi* have rough margins.

6. Ciliate-leaved Bellevalia *Bellevalia ciliata*   Short to medium plant 15–35cm tall. Leaves 3–5, lanceolate, shorter and broader than in *B. romana*, and with *distinctly hairy margins*. Flowers pale purple, becoming greenish-brown, about 10mm long, carried in a very *broad cone-shaped raceme* on flower-stalks usually 3–4cm long. Cultivated land and fields, to 300m. March–April. GR, ʃI, TR.

7. *Bellevalia sarmatica*   Very similar to the previous species but the flowers are generally carried on longer *stalks, up to 10cm* and they have creamy tepal lobes. C,SW&SERS.

The last two species are the only Bellevalias in Europe which carry their flowers in broad cone-shaped racemes. The rest have narrower, cylindrical racemes.

8. Short-stalked Bellevalia *Bellevalia brevipedicellata*   Short plant to 15cm. Leaves 2–3, linear or narrowly lance-shaped. Flowers whitish, about 7mm long, *on flower stalks only 1mm long*; raceme cylindrical. Rocky places, to 200m. February–March. SWCR.

Easily distinguished from all other European Bellevalias by its nearly stalkless flowers.

STRANGWEIA

Strangweia spicata [19]   Low hairless bulbous perennial. Leaves 4–5, basal, narrowly linear, dark green, often with undulate-margins. Flowers china-blue to deep violet-blue, 5–10mm long, more or less erect, bell-shaped, carried in a dense spike; the slightly spreading tepals are joined into a tube in their lower half; stamens deep violet-blue, the filaments flattened, with a prominent tooth on each side of the anther. Rocky and grassy places, 250–1000m. January–March. cGR – Attica.●

Although rather restricted in its distribution, *S. spicata* is not uncommon in certain well-known places such as Delphi and Mt Parnassus. It is a Scilla-like plant, but the tepals are joined into a tube whereas in *Scilla* they are free from one another. Some botanists now regard this plant as a species of *Bellevalia*.

Grape Hyacinths MUSCARI

The Grape Hyacinths need little introduction as several species are grown in our gardens, especially *M. armeniacum* which is often sold as a cut flower in early spring. They are mostly easy to grow and often multiply rapidly, both by the production of bulblets and by copious seeds. Most of the common species have blue flowers and it may surprise some to discover that one European species *M. macrocarpum* has yellow flowers.

The Grape Hyacinths are related to the Hyacinths and Bellevalias, but are readily recognised by the flowers which are restricted or crimped in towards the mouth. When identifying the species it is necessary to note the colour of the tepals, or 'teeth', as they are often referred to, and the colour of the fertile flowers; those are the lower flowers in the raceme. The uppermost flowers are generally sterile, or infertile, and a different colour.

Small hairless bulbous perennials. Leaves narrow, linear, all basal. Flowers carried in short, usually dense racemes or spikes, each urn-shaped, bell-like or nearly globose with a sharply contracted mouth; tepals separate for a very short distance so that they resemble 6 tiny teeth at the apex of the flower tube. Fruit a small 3-valved capsule, papery when ripe.

Key to European Species of Muscari

1. Autumn-flowering plant   5. *M. parviflorum*
   Spring flowering plants   **2**

2. Mature flowers yellow   12. *M. macrocarpum*
   Mature flowers blue, greenish, whitish or brown   **3**

3. Flowers pale to deep blue or blackish-blue   **4**
   Flowers other than blue (uppermost sterile ones
      sometimes blue)   **6**

4. Teeth, or tepal lobes, the same colour as the tube   4. *M. commutatum*
    Teeth, or tepal lobes, whitish   **5**

5. Flowers urn-shaped; leaves parallel-sided   2. *M. neglectum* &
                                               3. *M. armeniacum*

    Flower globular; leaves broader towards the tip   1. *M. botryoides*

6. Teeth, or tepal lobes, blackish-brown   7. *M. tenuiflorum*
    Teeth white or yellowish   6. *M. comosum* (and four
                                     allied species, 8, 9, 10, 11
                                           – see text)

1. *Muscari botryoides* [19]   Low to short plant 5–10cm tall. *Leaves 2–3, widest at the tip*, 5–10mm wide, grey-green on the upper surface, usually shorter than the flower stem. *Flowers vivid blue with white teeth*, 3–5mm long, nearly globular; upper sterile flowers usually paler and rather few in number. Mountain meadows, often in damp situation, 500–2000m. April–June. A, AL, BG, CH, CO, CS, D, E, F, GR, H, I, PL, R, *w*RS, SC, YU.*

An attractive species easy to recognise because of its short spike of nearly round flowers and leaves which become wider towards the tip.

2. Common Grape Hyacinth *Muscari neglectum* [19]   Low to short plant 5–30cm tall; bulb often with blackish tunics and usually producing many small offsets. *Leaves 3–6, narrowly linear, 2–8mm wide*, bright or deep green, usually as long, or longer, than the flower stem. *Flowers deep-blue to blackish-blue, with white teeth* and with a greyish waxy 'bloom' on the outside, urn-shaped, 4–8mm long; upper sterile flowers paler blue, 10–20 in number. Open grassy or rocky places, or in woods, to 2000m. March–May. A, AL, BAL, BG, CH, CO, CR, CS, D, E, F, GR, H, I, K, P, PL, R, *w,s&e*RS, SA, SC, TR, YU.*

Common Grape Hyacinth fruit capsule, × 3

Muscari neglectum is the commonest species in Europe and the most well-known in gardens. It can become a pest in cultivation because of its ability to produce many offset bulblets around the parent bulb. Several names have been applied to forms of *M. neglectum*, including *M. racemosum* and *M. atlanticum*, for the deep blue-flowered forms. *Muscari pulchellum* is the very dwarf narrow-leaved variant from Greece which has only a few flowers in the raceme.

3. Armenian Grape Hyacinth *Muscari armeniacum* [19]   Very similar to the previous species but with *bright blue flowers* of a paler shade and wider leaves which are grey-green on the upper surface. Grassy places, to 1000m. April–May. BG, GR, TR, YU.*

A popular garden plant for its long striking spikes of blue flowers.

4. *Muscari commutatum* [19]   Similar to M. *neglectum* but easily recognised by its rather angular *violet-black flowers* with *no white teeth*. Grassy or rocky places, to 1000m. April–May. CR, GR, I, SC, YU.

5. Autumn Grape Hyacinth *Muscari parviflorum* [19]   Short plant, 15–30cm tall. Leaves 3–5, less than 3mm wide, shorter than the flower stem. *Flowers appearing in the autumn,* pale blue or lilac blue, 3–5mm long, bell-shaped and only slightly constricted at the mouth, carried in a loose raceme with a few sterile flowers at the apex. Grassy or rocky places, often near the sea, to 500m. September–November. BAL, ɟE, GR, I, SC, YU.

This is the only autumn-flowering species of Grape Hyacinth. It is not very showy with its small rather dull bluish flowers.

6. Tassle Hyacinth *Muscari comosum* (=*Leopoldia comosa*) [19]   Short to medium plant, 20–60cm tall; bulb often pinkish-tinged. Leaves 3–6, linear or tapering gradually to the tip, 5–20mm wide. *Flowers brownish with creamy or pale yellowish-brown teeth,* 5–10mm long, urn-shaped, carried on stalks up to 15mm in length in a long loose raceme; upper *sterile flowers blue or violet, held erect* on long slender violet-blue stalks. Often on cultivated land but also on stony or grassy hillsides, or in sparse scrub, to 1500m. April–June. A, AL, BAL, BG, CH, CO, CR, D, E, F, GR, I, K, PL, R, *C&W*RS,SA, SC, TR, YU.*

This is one of the commonest species of *Muscari* in Mediterranean regions. It is easy to recognise with its dull brownish flowers and the striking tuft of blue-violet sterile flowers at the top of the raceme. Although not a showy plant it is cultivated to some extent, particularly in the form known as 'Plumosum' which produces large broad spikes of feathery purple growths consisting almost entirely of sterile flowers.

7. *Muscari tenuiflorum*   Similar to *M. comosum* but the bulb is normally not pinkish and the flowers are more angular-looking at the mouth and the tepal lobes or *teeth are blackish-brown,* not whitish or yellowish. Grassy places, to 500m. May–July. A, AL, BG, CS, D, GR, H, R, *W*RS, TR, YU.

In addition to *M. comosum* and *M. tenuiflorum* there are four similar and closely allied species which have limited distributions in the Greek Islands and southern Italy. They are –

8. *Muscari cycladicum*   Like *M. comosum* but the fertile flowers have yellowish teeth and are stemless, or on stalks only about 1mm long; *sterile flowers also carried on very short stalks* which are not erect. Limestone cliffs and rocky hillsides, to 500m. April. CR, GR – Cyclades.

9. *Muscari weissii*   Like *M. comosum* but fertile flowers with yellowish teeth; *sterile flowers many, not erect*, and carried on stalks 5–10mm long. Sandy places near the sea or in low scrub, to 300m. March–April. CR, GR.

10. *Muscari spreitzenhoferi*   Like *M. comosum* but fertile flowers with yellowish teeth, carried on stalks more than 5mm long; *sterile flowers very small and few* in number, sometimes absent. Rocky places or in scrub, to 2300m. March–July. CR.

11. *Muscari gussonei*   Like *M. comosum* but fertile flowers with yellowish teeth, carried on *stalks less than 5mm long*; sterile flowers few, stemless. Sandy places near the sea, to 50m. April. I, SC.

12. Yellow Grape Hyacinth *Muscari macrocarpum* [19]   Low to short plant 10–20cm tall; bulb with persistent fleshy roots. Leaves 2–6, linear, grey-green, strongly channelled and often recurved. *Flowers yellow with brownish teeth*, 10–12mm long, rather tubular, carried on very short stalks in a dense raceme, very sweetly scented; sterile flowers absent or very few. Limestone rock crevices and stony scrub, to 500m. April. GR – Amorgos Island.*

This beautiful species is instantly recognisable by its yellow strongly scented flowers and is sometimes seen in cultivation. It is closely related to the Turkish Musk Hyacinth, *M. moschatum*, which is cultivated for its sweet scent and is naturalised in parts of Italy; it has pale purplish flowers, fading to white.

DIPCADI

Dipcadi *Dipcadi serotinum* (=*Uropetalum serotinum*) [20]   Short to medium, hairless, bulbous, perennial to 40cm tall. Leaves 3–5, all basal, linear, grooved, rather shorter than the flower stem. Flowers *brownish, yellowish-brown or greenish-brown*, sometimes flushed with red, drooping bells, 12–15mm long, in a lax one-sided raceme; outer tepals recurved from the middle, the inner ones straight, all fused together in the basal third. May–July. Rocky, stony or sandy places in dry sunny positions, to 2400m. E, SF*, c&SI, P.●

A curious plant confined to south-west Europe and North Africa where it is often local and certainly rather rare in the northern part of its range. It is sometimes seen in cultivation, though its rather sombre colouring makes it a plant primarily for the specialist collection.

STREPTOPUS

Streptopus *Streptopus amplexifolius* [20]   Medium to tall erect perennial to 80cm tall with leafy zig-zagged stems, branched in the upper part. Leaves bluish-green above, oval-heart-shaped, alternate, clasping the stem, hairless. Flowers

Streptopus fruit, × 1½

small, greenish-white, bell-shaped, 8–10mm long, solitary or in pairs on slender stalks *bent in the middle*. Fruit a small red berry. June–August. Damp woods and rocks in hilly and mountainous districts, to 2300m. A, BG, CH, CO, CS, *c&s*D, *n*E, F, I, PL, R, YU.

Solomon's Seals POLYGONATUM

Perennials with a thick whitish rhizomatous rootstock, forming patches; stems erect and arching, unbranched. Leaves alternate or whorled, generally bluish-green beneath, short-stalked or stalkless. Flowers greenish or whitish, long pendent bells, solitary or in small clusters on short stalks at the nodes; tepals fused into a tube in the lower two-thirds. Fruit a small rounded berry.

The Solomon's Seals are amongst the most graceful of European monocots and several are widely grown in our gardens.

1. Whorled Solomon's Seal *Polygonatum verticillatum* [20]   Short to tall plant to 80cm tall; stems angled, usually hairless. Leaves *in whorls* of 3–8, linear to narrowly lance-shaped. Flowers greenish-white, 5–10mm long, in clusters of 2–4, or solitary. Berry reddish-violet. May–July. Woods, meadows and rocky places in mountainous areas, to 2400m. A, B, BG, CH, CS, D, DK, E, F, GB*, H, I, N, NL, P, PL, R, RS, SF, YU.*

An attractive species quite commonly seen in cultivation. The range of this species extends into Asia, including the Himalaya.

Common Solomon's Seal fruit, × 1½

2. Sweet-scented Solomon's Seal *Polygonatum odoratum* (=*P. officinale*) [20] Short to medium plant to 65cm tall; *stems angled*, hairless. Leaves alternate, elliptical to oblong or lance-shaped, hairless. Flowers white tipped green, scented, 12–27mm long, generally solitary or in pairs. Berry bluish-black. May–June. Woods and rocky places, to 2200m. T – except AZ, BAL, CR, FA, IRL, IS, SA, TR.*

One of the most widespread species and widely cultivated. It is the only Solomon's Seal with attractively fragrant flowers.

3. Common Solomon's Seal *Polygonatum multiflorum*   Similar to the previous species but often taller, to 80cm; stems rounded, hairless. Flowers 9–20mm long, not scented and *in clusters of 2–6*. April–June. Woods and scrub. T – except AZ, BAL, CO, CR, FA, IRL, IS, P, *n*RS, SA.*

The rhizomes of this species were once used in herbal remedies. Hybrids between this and previous species are commonly cultivated and are naturalised in parts of western Europe.

4. Broad-leaved Solomon's Seal *Polygonatum jacquinii* (=*P. latifolium*) [20] Short to tall plant to 100cm tall, though often less; stems angled, finely downy in the upper part. Leaves alternate, elliptical to oval or lance-shaped, *finely downy beneath*. Flowers white tipped green, 10–18mm long, solitary or in clusters of 2–5. Berry bluish-black. April–June. Woods, shrubby and rocky places. A, BG, CS, GR, H, I, K, R, RS – except *n*.●

The distribution of this species extends into the Caucasus Mountains. It is rather rare in cultivation but is readily recognised by the downy undersurface to the leaves.

5. Oriental Solomon's Seal *Polygonatum orientale* (=*P. polyanthemum*) is like the previous species but the stems and flower stalks are hairless and the flowers smaller, only 8–12mm long. K, also found in Asia Minor, the Caucasus and Iran.

False Helleborines VERATRUM

Robust tufted perennials with alternate elliptical or lance-shaped, pleated leaves, often rather crowded and overlapping and with sheathing bases. Flowers numerous in dense terminal racemes or panicles, sometimes only male, each with 6 spreading tepals (persisting in fruit) and 6 stamens. Fruit a 3-valved capsule. *Poisonous.*

1. Black False Helleborine *Veratrum nigrum* [20]   Medium to tall plant to 1m, sometimes slightly more. Leaves broadly elliptical, the upper small and linear-lance-shaped, all hairless. Bracts coloured. Flowers *reddish-brown to blackish*, 9–15mm, in branched clusters or a simple raceme. Fruit capsule hairless. June–August. Mountain meadows, woodland fringes and scrub, to 1600m. Central and south-east Europe – A, AL, BG, CH, *e*F, *n*GR, H, I, R, *c*&*w*RS, YU.*

2. White False Helleborine *Veratrum album* [20]   Tall plant to 1.75m. Leaves broadly elliptical, the upper smaller and lance-shaped, all finely downy beneath. Bracts green. Flowers *white to greenish or greenish-yellow*, whitish outside, 15–25mm. Fruit capsule slightly downy. June–August. Damp grassy places, particularly meadows and pastures in the mountains, 700–2700m. Much of central and southern Europe and part of the north – A, AL, BG, CH, CS, D, E, F, GR, H, I, N, PL, R, RS, YU.*

A very poisonous species used in the past as an arrow poison. It frequently occurs in mountain meadows with the Great Yellow Gentian, *Gentiana lutea*, and the two are rather similar with their large elliptical leaves. However, the gentian can be readily distinguished by its opposite bluish-green leaves when not seen in flower.

Veratrum lobelianum from Switzerland is sometimes said to be a distinct species with the flowers greenish on both surfaces. Its status is doubtful and intermediates are frequently seen. *Veratrum misae* from arctic Russia is similar to *V. album* but a smaller plant, not more than 40cm tall, with hairless leaves and yellowish-green flowers.

Sea Squills URGINEA

Bulbous perennials with basal linear or linear-oblong leaves which appear after the flowers. Flowers in few- to many-flowered spike-like racemes, white, greenish or pinkish, each with a bract and often a bracteole at the base; tepals separate, spreading, each with a dark mid vein. Fruit capsule 3-sided, containing flattened winged seeds.

1. Sea Squill *Urginea maritima* [20]   Medium to tall plant to 1.5m, though often less. Leaves long, narrow lance-shaped, rather fleshy, flat and shiny-green, appearing after the flowers but lasting into the following summer. Flowers *whitish*, each tepal with a green or purplish mid vein, 10–16mm, *in dense spikes*. August–October. Dry rocky hills, stony and sandy places. Mediterranean Europe – AL, CO, CR, E, SF, GR, I, C&SP, SA, W&CYU.

A rather poisonous plant used medicinally since classical times. The bulbs are large, often 8–15cm in diameter, and frequently exposed at the soil surface. This species is also found in N. Africa and the Middle East.

2. Red Sea Squill *Urginea fugax*   Short plant to 35cm tall. Leaves linear, appearing after the flowers. *Bracts tiny*, 1mm long. Flowers pale pink, each tepal with a red mid vein, 18–20mm, 5–10 in a lax 'spike'; style as long as the stamens. Dry hillslopes. CO, I, SA. Also distributed in North Africa, Cyprus, Asia Minor and Syria.

3. Undulate Sea Squill *Urginea undulata*   Short to medium plant to 50cm tall. Leaves linear-oblong with wavy margins, appearing after the flowers. Bracts larger than the previous species, 4−5mm long. Flowers dull pink or grey or greenish-purple, each tepal with a red mid vein, 8−30 in a rather lax 'spike'; style longer than the stamens. Rocky ground. *s*CO, SA. Also found in North Africa.

PARIS

Herb Paris *Paris quadrifolia* [20]   Short to medium hairless perennial with a creeping rootstock, stem up to 40cm tall, often less. Leaves green, usually 4 but sometimes up to 8, all in *a single whorl* towards the top of the stem, oval, broadest above the middle, pointed, short-stalked. Flowers green or greenish-yellow, solitary, star-like, 40−60mm, sepals and petals 4−6, the sepals lance-shaped, the petals thin and thread-like. Fruit a black 'berry', eventually splitting. May−July. Damp woods, often on calcareous soils, to 2000m. T − except AL, AZ, BAL, CR, FA, GR, IRL, K, P, *s*RS, SC, TR.●

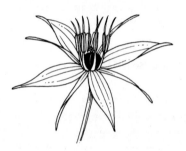

Herb Paris flower, × 1

A fascinating plant once placed in a separate family, the Trilliaceae, and with relatives in places as far apart as the Himalayas, Japan and North America. Herb Paris is a poisonous plant much used in herbal remedies in the past.

ZIGADENUS

A small genus of plants found mainly in North and Central America. Most of the species have rather dingy greenish-white flowers of no great beauty.

Zigadenus sibiricus [20]   Medium to tall slender, hairless, bulbous perennial to 80cm tall. Leaves mostly basal, linear, pointed. Bracts dark violet, elliptical. Flowers greenish, whitish within, 5−8mm long, narrow bell-shaped, few in a rather lax raceme; tepals united into a tube in the lower half; anthers reddish-violet. Sparse woodland, scrub or rocky places. June−August. *c*&*e*RS.

This rather unusual plant is known only from the Ural Mountains in the area covered by this book, however, the distribution of the species extends into parts of temperate Asia.

TOFIELDIA

A small genus of about 20 non-bulbous tufted evergreen plants, spread right round the temperate Northern Hemisphere and in South America. They are mostly not very showy with dense spikes or heads of very small white or greenish flowers.

Low perennial rhizomatous plants with flat fans of leaves and sometimes a few smaller leaves on the flowering stems. Flowers small, usually white stemless in dense racemes or spikes, sometimes so short as to appear head-like; tepals six, stamens six with hairless filaments. Fruit consisting of three free carpels with many seeds.

In Europe there are only two species.

1. Scottish Asphodel *Tofieldia pusilla* (=*T. borealis*)   Low to short plant, usually 4–15cm tall. Leaves about 3–5cm long, *all basal*, linear with 3–4 veins; stem leaves absent. *Flowers white or greenish-white*, about 2mm long in *dense heads or spikes*, generally 0.5–1.5cm long. Wet places in the mountains, to 2200m, but often near sea level in the north of its range. June–August. A, CH, CS, D, F, FA, GB, I, IS, N, PL, *n&c*RS, S, SF, YU.●

An easily recognised little plant, with its flat fans of tough evergreen leaves, occurring in bogs and wet peaty rocky places. The distribution of *T. pusilla* extends into Arctic Asia and the United States.

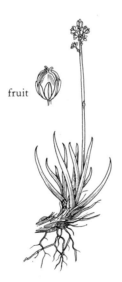

fruit

Scottish Asphodel, × ½

1a. *T.p.* subsp. *austriaca*   Like *T. pusilla* but usually with slightly longer leaves each with 5–7 veins. Mountains, to 2200m. Mainly A, YU.

2. *Tofieldia calyculata* (= *T. palustris*)   Similar to *T. pusilla* but usually more robust, to 30cm tall. *Leaves basal, and with 1–3 on the stem. Flowers yellowish* or occasionally reddish, produced in *racemes 2–6cm long.* Wet pastures, margins of damp woods and alpine turf, to 2300m. June–August. A, CS, D, E, F, I, PL, R, *nw,c&sw*RS, S, YU.●

Bog Asphodels NARTHECIUM

Small hairless perennials with a creeping rhizomatous rootstock and flattened sword-shaped leaves like a small flag iris. Flowers in terminal racemes, starry, each with 6 persisting tepals; stamens 6 with hairy stalks (filaments). Fruit an oblong capsule.

1. Bog Asphodel *Narthecium ossifragum* [21]   Low to medium plant up to 45cm tall, though generally less. Leaves pale green, often tinged orange, those on the flowering stems different and *much smaller* than the basal fan-shaped

Bog Asphodel flower, × 1½

clusters. Flowers bright yellow, greenish outside, 12–18mm, in racemes of 6–20; anthers orange with yellow-hairy stalks. Capsule orange, 12mm. July–August. Wet places, particularly heaths and acid bogs. B, *nw*D, DK, *c&n*E, F, FA, GB, H, IRL, N, *n*P, *w*RS, *s*S, SF.

    A common plant of bogs and heathy places throughout much of Britain but absent from central England and most of East Anglia.

2. Corsican Bog Asphodel *Narthecium reverchonii*   Short to medium plant to 40cm tall. Leaves all similar except that the upper are rather smaller than the lower. Flowers yellow, 12–16mm, in racemes of 10–24. Capsule 10–13mm. Moist places by mountain streams. CO*.

3. Scardic Bog Asphodel *Narthecium scardicum*   Low to short plant to 27cm tall. Leaves all similar, though the upper smaller than the lower. Flowers *yellow*, small, 8–10mm, in racemes of 5–13. Capsule 8–10mm. Damp places by mountain streams and lakes, 1600–2300m. *ne*AL, *sw*YU.

APHYLLANTHES

Aphyllanthes monspeliensis [21]   Short to medium perennial to 40cm tall, though often less, forming tough rush-like tufts. Stems bluish-green, linear, rounded in section. Leaves reduced to reddish-brown membranous sheaths at the base of each stem. Flowers blue, rarely white, 25–30mm, in a head of 2–3 surrounded at the base by small overlapping papery bracts. Fruit a small capsule containing 3 seeds. April–July. Dry grassy and rocky places, to 1500m. E, *s*F, *n*I, *n*P.*

A beautiful plant with tough rush-like stems often occurring in large colonies, though local. The flowers open in the sun, each tepal with a prominent dark mid vein. Several good forms are in cultivation, some with intensely blue flowers.

MAIANTHEMUM

May Lily *Maianthemum bifolium* [21]   Low to short, patch forming, hairless perennial, with a thin creeping rhizomatous rootstock; stems erect to 15cm tall. Basal leaves green and shiny, heart-shaped, long-stalked, often withered at flowering time; *stem leaves 2, alternate*, heart-shaped, short-stalked. Flower white, very small, 4–6mm, in a compact oblong or rounded head, each with 4 tepals and 4 stamens. Fruit a small pale mauve or red-spotted berry, 5mm. May–July.

May Lily fruit, × 4

Woods and shady places, often on slightly acid soils, to 2100m. A, B, CH, CS, D, DK, *n*E, *c*GB*, H, *n*I, K, *c*&*s*N, *n*NL, PL, R, RS, S, SF, YU.*

In Britain this attractive little plant is mainly confined to a few localities in the east and north of England.

CONVALLARIA

Lily of the Valley *Convallaria majalis* [21]   Short, hairless, patch-forming perennial with a creeping rhizomatous rootstock, to 37cm tall, though often less. Leaves often 2, sometimes up to 4, broad elliptical, sheathing around each other at the base, deep shiny-green above. Flowers white, sometimes pink, very fragrant, drooping rounded bells, 5–9mm long, in slender one-side racemes; tepals united to about the middle. Fruit a small red berry. April–June. Woods, scrub and mountain meadows, to 2300m, often on rather calcareous soils. T — except AZ, ?CO, CR, FA, IRL, IS, P, SA, SC, TR.*

A well known and much loved plant frequently seen in gardens and grown for its pleasant ground covering habit as well as for the delightful fragrance of its flowers. In the past it has been used medicinally for heart disease as well as the source of a green dye prepared from the leaves. Pink-flowered forms occur mainly in central and eastern Europe. In Britain the species is confined mainly to England and eastern Wales and a few scattered localities in Scotland.

ASPARAGUS

Hairless rhizomatous perennials with woody or herbaceous stems, often with a rather ferny appearance. The leaves, or green structures that function as leaves, are in fact slender reduced stems, or cladodes and generally occur in clusters, each rarely more than 2mm broad; the true leaves are reduced to small papery bract-like structures at the base of cladodes and sometimes have a spiny base. Flowers small, whitish or greenish, bell-shaped, each with 6 tepals fused together at the base; flower stalk jointed near the middle usually. Fruit a small berry. All the species except *A. albus* have the male and female flowers on separate plants.

A complicated genus with some 14 species in the region covered by this book. They are difficult to identify often and some are very limited in distribution; these are dealt with at the end of the account. All leaves referred to in the descriptions are in fact the false leaves or cladodes mentioned above.

1. White Asparagus *Asparagus albus* Tall plant to 90cm; stems woody, flexuous, white, spiny but otherwise smooth. Leaves 5–25mm long, in clusters of 10–20, sharply pointed, soon deciduous leaving bare spiny stems. Flowers white, sweetly scented, 2–3mm long, *bisexual*, in groups of 6–15, rarely fewer. Berry black, 4–7mm. April–June. Hedges and scrub. BAL, CO, ꞩF, I, ꞩ&ᴄP, SA, SC.

2. *Asparagus acutifolius* [21] Tall plant often reaching 2m; stems woody, much branched, spiny, grey or whitish. Leaves in clusters of 10–30, each 2–8mm long, *sharply pointed*. Flowers yellowish-green, sweetly scented, 3–4mm long, in groups of 2–4 mixed with the leaves. Berry black, 4.5–7.5mm. April–June. Dry rocky places and hedges. AL, BAL, BG, CO, CR, E, ꞩF, GR, I, P, SA, SC, TR, YU.*

One of the commonest species in southern Europe, but also found in Asia Minor and generally recognised by its short spiny leaves. The young shoots are often eaten as a vegetable though the plant is not cultivated as such.

3. *Asparagus aphyllus* [21] Medium to tall plant to 1m; stems woody, much branched, spiny, green. Leaves 10–20mm long, *in clusters of 3–7*, sharply pointed. Flowers greenish, 3–4mm long, in groups of 3–6 mixed with the leaves. Berry black, 7–8mm. April–June. Rocky places and scrub. CO, CR, *nw*E, GR, I, P, SA, SC, TR.

4. *Asparagus stipularis* Medium plant up to 60cm tall; stems woody with numerous smooth or rather rough ridges. Leaves 15–30mm long, *solitary or in clusters of 2–3*, spreading, sharply pointed. Flowers greenish, 3–4mm long, in groups of 2–8 mixed with the leaves. Berry black, 5–8mm. Rocky places and scrub. BAL, CR, E, GR, I, *c*&*s*P, SA, SC.

5. *Asparagus verticillatus* [21] Tall stout plant to 2.5m; stems spreading or deflexed, strongly ridged. Leaves long, 20–50mm, in clusters of 10–20, *triangular in cross-section*, hairy-edged. Flowers greenish, 2–3.5mm, in groups of 2–10, mixed with the leaves. Berry black, 5.5–8mm. Rocky places and scrub, mainly in south-eastern Europe. BG, GR, K, R, *w*&*e*RS, TR, YU.

6. Maritime Asparagus *Asparagus maritimus* Medium to tall erect plant to 1m; stems herbaceous, ridged. Leaves 10–30mm long somewhat flattened, in clusters of 4–7, erect or spreading. Flowers greenish-white, 4–6mm, *generally in pairs and not mixed with the leaves*. Berry red, 6–12mm. Sandy soils, coastal regions. AL, BG, CO, *s*F, GR, I, K, *w*RS, SA, YU. Also found in North Africa.

Maritime Asparagus, × ¾

7. Wild or Common Asparagus *Asparagus officinalis* Very variable medium to tall plant to 2m, though often less; stems herbaceous, erect, smooth, green, much branched in the upper part. Leaves 10–25mm long, in clusters of 4–15, flattened or thread-like, not spreading much. Flowers yellowish or greenish-white, 4.5–6.5mm long, usually in pairs, sometimes solitary, not usually mixed with the leaves; flower stalks jointed near the middle. Berry red, 6–10mm. June–August. Hedges, grassy and waste places. T – except AZ, BAL, CO, CR, CS, FA, IS, (N), *n*RS, (S), SA, SF.*

A widely cultivated plant, the young shoots being gathered early in the season. It is considered as one of Europe's most delicious vegetables. Later in the season the ferny foliage is often cut for floral arrangements. In Britain it is confined mainly to southern Wales and parts of the south-west, though it is naturalised in many places.

7a. *A.o.* subsp. *prostratus* is a lower plant, only to 30cm, with decumbent stems. Leaves 5–10mm long. Flowers often mixed with the leaves. Coastal rocks and sands along the Atlantic seaboard.

8. *Asparagus tenuifolius*   Tall plant to 1m; stems herbaceous, erect, smooth. Leaves 10–25mm, in clusters of 15–40 or more, thread-like, *spreading*. Flowers greenish-white, 6–8mm, solitary or in pairs mixed with the leaves; flowerstalks jointed near the top. Berry red, 10–16mm. A, BG, CH, s&neF, H, I, K, R, wRS, TR, YU.

   The remaining species have a very limited distribution at least in the area covered by this book.

9. *Asparagus bresleranus*   Short to medium plant, to 50cm tall; stems herbaceous, flexuous. Leaves 10–20mm, *very unequal*, usually in clusters of 3, sharply pointed. Flowers 3.5–5mm, solitary or in pairs. Berry black, 6–7mm. seRS – also occurs in south-west and central Asia.

10. *Asparagus kasakstanicus*   Similar to the previous but to 70cm tall and stems ridged. Leaves 20–40mm long, in clusters of 3–6. Flowers 5–6mm long, in groups of 2–4. *Berry red*, 6–8mm. Calcareous soils. K, seRS.

11. *Asparagus persicus*   Similar to (9) but much taller, to 2m often; stems smooth. Leaves 10–40mm, in clusters of 2–6 or solitary, flattened or rounded. Flowers 3–5mm long, in pairs or solitary. Berry red, 5–7mm. Saline or calcareous soils. seRS – also found in west and central Asia.

12. *Asparagus brachyphyllus*   Medium to tall plant to 80cm; stems herbaceous, flexuous, ridged, with spreading branches. Leaves small, 4.5–10mm long, in clusters of 3–5, *sword-shaped*. Flowers 4–6mm, usually in pairs and not mixed with the leaves. Berry red, 4.5mm. Calcareous and saline soils, in south-east Europe mainly. BG, K, R, w&eRS, ?TR.

13. *Asparagus littoralis*   Medium plant to 60cm tall; stems herbaceous, straight, smooth. Leaves 15–30mm long, in clusters of 4–8, flattened. Flowers 5–6.5mm long, in groups of 2–4 or solitary, usually mixed with the leaves. Berry red, 5–7mm. Coastal rocks. K.

14. *Asparagus pseudoscaber*   Tall erect plant to 2m; stems herbaceous, ridged. Leaves 5–15mm long, in clusters of 10–20. Flowers 4–6mm long, solitary or in pairs, usually mixed with the leaves. Berry red, 7–11mm. R, wRS, YU.

PLATE 1

Luronium natans p.25

*lia
culoides* p.25

*Alisma plantago-
aquatica* p.26

*Sagittaria
sagittifolia* p.27

gramineum p.26

*Damasonium
alisma* p.27

PLATE 2

Caldesia
parnassifolia p.28

Borderea pyrenaica p.31

Stratiotes
aloides p.29

Butomus umbellatus p.28

Hydrocharis
morsus-ranae p.29

Tamus communis
p.30

PLATE 3

Lilium bulbiferum p.37

L.m. var. *cattaniae* p.36

martagon p.36

L. candidum p.37

L. pyrenaicum p.38

PLATE 4

Lilium chalcedonicum p.38

L. rhodopae

L. pomponium p.39

L. carniolicum p.38

Erythronium dens-canis p.40

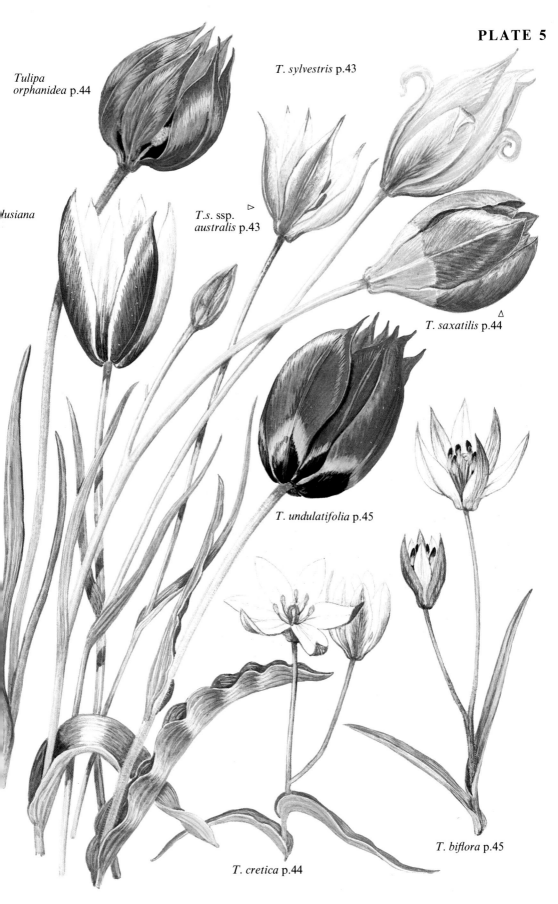

PLATE 5

Tulipa orphanidea p.44

T. sylvestris p.43

lusiana

T.s. ssp. *australis* p.43

T. saxatilis p.44

T. undulatifolia p.45

T. cretica p.44

T. biflora p.45

PLATE 6

Tulipa gesnerana p.46

T. hungarica p.4?

T. urumoffii p.47

T. praecox p.47

T. shrenkii p.47

T. agenens p.48

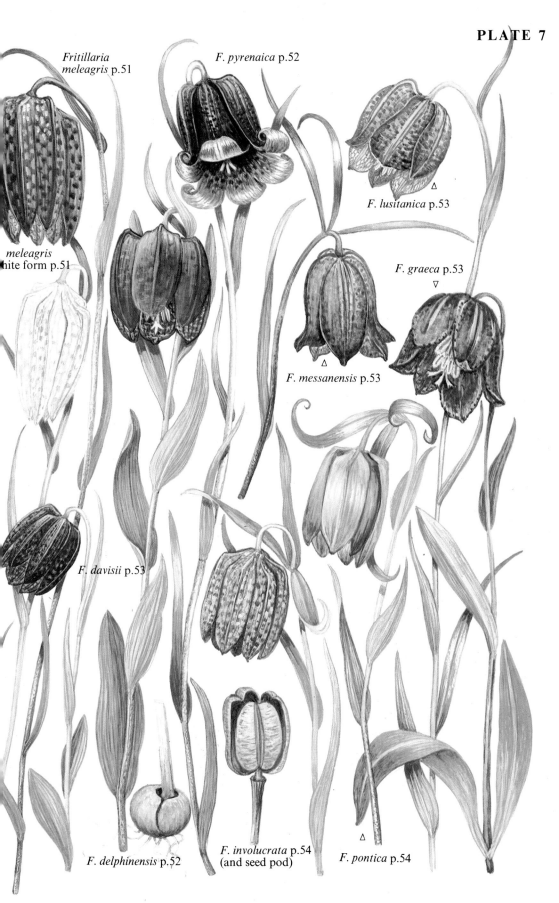

PLATE 7

Fritillaria meleagris p.51

F. pyrenaica p.52

F. lusitanica p.53

△

meleagris white form p.51

F. graeca p.53

▽

F. messanensis p.53

△

F. davisii p.53

F. delphinensis p.52

F. involucrata p.54 (and seed pod)

F. pontica p.54

△

PLATE 8

Fritillaria ruthenica p.55

F. gussichae p.54

F. tuntasia p.55

F. drenovskyi p.54

F. ehrhartii p.55

F. conica p.55

F. stribryni p.56

F. rhodokanakis p.56

PLATE 9

C. alpinum p.60

C. lusitanum p.61

lchicum autumnale p.60

C. variegatum p.61

C. macrophyllum p.61

C. bivonae (& corm) p.61

PLATE 10

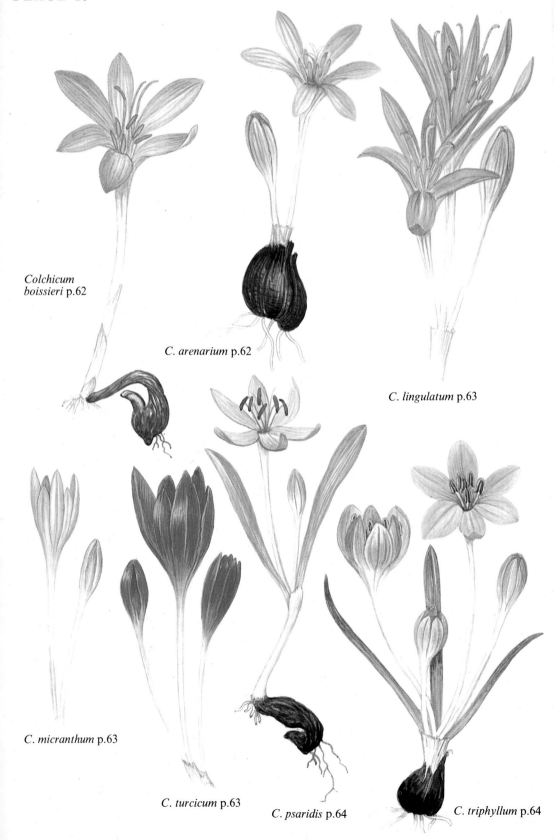

Colchicum boissieri p.62

C. arenarium p.62

C. lingulatum p.63

C. micranthum p.63

C. turcicum p.63

C. psaridis p.64

C. triphyllum p.64

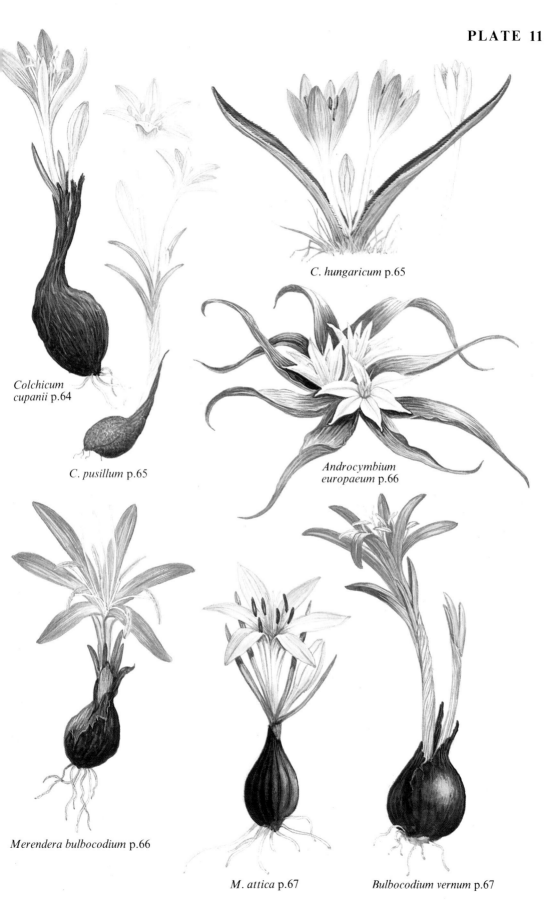

PLATE 11

Colchicum cupanii p.64

C. pusillum p.65

C. hungaricum p.65

Androcymbium europaeum p.66

Merendera bulbocodium p.66

M. attica p.67

Bulbocodium vernum p.67

PLATE 12

Anthericum liliago p.69

Simethis planifolia p.69 ▷

Paradisea liliastrum p.68

Eremurus spectabilis ▷ p.72

△

Asphodelus fistulosus p.72

Asphodelus albus p.71

Nectaroscordum siculum p.73

Asphodeline lutea p.70

PLATE 13

A. angulosum p.76

A. atropurpureum p.76

um
peloprasum p.75

A.
callimischon
p.77

. carinatum p.77

A. atroviolaceum
p.76

A. moly
p.81

A. guttatum p.80

A.
moschatum
p.81

cupanii
8

A. ericetorum p.79

A. flavum p.79

A. narcissiflorum
p.82

A. neapolitanum
p.82

PLATE 14

Allium paniculatum p.84 ▷

A. roseum p.85 ▽

A. nigrum p.83

A. ▷ *schoeno-prasum* p.86

A. scorodoprasum p.86 △

A. senescens p.87

A. vineale p.91

A. sphaero-cephalon p.88

A. ursinum p.90

A. rotundum p.85

A. subhirsutum p.89 △

A. oleraceum p.83

A. triquetrum p.90 △

A. victorialis p.90 △

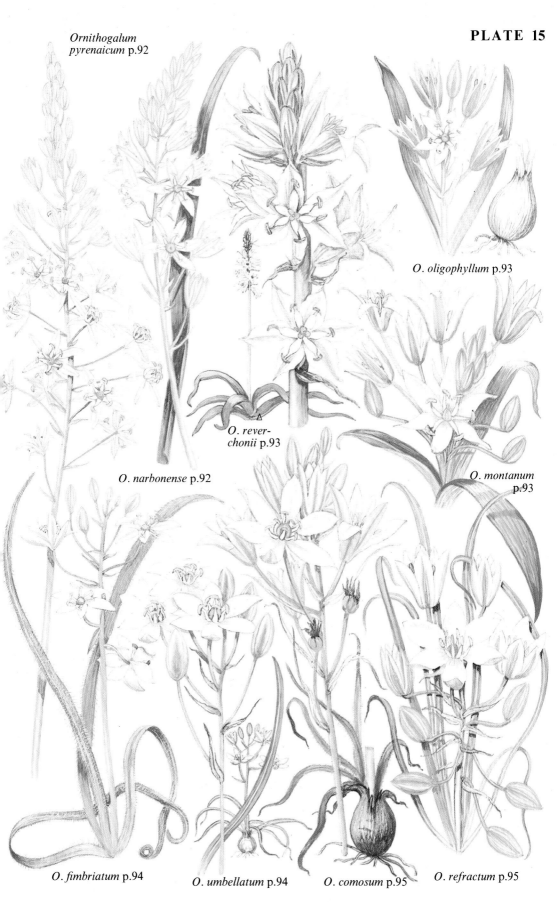

PLATE 15

Ornithogalum pyrenaicum p.92

O. oligophyllum p.93

O. rever-chonii p.93

O. narbonense p.92

O. montanum p.93

O. fimbriatum p.94

O. umbellatum p.94

O. comosum p.95

O. refractum p.95

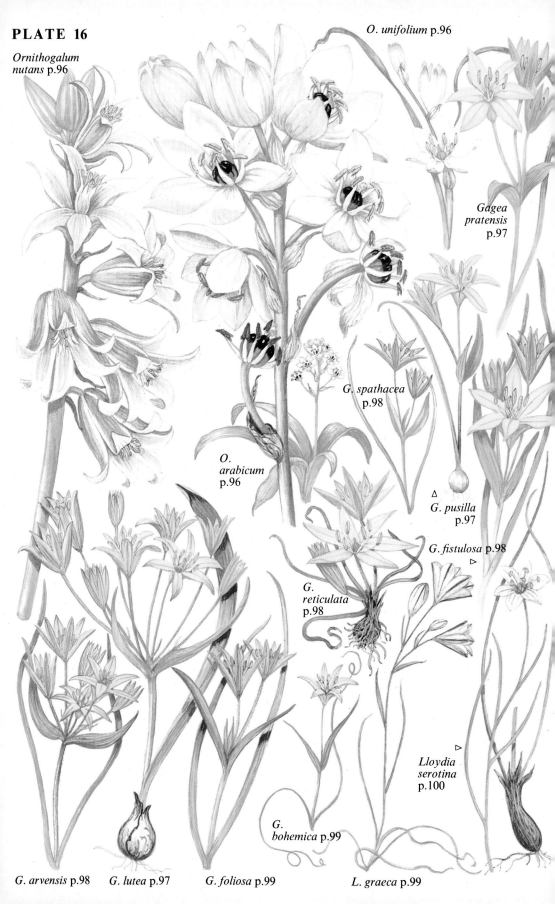

PLATE 16

Ornithogalum nutans p.96

O. unifolium p.96

Gagea pratensis p.97

O. arabicum p.96

G. spathacea p.98

△ *G. pusilla* p.97

G. fistulosa p.98 ▷

G. reticulata p.98

▷ *Lloydia serotina* p.100

G. bohemica p.99

G. arvensis p.98   *G. lutea* p.97   *G. foliosa* p.99   *L. graeca* p.99

PLATE 17

Scilla sibirica p.103

S. bifolia p.103

...iondoxa ...tica p.101

S. ramburei p.104

S. verna p.103

S. pratensis p.105

S. bithynica p.105

S. monophyllos p.104

S. autumnalis p.105

PLATE 18

Scilla hyacinthoides p.106

S. peruviana p.106

S. lilio-hyacinthus p.106

Δ *Hyacinthella leucophaea* p.109

Hyacinthoides non-scripta p.107

Hyacinthoides hispanica p.107

Hyacinthoides italica p.108

Hyacinthella dalmatica p.*

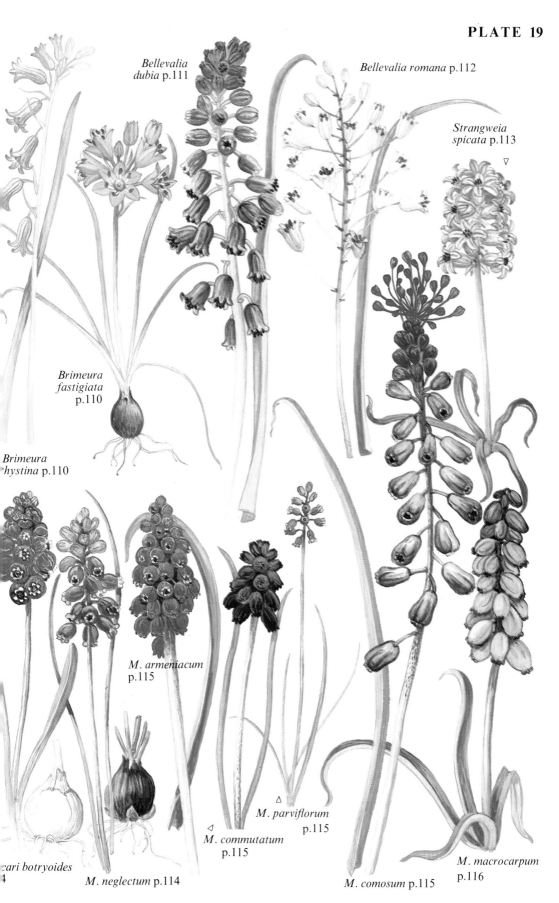

PLATE 19

*Bellevalia
dubia* p.111

Bellevalia romana p.112

*Strangweia
spicata* p.113

*Brimeura
fastigiata*
p.110

*Brimeura
hystina* p.110

M. armeniacum
p.115

M. parviflorum
p.115

M. commutatum
p.115

cari botryoides

M. neglectum p.114

M. comosum p.115

M. macrocarpum
p.116

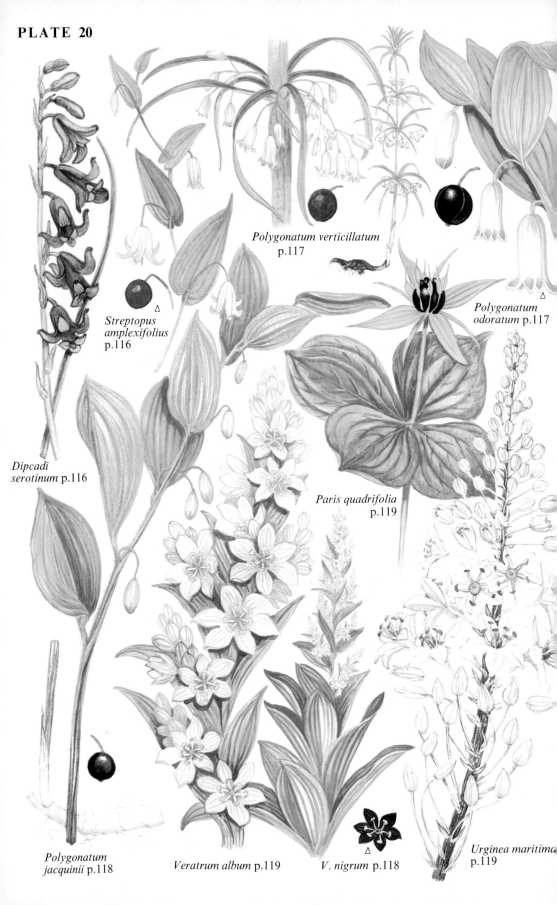

PLATE 20

Polygonatum verticillatum
p.117

*Streptopus
amplexifolius*
p.116

*Polygonatum
odoratum* p.117

Paris quadrifolia
p.119

*Dipcadi
serotinum* p.116

*Polygonatum
jacquinii* p.118

Veratrum album p.119

V. nigrum p.118

Urginea maritima
p.119

PLATE 21

Asparagus acutifolius p.124

Maianthemum bifolium p.123

Convallaria majalis p.123

Aphyllanthes p.123
monspeliensis

rthecium
fragum p.122

paragus
yllus
24

Smilax △
aspera p.128

paragus
rticillatus p.125

Ruscus aculeatus p.127

R. hypoglossum p.127

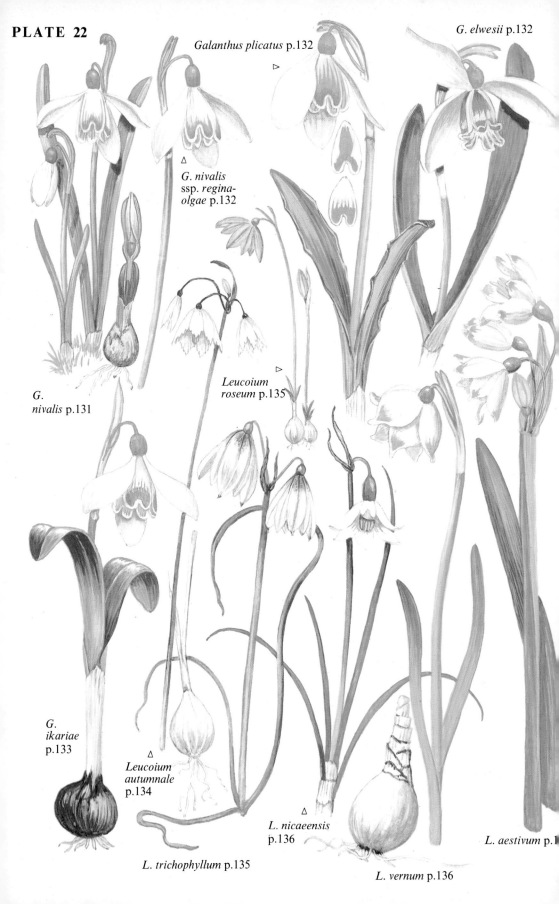

PLATE 22

Galanthus plicatus p.132

G. elwesii p.132

G. nivalis ssp. *regina-olgae* p.132

G. *nivalis* p.131

Leucoium roseum p.135

G. *ikariae* p.133

Leucoium autumnale p.134

L. trichophyllum p.135

L. nicaeensis p.136

L. vernum p.136

L. aestivum p.1

PLATE 23

Lapiedra martinezii p.138

Pancratium maritimum p.139

P. illyricum p.139

Sternbergia lutea p.138

S. colchiciflora p.137

PLATE 24

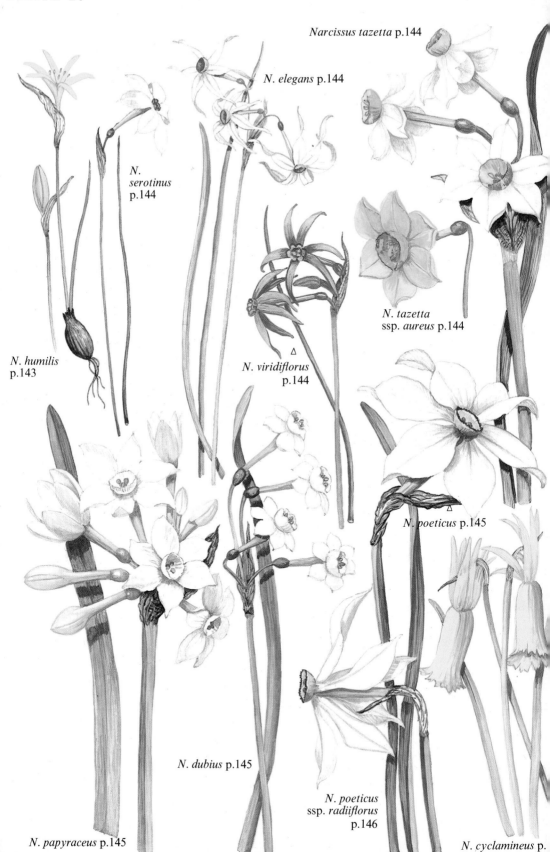

Narcissus tazetta p.144

N. elegans p.144

N.
serotinus
p.144

N. tazetta
ssp. *aureus* p.144

N. humilis
p.143

N. viridiflorus
p.144

N. poeticus p.145

N. dubius p.145

N. poeticus
ssp. *radiiflorus*
p.146

N. papyraceus p.145

N. cyclamineus p.

rcissus
quilla p.146

N. requienii p.147

N. pusillus p.147

N. rupicola p.147

PLATE 25

N. triandrus p.148

△
N. triandrus ssp. *concolor* p.148

ulbocodium p.148

△
N. hedraeanthus p.149

N. calcicola p.147

N. cantabricus p.149

N. bulbocodium ssp. *obesus* p.149

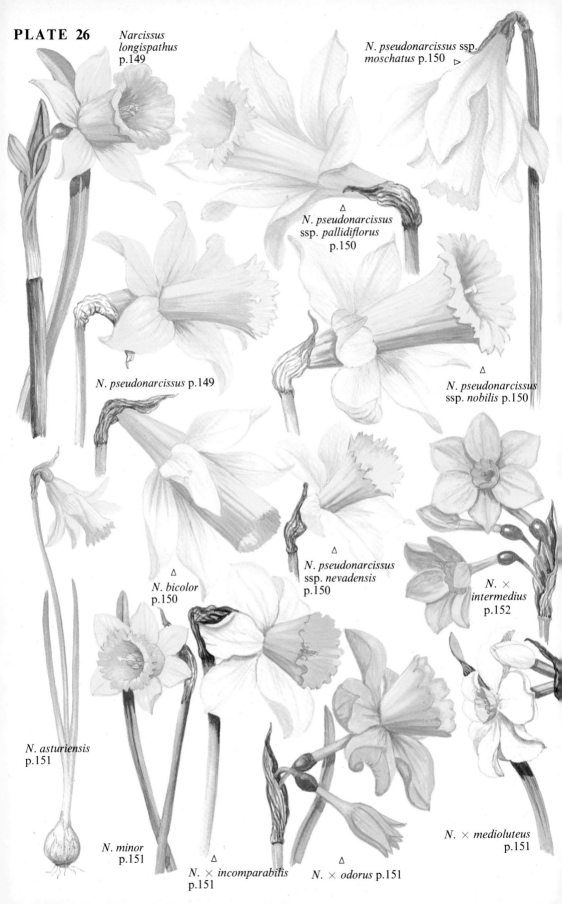

PLATE 26

Narcissus longispathus p.149

N. pseudonarcissus ssp. *moschatus* p.150 ▷

N. pseudonarcissus ssp. *pallidiflorus* p.150
△

N. pseudonarcissus p.149

N. pseudonarcissus ssp. *nobilis* p.150
△

N. bicolor p.150
△

N. pseudonarcissus ssp. *nevadensis* p.150
△

N. × *intermedius* p.152

N. asturiensis p.151

N. minor p.151

N. × *incomparabilis* p.151
△

N. × *odorus* p.151
△

N. × *medioluteus* p.151

PLATE 27

Iris germanica p.156

I. albicans p.157

△ *I. pallida* p.157

I. variegata p.157

I. aphylla p.158

I. lutescens p.158

▷ *I. pumila* p.158

I. reichenbachii p.159

PLATE 28

Iris sibirica p.159

I. humilis
p.159

I. unguicularis p.160

I. spuria p.161

I. pseudacorus p.161

I. graminea p.162

I. sintenisii p.162

I. foetidissi
p.

PLATE 29

*ris
atifolia* p.163

I. filifolia p.163

I. boissieri p.164

I. serotina
p.164

I. xiphium
p.163

I. planifolia p.165

PLATE 30

Gladiolus byzantinus
p.168

Gynandriris
sisyrinchium p.165

Romulea
columnae p.171

Hermodactylus
tuberosus p.166

R.
ramiflora
p.171

Sisyrinchium
bermudianum p.167

R. bulbocodium
p.170

Gladiolus italicus
p.168

Gladiolus illyricus p.168

Gladiolus imbricatus p

R. requienii p.172

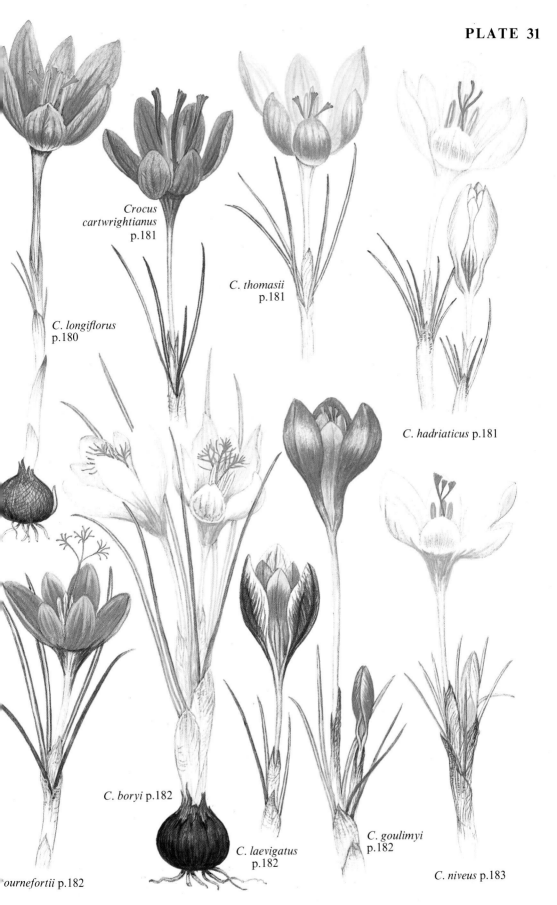

PLATE 31

Crocus
cartwrightianus
p.181

C. thomasii
p.181

C. longiflorus
p.180

C. hadriaticus p.181

C. boryi p.182

C. laevigatus
p.182

C. goulimyi
p.182

ournefortii p.182

C. niveus p.183

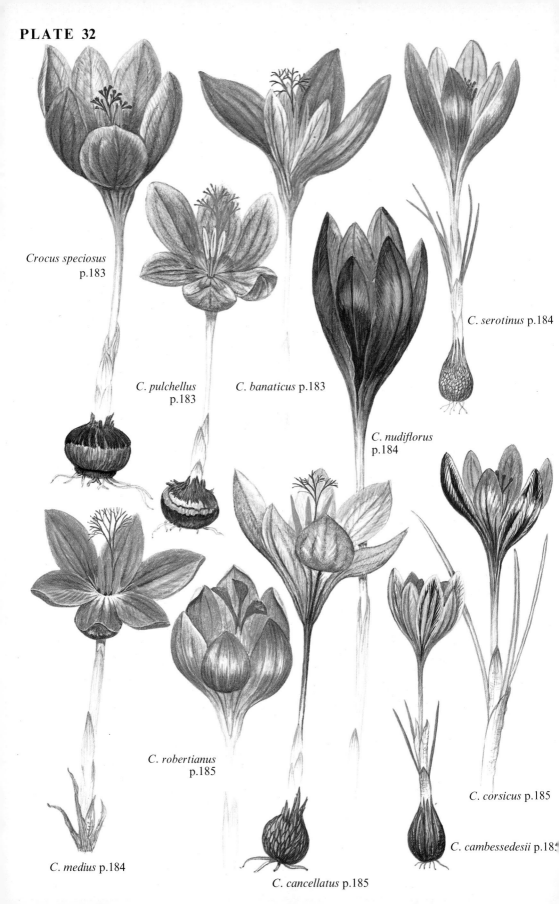

PLATE 32

Crocus speciosus
p.183

C. pulchellus
p.183

C. banaticus p.183

C. serotinus p.184

C. nudiflorus
p.184

C. robertianus
p.185

C. corsicus p.185

C. cambessedesii p.18?

C. medius p.184

C. cancellatus p.185

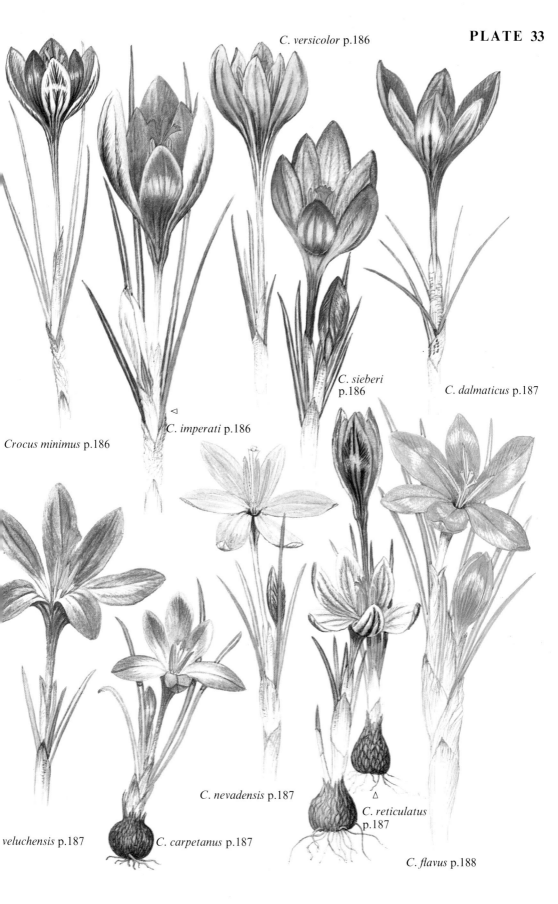

PLATE 33

C. versicolor p.186

C. sieberi p.186

C. dalmaticus p.187

C. imperati p.186

Crocus minimus p.186

veluchensis p.187

C. carpetanus p.187

C. nevadensis p.187

C. reticulatus p.187

C. flavus p.188

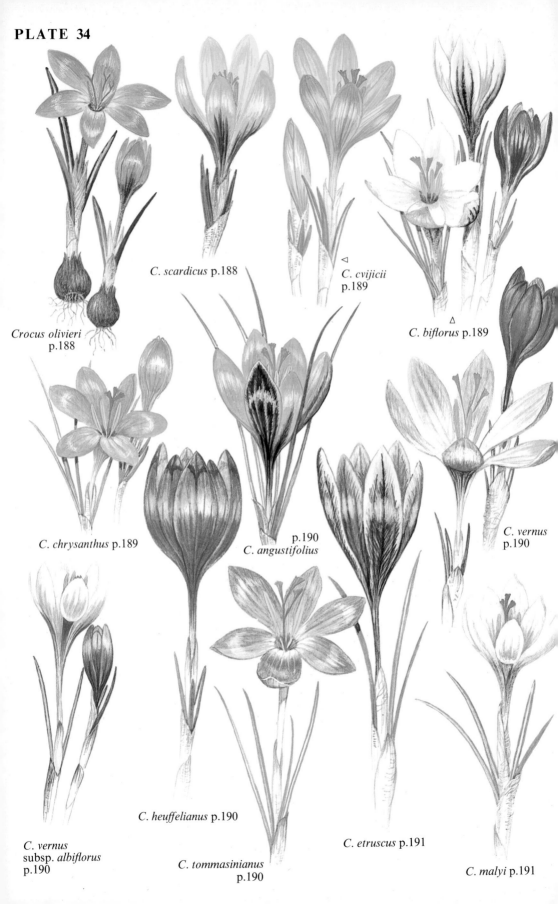

PLATE 34

Crocus olivieri
p.188

C. scardicus p.188

C. cvijicii
p.189

C. biflorus p.189

C. chrysanthus p.189

p.190
C. angustifolius

C. vernus
p.190

C. vernus
subsp. *albiflorus*
p.190

C. heuffelianus p.190

C. tommasinianus
p.190

C. etruscus p.191

C. malyi p.191

PLATE 35

...sarum vulgare
...92

Arisarum proboscideum p.193

Biarum tenuifolium p.193

Arum maculatum p.196

...um ...grum p.196

Arum italicum p.195

Arum creticum p.196

Arum pictum p.196

PLATE 40

Serapias parviflora
p.221

*S.
neglecta*
p.220

H. hircinum
ssp. *calcaratum*
p.222

△

*Barlia
longibracteata*
p.223

△

S. vomeracea
p.220

S. lingua
(& colour forms) p.221

S. cordigera p.222

△

*Anacamptis
pyramidalis* p.224

◁

Himantoglossum hircinum p.222

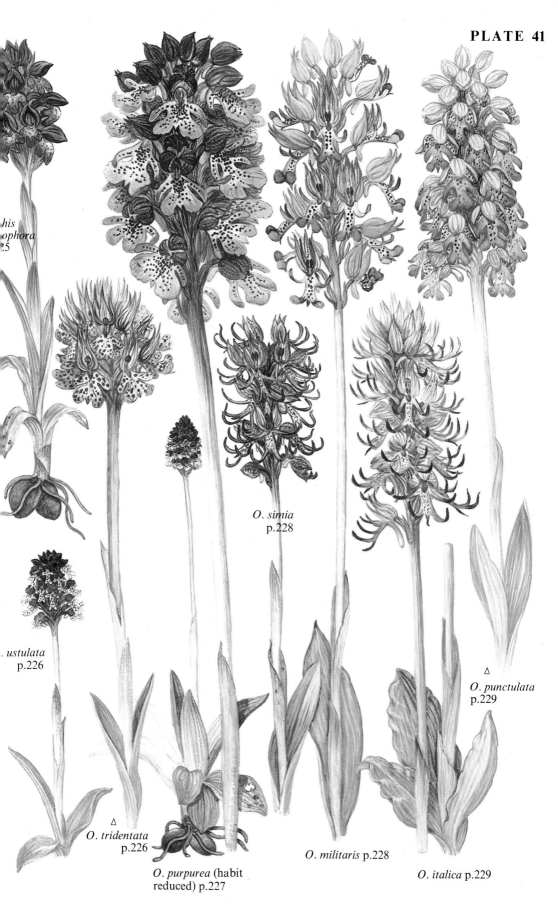

PLATE 41

*his
ophora
.5*

ustulata
p.226

O. simia
p.228

Δ
O. punctulata
p.229

Δ
O. tridentata
p.226

O. purpurea (habit
reduced) p.227

O. militaris p.228

O. italica p.229

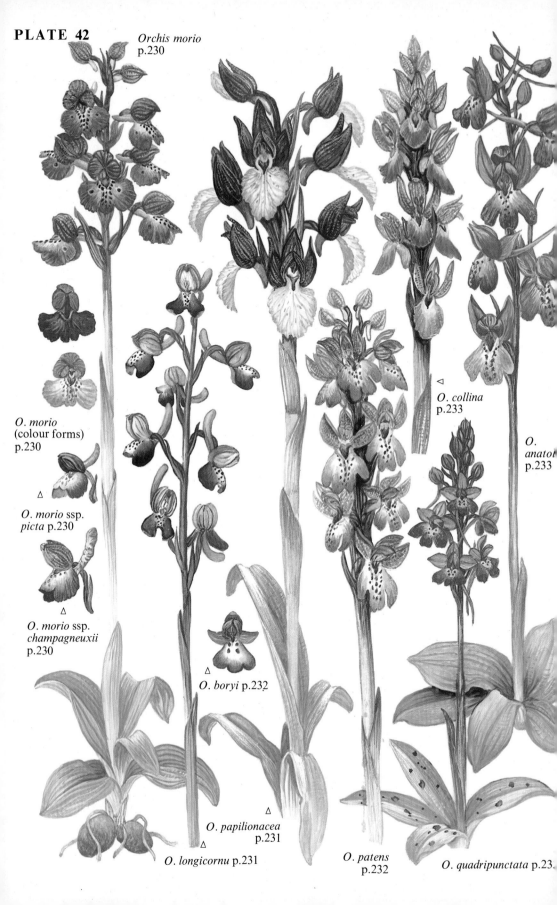

PLATE 42

Orchis morio p.230

O. morio (colour forms) p.230

△

O. morio ssp. *picta* p.230

△

O. morio ssp. *champagneuxii* p.230

△

O. boryi p.232

O. collina p.233

◁

O. anatol p.233

△

△

O. papilionacea p.231

O. longicornu p.231

O. patens p.232

O. quadripunctata p.23

PLATE 43

*Orchis
ula* p.234

O. pallens p.235

*Traunsteinera
globosa* p.237

O. provincialis
p.235

Δ

Δ

Comperia comperiana
(fl. ×1 & reduced plant) p.238

*Dactylorhiza
iberica* p.239

O. laxiflora
p.236

*Dactylorhiza
sambucina* (2 colour
forms) p.239

PLATE 44

D. traunsteinera
(fl.) p.243

▷
D.
majalis
p.241

D. purpurella
p.242

△
D. cruenta
p.241

Dactylorhiza incarnata
(& colour forms) p.240

△
D. cordigera
p.243

△
D. lapponica
p.243

△
D. fuchsii
p.245

D. maculata p.244

D. el
p.246

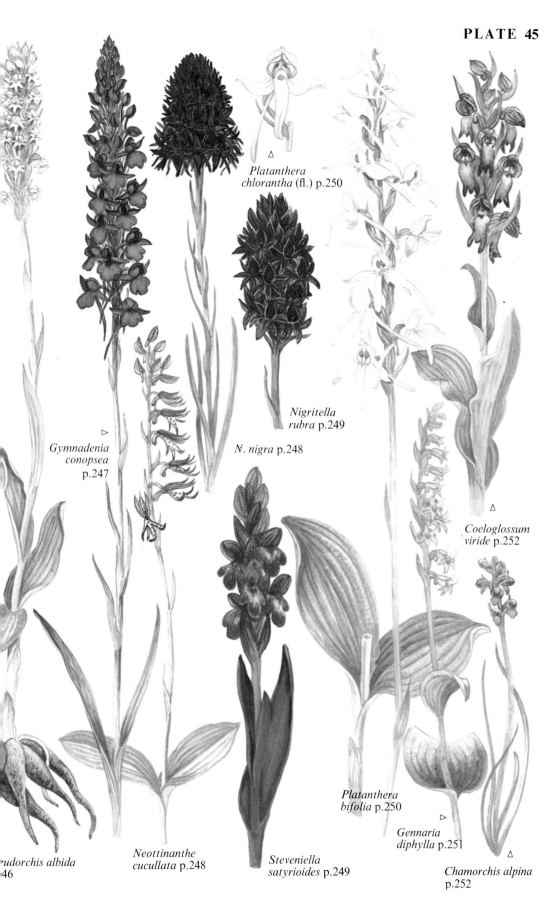

PLATE 45

Platanthera
chlorantha (fl.) p.250

Nigritella
rubra p.249

N. nigra p.248

Gymnadenia
conopsea
p.247

Coeloglossum
viride p.252

Platanthera
bifolia p.250

udorchis albida
46

Neottinanthe
cucullata p.248

Steveniella
satyrioides p.249

Gennaria
diphylla p.251

Chamorchis alpina
p.252

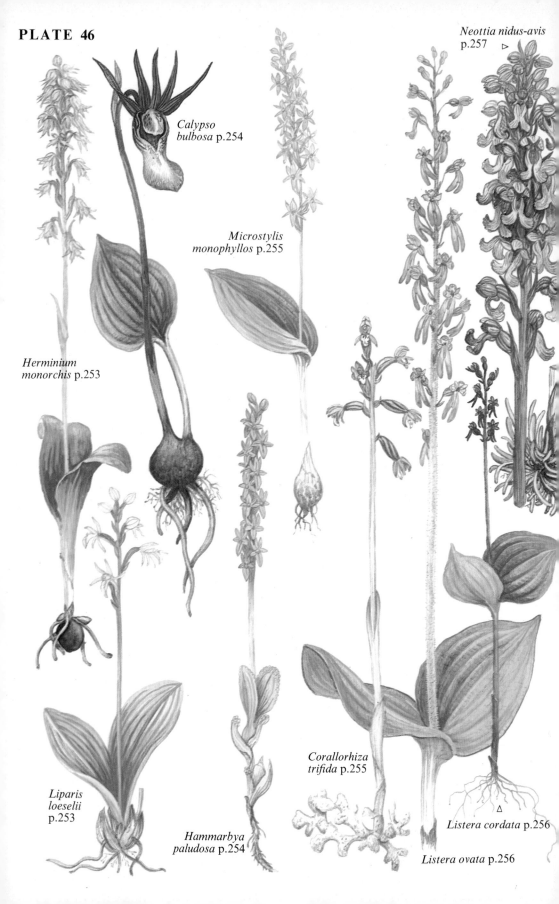

PLATE 46

Neottia nidus-avis p.257 ▷

Calypso bulbosa p.254

Microstylis monophyllos p.255

Herminium monorchis p.253

Liparis loeselii p.253

Hammarbya paludosa p.254

Corallorhiza trifida p.255

Listera cordata p.256 △

Listera ovata p.256

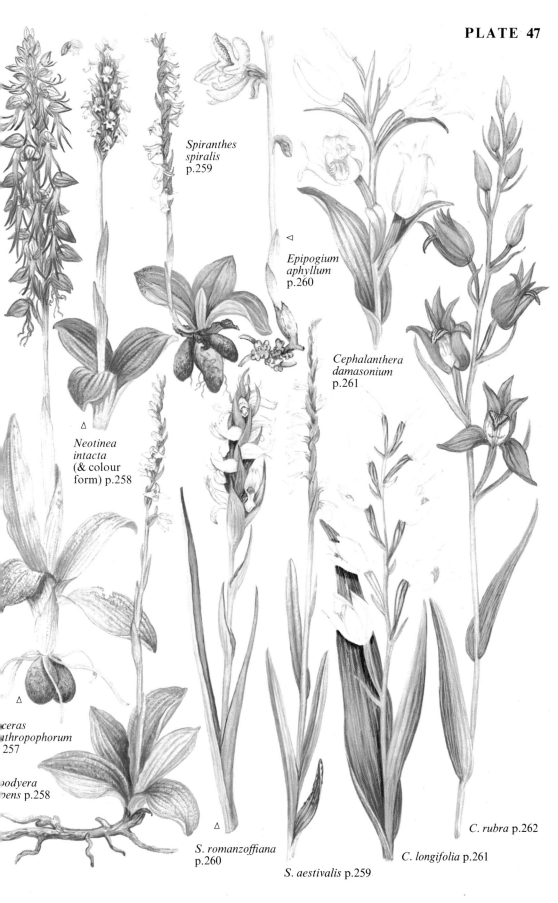

PLATE 47

Spiranthes spiralis p.259

◁ *Epipogium aphyllum* p.260

Cephalanthera damasonium p.261

△ *Neotinea intacta* (& colour form) p.258

△

ceras thropophorum 257

odyera ens p.258

△

S. romanzoffiana p.260

S. aestivalis p.259

C. longifolia p.261

C. rubra p.262

PLATE 48

Epipactus palustris p.264

E. phyllanthes p.266

Limodorum abortivum p.263

E. microphylla p.266

E. dunensis p.265

E. helleborine p.264

E. purpurata p.265

E. atrorubens p.

Butcher's Brooms RUSCUS

Evergreen shrub-like plants producing shoots annually from below ground, but these not continuing to grow in following seasons. The alternate, leathery leaf-like structures are flattened modified stems, which are called cladodes or false-leaves. The true leaves are small and scale-like and are generally only observable on young shoots. Flowers small, dull green, spotted purple, arising from the middle of the false leaves, either male or female on the same or on separate plants; tepals 6 separate, but the stamens only 3 and fused together into a short tube. Fruit a red berry.

1. Butcher's Broom *Ruscus aculeatus* [21]   Short to tall hairless shrub from 10–100cm; stems branched. False leaves dark green, oval, 1–4cm long, *spine-tipped*. Flowers greenish-white, 3mm, solitary or in pairs on the upper surface of the false leaves; male and female flowers on separate plants. Berry red, globular, 12–15mm. Woods, shrub, hedgebanks and sea cliffs. January–April. A, AZ, BAL, BG, CH, CO, CR, E, F, GR, *c&s*GB, H, I, *sw*IRL, K, P, R, SA, SC, YU.*

A very characteristic plant forming dense dark spiny bushes. It is widely cultivated and naturalised in many parts of western Europe. The young shoots can be cooked and eaten and resemble asparagus in flavour.

2. Large Butcher's Broom *Ruscus hypoglossum* [21]   Short to medium, shrub-like plant to 40cm tall, rarely more; stems generally unbranched. False leaves mid-green, elliptical to lance-shaped, 3–10cm long, *not spine tipped or rigid* like the previous species. Flowers greenish, 3–5mm, borne in clusters of 3–5 on the upper surface of the false leaves; male and female flowers on separate plants. Berry scarlet, 18–20mm. Deciduous woods and scrub. January–April. A, BG, CS, GR, H, I, K, R, SC, TR, YU.*

A species confined chiefly to eastern and south-eastern Europe but also found in Asia Minor. It is quite often cultivated in western Europe.

Spanish Butcher's Broom, × ½

3. Spanish Butcher's Broom *Ruscus hypophyllum*   Short to medium shrub-like plant from 10–70cm tall, sometimes more; stems usually unbranched, erect. False leaves flexible, oval or lance-shaped, 5–9cm long. Flowers greenish, 3–4mm, borne on the upper or lower surface of the false leaves; male and female flowers on the same plant. January–March. Woodland. *sw*E, (*se*F), *se*C.●

A rather rare species whose distribution extends into north-west Africa. It is apparently naturalised in south-eastern France – Isle d'Hyeres.

SMILAX

An interesting genus of trailing shrubs or climbers sometimes placed in a separate family, the Smilacaceae. Plants are often prickly, but hairless, with alternate leaves which are untoothed and with a rounded, heart-shaped or arrow-shaped base with the main veins parallel; near the base of the leaf-stalk there are two characteristic simple tendrils which help the plants to climb. The flowers are tiny, white, yellowish or greenish in clusters or umbels, each with 6 separate tepals; the male and female on different plants. Fruit a small, shiny, smooth berry.

1. Common Smilax *Smilax aspera* (=*S. mauritanica, S. nigra*) [21]   Variable creeping or climbing shrub, to 15m; stems angled, smooth or with prickles. *Leaves leathery*, shiny-green, oblong, triangular, oval or lance-shaped with a heart or arrow-shaped base, smooth or with prickles on the stalk and margin, and on the main veins beneath; stalk thickened towards the top. Flowers greenish-white or greenish-yellow, 3–5mm, in branched clusters. Berry red or black, 7mm. August–October. Scrub and bushy places. AL, BG, CO, CR, E, F, GR, I, P, SA, SC, TR, YU.

The distribution of this species extends into western Asia. The young asparagus-like shoots are edible when cooked.

2. Larger Smilax *Smilax excelsa*   Climbing shrub up to 20m; stems angled, prickly. Leaves membranous or slightly leathery, oval to rounded with *a rounded or somewhat heart-shaped base*, smooth or with tiny prickles on the margin and on mid vein beneath; stalk *not thickened* towards the top. Flowers greenish, 6–9mm, in long-stalked umbels. Berry red. Scrub and bushy places. AEG, BG, GR, R, TR, YU.

3. Canary Isles Smilax *Smilax canariensis*   Like the previous species but *stems rounded and without prickles*. Leaves leathery, oval to lance-shaped, smooth; stalked slightly thickened and rough towards the top. AZ. Also known from the Canary Isles.

Daffodil Family AMARYLLIDACEAE

The Daffodil Family contains only six genera in Europe, though several can be rated amongst the most appealing and beautiful of bulbous genera. Among these the daffodils and narcissi, together with the snowdrops and snowflakes and the striking 'crocus-like' Sternbergias are most noteworthy.

The Amaryllidaceae is primarily a tropical or subtropical family, particularly in Africa and South America where such well known plants as the Hippeastrum, Amaryllis, Nerine and Crinum originate. These are widely cultivated in Europe and indeed the Amaryllis Lily (*Amaryllis belladona*) is naturalised in parts of Portugal and in the Azores.

Bulbous, hairless perennials with scapes (leafless stems). The leaves are basal, linear to strap-shaped and generally rather fleshy; they may be present or absent, or only partially developed at flowering time, depending on the particular species. The flowers may be solitary or clustered into an umbel, and they are subtended by one or several 'bract-like' spathes which cover and protect the flowers in bud. The 6 tepals are all petal-like and, as with the other flower parts, they arise from the top of the ovary; the ovary is inferior in contrast to the Lily Family in which it is always superior. In the genus *Narcissus* and *Pancratium* a conspicuous 'cup' or 'trumpet-shaped' corona is present inside the tepals. The stamens are 6 in number, one opposite each tepal – in *Pancratium* they are borne on the rim of the corona. The stigma is solitary but swollen or 3-lobed at the tip. The fruit is a three-valved capsule, generally containing many seeds.

Key to Genera of Amaryllidaceae native to Europe

1. Flowers with a well developed cup or trumpet
   (corona)   2
   Flowers without a cup or trumpet   3

2. Flowers always white, with the stamens joined to
   the rim of the corona   *Pancratium* p.139
   Flowers yellow, cream or white, with the stamens
   inside the corona   *Narcissus* p.140

3. Flowers yellow, 'crocus-like'   *Sternbergia* p.137
   Flowers white or pink, not 'crocus-like'   4

4. Inner tepals half the length of the outer; flowers
   always solitary   *Galanthus* p.130
   Inner tepals equal to the outer; flowers often
   clustered, sometimes solitary   5

5. Flowers nodding, bell-shaped   *Leucojum* p.133
   Flowers more or less erect, open and starry   *Lapiedra* p.138

Snowdrops GALANTHUS

One of the earliest harbingers of spring, the snowdrop must surely be among the best loved of all plants. Early in the new year, still in the depths of winter, the pale shoots can be seen pushing through the earth and at the first hint of warmer weather the flowers appear, shy closed drops at first which slowly open to the sunshine.

Perhaps surprisingly there are almost a dozen species of snowdrop, even including autumn flowering forms, and although they look superficially alike they can be readily split on various characters of both the leaf and flower. The genus has its centre of distribution in N. Turkey and the Crimea extending eastwards as far as the Lebanon and N.W. Iran.

The exact origin of the Common Snowdrop, *Galanthus nivalis*, is rather uncertain, because the plant has been cultivated for many centuries and as a result has become widely naturalised. It is certainly not native to Western Europe but more probably to the region encompassing E. Switzerland, Austria and Yugoslavia eastwards. The species was probably brought into Britain by the Romans.

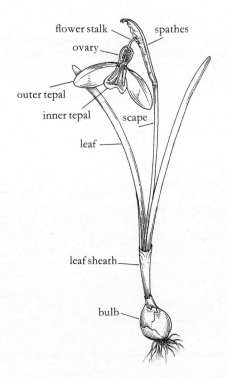

Cross-section of a typical Snowdrop to illustrate the botanical details

Snowdrops are hairless bulbous perennials, often forming small tufts. Each bulb has two basal leaves enclosed at the base in a whitish tubular-sheath. Flowers solitary, pendulous on slender stems or scapes with a 'bract-like' spathe near the apex which encloses the flower in a membranous sheath while in bud. The six white tepals are of two sorts, the outer three large oval and petal-like, whilst the inner three are about half the size, notched at the end and with a characteristic green patch or sinus near the apex, but also at the base sometimes, depending on the species. There are six stamens hidden within the inner tepals.

Key to European Species of Galanthus

1. Flowers appearing in winter (October–December)
before the leaves ... 1a. *G. nivalis* subsp. *reginae-olgae*

Flowers appearing in spring (January–April) with the young leaves ... 2

2. Leaves folding around each other at the base (just above the sheath) ... 3
Leaves held flat against one another at the base, *not* folding around each other ... 5

3. Inner tepals with a green patch at the notch end only; leaves bright shiny-green, recurved at the tip ... 4. *G. ikariae*
Inner tepals with a green patch at the base *as well* as at the notch end; leaves grey-green, not recurved at the tip ... 4

4. Leaves 12mm wide or more; outer tepals 7–14mm wide, strongly convex ... 3. *G. elwesii*
Leaves never more than 12mm wide; outer tepals 4–10mm wide, only slightly convex ... 3a. *G. elwesii* subsp. *graecus*

5. Leaves broad with back-folded margins (revolute) ... 2. *G. plicatus*
Leaves narrow with parallel edges, margins *not* back folded ... 1. *G. nivalis* subsp. *nivalis*

1. Common Snowdrop *Galanthus nivalis* [22] Low to short, usually tuft forming plant, rarely more than 12cm tall. Leaves grey-green or bluish-green, linear-strap-shaped, *pressed flat against each other* in bud, partly developed at flowering time. Spathe as long as the flower-stalk. Flowers 12–25mm long, the inner tepals with a green patch at the notch end only. Deciduous woods, streamsides, banks and shady places, to 2200m. January–April. Widespread in central and southern Europe and naturalised in many places besides. A, AL, (B), BG, CH, CS, D, *n&cE*, (*c&sF*), (GB), GR, H, I, K, N, PL, R, *c,e&wRS*, YU.*

1a. *G.n.* subsp. *reginae-olgae* (=*G. corcyrensis*) [22] is an earlier flowerer, the flowers appearing *before the leaves* and rather larger, 20–35mm long. October– December. *w*GR, SC, *sw*YU.*

The Common Snowdrop, as the name implies, is the most frequently seen species, widely planted and naturalised and often sold in bunches in the early spring, making a delightful small cut flower. There are a large number of forms sold in the trade, some being particularly vigorous and large flowered. In the garden they are best moved and planted in full growth, immediately after flowering, and rather resent being moved in the dormant state, which is the best time for most other bulbous species.

In the wild it is often locally common, sometimes occurring in large numbers, particularly in open deciduous woodland. It is readily recognised by its narrow, strap-shaped leaves.

Common Snowdrop, × ½.
Subsp. *reginae-olgae* on right

Plicate-leaved Snowdrop,
× ½

G. elwesii, left; *G. ikariae*,
right, × ½

2. Plicate-leaved Snowdrop *Galanthus plicatus* [22]   Short, often tufted plant to 15cm tall. Leaves grey or bluish-green, broad strap-shaped or oblong, usually broadest above the middle, *the margin folded back*, remaining like this at maturity. Spathe shorter or longer than the flower-stalk. Flowers 14–28mm long, the inner tepals with a green patch only at the notch end, but this often extending back beyond the middle. Woodlands, scrub and shady places. February–April. K, *e*R, *w*RS.*

An eastern European species readily recognised by its rather broad leaves which have their margins folded or rolled backwards. *G. plicatus* is sometimes cultivated.

3. *Galanthus elwesii* [22]   Short, often tufted plant sometimes reaching 18cm in height. Leaves grey-green, oblong, *folded around each other* in bud, at the base only at maturity, 12mm or more wide, ridged on the back in the lower half. Spathe longer than the flower-stalk. Flowers 15–28mm long, the outer tepals strongly convex, 7–14mm wide, the inner tepals with a green patch at both the base and at the notch ends. Woods, scrub, banks and rocky meadows – east and south-east Europe, extending into W. Turkey. February–March. BG, *n*GR, R, *w*RS, *s*YU.*

3a. *G.e.* subsp. *graecus* has the leaves only slightly overlapping in bud, *rather twisted* at maturity and never more than 12mm wide; outer tepals only slightly convex; 4–10mm wide. BG, *n*GR – including the N. Aegean Islands of Samos and Thasos.

A rather vigorous snowdrop, readily recognised by its leaves which wrap around one another in the young state and at the base at maturity. Hybrids occur occasionally in the wild (BG & *n*GR) between the species and its subspecies, *graecus*, and these have been recognised in the past as a separate species, *G. maximus*, though quite erroneously so.

4. *Galanthus ikariae* [22]   Short plant to 15cm tall. Leaves *bright shiny-green*, oblong-elliptical, recurved at the top and overlapping slightly at the base. Spathes longer than the flower-stalks. Flowers 15–25mm long, the inner tepals with a green patch at the notch end only, but this often extending back beyond the middle. Rocky places. GR* – Kikladhes, Andros and Nikaria (=Ikaria).*

A handsome and rather rare snowdrop with distinctive glossy leaves, a plant seldom seen in cultivation. The distribution of this species extends eastwards into Turkey, the Caucasus and N.W. Iran.

Snowflakes LEUCOIUM or LEUCOJUM

The snowflakes are slightly less well known, but equally as delightful, as their cousins, the snowdrops. Like them, the snowflakes include both autumn and spring flowering species, but whereas the snowdrops have an easterly Mediterranean distribution the snowflakes have a centre of distribution in the western Mediterranean.

Snowflakes are readily distinguished from snowdrops in having six equal tepals rather than the three inner ones being only half the size of the three outer. The flowers are often in small clusters rather than solitary, but like the snowdrop are borne on leafless scapes with a spathe or spathes near the top, which enclose the flowers in bud.

Snowflakes can be divided into two main groups. Firstly the linear-leaved species, which have in addition, solid scapes and white or pale pink flowers. Secondly the strap-leaved species with hollow scapes and white flowers whose tepals are green or yellow spotted near the tip. This latter group contains the two most widespread and best known species, the Spring and Summer Snowflakes. The remaining species belong to the first group.

The name *Leucoium* was originally *Leucoeion* or 'white eye', an allusion to the white flowers of the Spring Snowflake, *L. vernum*.

Key to European Species of Leucoium

1. Flowers appearing in late summer and autumn
   (August–October) before the leaves   2
   Flowers appearing in the spring (January–May)
   with the leaves   4

2. Flowers pure white   3. *L. valentinum*
   Flowers pink, or white tinged pink at the base   3

3. Flowers 9–14mm long, usually white tinged pink
   at the base; flower-stalks 12–25mm long   1. *L. autumnale*
   Flowers 5–9mm long, pink; flower-stalks 1–5mm
   long   2. *L. roseum*

4. Flowers white with a greenish or yellow spot near
   tip of each tepal; scape hollow; leaves
   strap-shaped   5
   Flowers plain white; scape solid; leaves linear   6

5. Flowers solitary usually on scapes longer than
   leaves at flowering time; scapes to 35cm long   7. *L. vernum*
   Flowers in clusters of 2–7, on scapes generally
   shorter than leaves at flowering time; scapes
   35cm long or more   8. *L. aestivum*

6. Flower-stalks mostly longer than spathes; flowers
   12–20mm long   4. *L. trichophyllum*
   Flower-stalks shorter than spathes; flowers 8–12mm long   7

7. Flowers usually solitary; style slightly longer than
   the stamens   6. *L. nicaeensis*
   Flowers usually in clusters of 2–4, rarely solitary;
   style shorter than the stamens   5. *L. longifolium*

1. Autumn Snowflake *Leucoium autumnale* [22]   Low/short, often tuft form-ing perennial, rarely more than 15cm tall. Leaves linear, generally appearing after the flowers. Flowers white, *tinged pink* at the base, more rarely all pink, 9–14mm long, solitary or 2–3 together on *long thin stalks* 15–25mm long; spathe solitary. Rocky and stony hillslopes. August–September. W. Mediterranean region – CR, E, P, SA, SC.*

A very beautiful plant which will succeed in warm sunny spots in southern gardens. It is readily distinguished from other species by its pink tinged flowers and solitary spathe.

2. Rose Snowflake *Leucoium roseum* [22]   A smaller plant than the previous species, not more than 12cm tall. Leaves linear, generally appearing after the flowers. Flowers pink, small 5–9mm long, *solitary, usually on short stalks*, 1–5mm long above the spathe; spathes two. Rocky ground and dry pastures. September–October. CO, SA.*****

The daintiest of the autumn snowflakes and a plant unsuitable for outdoor cultivation, and indeed not always easy even with the protection of a frame or greenhouse.

3. *Leucoium valentinum*   Low plant rarely more than 12cm tall. Leaves linear, thread-like, appearing after the flowers. Flowers *milky-white*, 8–12mm long, solitary or 2–3 together; spathe solitary or two together. Ovary disc-like, 6-lobed. Rocky pastures. August–September. *e*E*, *nw*GR*●

A rare and little known species readily distinguished from the other autumn flowering snowflakes by its small pure white flowers. This species is rather like the spring flowering *L. nicaeensis*.

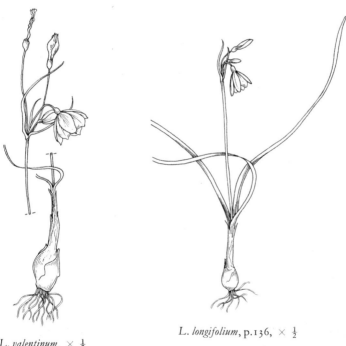

L. longifolium, p.136, × ½

L. valentinum, × ½

4. Three-leaved Snowflake *Leucoium trichophyllum* (= *L. grandiflorum*) [22] Short perennial up to 30cm tall, but often less. Leaves *generally three* per bulb, narrow linear, developed at flowering time. Flowers white, *sometimes tinged pink*, 12–20mm long; *broad bells*, in clusters of 2–4, each on long slender stalks up to

60mm long; spathes two, shorter than the individual flower-stalks. Dry sandy ground. January–April. *sw*&*scE*, *s*&*cP*.●

An attractive species with its wide opening flowers appearing very early in spring, often shortly after Christmas. The distribution of this species extends to Morocco in North Africa.

5. *Leucoium longifolium*   Like the previous species but shorter and more slender. Flowers white, *small*, 8–11mm long; *in clusters* of 2–4, rarely solitary, each on slender stalks up to 25mm long; spathes two, *longer than* the individual flower-stalks; style *shorter than* the stamens. Rocky ground and dry mountain slopes, often partially shaded, to 450m. April–May. CO*●

A small white-flowered snowflake endemic to Corsica, and rarely seen in cultivation. Later flowering than the previous species and certainly a rarer one.

6. French Snowflake *Leucoium nicaeensis* (= *L. hiemale*) [22]   Low/short generally tufted perennial up to 18cm tall, though usually less. Leaves linear, developed at flowering time. Flowers white, small, 8–12mm long, *usually solitary*, sometimes 2–3 together, on rather short flower stalks, 10–18mm long; style *slightly longer* than the stamens. Ovary disc-like, 6 lobed. Rocky places. March–May. *seF* – Maritime Alps and the neighbouring Mediterranean coast.*

7. Spring Snowflake *Leucoium vernum* [22]   Short often tufted perennial up to 35cm tall, though generally less. Leaves strap-shaped, broad, deep green, partly developed at flowering time. Flowers white, each tepal with a *greenish* or *yellowish* spot below the tip, 15–25mm long, *solitary* or rarely 2 together; spathe one, membranous. Damp and shady places, often wooded, to 1600m. February–March. Widespread in central and parts of south and west Europe. A, B, CH, CS, F, D, (DK), *n*E, (GB), H, I, (NL), PL, R, *w*RS, *n*&*c*YU.*

The best loved and, together with the Summer Snowflake, the most widespread and easily grown species. It is readily distinguished by its broad deep green leaves and early flowering habit, besides having the largest flowers of any species. In Britain it has become naturalised in south Devon.

The Carpathian plant which has yellow markings near the tips of the tepals is sometimes distinguished as var. *carpathicum*, whilst the Hungarian plant, with two-flowered scapes, as var. *vagneri*. This last named is the best of all to cultivate, if obtainable.

8. Summer Snowflake *Leucoium aestivum* [22]   Rather robust, short/medium, perennial, forming large tufts, up to 60cm tall. Leaves broad, strap-shaped, bright green, well developed at flowering time. Flower white, each tepal with a green spot near the tip, 13–22mm long, *in clusters* of 3–5 or more, each with a different length flower stalk; *scape winged*, with transparent margins. Damp meadows, swampy places and ditches to 1300m. April–June. Widespread in West, Central and S. Europe – A, AL, B, BG, CH, CS, D, (DK), (E), F, *s*GB, GR, H, I, *w*IRL, K, NL, R, *w*RS, TR, YU.*

Though called the Summer Snowflake the flowers actually appear in the late spring. Like the previous species the Summer Snowflake is widely cultivated and is naturalised in many places. Some forms are rather coarse with small flowers, whilst the larger flowered ones are more worth cultivating. The distribution of this species extends eastwards into Asia Minor and the Caucasus.

9. *L.a.* subsp. *pulchellum* is a less robust plant with more slender leaves, the scape *without transparent wings*. Flowers small, 8–14mm long, in clusters of 2–4. Late March–early April. BAL, CO, SA.

STERNBERGIA

The genus *Sternbergia* contains six species of delightful bulbous plants, although only two are native to Europe. The centre of distribution is to the east of the Bosphorus, in Turkey, the Caucasus and western Iran.

Sternbergias are readily recognised by their yellow or golden 'crocus-like' flowers, which in the European species appear in the autumn. They are readily distinguished from Crocuses in having six rather than three stamens. Each bulb produces only a single flower usually, which has a characteristic papery spathe at the base of the ovary immediately beneath the tepals. The bulbs are poisonous.

1. Slender Sternbergia *Sternbergia colchiciflora* [23]   Low plant rarely more than 5cm tall. Leaves linear, keeled, twisting, deep green, *appearing in the spring* and dying away before the flowers appear. Flowers pale yellow or whitish-yellow, *at ground level*, 3–4cm long; tepals linear, broadest above the middle. September–October. Dry stony ground. Southern Europe mainly – BG, E, G, GR, H, I, K, R, *w*RS, SC, YU.●

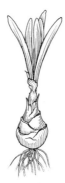

Slender Sternbergia, × ½

The smallest species of *Sternbergia* with dainty flowers, but it has little general appeal to the gardener compared to its larger-flowered cousins. Besides this, it is reputably a difficult plant to keep in cultivation. The distribution of *S. colchiciflora* extends eastwards into Asiatic Turkey and the eastern Mediterranean countries.

2. Common Sternbergia *Sternbergia lutea* [23]　Low to short plant up to 12cm tall. Leaves strap-shaped, slightly channelled, deep green, 8–15mm broad *appearing before or with* the flowers. Flowers golden-yellow, crocus-like and goblet-shaped, 4–5cm long, borne on slender scapes; tepals oblong-elliptical, 7–15mm broad, fused at the base into a short tube. August–October. Dry scrub, short grass meadows, stony and rocky places generally in the mountains, to 1000m. Mediterranean Europe – AL, BAL, CR, E, (SF), GR, I, SA, SC, YU.*

Common Sternbergia, subsp. *sicula* on right, × ⅓

2a. *S.l.* subsp. *sicula* (= *Sternbergia sicula*) is an altogether more slender plant, the leaves only 3–5mm broad and linear, the flowers smaller with linear-oblong tepals, 4–8mm broad. AEG, SGR, SI, SC.*

One of the finest autumn flowering bulbous plants, thriving in our gardens in warm, sunny spots, especially at the base of a wall, and doing particularly well on chalky soils. The more slender subsp. *sicula* does equally as well in cultivation as the type.

In the wild the Common Sternbergia often occurs in large numbers, the distribution of the species extending into Asia Minor eastwards to western Iran.

LAPIEDRA

A genus of one species, not obviously related to any other member of the family. The bulb is like that of a small Daffodil with dark papery tunics, while the leaves resemble those of a Snowdrop.

Lapiedra martinezii [23]　Short plant to 25cm tall. Leaves linear, to 10mm wide, *appearing after the flowers*, deep with a greyish central stripe. Umbel with 4–9 flowers on stalks 10–20mm long. Flowers white, flat and starry, about 15–20mm across, each tepal with a green stripe on the outside. Rock crevices. August–September. S&SEE.●

The umbel of small white flattish flowers immediately serve to distinguish this from all other Amaryllids.

Sea Lilies PANCRATIUM

The Sea Lilies are amongst the most beautiful plants in the Daffodil Family, indeed they can be likened to large white trumpet daffodils in flower. The leaves are strap-shaped, greyish or bluish-green and present throughout the year. The flowers are borne in stout umbels, each with 3–15 flowers enclosed by two half-membranous spathes in bud. The blooms are white marked with green, each with a conspicuous tepal tube and a corona; the corona supports the stamens which adhere to its perimeter. Fruit a rounded, rather smooth, capsule. The bulbs are slightly poisonous.

1. Sea Daffodil or **Sea Lily** *Pancratium maritimum* [23]   Medium plant to 6ocm tall. Leaves 5–20mm wide. Flowers very fragrant, 10–15cm long with a long thin tepal tube over half the length of the flower, the tepals linear lance-shaped, half-spreading; corona 20–34mm long, the margin with twelve small triangular teeth. Coastal sand, mainly in southern Europe. July–September. AL, AZ, BAL, BG, CO, CR, E, *W&SF*, GR, I, P, SA, SC, TR, YU.●

A beautiful and highly perfumed plant of the seashore which is found around most of the Mediterranean coast.

Sea Lily flower × $\frac{1}{3}$

2. Illyrian Sea Lily *Pancratium illyricum* [23]   A stouter species than the previous, to 45cm tall, sometimes more. Leaves 15–30mm wide. Flowers fragrant, 6–9cm long, with a short stout tepal tube about a quarter the length of the flower, the tepals lance-shaped, spreading; corona 15–25mm long, consisting of six deeply cleft lobes. Rocky places, generally near the sea. May–June. CO, SI – Capri, SA.●

Daffodils and Jonquils NARCISSUS

Of all the bulbous plants the daffodil is probably the most widely planted and best loved. The Wild Daffodil, *Narcissus pseudonarcissus*, is widely naturalised in Europe and it has been used a great deal horticulturally in the breeding of numerous cultivars which are available in the trade today. Besides the Wild Daffodil itself, however, the genus *Narcissus* consists of over twenty species, including both spring and autumn flowering ones. It is a genus of the Mediterranean region primarily, especially Spain and Portugal where they are often to be found growing in large numbers. There are few more breathtaking sights than a Pyrenean or Lake District meadow crowded with pale or deep yellow daffodils, or a valley snowy with the sweetly scented blooms of the Poet's Narcissus. As a genus of garden worthy plants they are difficult to rival, being easy to cultivate and quick to multiply in many instances.

The genus has been classified and reclassified a number of times during the past century. Some of the species seem fairly clear cut, but others, notably the larger flowered ones, present numerous problems of interpretation and botanists are not generally agreed on the best way to treat these. The problem is exemplified by *N. pseudonarcissus* itself where, as in the *Tulipa gesnerana* complex (p.46) there has been a long history of cultivation in southern and south-western Europe. This has tended to obscure the exact delimitation of the various forms and subspecies. Man has been able to select vigorously various forms due to their natural capacity for variation and these in their turn have often become naturalised in areas adjacent to their wild habitat. This has confused the picture still further.

Narcissi are bulbous perennials, tufted or solitary, with basal strap-shaped or thread-like leaves, flat, channelled or rounded in cross-section. Flowers solitary or in one-sided, umbel-like, clusters, on leafless scapes, with a green or papery spathe enclosing the flowers in bud. Tepals 6, all alike, united at the base into a short or long tube, the tepal tube, and with a corona extending outwards from the centre (described as a 'cup' if broader than long, or a 'trumpet' if longer than broad). Stamens 6, joined to the top of the tepal tube, included within the corona in most instances. Fruit a 3-valved capsule.

Key to European Species of Narcissus

1. Autumn flowering species (September–October),
flowers usually appearing before the leaves 2
Spring flowering species (January–June), flowers
appearing with the leaves 5

2. Flowers yellow, the cup consisting of 6 'teeth-like'
scales .... 1. *N. humilis*
Flowers greenish or white with an orange or
yellow 6-lobed cup 3

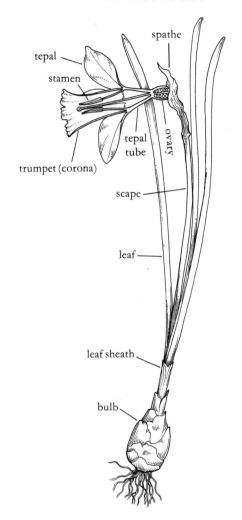

tepal

spathe

stamen

tepal
tube

ovary

trumpet (corona)

scape

leaf

leaf sheath

bulb

Cross-section of a typical Daffodil to illustrate the botanical details

3. Flowers dull olive-green, rather foetid   4. *N. viridiflorus*
   Flowers white with a yellow or orange cup,
   fragrant   **4**

4. Flowers solitary, rarely 2 together; leaves 1mm
   broad   2. *N. serotinus*
   Flowers in clusters of 3–7; leaves 2–4.5mm broad 3. *N. elegans*

5. Flowers with a cup (corona wider than long)   **6**
   Flowers with a trumpet (corona noticeably longer
   than wide), usually flared at the end   **24**

6. Small plants, leaves not more than 5mm wide   **7**
Medium plants, 10cm tall or more, leaves 6–15mm
   wide   **18**

7. Tepals strongly reflexed   18a. *N. triandrus*
    concolor
   Tepals not reflexed   **8**

8. Leaves 'rush-like', rounded in cross-section   **9**
Leaves flat, ridged beneath, square or rectangular
   in cross-section   **15**

9. Cup deep, 7–25mm; flowers solitary; tepals linear   **10**
Cup shallow, not more than 7mm deep; flowers in
   clusters of 2–5, sometimes solitary; tepals
   rounded to oval   **12**

10. Flowers white   21. *N. cantabricus*
Flowers pale to deep yellow or orange-yellow   **11**

11. Stamens not protruding from cup   19. *N. bulbocodium*
Stamens protruding from cup   20. *N. hedraeanthus*

12. Tepal-tube curved   13. *N. pusillus*
Tepal-tube straight   **13**

13. Leaves 1–2mm wide; flowers often solitary;
   flower-stalk less than 18mm long   11. *N. requienii*
Leaves 2–4mm wide; flowers in clusters of 2–5;
   flower-stalk 20mm or more long   **14**

14. Flowers orange-yellow, 22mm or more in diameter   10. *N jonquilla*
Flowers deep yellow, less than 22mm in diameter   12. *N. willkommii*

15. Flower-stalk 1–3mm long; flowers usually solitary   14. *N. rupicola*
Flower-stalk 6mm long or more; flowers usually in
   clusters of 2–5, sometimes solitary   **16**

16. Leaves 1–2mm wide, curling on the ground   16. *N. scaberulus*
Leaves 2–5mm wide, erect or spreading   **17**

17. Flowers in clusters of 2–5, 17–25mm in diameter   15. *N. calcicola*
Flowers usually solitary, 22–30mm in diameter   17. *N. cuatrecasasii*

18. Flowers solitary, 40–50mm in diameter, white
   with an orange or brown edged shallow cup   8. *N. poeticus*
Flowers in clusters of 2–20, 12–38mm in diameter   **19**

19. Tepals white   **20**
Tepals creamy-yellow to deep yellow   **23**

20. Cup white   **21**
Cup bright or deep yellow   **22**

21. Flowers 20mm in diameter or more, often in
    clusters of 7 or more   6. *N. papyraceus*
    Flowers 12–16mm in diameter, never more than 6
    to a cluster   7. *N. dubius*

22. Leaves 10mm wide or more; flowers in clusters of
    2–7   5. *N. tazetta*
    Leaves 7–10mm wide; flowers generally in pairs   29. *N. × medioluteus*

23. Leaves 5–8mm wide; flowers bright yellow, the
    cup 3–4mm deep   30. *N. × intermedius*
    Leaves 10mm wide or more; flowers all yellow, or
    cream with a yellow cup, the cup 5mm or more
    deep   5. *N. tazetta*

24. Tepals strongly reflexed   **25**
    Tepals forward directing or spreading outwards   **26**

25. Flowers deep yellow, solitary   9. *N. cyclamineus*
    Flowers white or creamy-white, in clusters of 2–6,
    rarely solitary   18. *N. triandrus*

26. Spathe green, exceeding 60mm long; flowers
    pointing upwards   22. *N. longispathus*
    Spathe papery-brown, less than 60mm long;
    flowers horizontal or pointing downwards   **27**

27. Dwarf plants, not more than 10cm tall; leaves
    2–6mm wide   26. *N. asturiensis*
    Short to medium plants more than 15cm tall   **28**

28. Trumpet exceeding 25mm long   **29**
    Trumpet less than 25mm long   **30**

29. Trumpet not flared, parallel side to the end;
    tepal-tube 8–12mm long   24. *N. bicolor*
    Trumpet flared towards the end; tepal-tube more
    than 15mm long   23. *N. pseudonarcissus*

30. Tepal-tube 9–15mm long   25. *N. minor*
    Tepal-tube more than 15mm long   23. *N. pseudonarcissus*

Autumn Flowering Narcissi – leaves usually absent at flowering time, appearing after flowering, or in the spring.

1. Tapeinanthus *Narcissus humilis* (= *Tapeinanthus humilis, Braxireon humile*)
[24]   Short slender plant. Leaves rush-like to 1mm wide, generally only one from each bulb. Flowers *yellow*, 18–22mm across, solitary or sometimes two together, the tepals narrow oblong, pointed; cup very shallow, consisting of

6 small scales. Grassy places and open woods, at low altitudes. September–October. swE.●

2. *Narcissus serotinus* [24]   Short slender plant. Leaves rush-like, to 1mm wide, rather bluish-green, one or two from each bulb. Flowers *bi-colored* 20–30mm across, solitary or sometimes two together, the tepals white, oblong, pointed; cup shallow, orange, 6-lobed. Dry places, stony hillslopes, particularly around the Mediterranean, to 250m. September–October. BG, CO, CR, E, GR, I, P, SA, SC, YU.●

3. *Narcissus elegans* [24]   Short, rather slender plant. Leaves linear, 2–4.5mm wide, channelled, bluish-green; appearing before or with the flowers. Flowers bi-colored, 22–38mm across, *in clusters* of 3–7, fragrant, the tepals white or slightly greenish, narrow-oblong, pointed, often pointing backwards slightly; cup shallow, yellowish or orange-brown. Dry and rocky places, at low altitudes. September–October. SI, SC.●

Tapeinanthus flower, p. 143, × 1

N. *tazetta* flower, × 1

4. Green-flowered Narcissus *Narcissus viridiflorus* [24]   Short, rather slender plant. Leaves rush-like, to 4mm wide, hollow, generally only one from each bulb; appearing shortly after the flowers. Flowers *dull olive-green*, 20–30mm across, rather foetid, in clusters of 2–5, the tepals narrow-oblong, pointed, often backward pointing; cup shallow, 6-lobed. Damp sandy places, at low altitudes. September–October. swE, GBZ – Gibralta.*

Spring Flowering Narcissi – leaves and flowers appearing together.

5. *Narcissus tazetta* [24]   Medium, often tufted plant. Leaves broad, strap-shaped, slightly channelled. Flowers *bi-colored*, 15–40mm across, in clusters of 2–7, fragrant, the tepals white, broad-oval; cup deep yellow. Meadows and pastures, sometimes in cultivated fields, to 500m. January–March. BAL, CO, CR, E, F, GR, I, SA, SC, YU.*

5a. *N.t.* subsp. *italicus* has cream coloured tepals and a bright orange-yellow cup. GR, I, YU.*

5b. *N.t.* subsp. *aureus* [24] has bright yellow tepals and a deep yellow or orange cup. *se*F, *nw*I, SA.*

Subspecies *aureus* is frequently naturalised in other parts of southern Europe.

This sweetly scented narcissus has been known and widely cultivated for centuries. It is certainly by far the widest in distribution occurring through much of southern Europe and North Africa and extending eastwards into Asia Minor, Syria, Iran and as far as China and Japan. Whether it is native in these eastern countries or has been delivered there by the hand of man it is difficult to say. Certainly the plant has been cultivated for its fragrance for a long time, and indeed has been used in some Moslim countries as a graveside flower.

6. Paper-white Narcissus *Narcissus papyraceus* [24]   Medium, often tufted, plant. Leaves bluish or greyish-green, broad strap-shaped. Flowers *pure white*, 25–40mm across, in clusters of 3–20, fragrant, the tepals oval, pointed; cup deep with rounded teeth along the edge. Meadows and fields, particularly close to the Mediterranean. February–April. (CO), E, F, GR, I, P, SC, YU.*

6a. *N.p.* subsp. *polyanthus* has *green leaves* and an untoothed cup. *s*F, (E, I).

6b. *N.p.* subsp. *panizzianus* has smaller flowers than (6), 20–25mm across. *se*F, *n*I, (P).●

Like the preceding species the Paper-white Narcissi are widely grown in the horticultural trade as a cut flower, appearing in the shops at Christmas time or shortly afterwards. Their numerous flowers and haunting fragrance makes them amongst the most popular cut flowers. Unfortunately as outdoor plants they are unsuitable in much of the British Isles though they make excellent pot plants for early forcing.

7. Doubtful Narcissus *Narcissus dubius* [24]   Short to medium plant. Leaves bluish or greyish-green, narrow strap-shaped, flat. Flowers white, *small* 12–16mm across, in clusters of 2–6, the tepals broad-elliptical; cup deep. Rocky calcareous slopes, generally amongst low scrub. March–April. *ne*E, *s*F.*

This slender and rather elegant little plant is very local in distribution. Its exact status is rather uncertain but it is believed to be a natural hybrid between *N. papyraceus* and *N. requienii*, although not all authorities are agreed on the parentage. It is a difficult plant to grow and maintain in cultivation.

8. Poet's or **Pheasant's Eye Narcissus** *Narcissus poeticus* [24]   Short to medium, often tufted, plant. Leaves bluish or greyish-green, strap-shaped, flat, 6–10mm wide. Flowers bi-colored, *large*, 40–50mm across, *solitary*, fragrant, the tepals white, rounded and overlapping; cup small and shallow, yellow with an orange or brownish rim. Damp meadows, usually in the mountains and often in large numbers, to 2300m. April–May. A, AL, (B), CH, (CS), (D), *n&c*E, *c&s*F, (GB), *nw*GR, H, I, YU.*

8a. *N.p.* subsp. *hellenicus* has broader leaves and *smaller* flowers, 30–35mm across. Meadows. *c*GR.

8b. *N.p.* subsp. *radiiflorus* (=*Narcissus radiiflorus*) [24]   Like (**8**) but tepals oval and distinctly *narrowed* into a 'claw' at the base. Meadows. AL, *s*CH, *w*GR, I, *s*YU.●

The Poet's Narcissus has been known for a long time, indeed the name was mentioned by Lobel as long ago as 1570. With its large white sweetly scented flowers it is frequently grown as a cut flower. In the wild it is often to be seen in large numbers, particularly in the bottoms of mountain valleys. In cultivation it is a good species for naturalising in grass, increasing steadily in numbers through the years.

9. Cyclamen-flowered Narcissus *Narcissus cyclamineus* [24]   Short slender plant. Leaves bright green, slender strap-shaped. Flowers deep yellow, 35–40mm long, solitary, the tepals lanceolate, *bent backwards* like the petals of a cyclamen flower; trumpet long and narrow, the same length as the tepals. Damp mountain pastures, often shaded, stream and river banks, to 1000m. February–March. *nw*E, *nw*P.＊

Cyclamen- flowered Narcissus flower, × $\frac{3}{4}$

N. *cyclamineus* is a plant of damp meadows and moist places, a very distinct plant with its strongly reflexed tepals and narrow trumpets. A delightful plant to grow in the garden, often succeeding in semi-shaded positions.

10–13 Jonquils   Variable plants characterised by their smooth slender rush-like leaves which are rounded in cross-section. The flowers are all of one colour, yellow, and are borne either in small clusters or are solitary. The cup is small, twice as wide as long.

10. Common Jonquil *Narcissus jonquilla* [25]   Short often tufted plant. Leaves deep green, 2–4mm wide, slightly channelled. Flowers in clusters of 2–5, rich golden-yellow, *sweetly scented*, 22–32mm across, the cup 3–4mm deep; tepal-tube 20–30mm long. Meadows and damp places. March–April. *c&s*E, (F), (I), *c&s*P, (YU).＊

The Common Jonquil is one of the daintiest and sweetest scented of all narcissi. It has been cultivated since the sixteenth century and is much prized for its perfume which is used in perfumery. As a result it has become widely naturalised in southern Europe. The natural distribution of the species extends southwards into North Africa.

11. Rush-leaved Narcissus *Narcissus requienii* (=*N. juncifolius*) [25]   Low to short, often tufted, plant. Leaves very slender, deep green, 1–2mm wide, more or less upright. Flowers small, solitary or two together, deep yellow, sweetly scented, 17–22mm across, the cup 4–6mm deep; tepal-tube 12–18mm long, straight; flower-stalk above spathe 11–22mm long. Rocky mountain and hill slopes, to 1600m. March–May. *n&eE, sF.* *****

12. *N. willkommii* (=*N. jonquilloides*) has slightly *grey-green* leaves, 2–3mm wide and rather smaller flowers than (**11**), in clusters of 2–3; flower stalks 20–45mm long. Damp grassy places. *swE, sP.* **●**

13. *Narcissus pusillus* (=*N. minutiflorus*) [25]   Low plant. Leaves very slender, deep green, 1–2mm wide, *prostrate*. Flowers small, usually in clusters of 2–5, deep yellow, fragrant, 12–20mm across, the cup 2.5–7mm deep; flower tube *curved*. Damp grassy places. March–April. *swE, sP.* **●**

14–17 Rock Narcissus Group. Superficially resembling the Jonquil Group but the leaves are greyish-green, distinctly ridged on the back and 4-angled in cross-section. Flowers are all of one colour, yellow, solitary or in small clusters. The cup is small and less than twice as wide as long.

14. Rock Narcissus *Narcissus rupicola* [25]   Short, often tufted plant. Leaves 1.5–3mm wide, with two keels on the back. Flowers *usually solitary*, deep yellow, slightly fragrant, 15–30mm across, the cup 2–4mm deep, usually with 6 shallow

Rock Narcissus flower, × ¾

lobes; tepal-tube 18–25mm long, straight; flower-stalk above spathe very short, never more than 3mm long. Rock crevices and stony mountain pastures, generally on calcareous soils, 1000–2300m. April–May. *n&cE, n&cP.* *****

15. *Narcissus calcicola* [25]   Low tufted plant. Leaves 2–5mm wide with two keels on the back, erect or spreading; edge smooth. Flowers in clusters of 2–5, rarely solitary, deep yellow, scented, 17–25mm across, the cup 5–8mm deep, as wide as deep, wavy-edged; *flower-stalk* above spathe 6–15mm long. Limestone rock crevices, March–April. *wc*P.*

16. N. scaberulus   Like (**15**) but with prostrate and curling 4-angled leaves, 1–2mm wide; flower solitary or 2–3 together. Cultivated or disturbed ground, to 500m. March–April. *c*P* – Mondego Valley.●

17. *N. cuatrecasasii* (=*N. rupicola* subsp. *pedunculatus*)   Like (**15**) but flowers *usually solitary* and rather larger, 22–30mm across, the cup almost twice as wide as deep. Limestone rock crevices in the mountains, *c*&*s*E.

18. Angel's Tears *Narcissus triandrus* (=*N. calathinus, N. cernuus, N. pulchellus* and *N. capax*) [25]   Low to short, often tufted, plant. Leaves dark green, flattish or half-rounded in cross-section, 1.5–3mm wide. Flowers white or very pale creamy-yellow, *drooping* in clusters of 2–6, sometimes solitary, the tepals lanceolate, *strongly reflexed*; cup deep, downward pointing, 13–25mm long.

Meadows, mountain pastures and hedgerows, 100–1200m. March–May. *n*&*nc*E, *sw*F, *n*&*nc*P.*

18a.   *N.t.* subsp. *concolor* [25] has solitary *bright yellow* smaller flowers, the cup 5–10mm long. Stony mountain pastures and woods. *c,s*&*e*E, *c*P.*

19-21 Hoop Petticoat Narcissi   Easily recognised by their solitary flowers and large broad petticoat-like cups and the small slender tepals. Leaves rush-like, rounded in cross-section.

19. Hoop Petticoat Narcissus *Narcissus bulbocodium* [25]   Variable low to short, often tufted, plant. Leaves deep green, more or less upright, 1–1.5mm wide, 2–4 from each bulb. Flowers held horizontally, pale yellow to deep orange-yellow, tinged with green on the outside, the tepals linear to narrow-triangular, pointed; the cup cone-shaped 7–25mm long, the stamens not protruding beyond the rim. Mountain pastures, rocky places and scrub, 200–1800m. February–April. E, *sw*F, P.*

A beautiful and widely cultivated plant which multiplies freely once established, especially on grassy slopes.

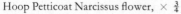

Hoop Petticoat Narcissus flower, × ¾   Subsp. *obesus*, × ¾

19a. *N.b.* subsp. *obesus* [25] has *semi-prostrate and twisting leaves*, the cup-cone narrowed slightly at the rim. *sw*E, *w*&*s*P.*

20. *Narcissus hedraeanthus* [25]   Low plant. Leaves dark green, 1mm wide, *only one* to each bulb. Flower scapes prostrate in the lower half. Flowers upward directing, pale yellow, slightly green tinged outside, the tepals oblong, blunt; the cup cone-shaped, 10–15mm long, the *stamens protruding beyond the rim*; flower-stalk above the spathe absent. Meadows and rocky ground in the mountains. *se*&*sc*E*.●

N. hedraeanthus flower, × ¾

N. cantabricus flower, × ¾

21. *Narcissus cantabricus* [25]   Low to short plant. Leaves dark green, 1–1.5mm wide, usually only one to each bulb. *Flowers held horizontally, white*, the tepals lanceolate, pointed; the cup quite large, cone-shaped, 12–18mm long, with a rather flared and toothed rim, the stamens not protruding beyond the rim. Scrubby places, to 1250m. February–March. E.*

This dainty white Hoop Petticoat is one of the very earliest species to flower in the new year. The distribution of the species extends into North America.

22. *Narcissus longispathus* [26]   Variable medium to tall plant. Leaves greyish-green, 10–15mm wide. Spathe *large and green*, 60mm long or more. Flowers large, solitary or sometimes 2 together, rather upward directing, the tepals medium yellow, trumpet darker, 25–30mm long, flared at the end. On the margins of, or actually in, mountain streams. *se*E* – Sierra de Cazorla.

A fairly recently discovered species which is easily recognised by its large, rather upward pointing, flowers, and long leaf-like spathes which are quite unlike those of any of the other trumpet daffodils.

23. Wild Daffodil or **Lent Lily** *Narcissus pseudonarcissus* [26]   Short/medium, often tufted, plants. Leaves grey- or bluish-green, 6–12mm wide. Spathe *papery-brown*, 20–60mm long. Flowers usually solitary, horizontal or drooping, bi-colored, the tepal-tube 15–25mm long; tepals pale to mid-yellow, usually rather twisted, trumpet pale to deep yellow, 20–35mm long, only *slightly flared* at the end. Flower-stalk above the spathe 3–12mm long. Meadows, woods and rocky ground. Widely naturalised. March–April. CH, D, *n&cE*, F, GB, NL. Widely naturalised in Britain and southeast Ireland.*

The Wild Daffodil is one of the widest grown and naturalised of all bulbous plants, a harbinger of spring throughout much of Europe and widely used by commercial growers and hybridisers to produce the enormous range of form seen in many daffodil cultivars commonly grown in our parks and gardens. The species is extremely variable and numerous forms can be recognised in the wild. Botanists disagree widely on how to treat this complex, some recognising numerous separate species, others a series of subspecies or varieties within the one species. Following *Flora Europaea* seven subspecies are here recognised.

23a. subsp. *pallidiflorus* (=N. *pallidiflorus*) [26]   Like (**23**) but flowers often very pale, the trumpet somewhat darker, 30–40mm long, distinctly *flared and lobed* at the end, the margin often rather recurved. Grassy and rocky places in the mountains, to 2200m. April–June. *n*E, *s*F – Pyrenees and Cordillera Cantabrica.*

23b. subsp. *moschatus* (=N. *moschatus*) [26]   Like (**23**) but flowers *all the same* colour, cream to pale yellow; flower-stalk above the spathe long, 10–25mm. Grassy and rocky places in the mountains, to 2200m. April–June. *n*E, *s*F – Pyrenees and Cordillera Cantabrica.●

23c. subsp. *nobilis* [26] has horizontal or upward directed flowers, the tepals pale yellow pointing slightly backwards, the *trumpet deep golden-yellow* and flared at the end, 30–45mm long; flower-stalk above the spathe 8–15mm long. Meadows and rocky pastures in the mountains, to 2200m. *nw&ncE*, P.●

23d. subsp. *major*   Like (**23c**) but flowers slightly smaller and *all one* colour, deep golden-yellow; flower-stalk above the spathe 8–30mm long. Meadows and rocky places. E, *s*F, P – occasionally naturalised elsewhere in W. Europe.●

23e. subsp. *portensis*   Like (**23**) but *with narrower leaves*, not more than 7mm wide, and flowers all one colour – deep golden-yellow; trumpet *not flared* at the end. Meadows and rocky places. *nw&cE*, *n*P.

23f. subsp. *nevadensis* [26]   Like (**23**) but flowers often horizontal or upward directed, in clusters of 2–4, the tepals pale yellow, the trumpet mid to bright yellow, smaller than all the other subspecies, 15–25mm long. Meadows and rocky places. *s*E – Sierra Nevada.●

The Tenby Daffodil, *N. pseudonarcissus* subsp. *obvallaris* is an intermediate between (**23d**) subsp. *major* and (**23e**) subsp. *portensis* and is naturalised in southwest Wales.

24. *Narcissus bicolor* (=N. *abscissus*) [26]   Medium plant, often tufted. Leaves greyish-green, 10–14mm wide. Spathe papery-brown, 25–40mm long. Flowers solitary, horizontal, bi-colored, the tepals creamy-white to pale yellow, trumpet deep yellow, 35–40mm long, *not flared* or lobed at the end; tepal-tube *shorter than* in (**23**), 8–12mm long. Mountain meadows, to 2200m. *n*E, *s*F – Pyrenees and Corbières.●

Superficially like the preceding species but readily distinguished by its un-flared trumpet and short tepal-tube.

25. Small Wild Daffodil *Narcissus minor* [26]   Short, often tufted, plant, 10–20cm tall. Leaves narrow, greyish- or bluish-green, 3–10mm wide. Spathe papery-brown. Flowers rather small, scented, horizontal or drooping, usually but not always bi-colored, the tepals pale to deep yellow, trumpet deep yellow, 16–25mm long, *flared and toothed* at the end; tepal-tube 9–15mm long. Meadows, grassy and scrubby places in the mountains, to 2200m. March–April. *n*E, *sw*F, P.* Often hybridises with N. *pseudonarcissus*, and naturalised in south-eastern France.

A small trumpet daffodil most readily recognised by its slender leaves and small flowers. Commercially it is often sold under the name N. *nanus*.

26. Asturian Daffodil *Narcissus asturiensis* [26]   Low plant rarely more than 10cm tall. Leaves slender, greyish-green, 2–6mm wide. Spathe green at first, but becoming brown and papery. Flowers small, solitary, drooping, mid-yellow; tepal-tube 5–9mm long, the trumpet 8–16mm long, somewhat waisted in the centre but flared towards the end. Grassy and rocky places in the mountains, to 1800m. February–March. *nw*&*nc*E, *n*&*c*P.* A perfect miniature Daffodil flowering very early in the year and frequently cultivated in this country, though it is best suited to the alpine house or frame. It will sometimes be found in catalogues as N. *minimus*.

Natural Hybrids. Although numerous narcissi hybrids exist four important ones are found commonly in the wild.

27. *Narcissus × incomparabilis* (*N. poeticus × N. pseudonarcissus*) [26]   Short to medium often tufted plant. Leaves 8–12mm wide, rather greyish-green. Spathe papery-brown. Flowers *solitary,* bi-colored, faintly fragrant, the tepals pale yellow, oval, broadest above the middle, the trumpet orange-yellow, 13–22mm long, lobed and wavy-edged. Meadows and grassy places, to 1850m. April–May. *s*&*sc*F – widely naturalised elsewhere in central and southern Europe.*

28. *Narcissus × odorus* (*N. jonquilla × N. pseudonarcissus*) [26]   Medium plant. Leaves *bright green*, ridged on the back, 6–8mm wide. Spathe papery-brown. Flowers solitary or in clusters of 2–4, *all one colour*, bright yellow, fragrant, tepals oval, the trumpet 13–18mm long, slightly lobed at the end. (*s*F, 1).* A plant originating in gardens, occasionally naturalised.

29. *Narcissus × medioluteus* (= N. *biflorus*, N. *poeticus × N. tazetta*) [26]   Medium plant. Leaves greyish-green, flat, 7–10mm wide. Spathe papery-brown. *Flowers usually 2,* bi-colored, fragrant, tepals white, almost rounded, the cup bright yellow, shallow, 3–5mm long. Meadows and rocky places, to 500m. *s*F, but widely grown and naturalised in central and western Europe including Great Britain.*

30. *Narcissus × intermedius* (*N. jonquilla × N. tazetta*) [26]   Medium plant, often tufted. Leaves bright green, *deeply channelled*, 5–8mm wide. Spathe papery-brown. Flowers *in clusters* of 3–6, fragrant, bright yellow, tepals oval, the shallow cup often rather deeper in colour, 3–4mm long. *ne*E, *s&se*F – occasionally naturalised elsewhere, especially in Italy and the Balearic Isles.●

Iris Family IRIDACEAE

A large family of monocotyledons, the representatives of which are mostly of great ornamental value. There are about 70 genera with a worldwide distribution in temperate and tropical regions, but in Europe the most interesting and useful members for our gardens belong to three genera, *Iris, Gladiolus* and *Crocus*. Only seven genera are native in Europe.

Perennial herbs with rhizomes, corms or bulbs. Leaves alternate or in a basal fan or rosette, not separated into a blade and stalk and usually parallel-sided or sword-shaped. Flower stems well-developed and branched with several flowers, or much reduced with only one or two flowers; buds usually enclosed within a bract and bracteole, sometimes referred to as spathes or spathe valves. Flowers regular or irregular; tepals six, free of joined into a tube, either equal, unequal or with the inner 3 equal and very different in size to the 3 outer ones; stamens 3, opposite to the outer tepals; ovary inferior; style divided into 3-many branches, these sometimes thread-like and sometimes wide and flattened so that they are tepal-like, or 'petaloid' as they are often called. Fruit a 3-valved capsule containing many seeds.

Key to genera of Iridaceae native in Europe

1. Flowers horizontal and irregular, produced in a
     spike   *Gladiolus* p.167
     Flowers upright and regular, solitary to several on
     branched or simple stems   **2**

2. Style branches slender, not widened and tepal-like   **3**
     Style branches expanded and coloured like the
     tepals   **5**

3. Tepal tube at least 2cm long   *Crocus* p.173
     Tepal tube less than 1cm long   **4**

4. Plant 15–45cm tall; rhizomatous with fibrous
     roots   *Sisyrinchium* p.166
     Plant usually less than 10cm; rootstock a corm   *Romulea* p.170

5. Rootstock a netted corm   *Gynandriris* p.165
     Rootstock a rhizome, horizontal tuber or bulb with
     papery tunics   **6**

6. Flowers translucent greenish-yellow, blackish-
   brown on 3 outer tepals; leaves square in section   *Hermodactylus* p.166
   Flowers white, blue, lilac or yellow; leaves flat or
   channelled   *Iris* 153

⁑ IRIS

A large and extremely well-known genus which is among the most important
horticulturally, of all the monocotyledons. Undoubtedly the group of species
which has received most attention is the bearded or Pogon Iris section since the
species are very easily grown and hybridise freely. Thus from relatively few wild
species there are now a host of colourful hybrids which contain colours unknown in their parents. Apart from their value as ornamental plants, irises have
not been used very much, although the rhizomes of *I. germanica* subsp. *florentina*,
known as 'Orris Root', yield a perfume not unlike that of violets.

Iris have rather complicated flowers, basically made up of six tepals joined
into a tube at the base. The three outer tepals stand out horizontally and have a
deflexed blade (the 'falls') and the three inner are usually erect or incurved (the
'standards'). The lower, narrower part of the falls is known as the 'haft'. In
addition to these six colourful tepals, the three branches of the style are also
expanded and coloured so that they resemble tepals. These curve outwards over
each of the falls and are usually referred to as the style arms. Each style arm is 2-
lobed at its apex and has a stigma hidden from view on the underside, just by the
base of the two lobes where it is close to the stamen. There are three stamens, one
in each of the tunnel-like spaces formed by the falls and style branches. This
curious formation is suited to bee pollination, the bees being attracted by a little
nectar at the base of the falls. To get access to this the bee must squeeze into the
tunnel and on its way out again gathers pollen on its back. Visiting another *Iris*
flower, the bee then deposits some pollen on to the flap-like stigma as it makes its
way into one of the corresponding tunnel on that flower.

The flowers are protected in the bud stage by two 'spathe valves' which can be
wholly green, wholly white and papery or partly green with a papery margin and
apex. This is a useful diagnostic feature, especially in the bearded irises. It is also
useful to know if the spathe valves have an angular keel along the centre.

In Europe, *Iris* has only about 30 species but over its whole range, that is the
entire Northern Hemisphere, there are over 250 species. The European ones are
not the most spectacular in the genus although the Xiphium group is important
since it has given us all the bulbous 'English' 'Dutch' and 'Spanish' hybrids
which are so popular as cut flowers. Several of the Pogon Iris have been the
parents of some of the bearded hybrids, while in the beardless group *I. sibirica*,
with its many forms and hybrids (with other Asiatic species) is important
horticulturally. *I. unguicularis* (=*I. stylosa*) is one of our best winter-flowering
plants but it is probable that the plant in general cultivation is of North African
rather than European origin, since it is of a more vigorous nature than the
delicate smaller form which grows in Greece.

The species of *Iris* can be divided into several distinct groups depending largely upon their habit of growth and flower characters. In Europe some of the groups are absent, but the following four can be recognised.

A. Bearded or *Pogon Iris*   Rhizomatous; flowers with a beard in the centre of the falls; leaves flat. Widespread in Europe and Asia.

B. Beardless or *Apogon Iris*   Rhizomatous; flowers with hairless falls; leaves flat. Widespread in Europe, Asia and N. America.

C. Xiphium Iris   Bulbous with no fleshy roots; standards well developed and erect (except *I. serotina*); falls with no beard (except *I. boissieri*); leaves channelled. S.W. Europe, N. Africa.

D. Juno or *Scorpiris Iris*   Bulbous, with fleshy roots; flowers with the standards reduced in size and held out horizontally or deflexed; falls with no beard; leaves channelled. One European species only, the rest Asiatic.

Keys to European Iris

Group A – Bearded Iris

1. Stems branched and well-developed   2
   Stems unbranched and often very short   7

2. Stems branched below the middle, often at ground
      level   6. *I. aphylla*
   Stems branched above the middle   3

3. Spathes entirely silvery-papery   4. *I. pallida*
   Spathes partly green at flowering time   4

4. Flowers white or yellow, strongly veined brown
      or violet   5. *I. variegata*
   Flowers white or bluish-purple not very heavily
      veined   5

5. Flower-tube 1.5–2.5 cm long; spathes 3.5–5.5 cm
      long   6
   Flower-tube 3–3.5 cm long; spathes 5.5–6.5 cm
      long   2. *I. marsica*

6. Lower flowers on distinct branches; flowers
      usually bi-colored pale and deep purple   1. *I. germanica*
   Lower flowers stemless; flowers white or
      sometimes pale lilac   3. *I. albicans*

7. Rhizome very thin and wiry; flower-tube 1cm or
      less long   14. *I. humilis*
   Rhizome thick; flower-tube more than 1cm long   8

8. Stem almost absent; spathes with no sharp keel   9
Stem usually 3cm or more long; if less then spathes
   with a sharp keel   10

9. Leaves straight or slightly curved, 1–1.5cm wide   10. *I. pumila*
Leaves strongly curved, less than 1cm wide   11. *I. attica*

10. Spathes with a sharp angular keel   11
Spathes rounded or occasionally the outer one
   slightly keeled   12

11. Flower-tube usually 3.5–5cm long   13. *I. suaveolens*
Flower-tube usually 1.5–2.5cm long   12. *I. reichenbachii*

12. Flower-tube more than 5cm long   9. *I. pseudopumila*
Flower-tube less than 5cm long   13

13. Beard yellow; flowers yellow, mid-violet, white
   or bi-colored   7. *I. lutescens*
Beard violet; flowers deep violet-blue   8. *I. subbiflora*

Group B – Beardless Iris

1. Stem 20cm or less tall   2
Stem more than 20cm tall   7

2. Flower-tube 5cm or more long   3
Flower-tube less than 4cm long   4

3. Flowers bluish or lilac; stem 3–15cm long (*se*RS)   16. *I. tenuifolia*
Flowers with purple apex to falls, whitish and
   veined on the haft; stem nearly absent (CR, GR)   17. *I. unguicularis*

4. Stem flattened; flowers fruit-scented   22. *I. graminea*
Stem rounded; flowers not fruit-scented   5

5. Ovary narrowed at apex, like the neck of a
   bottle, the narrow part 1–2.5cm long   6
Ovary ending abruptly at the apex where it meets
   the flower-tube   18. *I. ruthenica*

6. Stem 10–20cm long   23. *I. sintenisii*
Stem up to 4cm long   24. *I. pontica*

7. Plant of watersides or wet salt marshes   8
Plants not growing by water but sometimes in
   damp meadows   9

8. Flowers deep yellow; standards much shorter than
   falls   20. *I. pseudacorus*
Flowers lilac-blue, white or pale yellow; standards
   as long as falls, or nearly so   21. *I. spuria*

9. Stem strongly flattened and winged at its edges   22. *I. graminea*
  Stem rounded or only slightly flattened, not winged   **10**

10. Flowers violet-blue veined darker; leaves to
   1cm wide   15. *I. sibirica*
  Flowers dirty violet or yellowish; leaves 1–3cm
   wide   19. *I. foetidissima*

Group C & D – Xiphium and Juno Iris (Bulbous Irises)

1. Falls with a beard in the centre   29. *I. boissieri*
  Falls with no beard   **2**

2. Flower-tube more than 1cm long   **3**
  Flower-tube less than 1cm long   **5**

3. Flowers yellow   28. *I. juncea*
  Flowers not yellow   **4**

4. Flowers bluish, violet or lilac, rarely white;
   stem very short   31. *I. planifolia*
  Flowers rich purple; stem at least 25cm   27. *I. filifolia*

5. Standards very small and bristle-like;
   flowering late summer   30. *I. serotina*
  Standards large (4–5cm long); flowering early
   to mid-summer   **6**

6. Haft of falls at least 2.5cm wide; leaves appearing
   in spring   25. *I. latifolia*
  Haft of falls less than 1cm wide; leaves appearing
   in autumn   26. *I. xiphium*

Group A – Bearded Iris

1. Tall Bearded Iris *Iris germanica* [27] Tall plant to 50–100cm. Rootstock a thick spreading rhizome; leaves erect, grey-green, 30–70cm long, 2–3.5cm wide; stem with a few short branches. Spathes green in the lower half, papery and often tinged purplish in the upper half. Flowers up to five, usually violet-blue, the falls normally darker than the standard; beard yellowish; flower-tube 1.7–2.5cm long. The standards also have a few hairs near the base of the haft. Rocky places and in sparse scrub, to 1000m. April–June.*

 Cultivated all over Europe and often naturalised, especially in the Mediterranean region.

 Iris germanica is of unknown origin and it is generally accepted that it is a hybrid. It does however, naturalise easily and thus often appears to be wild.

1a. Florentine Iris *I.g.* subsp. *florentina* This is very like *I. germanica* but has whitish flowers with a very faint tinge of blue or lilac. It is often cultivated in the

Mediterranean region and in Italy a violet-scented perfume is extracted from the rhizome, which is known as 'Orris Root'.*

2. *Iris marsica* Similar to *I. germanica* but is shorter with leaves 3–5 cm wide and rather curved. The spathes are up to 6.5 cm long and the flower-tube about 3–3.5 cm long. Rocky hillsides, 1100–1700m. 1 – Appennines.

3. *Iris albicans* [27] Like *I. germanica* but usually shorter, up to 60cm tall and with *pure white flowers*, the lower ones stemless rather than on short branches. *Spathes green* at flowering time, or with only a very small papery tip. Often planted in cemeteries and naturalised locally (C, F, E, P, YU).*

  I. albicans occurs wild in southern Arabia and Yemen and it is thought that it has been distributed by pilgrims returning from Mecca. It is now widespread in many Moslem countries and is also common in parts of southern Europe, especially in or near cemeteries. It is easily confused with *I. germanica* subsp. *florentina* because of the white flowers, but in *I. albicans* they are more pure white and there are no hairs at the base of the standards. There is a very pale lavender-blue form of *I. albicans* which is occasionally seen in Europe.

4. Dalmatian Iris *Iris pallida* [27] Similar to *I. germanica* in general appearance but with uniformly pale lilac-blue flowers and the spathes are wholly papery and silvery-white. Rocky places and in scrub, to 1000m. April–June. *w*YU–Dalmatian coast.*

  I. pallida is very easy to recognise because of its very silvery spathes , even in the bud-stage. It grows in large colonies on the limestone slopes of the Adriatic coastal mountains of Yugoslavia. It is often cultivated under the name of *I. pallida dalmatica*.

4a. *I.p.* subsp. *cengialtii* Similar to *I. pallida* but of *much shorter habit* with rather greener leaves and darker violet flowers; spathes wholly papery but brownish. Dry grassy and rocky places, to 1000m. *n*I, *nw*YU.*

  Some of the plants from north-west Yugoslavia are rather intermediate between *I. pallida* and *I.p.* subsp. *cengialtii*, having the darker flowers but with silvery spathes. The beard hairs vary from yellow to white.

5. Variegated Iris *Iris variegata* [27] Short to medium plant, 15–45cm tall. Rootstock a thick rhizome. Leaves green, 10–30cm long, 0.5–3cm wide, rather curved; stems branched above the middle. Flowers three to six, very colourful with whitish or yellowish falls with pronounced violet veins and a white or yellow beard, standards white or yellow; flower-tube about 2–2.5cm long. Rocky and grassy places and in lightly wooded places, 400–1000m. May–June. A, BG, CS; D, H, R, *sw*RS, YU.*

  Various forms of this variable species have been described as separate species, for example *I. reginae* which has a white background colour and *I. rudskyi* with a yellow ground colour.

6. *Iris aphylla* [27]   Short to medium plant, 15–30cm tall. Rootstock a thick rhizome. Leaves greyish-green, 15–30cm long, about 0.5–2cm wide, somewhat curved, dying away in winter; stems branched very low down, at least below the middle and sometimes at ground level. Flowers three to five, purplish-violet with a whitish or yellowish beard on the falls; flower-tube about 1.5–2cm long. Rocky and grassy places, 400–1000m. May–June. A, CS, D, F, H, I, PL, R, *c,w*&*sw*RS, YU.●

Easily recognised by its habit of branching very low down, the only species to do this. *I. aphylla* hybridises with other species in the area, a point to be remembered when trying to identify eastern European Irises.

7. *Iris lutescens* (=*I. chamaeiris*) [27]   Low to medium plant, 5–25cm tall. Rootstock a thick rhizome. Leaves greyish-green, 5–25cm long, 0.5–2.5cm wide, more or less straight, not dying away in the winter; stems not branched. Flowers one or two, mid-violet, yellow, whitish or bi-colored, with a yellow beard in the centre of the falls; flower-tube usually 2–3cm long. Stony or sandy soils in scrub, to 1000m. March–May. *ne*E, *s*F, I.*****

I. lutescens is often called *I. chamaeriris* in gardens. The spathes of this species are not keeled on the backs and in this way *I. lutescens* can be separated from *I. reichenbachii*. It is distinguished from *I. pseudopumila* by the length of the flower-tube and by having generally wider leaves. The spathes do not tightly clasp the tube as in *I. pseudopumila*. The next species, *I. subbiflora* has darker coloured flowers and a different distribution.

8. *Iris subbiflora*   Similar to *I. lutescens* but usually taller, 25–40cm tall, and with deep violet-blue flowers; the spathes are generally longer, up to 8cm (not more than about 5cm in *I. lutescens*); flower-tube longer, normally more than 3.5cm. The beard is violet-blue. *sw*E, P.*****

9. *Iris pseudopumila* [27]   Similar to *I. lutescens* but with only one flower per stem. Leaves usually less than 1.5cm wide; spathes tightly sheathing the flower-tube which is 5–7cm long. Rocky places, to 300m. February–April. *se*I, SC, M – and Gozo.●

The solitary flowers, rounded spathes without a keel and long flower-tube make this an easily recognised species. It is very variable in flower colour, purple and yellow or bi-colored variants occurring as in *I. lutescens*.

10. Dwarf Bearded Iris *Iris pumila* [27]   Low plant, to 5cm tall. Rootstock a thick short rhizome. Leaves greyish-green, straight or slightly curved, 5–15cm long, 1–1.5cm wide, dying away in the winter; *stem unbranched, absent or at most 1cm long.* Flowers solitary, yellow, purple or bluish with the beard in the centre of the falls usually taking on the same colour as the flower; flower-tube about 5–10cm long. Dryish grassy or rocky places, to 500m. April–May. A, AL, BG, CS, H, K, R, *nw*RS, YU.*****

I. pumila has a very short stem and the only species which can be compared to it in this respect are *I. attica* and *I. suaveolens*. It can be separated from the former by having broader, straighter leaves and from the latter by having rounded spathes with no sharp keel.

11. Iris attica Similar to *I. pumila* but is even more dwarf and has *sickle-shaped leaves* only 5–10cm long and less than 1cm wide. Limestone crevices and screes, to 1000m. GR, *s*YU.*

This is sometimes regarded as a subspecies of *I. pumila*.

12. Iris reichenbachii [27] Low to short plant, 5–30cm tall. Rootstock a thick rhizome. Leaves grey-green, about 10–30cm long, 5–15cm wide, slightly curved, stem unbranched. Flowers one or two, violet blue, dirty purplish-brown or dull yellow with darker veins; beard yellow or purplish; flower-tube 1.5–3cm long. Rocky or grassy places in the open or in light woodland, 100–2300m. May–July. BG, *n*&*c*GR, *sw*R, *c*&*s*YU.*

The spathes of *I. reichenbachii* have a sharp keel and in this way it may be distinguished from the other European bearded irises, except for *I. suaveolens* which has a longer flower-tube and dwarfer habit.

13. Iris suaveolens (=*I. mellita, I. rubromarginata*) Similar to *I. reichenbachii* but with stems only 1–5cm (occasionally more) long. Leaves *less than* 1cm wide. Flower-tube usually 3.5–5cm long. Rocky and grassy places, to 1000m. April–May. BG, *se*R, *w*TR, *s*YU.*

Like most of the dwarf bearded irises this occurs in purple and yellow forms. The spathes are keeled as in *I. reichenbachii* but the more dwarf habit and the long slender flower-tube help to distinguish between them. The leaves of *I. suaveolens* sometimes have purple margins and this form has been given the name *I. rubromarginata*. It is not a consistent feature however, and the plants are in all other ways inseparable from *I. suaveolens*.

14. Iris humilis (=*I. arenaria*) [28] Low plant, 5–10cm tall. Rootstock a slender wiry rhizome. *Leaves grassy-looking*, 5–15cm long, 1–7mm wide; stems unbranched. Flowers one or two, yellow with brownish-purple veins on the falls and a yellowish-brown or orange beard; flower-tube 0.5–1cm long. Sandy or stony places, to 500m. A, CS, H, R, RS. 9

A low clump-forming iris which bears little resemblance to any other European species. It is indeed often placed in section *Regelia* rather than with the bearded irises, a section associated with central Asia rather than eastern Europe. The seeds have a fleshy whitish attachment, or aril, which makes it unlike any of the species of the bearded group.

Group B – Beardless Iris

15. Siberian Iris *Iris sibirica* [28] Medium to tall plant to 30–130cm. Rootstock a fairly slender compact rhizome *forming a dense clump*. Leaves up to 90cm long and 1cm or less wide, erect; *flowers one to five*, bluish-violet with distinctly darker veins and often with brownish suffusion towards the base of the tepals; flower-tube 5–7mm long. Damp meadows or in moist lightly wooded places, to 1000m. June–July. A, BG, CH, CS, D, *w*F, H, I, PL, R, *n,c*&*s*RS, YU.*

Iris sibirica is a very well known garden plant for growing around ponds and at the edge of streams, although it also makes a satisfactory herbaceous border plant in rather drier conditions. It is available to gardeners in a great range of shapes and sizes and in colours from white to deep violet or blue. It is frequently crossed with the Oriental Iris, *I. sanguinea (= I. orientalis)*.

16. *Iris tenuifolia   Low plant to 10cm.* Rootstock a compact rhizome, densely tufted and covered in old dead leaf bases. Leaves stiff and greyish green, up to 35cm long, 3–5mm wide. Flowers one or two, bluish-lilac to violet, scented; flower-tube 5–8cm in length. Dry stony and sandy places, 1500–2000m. April–May. *se*RS – but mainly Asiatic.●

A rather distinctive Iris, its wiry leaves and fibrous leaf bases persisting around the base of the stem in a tuft.

17. Algerian Iris *Iris unguicularis (= I. stylosa)* [28]   Low plant to 15cm. Rootstock a rough rhizome with wiry roots, forming dense clumps. Leaves tough, up to 30cm long, 1–5mm wide; *flower stem absent or extremely short.* Flowers solitary, scented, lilac or violet at the tips of the falls and standards, becoming nearly white but heavily veined violet on the haft; falls with an orange band in the centre; flower-tube about 10–20cm long. Stony places in scrub or on ledges, to 1800m. February–May. CR, *s*GR.*

In Europe this plant is rather smaller than its well-known North African form and is often known as *I. cretensis*. It is difficult however to separate the plants from different areas since there are many intermediates.

The Algerian Iris is very popular for its fragrant flowers around Christmas and is widely grown in gardens. It is extremely variable in habit and colouring.

18. *Iris ruthenica   Low to short plant, 15–30cm tall.* Rootstock a compact rhizome. Leaves erect, up to 30cm long and about 5mm wide. *Flowers solitary,* lilac or violet shading to nearly white with violet veins in the centre of the Falls; flower-tube 0.8–1cm long. Light woods and grassy places, 300–1000m. April–May. *c*&*e*R.*

Iris ruthenica is mainly Asiatic in distribution.

19. Roast Beef Plant or **Stinking Iris** *Iris foetidissima* [28]   Medium plant usually 30–50cm tall. Rootstock a tough, compact rhizome. Leaves shiny green, not dying away in winter, 30–60cm long, 1–2.5cm wide, with a rather strong smell when crushed. Flowers one to five, dull purplish, dirty violet tinged with yellow or less frequently wholly yellow; flower-tube 1cm long. Capsule splitting open to reveal rows of large bright orange seeds which persist through the winter. Woods and scrub and hedgerows, especially on alkaline soils, to 500m. May–August. AZ, CO, E, F, GB, I, P, SA, SC – naturalised in some other countries.*

I. ruthenica, p. 160, × ½   *I. foetidissima* fruit capsule, × ¾

This is a popular iris in gardens for the bright fruit capsules, often used for winter decoration. The flowers, however, are very dull compared to most iris species.

20. Yellow Flag *Iris pseudacorus* [28]   Tall plant to 70–180cm. Rootstock a thick rhizome, often covered with the remains of old leaves. Leaves slightly greyish-green, sword-shaped, 50–100cm long, 1–3cm wide, rather tough, with a prominent mid-rib. Flowers stem with a few long branches, flowers usually 5–10, bright yellow with brown markings in the centre of the falls; flower-tube 1–1.5cm long. Standards much smaller than the falls. Near water, especially by rivers, canals or ponds, or in marshy land, to 500m. May–August. T – probably in all countries.＊

This is perhaps the best-known of all European irises, often occurring in great quantity near streams and ponds and damp sea-cliffs. The distribution of the species extends into Asia.

21. Salt Marsh Iris *Iris spuria* [28]   Tall plant, usually (20–) 40–80cm tall. Rootstock a thick brown rhizome covered with old leaf bases. Leaves erect and rather tough, often grey-green, 50–70cm long and usually 0.8–12mm wide. Flower stem with short branches; flowers 2–4, lilac or greyish-blue with darker veins and with a yellow stripe in the centre of the falls; flower-tube 7–15mm long, not to be confused with the apex of the ovary which is also like a tepal-tube but is solid and about 4cm long. Damp places, usually salt-marshes or near the sea, to 300m. April–May. A, CS, D, DK, ?F, GB, H, R, S.●

A common iris distributed from Europe eastwards through Russia and Iran into the western Himalaya and nearly always associated with damp soils rich in salts. It is very variable in stature and colour, many of the variants having been given separate names as species or subspecies. In Britain it is probably naturalised and has been recorded in East Anglia and Wales.

21a. *I.s.* subsp. *maritima*　Like *I. spuria* but is generally more compact with leaves only 5–8mm wide. The spathes enclosing the buds are entirely green when the flowers open, whereas in *I. spuria* they are transparent and papery at the apex. The flowers are creamy coloured with lilac-blue veins and are a little smaller. Similar habitat to *I. spuria*. E, F, P.●

21b. *I.s.* subsp. *ochroleuca* (=*I. ochroleuca*)　Like *I. spuria* but with generally wider leaves and larger flowers which are *creamy-white* with a yellow centre to the falls. The falls turn downwards and often the blade curls under the haft. Similar habitat to *I. spuria*. neGR.*

Subsp. *ochroleuca* is known mainly from Asiatic Turkey.

21c. *I.s.* subsp. *halophila* (=*I. halophila*)　Like *I. spuria* but the flowers are *pale yellow*. Similar habitat to *I. spuria*. sR, swRS.*

This subspecies also occurs in western Asia where it can have lilac or whitish flowers. It differs from subsp. *ochroleuca* in having smaller flowers, not bi-colored white and yellow.

22. *Iris graminea* [28]　Short to medium plant usually 15–35cm tall. Rootstock a thin rhizome, much-branched to form dense clumps. *Leaves deep-green overtopping the flowers*, the branches usually up to 10cm long and 5–15mm wide and the one to three stem leaves narrower. Flowers *strongly scented*, 2 (rarely 1) violet with prominent whitish veining on the falls and usually brownish or yellowish on the haft; flower-tube 2–5mm long and the cylindrical apex of the ovary 5mm long. Grassy places and in light woodland, to 1500m. May–June. A, BG, CH, CS, sD, neE, swF, H, I, PL, R, swRS, YU.*

Unusually vigorous forms of this have been called *I. pseudocyperus* and one such plant is commonly cultivated in Britain. It does not however, have the fruity fragrance of *I. graminea*.

23. *Iris sintenisii* [28]　Similar to *I. graminea* but *usually more slender*. Leaves about 3–6mm wide, *strongly veined*. Flowers unscented, blue-violet, the centre and lower part of the falls whitish with strong violet veins; flower-tube 2–5mm long and the cylindrical apex of the ovary 10–20mm long. Woods, coppices and grassy places, to 1100m. May–June. AL, BG, GR, I, R, TR, YU.*

A slender little iris with very richly coloured flowers with an almost steel-like quality to their appearance.

23a. *I.s.* subsp. *brandzae* (=*I. brandzae*)　Like *I. sintenisii* but has generally narrower leaves with fewer veins. The spathes are said to be rather inflated in appearance. Damp places. neR, swRS.

24. *Iris pontica*　Slightly similar to *I. sintenisii* but with the stem only 1–4cm long. Leaves 10–45cm long, 2–5mm wide. Flowers solitary, very large for the size of the plant, about 7–8cm diameter, purple with white or yellowish markings; flower-tube 8–12mm long and the beak-like apex of the ovary 2–2.5cm long. Grassy places, to 1000m. cR, swRS.●

A compact iris with the flowers usually buried among the leaves. The flowers have a violet and white appearance. Its main distribution is in W. Asia.

Group C – Xiphium Iris

25. English Iris *Iris latifolia* (=*I. xiphioides*) [29]   Tall plant, 40–70cm tall in flower. Rootstock a bulb with non-persistent roots and papery tunics. Leaves produced in spring, silvery on the upper surface, channelled, the lower 30–70cm long and 5–8mm wide; stem leaves becoming gradually smaller towards the apex of the stem. Flowers large, usually two, *bluish-purple with a yellow blotch in the centre of the falls*, occasionally white; flower-tube about 5mm long; falls with a distinct wing about 2.5–3cm wide, on the haft. Dampish meadows, to 2500m. June– July. eE, swF. A common plant of Pyrenean and Cantabrian meadows.*

This is one of the largest-flowered of the bulbous irises in Europe and is easily recognised by the very wide wing on the lower part of the falls. The other large-flowered species in this group, *I. boissieri*, has a beard on the falls and occurs much farther to the west in the Iberian Peninsula. *I. xiphium* has no wing on the haft of the falls. *I. filifolia* has a much longer flower-tube.

I. latifolia is the species from which many large and variously-coloured forms have been raised and they are collectively known as English Irises.

26. Spanish Iris *Iris xiphium* [29]   Rather like *I. latifolia* but with the *leaves only 3–5mm wide*, appearing in the autumn and not silvery on the upper surface. Flowers usually solitary, blue or violet with a deep yellow ridge in the centre of the falls; or wholly yellow, or rarely bi-colored; flower tube only 1–3mm long; falls with a haft only 1cm or less wide. Scrub or grassy places, in sandy or rocky ground, sometimes in dunes, to 1500m. April–May. (–June). cO, E, swF, wI, P, sA.*

The Spanish Irises are very popular garden plants and are also useful for cutting, especially when forced for the winter months. A large number of hybrids have been raised between this species and *I. tingitana*, a N. African species, and possibly also with *I. latifolia*. These hybrids are known as the Dutch Irises and range in colour from white to yellow and bronze or purple with many intermediate colours also. In its wild state *I. xiphium* is normally violet but it does also occur in yellow forms, especially in Portugal where it is sometimes called *I. lusitanica* or *I. xiphium* var. *lusitanica*. *I. xiphium* is easily distinguished from *I. latifolia* by the narrow haft to the falls. *I. xiphium* var. *taitii* is a late-flowering form, often up to two months after the first *I. xiphium* appears, although it is a dune plant of low altitudes.

27. *Iris filifolia* [29]   Like *I. xiphium* but with *thread-like leaves* less than 3mm wide and deep reddish-purple flowers with a bright orange ridge in the centre of the falls; flower-tube about 1–3cm long. Dry, rocky places to 1500m. April–June. *sw*E, GBG – Gibraltar.●

The long tepal tube and very rich purple flowers distinguish this plant from the rest of the species in this group.

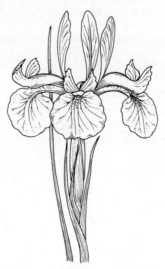

I. juncea flower, × ½

28. *Iris juncea*   Like *I. xiphium* but with leaves only 1–3mm wide and *deep yellow flowers* with faint brown veining near the base of the falls; *flower-tube long,* 3.5–5cm long. Stony places, to 1500m. *se*E, SC.

This resembles the yellow forms of *I. xiphium* but the very long flower-tube makes them easily separated.

29. *Iris boissieri* [29]   Like *I. xiphium* but with *flowers deep purple with a yellowish beard* on the falls; flower-tube 3–5cm long. On rocky acid soils in scrub, 600–900m. June. *nw*E*, *n*P*.●

This is a most interesting species, the only member of the group which possesses a thin beard of yellowish hairs on the falls. It is a very local and rather rare plant in the wild.

30. *Iris serotina* [29]   Similar to *I. xiphium* but with leaves 2–6mm wide, more or less shrivelled and brown at flowering time. Flowers violet-blue; flower-tube 0.5–1cm long; *standards very small and bristle like,* 1cm or less long and 1–2mm wide. In scrub or dry grassy places, about 1200m. August. *se*E.●

I. serotina is the most distinct of all the Spanish bulbous Irises. It flowers much later when the rest are dormant or in seed, and has tiny vestigial standards which are difficult to see at first. The leaves are green in winter and early spring but die away before flowering time leaving only the straw-like flower stem.

Group D - Juno Iris (Scorpiris)

31. *Iris planifolia (=I. alata)* [29]   Low to short plant, 10–15cm tall. Rootstock a bulb with persistent fleshy roots and papery tunics. Leaves all basal, shiny green, *produced in a fan* but channelled, not flat, 10–30cm long, and 1–3cm wide, arching somewhat. Flowers 1–3, stemless, bluish-violet with darker veining, or occasionally white, the ridge in the centre of the falls yellow; *flower-tube very long* usually 8–15cm long; standards much smaller than the falls and held horizontally, about 2–2.5cm long and 1cm wide. Rocky hillsides to 300m. November–February (–March). CR, SE, ?GR, SP, SSA, SC.*

This is not related to the other European bulbous irises but belongs to section Juno, the large number of species of which inhabit western Asia as far as Afghanistan and central Russia. Although the species in the Xiphium group are also bulbous there is no need for confusion since *I. planifolia* is stemless and the flowers have a very long tepal tube, much more than 5cm.

GYNANDRIRIS

An unusual genus in that it has only one representative in the northern hemisphere, all the rest being South African with no connecting links inbetween in tropical Africa. *Gynandriris sisyrinchium* occurs from western Europe eastwards into Russian Central Asia and western Pakistan and is also in N. Africa. It has been known as *Iris sisyrinchium* but is easy to distinguish from irises because it has a roundish corm with a netted coat and there is no flower-tube such as an iris has. It is of no great value as a garden plant since the individual flowers last only a few hours and in cooler northern countries, away from the Mediterranean, it does not flower very well unless grown in a greenhouse or frame.

Barbary Nut *Gynandriris sisyrinchium* [30]   Rootstock a corm covered with fibrous netted coats. Stem 10–60cm in height with a few linear channelled leaves, dark green on the upper side, usually 5–8mm wide and the two lowest often longer than the flower stem. Flowers 2–4cm in diameter, short-lived (less than 1 day each), rarely solitary and usually several in succession from papery bracts; in vigorous specimens there are often up to 4 sets of bracts, each enclosing several flowers; colour normally bluish-lilac, sometimes violet, usually with a yellow patch in the centre of the falls but sometimes with a white patch; falls obovate or elliptic, 2.5–3.5cm long and about 1cm wide; standard slightly shorter and about half as wide; style branches very deeply divided into two pointed lobes. Ovary with a slender solid neck-like part 2–3cm long and this should not be confused with a flower tube (which would be hollow) and which *Gynandriris* does not possess. Sandy or rocky places, to 1000m. April–May. AEG, AL, BAL, CO, CR, E, SF, GR, I, M, P, SA, SC, TR, YU.●

A very common plant around the Mediterranean, often not far from the sea. It is easily overlooked since its flowers are short-lived and usually open only in the afternoon and evening.

HERMODACTYLUS

This is a monotypic genus, the only species having been separated from iris from which it differs in having an ovary with only one chamber inside instead of three. The rootstock consists of finger-like tubers and the leaves are square in cross-section, rather like those of the often-cultivated *Iris reticulata*.

Snake's Head Iris, Widow Iris *Hermodactylus tuberosus* [30]   Leaves 2–4mm wide and up to 50cm long, greyish-green; stem 20–35cm in height with a solitary terminal flower of a greenish or yellowish shade, the falls dark velvety-brown towards the apex; flower-tube about 0.5cm long; falls about 5cm long the blade rounded or oblong; Standards about half as long as the falls and very narrow. Often in heavy red clay between limestone rocks or on sunny banks, at low altitudes. March–May. AEG, AL, CO, CR, SF, GR, I, M, SA, SC, TR, YU.*

   H. tuberosus is often sold in the late winter and early spring as a cut flower, for it lasts well and is beautifully scented. It is successful in gardens if given a warm dry place, especially on alkaline soils.

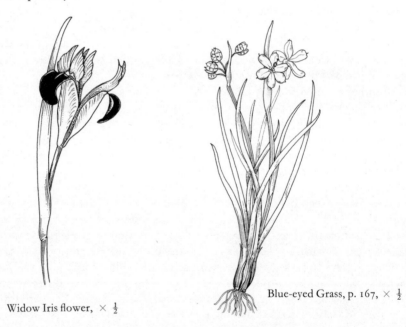

Widow Iris flower, × ½

Blue-eyed Grass, p. 167, × ½

SISYRINCHIUM

A large genus, almost all of the species of which are confined to North and South America. Although not as showy as the majority of members of the Iris family, their small bright starry flowers are often quite attractive and some of the species have considerable merit as garden plants. Only one species is thought to be native in Europe, that is in Ireland, and at least two more are naturalised to some extent.

Rootstock a slender rhizome. Leaves linear and flattish, mostly produced in a basal fan. Stem often flattened with a narrow wing on each side. Flowers small, regular, usually several produced from each set of bracts; tepals six, equal, joined into a short tube; stamens three, the filaments joined into a tube; style branches three. Fruit a 3-valved capsule containing many small rounded seeds.

Blue-eyed Grass *Sisyrinchium bermudianum (= S. angustifolium)* [30]   Short to medium plant, 15–45cm tall. Leaves narrowly linear, up to 20cm long and about 0.2–0.5cm wide. Flowers starry, about 8mm diameter, pale to mid-blue. In damp grass, often near water, to 100m. April–July. *n&wIRL.* *****

Sisyrinchium bermudianum is found mainly in the eastern states of N. America. This is the only species which is considered to be a native plant in Europe. *S. montanum* is similar in appearance but has darker flowers of a deep violet-blue. It is also a native of North America and is naturalised in several European countries. *S. californicum* with yellow flowers, is naturalised in Ireland but is a native of the western United States.

GLADIOLUS

A well known genus in gardens, the large flowered hybrids being very popular as bedding plants and for cut flowers. They are mainly hybrids between several of the South African species, the first crosses having been made in the mid nineteenth century. Nowadays there are a great many available in colour combinations not found in any wild species. In tropical and South Africa there are well over 100 species, but the genus also has representatives in Europe and western Asia. These are on the whole smaller and less showy than their African relatives and are very little grown in gardens, except for *G. byzantinus*. They are of course much hardier and can be grown out of doors in many European countries without lifting the corms for the winter, as is the case with the tender hybrids.

In Europe there are only seven species, although it is not easy to distinguish between them.

The rootstock of the *Gladiolus* is a corm covered with papery or rather fibrous coats. Leaves 3–5 usually, becoming narrower up the stem towards the flowers. Flowers usually 1–20 in a loose or dense spike which is either one-sided with the flower facing all in one direction (secund) or two-sided with alternate flowers facing in opposite directions (distichous); the flowers are held more or less horizontally and are very irregular in shape, with six tepals joined at the base together into a curved tube; stamens curved upwards and situated just below the upper tepal; stigma 3-lobed at the apex.

1. Flowers very deep dull violet (Greece and
      Turkey)   7. *G. atroviolaceus*
   Flowers pink to reddish or violet-purple   **2**

2. Spike markedly 1-sided   **3**
   Spike more or less 2-sided   **4**

3. Spike with 4–12 flowers; lowest leaf 1–1.5cm wide   6. *G. imbricatus*
   Spike with 1–6 flowers; lowest leaf up to 1cm wide   5. *G. palustris*

4. Plant usually less than 50cm tall with 3–10 flowers   3. *G. illyricus*
   Plant usually more than 50cm tall and usually with
      10 or more flowers   **5**

5. Anthers longer than filaments   1. *G. italicus*
   Anthers shorter than filaments, or equal   **6**

6. Flowers deep red-purple   2. *G. byzantinus*
   Flowers pink   4. *G. communis*

The leaf measurements given refer to the lowermost leaf.

1. Field Gladiolus *Gladiolus italicus (=G. segetum)* [30]   Plant 40–110cm in
height with 3–5 leaves, each usually 20–50cm long and about 0.5–1.7cm wide,
becoming narrower up the stem. Flowers (5–) 10–15 in a very loose, *more or less
2-sided spike* which is unbranched; tepals pinkish-purple to reddish, the lower
three with very narrow pinkish spear-shaped marks, outlined with purple;
flower-tube slightly curved; stamens with *anthers longer than filaments*. Seeds not
winged. Grassy places and in cultivated land, especially cornfields, to 1800m.
April–July. AL, AZ, BAL, BG, CH, CO, CR, E, F, GR, I, K, P, *w*&*e*RS, SA, SC, TR, YU.●
   A very common gladiolus in dryish Mediterranean cornfields often so plentiful
as to colour them pink. The flowers have narrow tepals which spread out a little
and do not overlap, thus giving a flower of rather poor substance.

2. Byzantine Gladiolus *Gladiolus byzantinus* [30]   Plant 50–100cm in height
with 4–5 leaves, each usually 30–70cm long and about 1–2.5cm wide. Flowers
10–20 in a moderately dense more or less 2-sided spike which often has one or
two branches; *tepals deep reddish-purple*, the lower three with narrow spear-shaped
marks outlined with deep purple; flower-tube only slightly curved; stamens with
anthers equal in length or shorter than the filament. Seeds winged. In scrub, to
500m. March–June. *s*E, SC.*
   This species is often cultivated and sometimes becomes naturalised. It is the
largest-flowered of the European gladiolus with broad tepals which meet or
overlap, giving a flower of substantial appearance.

3. *Gladiolus illyricus* [30]   Plant 25–50cm in height with 4–5 leaves, usually
10–40cm long and about 0.5–1cm wide. *Flowers 3–10* normally in an unbranched
(occasionally one branch) loose, more or less 2-sided spike; tepals reddish-

purple, the lower three with white spear-shaped marks and the central tepal of these three with a much narrower mark than the other two; flower-tube slightly curved; stamens with anthers equal to, or shorter than, the filaments. Seeds winged. Grassy or heathy places, sometimes in bracken, scrub or light woodland, to 500m. April–July. BAL, E, F, ʃGB*, I, P, SA, SC, YU.●

A slender species often with only a few flowers in the spike. It is extremely rare in Britain, where it probably only occurs in the New Forest.

4. *Gladiolus communis* Plant 50–100cm in height with 4–5 leaves, usually 30–50cm long and about 0.5–1.5cm wide. Flowers 10–20 in a loose, more or less 2-sided spike which *usually has two or three branches; tepals pinkish*, the lower ones often with red or white blotches or lines; flower-tube slightly curved; stamens with anthers equal in length or shorter than the filaments. Seeds winged. Dry grassy places or in scrub, to 500m. April–June. CO, E, F, GR, I, SC, YU.●

This is very similar to *G. byzantinus* but has on the whole narrower leaves and paler pinkish flowers in looser, often more branched, spikes.

5. *Gladiolus palustris* Plant 25–50cm in height with 2–3 leaves, 10–40cm long and about 0.5–1cm wide. Flowers 1–6 in a *loose 1-sided spike* which is unbranched; *tepals reddish-purple*; flower-tube slightly curved; stamens with anthers equal to, or shorter than, the filaments. Seeds winged. Damp meadows and in scrub, to 1000m. April–July. A, AL, CH, CS, D, F.●

Like the next two species, this has a 1-sided spike, but it is easily distinguished by the few red-purple flowers, rather loosely arranged.

6. *Gladiolus imbricatus* [30] Plant 30–80cm in height with usually 3 leaves, 15–35cm long and about 1–1.5cm wide, becoming narrower up the stem. Flowers 4–12 in *a dense 1-sided spike* which is unbranched or sometimes with 1–3 branches; tepals pale carmine to reddish-violet or reddish-purple, the lower three with white spear-shaped marks outlined in deep purple; flower-tube strongly curved near its apex; stamens with anthers equal to, or shorter than, the filaments. Seeds winged. Dampish meadows and in scrub, to 1000m, April–July BG, CS, D, F, GR, H, PL, R, *w,c&e*RS, YU.●

The dense 1-sided spike of reddish-purple flowers make this relatively easy to recognise. The tepals are broad and overlapping but the tips flare outwards to give a wide open flower.

7. *Gladiolus atroviolaceus* Plant 35–70cm in height with 3 leaves, 30–40cm long and only 4–8mm wide with strong parallel veins. Flowers 4–10 in a rather dense 1-sided unbranched spike; *tepals dark violet, often appearing blackish*; flower-tube distinctly curved; stamens with anthers longer than the filaments. Seeds not winged. Cultivated places, often cornfields or on grassy slopes, to 2000m. April–July. GR, TR.●

A striking plant with its very dark flowers, often very common in dryish fields. The distribution extends eastwards into Turkey, Iraq and Iran.

ROMULEA

Small plants with rather lop-sided corms and usually two roughly cylindrical basal leaves which have four grooves running along their length. In addition there are several stem leaves which often appear to be basal in the very dwarf specimens such as might be found in stony places. The flowers are crocus-like in shape but mostly smaller and have only a short flower-tube, the flower being carried on a green stem, although this is often very short and the flower appears to be produced almost at ground level; in crocus there is a long white or coloured flower tube which starts below ground, the stem being practically non-existent. Moreover, the leaves of a crocus are usually wider than those of romulea and have a whitish stripe along the centre. The flowers of romulea are produced singly from a bract and bracteole (sometimes these are called spathes) which can be green or papery. When identifying a romulea it is important to make a careful note of these. There are three stamens and the style is divided into six branches. In seed, romuleas are usually rather distinctive, as the flower stems curve over so that the capsule nearly touches the ground.

In Europe, N. Africa and western Asia there are probably not more than 20 species, although large numbers of names exist for the many minor variations of the species. A few species occur on the mountains of tropical Africa, while in South Africa there are about 70 species, many with large and beautifully coloured flowers.

European romuleas are all low-altitude plants, often occurring at sea level, on low hills, or on the lower slopes of coastal mountain ranges.

1. *Romulea bulbocodium* [30]   Flowers usually 2–3.5cm long with pointed tepals, varying from white to lilac, usually with a yellow throat and often with a greenish exterior, or striped violet outside; flower-tube 4–8mm long. Bract 1–2cm long, green with a brownish papery margin; *bracteole papery, brownish or reddish*. Rocky and grassy places. February–May. AEG, AL, BG, CR, E, F, GR, I, P, SA, SC, TR, YU.*

This is a common species in most of the Mediterranean area and is the one most often cultivated by bulb enthusiasts. It is extremely variable but can usually be recognised by the stigma being much longer than the anthers and the bracteole almost wholly papery, not green.

R. columnae has smaller flowers with a stigma shorter than the stamens. There are many named varieties but these are of little importance in such a variable species. Some of the most notable are:

1a. *R.b.* var. *clusiana*   This has large flowers 3–3.5cm long, rather colourful in being lilac with a large deep yellow centre. E, P.

1b. *R.b.* var. *leichtliniana*   The flowers are usually *white with a yellow throat* and with brownish or purplish veins on the outside. GR – Crete, Cyclades, Corfu.

1c. R.*b.* var. *subpalustris*   This has lilac flowers with *no yellow in the throat*. GR –
Cyclades.

2. Sand Crocus *Romulea columnae* [30]   *Flowers small*, 1–2cm long, with pointed
tepals, very pale lilac or purplish with darker veins and sometimes greenish on
the outside, with a yellow throat, occasionally the throat is very pale, nearly
white; flower-tube 2–5mm long. Bract 0.5–1.2cm long, green with a papery
rusty or purplish spotted margin; bracteole papery, rusty-spotted. In grassy
places, mainly near the sea. February–April. AZ, BAL, CO, CR, E, F, GB, GR, I, P, SA,
SC, TR.
  The very papery bracteole, yellowish throat and pale, dark-veined, flowers
distinguish this species. It usually has much smaller flowers than R. *bulbocodium*
with the stigma normally not reaching the tips of the anthers.

3. *Romulea rollii*   Very similar to R. *columnae* and may only be recognised by its
very long thread-like leaves, up to 30cm long and 0.5mm wide, or less. Sandy places
by the sea. February–March. CO, F, GR, I, SA, YU.

4. *Romulea ramiflora* [30]   Flowers 1–2cm long with pointed tepals, pale to deep
bluish-purple, sometimes with darker veins and sometimes greenish outside, the
throat with or without yellow colouration; flower-tube 2–6mm long. Bract
1–2cm long, green with a papery margin and prominent veins; *bracteole green*,
sometimes rust-spotted on the margin. Bare or grassy places usually near the sea.
February–March. BAL, CO, E, F, GR – Cyclades, I, SA, SC.
  Although rather similar to R. *columnae* in its flower size and colouring, this
species usually has much longer flower stems, up to 10cm long and becoming
longer in fruiting stage. The green bracteole is distinct from the almost entirely
papery one of R. *columnae*.

5. *Romulea gaditanus*   Like (**4**) but *with larger flowers*, 2–3cm long, pinkish-lilac
and often green on the exterior; the *stigma overtopping the anthers* slightly, whereas
in R. *ramiflora* it is just below the top of the anthers. Often in sandy places near
the sea. February–March. *w*&*s*E&P.●

6. *Romulea linaresii*   Flowers 2–2.5cm long with rounded tepals, *rich violet with
no yellow in the throat*; flower-tube 5–7mm long. Bract 1.2–2.2cm long, green with
a papery reddish-tinted margin; bracteole papery, rust-speckled, often with a
green line along the centre. In sandy places not far from the sea. February–
March. SC.●

6a. R.*l.* subsp. *graeca*   Like (**6**) but with *flowers smaller*, less than 2cm long, with
pointed tepals; bract up to 1.5cm long. Grassy and stony places. CR, GR, TR.

R. *linaresii* and its subsp. *graeca* can be recognised by their deep coloured flowers
with the throat the same colour or even darker. Most other romuleas have a
yellow or paler throat.

R. *linaresii*, × ½

R. *ligustica*, × ½

7. *Romulea melitensis*   Like (**6**) but flowers deep violet *with a yellow throat*. Moist sandy places near the sea. February–March. M – & Gozo.

8. *Romulea revelierei*   Flowers 1–1.5cm long with rounded to rather pointed tepals, purple-blue with darker veins and without *yellow in the throat*; flower-tube 3–5mm long. Bract 0.8–1.4cm long, green with a papery margin; bracteole papery with rust-coloured flecking and a green central band. Moist places near the sea. February–March. CO, I, Capri.
   This is rather similar to (**6**) but has the throat paler than the rest of the flower.

9. *Romulea ligustica*   Flowers 2–3.5cm long with rounded or rather pointed tepals, pale to very deep lilac with yellow in the throat; flower-tube 5–7mm long. Bract 1–2cm long; green with a papery rusty-speckled margin; bracteole papery and finely speckled with reddish-brown. Grassy or stony places near the sea. February–March. CO, *nw*I, SA.●
   R. *ligustica* differs from other species in that the stamens do not reach half way up the tepals.

10. *Romulea requienii*   Flowers 1.8–2.5cm long with rounded tepals, *dark violet* without yellow in the throat; flower-tube 5–9mm long. Bract 1–1.2cm long, green with a papery margin which is speckled or tinged with violet or brown; bracteole papery, reddish-brown speckled. Sandy places by the sea. February–March. CO, *sc*I, SA.●

A beautiful species which, with its deep purplish-blue flowers and rounded tepals looks more like a crocus than a romulea. The stigma projects well beyond the tips of the stamens which, combined with the dark flower colour and rounded tepals, makes it a distinctive plant.

CROCUS

A very popular genus among gardeners for the showy late autumn or early spring flowers which open like goblets in the sun. There is confusion over the name 'Autumn Crocus' for this is more commonly applied to *Colchicum autumnale*, a member of the Lily family. There are, however, true autumn-flowering Crocus as well and one of these, *C. sativus*, yields the dye and flavouring agent Saffron. The position is further complicated because another name for the Colchicum is 'Meadow Saffron'. Colchicum, however, is poisonous and should on no account be confused with Crocus.

Crocus often occur in very large numbers in the wild and they are among the very first flowers to appear near the melting snows in spring. Very few hybrids are known, although two or more species quite often occur together. Most of the crocuses which are cultivated are true wild species, or selections of them, perhaps for larger flowers or brighter colours. *C. vernus* is available in a wide range of cultivars, commonly known as the 'large Dutch' crocuses, but there is little doubt that they are derived from the common white and purple spring crocus of the central European mountains, here treated as *C. vernus* subsp. *vernus* and *C. vernus* subsp. *albiflorus*. The large 'Dutch Yellow' spring crocus is *C. flavus*, although in a rather more vigorous form than its wild predecessor, and it may be of hybrid origin. On the other hand the colourful range of plants well known as '*C. chrysanthus* cultivars' are either true *C. chrysanthus* (yellow) or *C. biflorus* (blue or white), or hybrids between them, which gives rise to a wide range of curiously striped and suffused colour forms which are used a great deal for an early rock garden display, or for growing in pots indoors. The majority of wild crocus species are not well known in gardens and may not be very easy to obtain, although they are mostly not difficult to cultivate or propagate.

C. sativus is one of the oldest of the crocuses in cultivation for it has been used for many centuries as a source of saffron. The useful part of the plant is the scarlet stigma which is plucked from the flower and dried for storage. The bright

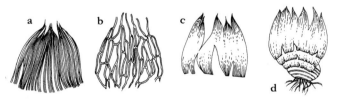

Types of Crocus corm tunics: **a**, parallel fibres; **b**, netted fibres; **c**, shell-like; **d**, annulate

yellow dye can be extracted in water and the resulting solution used for flavouring foods or dyeing textiles. It was formerly cultivated on a commercial scale in many European and Asian countries and even as far north as Britain in the Middle Ages, as at Saffron Walden, but nowadays it is rarely grown except for garden ornament. Since *C. sativus* is not a wild species but a sterile hybrid or form, it does not persist for very long in areas where it has been cultivated.

Crocus is a genus of about 100 species altogether, with 42 in Europe. Although many of them look similar, there are subtle and significant differences between them which will be appreciated only after a certain amount of familiarity with them. Unfortunately, some of the most important characters used in distinguishing between the species are rather difficult to observe – for example the type of coat or tunic enclosing the corm and the number of spathes, which are usually hidden from view. As far as possible the following guide-key and descriptions have been designed to avoid these, for it is not the author's wish to encourage the digging-up of crocuses to check the corm tunics or to dissect the plants in search of spathes. When identifying a species it is necessary therefore to pay attention to the locality in which it occurs, for this is often a useful short-cut.

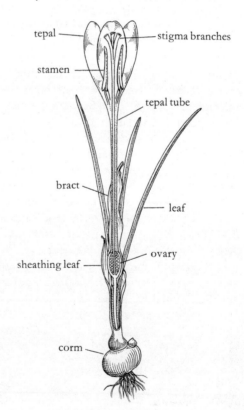

tepal — stigma branches

stamen

tepal tube

bract

leaf

ovary

sheathing leaf

corm

Cross-section of a typical Crocus to illustrate the botanical details

Low perennials, rarely more than 10cm tall with underground corms, usually solitary, leaves basal, grass-like, T-shaped in cross-section (except in *C. carpetanus*) and nearly always with a distinct whitish line along the centre of the upper surface. Flowers goblet-shaped, solitary or up to four, usually produced in succession, the stem very short and not visible above ground but elongating in the fruiting stage to push the seed capsule above the surface; tepals 6, obovate or oblanceolate, usually all alike but occasionally the inner 3 smaller than the outer, all united at the base into a long tepal or flower-tube; stamens 3, joined to the base of the tepals in the 'throat' of the flower. Style 3-branched to many-branched. Fruit a capsule splitting into 3 valves.

In the following key only the 'normal' forms of each species have been taken into account. Obviously it is always possible to find abnormal ones, such as albinos, which do not key out satisfactorily. Therefore when identifying a crocus growing wild, choose an average sized specimen with colouring which is typical of the majority of individuals. There is, however, allowance in the key for a certain amount of variation.

Key to Groups

1. Flowers in spring (January–July)   **2**
Flowers in autumn (September–January)   **6**

2. Flowers wholly yellow inside   *See key to Group A*
Flowers not wholly yellow inside   **3**

3. Flowers white inside, with or without a yellow
throat   **4**
Flowers lilac, blue or purple inside, with or without
a yellow throat   **5**

4. Throat yellow   *See key to Group B*
Throat not yellow   *See key to Group C*

5. Throat yellow   *See key to Group D*
Throat not yellow   *See key to Group E*

6. Stamens white or creamy   *See key to Group F*
Stamens yellow or blackish   **7**

7. Throat yellow   *See key to Group G*
Throat not yellow   *See key to Group H*

Key to Group A

1. Style with about 6 slender branches   32. *C. olivieri*
Style with 3 branches, or expanded and frilled at
apex   **2**

2. Flowers striped or stained bronze or purplish
outside. (Russia)   37. *C. angustifolius*
Flowers unstriped on the exterior   **3**

3. Tepals purple in the lower third   33. *C. scardicus*
   Tepals wholly yellow, sometimes purplish on the
   tube   4

4. Plant of alpine turf above 1800m; corm tunic finely
   netted   34. *C. cvijicii*
   Plant of woodland, scrub or open stony places,
   usually below 1800m; tunic papery or with
   parallel fibres   5

5. Leaves usually 5–8; corm with a long brown neck   31. *C. flavus*
   Leaves usually 3–4; corm with no long neck and
   with rings at the base   36. *C. chrysanthus*

Key to Group B

1. Stamens creamy white   9. *C. laevigatus*
   Stamens yellow   2

2. Stigma whitish or cream (Spain, Portugal)   3
   Stigma yellow or orange (France and eastwards)   4

3. Leaves rounded beneath, with a wide silver stripe
   above   28. *C. carpetanus*
   Leaves 2-grooved beneath, with a narrow white
   stripe above   29. *C. nevadensis*

4. Tepals plain white on outside but tube sometimes
   coloured   42. *C. malyi*
   Tepals stained or striped with purple or brown on
   outside   5

5. Throat very pale yellow   6
   Throat deep yellow   7

6. Leaves 2–3mm wide; corm tunic of parallel fibres   24. *C. versicolor*
   Leaves 0.5–1.5mm wide; corm tunic coarsely
   netted   30. *C. reticulatus*

7. Flowers stained or banded with purple outside
   (Crete, Yugoslavia)   8
   Flowers usually striped outside (Italy, Sicily,
   Turkey)   35. *C. biflorus*

8. Flowers heavily stained purple outside
   (S. Yugoslavia)   35c. *C. alexandri*
   Flowers banded, tipped or lightly stained purple
   (Crete)   25. *C. sieberi*

Key to Group C

1. Stigma whitish or pale cream (Spain, Portugal)   2
   Stigma yellow or orange   3

2. Leaves rounded below, with a wide silver stripe
   above   28. *C. carpetanus*
   Leaves 2-grooved beneath, with a narrow stripe
   above   29. *C. nevadensis*

3. Leaves usually 4–8mm wide. Woods or alpine
   meadows to 3000m   38. *C. vernus*
   Leaves usually 0.5–2.5mm wide. Open stony or
   grassy places to 1000m   4

4. Tepals less than 1.8cm long (Majorca)   20. *C. cambessedesii*
   Tepals more than 2cm long (N. Italy and
   eastwards)   5

5. Flowers white outside, sometimes blue on the tube   35b. *C. weldenii*
   Flowers usually striped outside   30. *C. reticulatus*

Key to Group D

1. Stigma whitish or pale cream (Spain, Portugal)   2
   Stigma yellow or orange   3

2. Leaves rounded below, with a wide silver stripe
   above   28. *C. carpetanus*
   Leaves 2-grooved beneath, with a narrow stripe
   above   29. *C. nevadensis*

3. Throat of flower pale yellow   4
   Throat of flower deep yellow   7

4. Tepals usually striped or veined on the outside   5
   Tepals unmarked on the outside (S. Yugoslavia)   41. *C. kosaninii*

5. Tepals usually less than 3cm long; leaves
   0.5–1.5mm wide (N.E. Italy and eastwards)   30. *C. reticulatus*
   Tepals usually more than 3cm long; leaves
   2–5mm wide   6

6. Leaves grey-green; corm tunic of parallel fibres
   (S. France, N.W. Italy)   24. *C. versicolor*
   Leaves green; corm tunic of netted fibres
   (W.C. Italy)   40. *C. etruscus*

7. Stamens white or cream   9. *C. laevigatus*
   Stamens yellow   8

8. Flower rich purple inside, buff or yellowish striped
    outside (Italy)   23. *C. imperati*
    Flower lilac-blue (Yugoslavia, Greece)   9

9. Tepals usually fawn or yellowish outside and
    slightly striped purple (W. Yugoslavia)   26. *C. dalmaticus*
    Tepals usually unmarked outside (S. Yugoslavia,
    Greece)   25. *C. sieberi*

Key to Group E

1. Flowers prominently striped or stained on the
    outside   2
    Flowers more or less uniform in colour   7

2. Tepals usually less than 1.8cm long (Majorca)   20. *C. cambessedesii*
    Tepals usually more than 2cm long   3

3. Leaves 0.5–1.5mm wide   4
    Leaves 2–8mm wide   6

4. Tepals usually blunt (Corsica, Sardinia)   5
    Tepals usually pointed (N.E. Italy and eastwards)   30. *C. reticulatus*

5. Stigma pale to deep yellow; corm tunic of parallel
    fibres   22. *C. minimus*
    Stigma deep orange or reddish; corm tunic netted
    at apex   21. *C. corsicus*

6. Leaves grey-green, 2–3mm wide (S.E. France and
    N.W. Italy)   24. *C. versicolor*
    Leaves deep green, 4–8mm wide   38. *C. vernus*

7. Stigma whitish; leaves with no white stripe
    (Macedonia)   33a. *C. pelistericus*
    Stigma usually yellow or orange; leaves with a
    white stripe   8

8. Spathe 1 (to be seen clasping the tepal tube)   9
    Spathes 2, about equal in length   27. *C. veluchensis*

9. Flowers with a coloured tube   38. *C. vernus*
    Flowers with a white tube   39. *C. tommasinianus*

Key to Group F

1. Flowers usually white without very prominent
    striping   8. *C. boryi*
    Flowers usually lilac, sometimes white with
    prominent striping   2

2. Flowers usually striped or stained on the outside   9. *C. laevigatus*
   Flowers usually not striped, stained or veined on
   the outside   **3**

3. Leaves produced at flowering time (Greek Is.)   7. *C. tournefortii*
   Leaves produced long after flowers   13. *C. pulchellus*

Key to Group G

1. Stamens blackish (before bursting – pollen is
   yellow)   35a. *C. melantherus*
   Stamens yellow   **2**

2. Style with many slender branches   **3**
   Style 3-branched or expanded and frilly at apex   **4**

3. Leaves usually appearing before or immediately
   after the flowers (Spain, Portugal)   16. *C. serotinus*
   Leaves appearing long after the flowers
   (Yugoslavia, Greece)   18. *C. cancellatus*

4. Flowers usually white, or at most very pale lilac   **5**
   Flowers mid-lilac to purple   **6**

5. Style deeply divided into 3 simple branches
   (W. & S. Greece)   6. *C. hadriaticus*
   Style branches 3 or more, subdivided into several
   shorter branches (S. Peloponnese)   11. *C. niveus*

6. Leaves appearing with the flowers; corm tunic
   finely netted   **7**
   Leaves appearing long after the flowers; corm
   tunic coarsely netted   19. *C. robertianus*

7. Throat pale yellow; spathe silvery-white   5. *C. thomasii*
   Throat deep yellow; spathe green tinged   1. *C. longiflorus*

Key to Group H

1. Style with more than 6 branches   **2**
   Style 3-branched or expanded and frilly at apex   **7**

2. Style branches lilac; inner tepals less than
   two-thirds size of outer (Roumania)   14. *C. banaticus*
   Style branches yellow or orange; all tepals more
   or less equal   **3**

3. Leaves appearing with flowers (W.,C.& S. Spain,
   Portugal)   16. *C. serotinus*
   Leaves appearing long after the flowers
   (N.E. Spain and eastwards)   **4**

4. Plant producing stolons; flowers purple (Spain,
   Pyrenees)   15. *C. nudiflorus*
   Plant with no stolons; flowers lilac-blue, purple
   or white   5

5. Corm tunic non-fibrous, with rings at its base;
   flowers often speckled outside with grey-purple
   (Crimea, Bulgaria)   12. *C. speciosus*
   Corm tunic netted-fibrous; flowers veined darker
   but not speckled   6

6. Flowers white, lilac or blue   18. *C. cancellatus*
   Flowers usually deep lilac or purple (N.W. Italy,
   S.E. France)   17. *C. medius*

7. Tepals usually less than 1.8cm long, striped on
   outside (Majorca)   20. *C. cambessedesii*
   Tepals usually more than 2cm long, often veined
   but not striped on exterior   8

8. Style deeply divided into 3 long red branches   9
   Style yellow or orange, expanded and frilled at
   apex, or only shortly divided   11

9. Style branches more than half as long as tepals   2. *C. cartwrightianus*
   Style branches less than half as long as tepals   10

10. Flowers usually plain white (C.&S. Greece)   6. *C. hadriaticus*
    Flowers lilac (N. Greece, Bulgaria, Roumania,
    Crimea, Turkey)   4. *C. pallasii*

11. Leaves appearing with the flowers; tunic
    non-fibrous (S. Peloponnese)   10. *C. goulimyi*
    Leaves appearing long after the flowers; tunic
    netted-fibrous (N. Greece, Pindus)   19. *C. robertianus*

1. *Crocus longiflorus* [31]   Leaves usually 3–4 from each corm, normally show-ing at flowering time but often very short, 1–3mm wide. *Flowers lilac to purple, often veined darker externally*, throat deep yellow, the tepals 2.2–4.3cm long, 0.7–1.6cm wide, blunt or rather pointed; stamens with yellow anthers and yellow filaments; *stigma divided into 3 orange-red* or rarely yellow branches, each of which may be expanded or shortly-lobed at the apex. Grassland and wood margins, 200–1900m. October–November. swi, sc, m.*

    The Maltese form, which has been given the name var. *melitensis*, is particu-larly colourful and probably the best form for cultivation. The outside of the tepals is often a pale almost biscuit colour with vertical strong purple veins. *C. longiflorus* is a beautiful autumnal species with a very sweet scent.

2. *Crocus cartwrightianus* [31]   *Leaves 5–11* from each corm, usually showing at flowering time, 1–2mm wide. Flowers lilac-purple, strongly veined darker, or pure white, or white with purple veins shading to purple at the base of the tepals outside, throat white or lilac, the tepals 1.5–3.2cm long, 0.7–1.3cm wide, rounded to blunt; stamens with yellow anthers and white or purplish filaments; *stigma divided into 3 very long deep red branches*, each branch 1.5–2.7cm long. Stony places to 1000m. October–December. CR, *c*&*s*GR – Attica, Cyclades.●

The Saffron Crocus, *C. sativus*, is not known as a wild plant but may be found as a relic of cultivation especially in Mediterranean regions where it has been grown for centuries to provide Saffron, the dye and colouring agent produced from the red stigma. It is a sterile plant and can only increase by division of the corms. In appearance it is like a large *C. cartwrightianus* with stigma branches 2.5–3.2cm long, which are too heavy to support themselves and thus flop sideways out of the flower.

3. *Crocus oreocreticus*   Like (**2**) but usually smaller and silvery or whitish on the exterior of the lilac tepals. The branches of the stigma are shorter than those of most *C. cartwwrightianus*. Rocky places, 1000–2200m. October–December. CR.●

A plant not differing greatly from the previous species, *C. cartwrightianus*, however, it always occurs at higher altitudes.

4. *Crocus pallasii*   Like (**2**) but flowers lilac, only slightly veined darker and with stigma branches 0.6–1.5cm long. Stony or grassy places, up to 1000m. October–December. *s*&*c*BG, K, *c*R, TR.●

This is easily confused with *C. cartwrightianus* but has a more northern distribution. The flowers are less heavily veined, rarely white, and the branches of the style are distinctly shorter.

5. *Crocus thomasii* [31]   Like (**2**) but flowers lilac, rarely white, and not or only slightly darker veined, the *throat pale yellow* and the tepals usually rather pointed; stamens with pale yellow filaments; stigma branches 1–1.6 (rarely to 2) cm long. Stony hills, up to 1000m. October–December. *s*I, *w*YU – Adriatic coastal mountains.●

This is easily distinguished from (**2**), (**3**) and (**4**) by its yellow throat. It may however, be confused with *C. longiflorus* which does have a yellow throat, but in *C. thomasii* the colour is very pale yellow while in the former it is deep yellow. The number of leaves per corm is an additional aid to identification. Both occur in southern Italy but otherwise have separate distributions.

6. *Crocus hadriaticus* [31]   Like (**2**) in leaf characters. *Flowers white*, very rarely flushed with pale lilac, sometimes brownish or purplish on the tube, throat *usually yellow* (on Mt Parnassus a wholly white form occurs), the tepals 2–4.5cm long, 0.7–1.8cm wide, blunt to rather pointed; stamens with yellow anthers and yellow or white filaments; stigma divided into 3 red or orange branches 1–1.6cm long. Fields and scrubland, 300–1500m. October–December. s&wGR – Corfu south to Peloponnese.●

Although this is easily recognised by its yellow throat from (2), the pure white form from Parnassus might be confused with the pure white forms of (2). The length of the stigma branches should help to distinguish them. It might also be confused with *C. boryi* which is also white with a yellow throat and which grows in the Peloponnese. This species, however, has white anthers and many more than 3 stigma branches. *C. niveus* from the southern Peloponnese has its 3 style branches expanded and lobed at the apex.

7. *Crocus tournefortii* [31]   Leaves 3–8 from each corm, present at flowering time, 1–3mm wide. Flowers usually unscented, *lilac, occasionally veined darker* outside, *throat yellow*, the tepals 1.5–3.5cm long, 0.4–1.3cm wide; blunt; *stamens with white anthers* and yellow densely hairy filaments; stigma divided into very many slender deep orange or yellow branches. Scrub and stony places, to 650m. September– December. CR, GR – Crete, Cyclades and Rhodes.●

A beautiful plant, unlike any other species in that the flowers do not close up at night or in dull weather.

8. *Crocus boryi* (=*C. cretensis*) [31]   Like (**7**) but *flowers normally white*, sometimes veined purple and rarely stained pale purple, throat deep yellow, the tepals 1.5–5cm long, 0.4–2.3cm wide, rounded to blunt; *stamens with white anthers* and sparsely hairy filaments. Olive groves, open stony hills and scrub, to 1500m. September– December. c&sGR, CR.●

The other similar white autumnal crocus in this area is *C. hadriaticus*, but this has yellow anthers and 3 stigma branches.

9. *Crocus laevigatus* [31]   Like (**7**) but flowers closing in dull light, sweetly scented and much more 'starry' in appearance when the flowers open out flat. Flowers *white or lilac usually strongly veined or stained purple on the outside*, the tepals 1.3–3cm long, 0.4–1.8cm wide, pointed to blunt; *stamens with white* anthers and filaments hairless or with hairs right at the base. Open stony places and in light scrub, to 1500m. October–December (less frequently to January). c&sGR, CR.*

The plants from Crete have often incorrectly been referred to as '*C. cretensis*'. They are often slightly smaller than the forms of *C. laevigatus* found in the rest of Greece. True *C. cretensis* is a synonym of *C. boryi*.

10. *Crocus goulimyi* [31]   Leaves 4–6 from each corm, showing at flowering time, 1–2.5cm wide. *Flowers lilac, often with the inner tepals paler and slightly smaller than the three outer*, throat white, the tepals 1.6–3.8cm long, 1–1.8cm wide, rounded to blunt; stamens with yellow anthers and white filaments; stigma white to yellow, divided into 3 branches which are each expanded and sometimes rather frilled at the apex. Olive groves and base of dry stone walls, 300–400m. October–November. sGR – only in the extreme south of Peloponnese.*

It is unlikely that this graceful species would be confused with any other, for its long slender flower-tube and smallish globular flower with unequal or slightly different coloured inner and outer tepals make it very distinctive.

11. *Crocus niveus* [31]   Leaves 5–8 from each corm, showing at flowering time but often rather short, 1–2mm wide. *Flowers white* or more uncommonly very pale lilac, *throat deep yellow*, the tepals 3–6cm long, 1.5–3.5cm wide, rounded to blunt; stamens with yellow anthers and yellow filaments; stigma divided into *3 orange to red branches*, each of which is often expanded and lobed at the apex. Olive groves and scrub hillsides, 50–400m. October–November. sGR – only in the extreme south of Peloponnese.*

Although occurring together with *C. goulimyi* and occasionally producing lilac forms there is no need for confusion since *C. niveus* is easily recognised by its yellow throat. Other white autumn crocuses in the area are *C. boryi* which has white anthers and *C. hadriaticus* which has its 3 style branches slender at the apex, not expanded as in *C. niveus*.

12. *Crocus speciosus* [32]   Leaves 3–4, absent at flowering time, appearing in late winter or early spring, about 5mm wide. *Flowers lilac-blue with very distinct darker veins*, often rather silvery on the exterior and sometimes speckled with grey, *throat white or faintly yellow*, the tepals 0.7–6cm long, 1.1–1.7cm wide, slightly pointed to rather blunt; stamens with *yellow* anthers and white or lilac, hairless or minutely hairy filaments; stigma with many yellow to deep orange thread-like branches. Woods and meadows. October–November. scBG, K.*

This is often confused with *C. pulchellus* and consequently there are dubious records of *C. speciosus* occurring in Macedonia and European Turkey. However, there is no real evidence that it occurs anywhere else in Europe other than the places stated.

C. speciosus is one of the easiest of all the autumn flowering crocus to grow and it seeds freely. Thus it is cheap to buy and can be used for naturalising in grass or under shrubs.

13. *Crocus pulchellus* [32]   Similar to (**12**) but differs in not having the flowers speckled on the outside, and in having a *deep yellow throat*, blunt to rounded tepals and densely hairy yellow filaments to the *white anthers*. Light woodland. September–October. BG, GR, TR, YU.*

Also a useful autumn-flowering species which is cheap to buy and easily grown. The deep yellow throat makes it a most attractive crocus when the flowers open fully on a sunny day.

14. *Crocus banaticus* (=*C. iridiflorus*) [32]   Leaves 1–3, absent at flowering time, appearing in late winter or early spring, 5–10mm wide. Flowers lilac to purple, slightly veined, throat lilac, the tepals pointed, *very unequal*, the 3 inner only a half to two-thirds the size of the outer, the outer ones 3.7–5cm long, 1.3–2.5cm wide; stamens with yellow anthers and white or lilac hairless filaments; *stigma with many lilac thread-like branches*. Meadows, woods and thickets. September–October. n&wR, RS – W. Ukraine, neYU.*

This beautiful species is rather rare in cultivation but is easily grown since it occurs in dampish situations in the wild and does not require a warm dry summer in order to ripen the corms. In full sun the large outer tepals tend to reflex leaving the inner ones standing up, the whole appearance then being rather that of a small Iris than a crocus. One of its synonyms is in fact *C. iridiflorus*.

15. *Crocus nudiflorus* [32]   *Plant stoloniferous, forming patches.* Leaves 3–4 from each corm, absent at flowering time, appearing in late winter to spring, 2–4mm wide. *Flowers deep lilac-purple or purple*, with little or no veining, throat white or lilac, the *flower-tube very long*, usually 10–22cm, the tepals 3–6cm long, 0.9–2cm wide, blunt; stamens with yellow anthers and white filaments; stigma divided into many short orange branches. Meadows, to 2000m. September–October. *sw*F, (GB), *n&c*E.*

This beautiful species is easily recognised by its long, slender flower-tube and rich purple flowers, together with the unusual feature of being stoloniferous – that is the corms produce offsets at the ends of 'stalks' enabling a colony to build up from one original corm. It has been cultivated in Britain for centuries and is naturalised in some places.

16. *Crocus serotinus* [32]   Corm coat made of coarse netted fibres. Leaves 4–7 from each corm, usually showing at flowering time but if not then appearing immediately afterwards, 1–3.5mm wide. *Flowers pale to deep lilac* often veined darker, *throat white, lilac or faintly yellow*, the tepals 2.3–5cm long, 0.6–1.5cm wide, pointed to blunt; stamens with yellow anthers and very pale yellow filaments; stigma with many short to long orange branches. Pinewoods, scrub and rocky grassland, below 500m. October–November. *c&s*P.●

16a. *C.s.* subsp. *clusii* (=*C. clusii*)   Like (**16**), differing only in having a corm coat consisting of finely netted fibres, the fibres rather silky and unlike the coarse ones of *C. serotinus*. Pinewoods and in scrub, to 900m. October–November. *n&c*P, *w*E.●

16b. *C.s.* subsp. *salzmannii*   Like (**16**), differing in having corm coat consisting of fine parallel fibres, not at all netted, becoming papery towards the apex of the corm. Open rocky places and in scrub, 100–2300m. September–December. *w,c&s*E.*

This has been cultivated for a long time and is still obtainable quite cheaply from nurseries as *C. salzmannii*. It is the most widespread of the subspecies of *C. serotinus* and occurs also in N. Africa.

There is a certain similarity between some forms of *C. serotinus* and *C. nudi-florus*, but the flower tube of the flower is usually below 11cm in length and the leaves are either visible at flowering time or emerge shortly after. The pale yellow filaments of *C. serotinus* also help in identification.

17. *Crocus medius* [32]   Leaves 2–3 from each corm, absent at flowering time, appearing in late autumn or winter, 2.5–4mm wide. Flowers lilac to deep purple, often veined darker; throat white; tepals 2.5–5cm long, 1.2–1.7cm wide, fairly pointed; stamens with deep yellow anthers and pale yellow filaments; *stigma with many spreading thread-like orange to scarlet branches.* Grassland and woods, 200–1400m. September–November. *nw*I, *se*F.*

It is probably more easy to confuse *C. medius* with the more eastern *C. cancellatus* than any other species, but the latter species is usually paler and has a pale yellow throat. Both have a coarsely netted bulb coat which distinguishes them from *C. nudiflorus*.

18. *Crocus cancellatus* [32]   Leaves 4–5 from each corm, absent at flowering time, 1–2mm wide, rather grey-green. Flowers white to deep lilac-blue, often veined purple-blue, throat usually pale yellow, the tepals 2.5–5cm long, 0.8–1.8cm wide, blunt or rather pointed; stamens deep yellow with pale yellow filaments; *stigma divided into many yellow to deep orange slender branches.* Rocky hills and open woods, to 1500m. September–November. GR, *s*YU.●

A very common species and very easy to recognise as a dormant corm, for it has a more *coarsely netted coat* than any other crocus. The large flowers, produced before the leaves, make it a very distinctive species when seen in the wild in Greece where it is unlikely to be confused with any other species.

19. *Crocus robertianus* [32]   Like (**18**), but differing in having 3–4 leaves, 4–6mm wide, green with a very distinct white stripe along the centre. Stigma large and frilly, usually orange, not divided into slender threads. Scrub clearings, 500–750m. October–November. *n*GR – Pindus Mts.●

A recently discovered species, apparently rather local in the wild although it may be more widespread in the relatively unknown Pindus range. It is a beautiful plant and should be a good garden crocus. Unlike *C. cancellatus* it is known only in a pale lilac colour.

20. *Crocus cambessedesii* [32]   Leaves 3–5 from each corm, showing at flowering time, 0.5–1mm wide. *Flowers very small, white or creamy to deep lilac, conspicuously striped purple* on the outside, throat white, the *tepals 1.4–1.8cm long,* 0.4–0.8cm wide, blunt; stamens with yellow anthers and white filaments; stigma usually shorter than the stamens but sometimes equal or overtopping them, divided into 3 orange to red branches, each of which is expanded or slightly lobed at the apex. Pinewoods and rocky hillsides, to 1000m. September–March. BAL.●

The only crocus occurring naturally in Majorca, flowering at various times throughout the autumn, winter and early spring. It is rather like a small *C. corsicus* or *C. minimus* but can be distinguished by its generally smaller size and by having two white papery spathes or bracts sheathing the flower-tube. In *C. minimus* there are two spathes also but the inner is very much narrower than the outer and is rather insignificant and they are brown or greenish spotted. In *C. corsicus* there is only one, brown-spotted, bract.

21. *Crocus corsicus* [32]   Like (**20**) but slightly larger and with only one brown-spotted spathe sheathing the flower-tube. Tepals usually 2–3.5cm long; style usually equal to or overtopping the stamens, orange to red. Scrub and mountain meadows, 500–2300m. January–April. *c*&*n*CO.*

C. corsicus and *C. minimus* are the only species occurring in Corsica and can be separated by the fact that *C. corsicus* has only one spathe whereas *C. minimus* has two, although the inner one is very narrow and difficult to see. In addition, *C. corsicus* has a slightly different corm tunic, netted at the apex of the corm, whereas that of *C. minimus* and *C. cambessedesii* have fibres which are parallel only. The stigma of *C. corsicus* usually varies from orange to red while that of *C. minimus* is yellow to orange.

22. *Crocus minimus* [33]   Like (**20**) but slightly larger and with the two spathes brown or greenish-spotted and very unequal, the inner very narrow and difficult to see, quite different to the equal white papery spathes of *C. cambessedesii*. Tepals usually 2–2.7cm long, sometimes stained with dark purple on the exterior; stigma usually equal to or overtopping the stamens, varying in colour from yellow to orange. In scrub, to 1500m. January–April. *s*co, sa.*

The only crocus growing in Sardinia, but also occurring in Corsica. It differs from *C. corsicus* in having a non-netted corm coat, two spathes and usually a paler stigma.

23. *Crocus imperati* [33]   Leaves deep glossy green, 3–6 from each corm, present at flowering time, 2–3mm wide. *Flowers purple, usually yellowish, silvery or buff on the outside striped with purple*, throat yellow to orange, the tepals (2.5–) 3–4.5cm long, 0.9–1.7cm wide, blunt to rounded; stamens with yellow anthers and pale yellow filaments; stigma deep orange or reddish divided into 3 branches, each branch expanded at the apex. Woods and grassy places, to 1100m. January–March. *w*i – near Naples and south to Sorrento.*

23a. *C.i.* subsp. *suaveolens*   Like (**23**) but differs in having only one spathe, whereas *C. imperati* has two. The stamens also differ in size; in (**23**) the filaments are 0.6–0.9cm long and the anthers 1.2–2.1cm long, while in (**23a**) the filaments are 0.3–0.5cm long and the anthers 0.8–1.2cm long. Stigma yellow to orange. Habitat as for (**23**). *w*i – near Rome southwards, not reaching Naples.*

C. imperati is a beautiful spring crocus with large flowers which look quite different when in bud to when they are fully open. This is because the outside of the tepals is often pale biscuit or silvery coloured and the inside is a strong lilac-purple.

24. *Crocus versicolor* [33]   Like (**23**) but with grey-green leaves. Flowers white to lilac, usually striped outside, throat pale yellow or nearly white; stamens with yellow or white filaments. Rocky places in scrub and open woodland, to 1200m. February–April. *s*cf, *n*wi.*

25. *Crocus sieberi* [33]   Leaves 2–7 (–10) per corm, showing at flowering time, 1.5–6mm wide. Flowers with a yellow throat, pale lilac to deep lilac-purple (var. *atticus*), sometimes with very dark tips to the tepals (mountains of the Peloponnese) and sometimes with a white zone separating the yellow throat from the lilac part of the tepals (var. *atticus* forma *tricolor*). [The Cretan form is white, usually with purple staining or banding on the exterior (var. *sieberi*, var. *versicolor*, var. *heterochromus*)]. Tepals 1.5–4.5cm long, 0.7–1.8cm wide, rather pointed to blunt or rounded, sometimes notched at the apex. Filaments and anthers yellow. *Stigma yellow to orange-red*, rather obscurely divided into 3 branches, *much expanded and frilled at the* apex. Mountain turf, scrub or conifer woods, 400–2800m. (January–) March–June (–July). AL, *s*BG, CR, GR, *s*YU.*

26. *Crocus dalmaticus* [33]   Like (**25**) but with leaves 1–2 (rarely –3)mm wide. Flowers lilac or purple-washed with silver or buff and usually veined with purple on the exterior of the tepals. Scrub and grassy places between rocks, 300–2000m. *n*AL, *w*YU.*

27. *Crocus veluchensis* [33]   Like (**25**) but with no yellow in the throat and with white filaments. Grass, usually near snow patches, 1200–2700m. AL, BG, GR, *s*YU.●

This is an extremely variable species both in flower size and colour. The smallest have tepals only 1.5cm long whilst in the largest specimens they may measure up to 5cm long. The colour ranges from pale silvery-lilac to a deep rich purple.

C. veluchensis also looks like some forms of *C. vernus*, but on inspection will be found to have 2 papery spathes clasping the tepal tube, not one as in the latter.

28. *Crocus carpetanus* [33]   Leaves 2–4 per corm, showing at flowering time, 1–2.5mm wide, *semi-cylindrical in cross-section*. Flowers pale lilac, often with finer darker veins, sometimes stained pinkish-purple on the tube and at the base of tepals, throat white or faintly yellow, the tepals 2–3.6cm long, 0.8–1.5cm wide, rounded; stamens with yellow anthers and white or very pale yellow filaments; *stigma divided obscurely into 3 white or creamy branches* which are much-expanded and frilled at the apex. Stony and grassy places in mountains, 1200–2000m. April–May. *c*&*nw*E, *n*P.●

C. carpetanus is one of the most distinct of all crocus with semi-cylindrical leaves which have a silvery upper surface rather than a narrow stripe along the middle. The frilled white stigma is also an easy means of identification, although *C. nevadensis* may be similar in this respect.

29. Sierra Nevada Crocus *Crocus nevadensis* [33]   Like (**28**) but leaves with 2 deeper grooves on the underside and with a narrower white stripe on the upper surface. Flowers cream, white or pale lilac with darker veining, the throat whitish or pale yellow. Alpine meadows and stony places, 1200–2300m. February–April. *ec*&*se*E.●

This species is rather similar to *C. carpetanus* but has a different distribution and can be distinguished by the leaves which are 2-grooved beneath. The corm tunic has parallel fibres, whereas *C. carpetanus* has a netted tunic.

30. Variegated Crocus *Crocus reticulatus* (=*C. variegatus*) [33]   Leaves 3–6 per corm, showing at flowering time, 0.5–1.5mm wide. Flowers white or lilac, strongly striped with purple on the outside, throat white or very pale yellow, the tepals usually 2–3.4cm long, 0.6–1.3cm wide, *usually rather pointed*; stamens with yellow anthers and pale yellow or white filaments; stigma divided into *3 yellow to deep orange branches*. Grassy or stony places, to 1000m. February–March. BG, H, *ne*I, K, R, *w*&*e*RS, YU.●

Some forms of *C. biflorus* resemble this species in colouring and it may be necessary to check the details of the corm tunic. *C. reticulatus* has a fibrous netted tunic, whereas *C. biflorus* has a smooth or papery one with rings at the base.

31. *Crocus flavus* (=*C. aureus*) [33]   Leaves erect, 5–8 per corm, showing at flowering time, 2.5–4mm wide. *Flowers pale to deep yellow throughout*, the tepals 1.5–3.5cm long, 0.5–1.2cm wide, blunt or slightly pointed; stamens with yellow anthers and filaments; *stigma obscurely divided into 3 short yellow or orange branches*. Woods, scrub and grassy places, to 800m. March–April. BG, GR, K, *s*R, RS, TR, *s*YU.*

A common yellow Crocus, very popular in gardens for its early bright golden flowers. It is usually cultivated in the form known as Dutch Yellow, although this may be a hybrid. *C. flavus* might be confused with *C. chrysanthus* but the former has wider green leaves whilst the latter usually has narrow greyish ones. Furthermore, the corm tunics of *C. flavus* have parallel fibres and a long brown 'neck' at the apex, while *C. chrysanthus* corms have rings at the base of their papery tunics and no neck. The leaves of *C. flavus* elongate enormously after flowering time and may reach 60cm long.

32. *C. olivieri* [34]   Like (**31**), but with leaves often spreading rather than erect, and only 2–4 per corm, they are generally wider, being 4–6mm wide. Style divided into 6 slender branches. Open woods, and grassy places, to 1000m. February–April. AL, BG, ?CR, GR, TR, *s*YU.*

C. olivieri is easily recognised since it is the only yellow European crocus with the style divided into 6 distinct branches.

33. *Crocus scardicus* [34]   Leaves 3–4 per corm, the tips just showing at flowering time, 0.5–1mm wide. *Flowers pale to deep orange-yellow, shading to purple on the lower part* of the tepals and on the tube, the tepals 2–4cm long, 0.8–1.1cm wide, blunt; stamens with yellow filaments and anthers; stigma obscurely divided into 3 short orange branches. Mountain turf near snow patches, 1700–2500m. May–July. *se*AL, *sw*YU.●

A very distinctive yellow crocus since it has a purplish base to the flowers. It is also very unusual in having no white stripe along the centre of the stiff narrow leaves. The following recently described species is apparently closely related:

33a. *C. pelistericus*   Like (**33**) in all its features except flower colour which is *uniform deep violet*; style whitish. Alpine meadows, 1900–2300m. May–June. *s*YU.●

34. *Crocus cvijicii* [34]   *Leaves 2–4 per corm*, just appearing at flowering time, 1.5–3mm wide. *Flowers pale cream to deep orange-yellow* throughout, rarely with a purple tube, the tepals 1.5–4cm long, 0.6–0.9cm wide, blunt; stamens with yellow filaments and anthers; stigma obscurely divided into 3 orange branches. *Alpine turf near snow patches*, 1800–2300m. May–June. AL, *n*GR, *s*YU. ●

Although similar to *C. scardicus*, this species usually has no purple at the base of the segments and its leaves have a white central stripe. If there is any confusion with *C. flavus* and *C. olivieri*, a check on the corm will show that it has a finely fibrous-netted tunic.

35. Scotch Crocus *Crocus biflorus* [34]   Leaves 2–5 per corm, appearing with the flowers, 0.5–2.5mm wide. *Flowers usually white, nearly always strongly striped* brown or purple on the exterior, throat yellow, the tepals usually 2–4.5cm long, 0.4–1.8cm wide, rounded to slightly pointed; stamens with yellow anthers and white or yellow filaments; stigma divided into 3 yellow or orange branches. Open stony places and in scrub, to 1000m. January–April. BG, GR, I, K, *w*RS, SC, TR, YU. *

In its striped forms *C. biflorus* is very similar to *C. reticulatus* and it may be necessary to dig up a corm for inspection. The former has a shell-like tunic with basal rings and *C. reticulatus* has a fibrous coarsely netted tunic. *C. biflorus* is a good garden plant. The origin of the name Scotch Crocus is not known.

The following are all part of the *C. biflorus* aggregate and are regarded as separate species by some authorities.

35a. *C. melantherus*   Like (**35**) but blackish stamens; flowers in the winter. October–January. *s*GR – Peloponnese. ●

This has been wrongly called *Crocus crewei* which is similar but spring-flowering and from Asia Minor.

35b. *C. weldenii*   Like (**35**) but flowers white, not striped on the outside, usually stained blue on the tube; throat white. *w*&*sw*YU. *

35c. *C. alexandri*   Like (**35**) but exterior of outer tepals stained an intense bluish-violet; throat white. *s*YU. *

35d. *C. adamii*   Like (**35**) but flowers lilac-blue with darker stripes on the outside; throat yellow. *s*YU. ●

35e. *C. pallidus*   Like (**35**) but flowers wholly white; throat white. *s*YU. ●

36. *Crocus chrysanthus* [34]   Like (**35**) but with wholly pale to deep yellow flowers, sometimes with a brownish or purplish tube. Open stony places and scrub, to 2000m. January–May. AL, BG, GR, R, TR, YU. *

C. chrysanthus is a common yellow-flowered species in the wild. It can be distinguished from other yellow species by the very slender, usually greyish leaves and by the corm tunics which have rings at the base. It is a popular garden plant and there are many colourful cultivars, some of them hybrids with *C. biflorus*.

37. Cloth of Gold Crocus *Crocus angustifolius* (=*C. susianus*) [34]   Leaves 3–6 per corm, appearing with the flowers, *0.5–1.5mm wide. Flowers yellow*, usually strongly suffused or striped externally with purple-bronze, the tepals 1.7–3.4cm long, 0.6–1.3cm wide, blunt or slightly pointed; stamens with yellow anthers and filaments; *stigma divided into 3 yellow to deep orange branches*. Hillsides, in scrub or light woods, to 1000m. February–March. K, *w*RS.*

This beautiful crocus has been known for many centuries in cultivation. The most striking form has the tepals almost mahogany on the exterior. It is unlikely that this species will be confused with any other yellow-flowered species, but if there is any doubt, a check on the corm tunic will show that it consists of very strongly netted-fibres.

38. Spring Crocus *Crocus vernus* (=*C. purpureus, C. napolitanus*) [34]   Leaves 2–4 per corm, the tips just visible at flowering time, usually *4–8mm wide. Flowers lilac, purple or striped*, sometimes white, *throat white or purple*, the tepals usually 3–5.5cm long, 0.9–2cm wide; stamens with yellow anthers and white filaments; stigma divided into 3 short yellow, orange or very rarely white, frilly branches, equal to or exceeding the stamens. Woods and mountain meadows, 150–1500m. March–June. AL, CH, D, (GB), I, YU.*

The common purple spring crocus of the Alps, and the species from which most of our very large-flowered garden crocuses have been raised.

38a. *C.v.* subsp. *albiflorus* [34]   Like (**38**) but smaller. Flowers often white but they may be purple, the tepals usually 1.5–3.5cm long, 0.4–1.2cm wide; style usually much shorter than the stamens. Short alpine turf, 600–3000m. March–June. A, AL, CH, CS, D, E, F, I, SC, YU.*

This is the tiny spring crocus of the Alps which often fills meadows with its small white or purple flowers soon after the melting of the snow. In Sicily it has been called *C. siculus* and in W. Yugoslavia, *C. vilmae*, but there is little difference between plants from these areas and those from the Alps.

The following are sometimes regarded as distinct species.

38b. *C. heuffelianus* [34]   Like (**38**) but flowers larger and rather globular with dark purple tips to the rounded tepals; throat without hairs. A, CS, H, PL, R, *w*RS, YU.●

38c. *C. scepusiensis*   Like (**38b**) but with a ring of hairs in the throat where the filaments join the tube. ?CS, PL, ?*w*RS.●

39. *Crocus tommasinianus* [34]   Like (**38**), but with a more slender flower. *Flowers lilac to purple with a white tube* and often with fawn or silvery coloration on the outside of the tepals. *Leaves only 2–3mm wide*, well developed at flowering time. Deciduous woods and shady banks, 300–1500m. March–May. *nw*BG, *w*&*sw*YU.*

A very popular crocus in gardens since it is the first to flower in the spring and it seeds freely so it is suitable for naturalising. The flowers are usually lilac but several colour forms are now available in the purple to reddish-purple colour range. Although similar to *C. vernus* it is easily recognised by its narrow leaves each with a very prominent silver stripe, and by its white tepal tube. *C. vernus* never has a white tube if the tepals are coloured.

40. Etruscan Crocus *Crocus etruscus* [34] Like (**38**) but the flowers with a yellowish throat, and the tepals often fawn on the outside with purple veins or stripes; stamens with pale yellow filaments. Corm tunic with strong netted fibres. Deciduous woods and fields, 300–1500m. *nw*I.*

C. etruscus* is similar in appearance to *C. dalmaticus* from Yugoslavia. However, in the latter there are two papery bracts clasping the tepal tube and only one in *C. etruscus*.

41. *Crocus kosaninii* Like (**38**) but with a yellow throat, the tepals mid-lilac-blue; stamens with yellow filaments. Leaves only 2 (rarely 3) per corm. Deciduous woods and scrub. *s*YU.●

42. *Crocus malyi* [34] Leaves 3–5 per corm, just visible at flowering time, 1.5–2.5mm wide. *Flowers white*, sometimes stained bluish or brownish at the base externally, *throat yellow*, the tepals 2–4cm long, 0.8–1.3cm wide, blunt to rather pointed; stamens with yellow anthers and filaments; style divided into *3 orange branches*. Coastal mountains in grassy places and at the edge of woods, 300–1000m. March–April. *w*YU.●

This species sometimes occurs near white-flowered forms of *C. vernus* and populations of *C. weldenii*, but it can be distinguished from both by its yellow throat.

Arum Family ARACEAE

Hairless perennials with tubers or rhizomes. Leaves all basal, varying from lanceolate to ovate, often with basal lobes giving an arrow-shape to the entire leaf. Flowers very small, produced in a dense spike or spadix which is elongated at the apex into a sterile pencil-like organ known as the appendix. The spadix is enclosed within an upright tubular or bottle-shaped spathe which often has a hooded apex; the appendix usually projects beyond the mouth of the spathe. Each flower is minute, often without tepals and is usually unisexual; the male flowers are generally carried in a cluster above the female ones and some sterile hair-like structures are often present as well. The fruit is a cluster of berries, sometimes brightly coloured.

The Araceae is a large family, especially well represented in the tropics, and although very diverse in appearance the plants are usually easily recognised because of the distinctive spathe and spadix, features which do not exist in any other family.

The flowers of the arums are often evil-smelling and pollinated by flies. The spathes are mostly greenish or brownish. On the whole they cannot be said to be very decorative although many of the tropical species are cultivated as house plants for their attractive foliage. *Philodendrons, Monstera deliciosa* (Cheese Plant) and *Zantedeschia aethiopica* (Common White Arum Lily) are typical tropical examples. In Europe the best known is *Arum maculatum*, the Common Cuckoo Pint or Lords and Ladies.

Key to Genera of European Araceae

1. Leaves digitately divided into ten or more
    oblong or lanceolate leaflets   *Dracunculus*, p.197
    Leaves entire, heart or arrow shaped, oblong or
    linear   2

2. Plants aquatic or semi-aquatic   3
    Plants not aquatic or semi-aquatic   4

3. Leaves sword-shaped, in a fan, iris-like; spathes
    green   *Acorus*, p.198
    Leaves heart-shaped; spathes white   *Calla*, p.198

4. Leaves heart-shaped   5
    Leaves ovate, oblong or linear   6

5. Spathes 4–5cm long only   *Arisarum*, p.192
    Spathes large, 8–40cm long   *Arum*, p.194

6. Spathes tube bent near the base   *Ambrosinia*, p.197
    Spathes tube not bent near the base, straight or
    slightly curved   7

7. Spathes stemless, held at ground level   *Biarum*, p.193
    Spathes stalked, held above ground level   *Arisarum*, p.192

ARISARUM

Small tuberous-rooted hairless perennials, among the smallest-flowered of all the European arums.

1. Common Arisarum or **Friar's Cowl** *Arisarum vulgare* [35] Short to medium plant 20–40cm tall. Leaves ovate or heart-shaped, plain green or spotted darker. *Spathe green or chocolate brown*, 4–5cm long, *hooded and short-pointed at the apex*; spadix greenish, slightly protruding from the mouth of the spathe. Berries greenish. Semi-shady and rocky places to 800m. December–April. AZ, BAL, CO, CR, E, F, GR, I, SA, SC, YU.*

A very common plant in the Mediterranean region. The tubers are often slender and stolon-like so that large patches may be formed.

1a. *A.v.* subsp. *simorrhinum* has the appendix much-swollen at the apex. s&eE.

2. Mouse Plant *Arisarum proboscideum* [35]   Short plant to 10–25cm tall. Leaves plain green, heart-shaped. *Spathe dark chocolate-brown, strongly hooded* at the apex and with a *long tapering point* up to 5cm long; spadix hidden within the spathe, whitish. Berries greenish. In slight shade, to 600m. March–May. swE, c&sI.*

A curious plant, the flowers resembling long-tailed mice burrowing down into the mass of leaves.

BIARUM

Low to short tuberous perennials; tubers rounded below, feathered above with the roots appearing from the upper surface at the base of the new shoot. Leaves not lobed or heart-shaped, usually linear to lanceolate, or oblong. Spathes stemless, produced at ground level, greenish, creamy-green or brownish; spadix maroon or blackish-purple, the male and female flowers separated by a group of hair-like sterile flowers. Fruit a cluster of white or greenish berries at or just above ground level.

1. Narrow-leaved Biarum *Biarum tenuifolium* [35]   Leaves very variable 5–20cm long and 1–2cm wide, *narrowly oblong to linear*, sometimes with very wavy margins, produced before or after the spathes appear. *Spathe pale brownish-green to deep chocolate, 8–30cm long*, the apex varying from erect and long-tapering, to hooded and rather blunt; spadix deep blackish-purple, projecting well beyond the spathe and carrying sterile flowers above and below the male flowers. Sparse scrub and in bare rocky places, to 1500m. July–November, occasionally also in spring. AL, CR, GR, E, I, P, SC, YU.*

A very variable and common plant in Greece and southern Yugoslavia. The shorter-spathed form is sometimes referred to as variety *abbreviatum*.

2. *Biarum bovei*   Similar to the previous species but the leaves are broadly oblong, about 5cm long and 1–1.5cm wide. The lower tubular part of the spathe is *rather inflated and there are no sterile flowers above the male ones*. October–December. sE, SA.●

B. carratracense from Malaga province of southern Spain is very like this and may be inseparable.

3. *Biarum spruneri*   Very like *B. tenuifolium* in appearance but the spadix *does not project beyond the spathe* and there are no sterile flowers above the male ones. Exposed sunny places in rocky ground. April–June. sGR.●

4. Cretan Biarum *Biarum davisii*   Low plant less than 10cm tall. Leaves produced after the flowers, only 1.5–3cm long, *ovate or elliptic* with an undulate edge. *Spathe creamy, 3–5cm long*, the lower closed part rather *swollen and bladder-like*, narrowing to the mouth, the tip hooded; spadix maroon, protruding out of the mouth of the spathe. Arid stony hillsides and rock crevices, to 1700m. November. CR.●

This is easily distinguished by its small creamy spathe, and unlike the other European species it does not have a disgusting smell!

leaf

Cretan Biarum, × ½

ARUM

Low to medium tuberous perennials, the tubers rather elongated with the shoot produced on one side. Leaves more or less arrow-shaped, spotted or unspotted. Spathes green, purplish, blackish or creamy, sometimes blotched, usually carried on a short stem which elongates in fruit; spadix carrying male, female and sterile hair-like flowers separately near its base, extended into a pencil- or club-shaped appendix at the apex. Fruit a cluster of red berries

The true arums are the commonest members of the family to be found in Europe and are readily recognisable by the arrow-shaped leaves and large, usually greenish, spathes which are not strongly hooded over at the apex as in *Biarum* and *Arisarum*.

Key to European species of Arum

1. Spathes produced in autumn, deep purple   7. *A. pictum*
   Spathes produced in spring, green or purplish   2

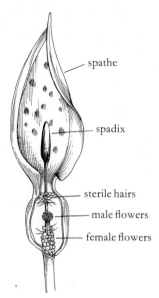

spathe

spadix

sterile hairs
male flowers
female flowers

Cross-section of an Arum inflorescence and spathe to illustrate the botanical details.

2. Spathes blackish-purple or brownish-purple inside   **3**
Spathes whitish, green or yellow, sometimes
    tinged or spotted deep purple   **4**

3. Spathes blackish-purple   5. *A. nigrum*
Spathes brownish-purple inside   4. *A. elongatum*

4. Spathe inflated at base. Crete   6. *A. creticum*
Spathe more or less tubular at base   **5**

5. Leaves produced in autumn   1. *A. italicum*
Leaves produced in spring   **6**

6. Spadix about half as long as spathe   2. *A. maculatum*
Spadix about two thirds as long as spathe   3. *A. orientale*

1. Large Cuckoo Pint *Arum italicum* [35] Short to medium plant to 45cm tall. Leaves shiny green, sometimes with dark spotting, usually with *prominent creamy veins*, appearing in autumn, 15–35cm long. Spathe large, upright, pale green or creamy, 15–40cm long; *spadix up to half as long as spathe, yellowish* in the upper part. Fruiting spike more than 10cm long. Hedges, light woodland and margins of cultivation, to 1000m. April–June. AL, BAL, BG, CH, CO, CR, E, F, GB*, GR, I, K, P, SA, SC, TR, YU.*

A very common arum in southern Europe, usually easy to recognise by its large triangular leaves and long pale spathe enclosing the yellowish spadix. The 'flowers' have a strong unpleasant smell which attracts flies for pollination purposes. There are some local variants which are sometimes treated as separate species: *A. albispathum* from the Crimea has whitish spathes, whilst *A. neglectum* from western Europe lacks the creamy veins to the leaves. *A. italicum* is frequently cultivated.

2. Common Cuckoo Pint or **Lords and Ladies** *Arum maculatum* [35] Short plant to 25cm tall. *Leaves appearing in spring*, deep shiny green, often with blackish spotting. *Spathe pale green*, sometimes tinged with purple, occasionally spotted purple, 10–25cm long; *spadix about half as long as the spathe*, usually deep purple, but rarely creamy. Fruiting spike less than 5cm long. Woods and hedgerows, to 1000m. March–May. T – except Fe, No, Su.●

This is the commonest European arum and the species most likely to be encountered in the more northern countries.

3. Eastern Arum *Arum orientale* Similar to the previous species but leaves dull or shiny, never black-spotted. Spathe less than 15cm long, pale green tinged with purple, never purple-spotted; *spadix more than half as long as the spathe*. Fruiting spike 5–10cm long. Woods, to 1000m. April–June. A, AL, BC, CS, DK, GR, H, I, K, PL, R, *c&w*RS, SC, SF, TR, YU.*

There are several geographical variants of this species, differing in the shape and size of the spadix and in the leaves which can be dull or shiny.

4. *Arum elongatum* Similar to *A. maculatum* but the *leaves appearing in autumn*. *Spathe brownish-purple*; spadix about the same length as the spathe. Fruiting spike 5cm or more long. In light woodland and scrub, to 1000m. April. BG, GR, K, *w&s*R, TR.

The equal spathe and spadix distinguish‘this species from other related species.

5. Dalmatian Arum *Arum nigrum* [35] Similar to *A. maculatum* but leaves appearing in the autumn and *spathes deep blackish-purple*; spadix blackish. Scrub and open stony places, to 1000m. March–April. AL, *w*YU, *n*GR.●

The very dark spathes make this easy to recognise since the only other species with spathes of this colour, *A. pictum*, is autumn flowering.

6. Cretan Arum *Arum creticum* [35] Medium plant 25–40cm tall. Leaves appearing in autumn, deep shiny green, unspotted. *Spathe white or yellow*, 8–13cm long with a rather *inflated tube* and a narrow blade which often folds back somewhat leaving the purple or yellow spadix protruding. Rocky hillsides, to 2000m. April–May. CR.*

This is the only arum to have a spathe with a swollen tube, but it is also distinct in having a narrow blade of white or yellow. It is unusual also in being sweetly scented and is an attractive garden plant, especially in its yellow form.

7. Autumn Arum *Arum pictum* [35] Medium plant to 50cm tall. Leaves appearing in autumn just before flowering time, thick and leathery, *deep shiny* *green with creamy veins. Spathe deep purple,* 15–25cm long; spadix deep purple, shorter than the spathe. Rocky ground in scrub and beneath pines, to 500m. October–November. BAL, CO, I, SA ●

The autumn-flowering habit separates this from the other European arums. The thick-textured leaves with creamy veins are very striking. It should not be confused with the creamy veined variant of *A. italicum,* known as variety *'pictum'* which is frequently cultivated.

AMBROSINIA

Ambrosinia *Abrosinia bassii* [36]   Low tuberous-rooted hairless perennial *less than 7cm tall.* Leaves elliptical or oblong, 2–7cm long and 1.5–3cm wide. *Spathe greenish-white* spotted red, 1.5–2cm long, the *tube inflated, with a sharp bend near its base* and an upturned pointed tip; spadix small, completely enclosed within the tube. Fruit a many-seeded berry. In dry scrub and grassy places, to 200m. October–December (–February). CO, I, SA, SC.

A tiny, rather insignificant plant, but with a very interesting flower structure.

DRACUNCULUS

Robust tuberous rooted perennials with much-divided leaves and enormous spathes. They are the largest members of the arum family in Europe and cannot be confused with any other species.

1. Common Dragon Arum *Dracunculus vulgaris* [36]   Tall plant to 100cm with a *robust, strongly blotched 'false stem'* formed by the leaf stalks and flower stem. *Leaves green,* up to 20cm long and 35cm wide, very deeply divided into 10–15 linear, lanceolate or oblong, *more or less equal segments. Spathe deep rich velvety reddish-purple,* broadly lanceolate, 25–40cm long and 10–20cm broad; *spadix deep black-maroon,* erect, very stout and rather shiny. Berries orange-red. In ditches, waste ground, hedges, scrubland, dry hillsides and rocky places, to 1000m. April–July. B, CO, CR, GR, I, SA, YU.*

Probably the most dramatic of the European arums with its purple or green spotted 'stem' and huge purple spathe. It is of considerable ornamental value, though the disgusting odour detracts from this somewhat.

In Crete there is a variant, var. *Creticus,* which has purple-blotched stems, and leaves with white markings. A white-spathed form of it is known.

2. Dragon's Mouth *Dracunculus muscivorus (= Helicodiceros muscivorus)* Medium plant to 45cm. *Leaves greyish-green,* deeply dissected into *very unequal linear-lanceolate segments. Spathe pale green with purple spots* and streaks, very hairy on the inner surface, 15–30cm long, 5–20cm broad, the blade reflexed, leaving the spadix protruding; *spadix purple covered with a mass of long hair-like sterile flowers.* Rocky and grassy places not far from the sea, to 200m. March–June. BAL, CO, SA.*

A striking plant with its enormous spathe and finely divided leaves. The hairy spadix and spathe distinguish it immediately from the other species. It also has an unpleasant odour like rotting meat which serves to attract flies and beetles which act as pollinators.

CALLA

Bog Arum *Calla palustris* [36]   Short hairless aquatic perennial to 30cm, with an underwater rhizomatous stock and trailing stems. Leaves carried above water, nearly round or broadly ovate, cordate at the base and with finely pointed tips, 5–10cm long. Spathe white inside, upright and flat with no tubular base, about 5–10cm long, borne on stalks up to 30cm above water; spadix shorter than the spathe, up to 3cm long with many yellowish flowers over its whole length. Fruit a cluster of red berries. Margins of fresh water ponds and lakes, to 1000m. June–August. A, B, CH, CS, DK, SF, F, D, (GB), NL, N, PL, R, RS, S.*

An attractive water plant sometimes grown in ornamental pools, although it can be very vigorous and trails across the surface of the water. The dried ground rhizomes have been used as a flour, but are poisonous when fresh.

ACORUS

Sweet Flag *Acorus calamus* [36]   Medium to tall hairless aquatic perennial to 1m, with a thick underwater rhizome. Leaves rather iris-like, linear or tapering gradually to the acute apex, 50–125cm long, up to 2cm wide. Flower-stem 3-angled, equalling or just exceeding the height of the leaves. Spathe green, resembling the stem and leaves; spadix 5–10cm long, densely covered in greenish flowers, *not enclosed at all by the spathe.* Fruits are not formed in Europe. In mud by fresh water ponds, lakes and rivers at low altitudes. May–July. Naturalised in most of Europe from introductions in the 16th Century from western Asia where it is native.*

The whole plant has a fruity smell when crushed, said by some to resemble tangerines. Calamus Oil is distilled from the plant and is used for flavouring certain alcoholic drinks such as gin and bitters. It is also used in perfumery, as an aid to digestion and for toothache. The powdered root has been used as an insect repellent.

Orchid Family ORCHIDACEAE

Orchids are amongst the most fascinating and bizarre of all flowers. The family contains an enormous range of flower types from the flamboyant exotic species to those with the tiniest flowers that can be easily overlooked. The Orchid Family occurs throughout the world except in extreme polar regions and is probably the second largest group of flowering plants with between 17–20,000 species, many of these being confined to the tropics. Many of the tropical species are epiphytes, anchoring themselves to the branches of trees, but they are adapted to a wide range of habitat. It is not generally realized that there are more than 120 species of orchid in Europe. All of these are terrestrial, inhabiting marshes, or grassland or woodland on many types of soil from the lowlands to high altitudes in the mountainous regions, depending on the species. Many are confined to the warm countries of southern Europe bordering on the Mediterranean, but others are only found in the north and they are some of the most fascinating flowers to be found in the region covered by this book.

Some, like the beautiful Lady's Slipper Orchid are becoming increasingly scarce due to habitat destruction and overpicking in the past. For this reason many are carefully protected, especially in the countries of Western Europe.

Orchids have an extraordinary and intimate partnership with various fungi in the soil in which they grow. This fungal association (known as a mycorrhizal association) is essential to the germinating seeds of orchids and to the young plants. The fungal strands, or hyphae, extract various nutrients essential to their growth from the surrounding humus and transfer them, in due course, to the roots of the developing orchid seedling, thereby assisting in their nourishment. What the fungus gets in return it is not known.

European orchids are slow growing and may take years to develop to flowering size. Some like the Bee Orchid die once they have flowered. Each fruit contains thousands of tiny 'dust-like' seeds which scatter easily in the wind.

Another curious feature of orchids is resupination which refers to the twisting of the flower. In most species the flower twists through a half circle, 180°, so that as seen, it is in fact upside down. This means that the upper petal, which is usually modified into a prominent lip, is in fact lowermost as seen. In some species resupination does not occur, or it revolves the flower through a full circle, 360°, so that the lip remains uppermost in the flower.

The European orchids are perennial with a thin rhizomatous or a tuberous rootstock. The leaves are spirally arranged, often aggregated towards the base of the plant into a loose rosette. The upper leaves may be similar to the lower or they may be sheath or bract-like. Some species are saprophytic and without chlorophyll, spending their lives on decaying vegetable matter or humus in close association with their fungal partners. The flowers may be solitary, or more frequently they occur in a globular head or a long spike. The ovary which is generally green, stalk-like and twisted is inferior and occurs at the base of the flower below the sepals and petals. There are 3 sepals which may be green or

variously coloured, equal in size, often as large as, or larger than, the petals.
Inside these there are 2 petals and a lip, which represents the third petal. The two
petals are usually coloured and are often smaller than the sepals. In quite a
number of species the sepals and petals, or at least the upper (middle) sepal and
petals are held close together, projecting forward to form a small 'hood' or
'helmet'. The lip or labellum is usually an elaborate structure, lowermost,
though occasionally uppermost, in the flower; it is often lobed and marked in
various ways with ridges, lines, dots or shiny zones and is generally a vital clue to
the identification of a particular species. The lip is frequently extended into a
short or long hollow spur which contains nectar and which projects backwards
behind the flower. One or two stamens occur and are fused to the stigma to
form a 'column', the pollen occurring in detachable masses or pollinia. The
column has two stigmas usually, the third being modified into a 'beak' or
rostellum which comes between the stigmas and the pollinia and this helps to
prevent self-pollination. The fruit is an elongated or rounded 3-valved capsule
containing numerous minute seeds.

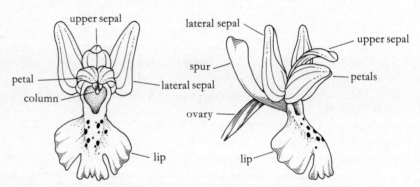

Front and side views of a typical orchid (*Orchis*) flower to illustrate the botanical details

    The highly specialised column and the prominent lip serve to distinguish
orchids from all the other plants in this book. The family is readily distinguished
though its member genera and species may often be very difficult to identify
accurately. The flowers are highly specialised to pollination by various insects
and other agents, though self-pollination is evident in *Epipactis* and has been
shown to occur in various species of *Ophrys*, particularly in the northern part of
their range.

    One final word here is needed. Please, please do not pick or dig up these
delightful plants. Many are scarcer now than they once were, and many are
protected by law in different countries and their survival depends on our
appreciation and our willingness to let others enjoy them in their wild habitats.
They do not take kindly to uprooting, nor are they easy to cultivate.

Key to Genera

1. Plants saprophytic, without green pigment
(chlorophyll); leaves absent but replaced by
bract-like sheaths or scales on the stem   **2**
  Plants with chlorophyll and leaves; leaves often
with a blade and stalk but in a number of genera
unsheathing or partly unsheathing the stem, or
both types on the same plant   **5**

2. Lip uppermost in flower   *Epipogium aphyllum*, p.260
  Lip lowermost in flower   **3**

3. Flowers with a distinct spur, lip 16−17mm long;
robust plant generally more than 40cm tall   *Limodorum abortivum*, p.263
  Flowers spurless, lip 5−12mm long; plants less
robust, rarely exceeding 40cm tall   **4**

4. Lip unlobed at tip, about 5mm long; flowers up
to 12 per stem   *Corallorhiza trifida*, p.255
  Lip 2-lobed at tip, 8−12mm long; flowers
numerous   *Neottia nidus-avis*, p.257

5. Flowers with a large pouch or slipper-like lip   **6**
  Flowers with a flat, concave or convex lip, lobed
or unlobed but not pouched or slipper-like   **7**

6. Stem leaves 2−4; lateral sepals pointing
downwards   *Cypripedium*, p.217
  Stem leaves absent but replaced by a solitary basal
leaf and one or two sheaths towards the base of
the stem; lateral sepals horizontal or erect   *Calypso bulbosa*, p.254

7. Flowers with a short or long spur, always distinct   **8**
  Flowers spurless   **27**

8. Lip large, 30−50mm long   **9**
  Lip smaller, less than 25mm long   **10**

9. Lip terminating in 4 long thread-like appendages   *Comperia comperiana*,
p.238
  Lip with two short basal 'arms' and a long strap-like
lobe notched at the tip, or divided up to halfway   *Himantoglossum
hircinum*, p.222

10. Lip entire, not lobed   **11**
  Lip 3-lobed, the middle lobe often itself 2−3-lobed   **12**

11. Spur and lip uppermost in flower, the lip similar in
shape and size to the petals; flowers blackish-
purple, reddish or yellowish, rarely white   *Nigritella*, p.248
   Spur and lip lowermost in flower, the lip longer
than the petals; flowers white or green or
yellowish-green   *Platanthera*, p.250

12. Spur long, as long as or longer than the ovary   **13**
   Spur short, rarely up to half the length of the ovary   **16**

13. Lip with 3 simple entire or more or less equal
lobes; spur considerably longer than the ovary, at
least 11mm, slender and pointed   **14**
   Lip variable, often toothed and/or lobed, if 3-lobed
then the lobes uneven, the central one often itself
lobed or toothed or reduced to a small 'tooth';
spur about as long, or slightly longer than the
ovary, broad and blunt, sometimes enlarged at
the tip   **15**

14. Flowers in a slender long spike; lip shallowly
3-lobed   *Gymnadenia conopsea*, p.247
   Flowers in broad conical or globose heads; lip
deeply 3-lobed   *Anacamptis pyramidalis*,
                                                                         p.224

15. Flower bracts membranous, each shorter than the
flower it subtends; upper leaves often sheathing
the stem   *Orchis* (in part), p.225
   Flower bracts leaf-like, the lowermost or all
longer than the flowers; upper leaves not
sheathing the stem except at the very base   *Dactylorhiza*
                                                          (in part), p.238

16. Sepals and petals all converging to form a hood   **17**
   At least the lateral 2 sepals spreading   **23**

17. Lip with three simple entire lobes, not necessarily
all the same size   **18**
   Lip variously lobed and toothed, the central lobe
generally broad, toothed, or notched and with a
small 'peg-like' tooth in the middle   **22**

18. Middle lobe of lip much smaller than the adjacent
lobes, the lip much longer than broad   *Coeloglossum viride*,
                                                                         p.252
   Middle lobe of lip as large or larger than the
adjacent lobes, the lip about as long as broad   **19**

19. Flowers tiny, lip not more than 3mm long, white,
    greenish-white or very pale pink   *Pseudorchis*, p.246
    Flowers larger, lip 4mm long or more, yellowish-
    green, lilac-pink or reddish-brown   **20**

20. Flowers lilac-pink, spur slender and incurved   *Neottianthe cucullata,*
                                  p.248

    Flowers greenish-yellow or reddish-brown, spur
    oblong or globular   **21**

21. Plant with a single basal lance-shaped leaf and
    usually two sheathing leaves above; flowers dull
    green to reddish-brown normally; lip lobes
    rounded   *Steveniella satyrioides,*
                              Crimea, p.249

    Plant with two heart-shaped leaves, no sheathing
    leaves above; flowers yellowish-green; lip with
    pointed lobes   *Gennaria diphylla,*
                        S.W. Europe, p.251

22. Lateral sepals and petals fused at the base   *Neotinea intacta*, p.258
    Lateral sepals and petals free from one another   *Orchis* (in part), p.225

23. Lip divided into two sections by a constriction in
    the middle, not lobed   *Cephalanthera*
                       (in part), p.261

    Lip not divided into two sections as above, but
    lobed   **24**

24. Sepals and petals all spreading, each with a
    spoon-shaped tip, appearing like a small
    elongated blob at the end of each   *Traunsteinera globosa,*
                          p.237

    Sepals and petals blunt to pointed but without a
    small expanded tip, only the lateral sepals
    spreading   **25**

25. Lip with three equal shallow rounded lobes   *Gymnadenia*
                      odoratissima, p.247

    Lip various lobed and toothed, if 3-lobed then the
    lobes not equal, the central one being longer   **26**

26. Flower bracts membranous, each shorter than the
    flower it subtends; upper leaves often sheathing
    the stem   *Orchis* (in part), p.225
    Flower bracts leaf-like, the lowermost or all
    longer than the flowers; upper leaves spreading
    and not sheathing the stem except only at their
    base sometimes   *Dactylorhiza*
                      (in part), p.238

27. Sepals and petals spreading, not forming a loose
hood   28
Sepals and petals forming a loose or tight hood   34

28. Flowers small, the lip 2–3mm long and
uppermost, green or yellowish-green   29
Flowers larger, the lip 5mm long or more and
lowermost, usually several-coloured rarely plain
green (except in *Liparis*)   31

30. Leaves 2–3, often with small bulbils along their
edges   *Hammarbya paludosa,*
p.254
Leaves solitary, without bulbils along the edge   *Microstylis monophyllos,*
p.255

31. Lip insect-like (bee, wasp or fly) or spider-like,
often velvety and with geometric markings in
various colours and with a small or large shiny
central zone or speculum   *Ophrys,* p.205
Lip not as above, neither velvety nor with a
speculum   32

32. Individual flowers with a stalk below the ovary,
horizontal or drooping   *Epipactis,* p.264
Individual flowers stalkless, erect or ascending   33

33. Leaves 2–3 basal; flowers plain green   *Liparis loeselii,* p.253
Leave 4 or more, spaced along the stem; flowers
white, pink or red   *Cephalanthera*
(in part), p.261

34. Lip entire, sometimes with a wavy edge   35
Lip clearly 3-lobed, not wavy edged   37

35. All leaves basal, stem without bract-like or
sheathing leaves; flowers yellowish-green   *Chamorchis alpina,* p.252
Leaves not all basal, stem with bract-like or
sheathing leaves; flowers white or pink,
sometimes greenish-white   36

36. Plants creeping by leafy runners; flowers in a more
or less one-sided spike   *Goodyera repens,* p.258
Plants not creeping; flowers spiralled in a spike *Spiranthes,* p.259

37. Middle lobe of lip 'tooth-like' much smaller than
the adjacent lobes; leaves oval or heart-shaped   *Listera,* p.256
Middle lobe of lip equal to or larger than the
adjacent lobes; leaves linear to lance-shaped   38

38. Leaves all linear and basal   *Chamorchis alpina,*

Leaves not all basal, the stem with one or more
bract-like or sheathing leaves, basal leaves
lance-shaped   **39**

39. Middle-lobe of lip entire; stem leaf or leaves
bract-like   *Herminium monorchis,*

Middle lobe of lip distinctly bifid; stem leaves
sheathing   *Aceras anthropophorum,*

OPHRYS

Of all genera of European orchids the genus *Ophrys* show the most extraordinarily complicated, almost bizarre, development of form. In the genus the most conspicuous feature of the flower is the large and curiously patterned and coloured lip. This often mimics insect bodies, thus earning some of the species common names such as the Bee, Fly and Spider Orchids. Evolutionarily such mimicry is not considered to be a coincidence but a special adaptation to ensure pollination – male insects or spiders are attracted, usually by scent which itself mimics that of the female, to their pseudomates to copulate, and having been so deceitfully lured, inadvertently pollinate the flower. Whether this evolutionary adaptation is still as important today as it once was is difficult to say for several species, including both the Bee and Late Spider Orchids, are known to be quite capable of self-pollination and this is probably the chief means of proliferation in these species in certain areas. Certainly as one moves northwards from the Mediterranean basin self-pollination becomes more apparent in *Ophrys*, a factor presumably associated with the decrease in the numbers and species of insects.

Ophrys are typical of the warm, dry, Mediterranean region, being particularly prolific in Italy, Greece, Southern France, Spain and many of the Mediterranean Islands, but also extending southwards into North Africa and eastwards into the Middle East. Moving northwards they become scarce and only a few species reach Great Britain and Northern Europe. The southern species often occur in large numbers, frequently with several different species growing together and the species can be very variable in both flower size and markings. To complicate matters hybridisation between species is common resulting in many intermediates. The parentage of such hybrids can often be deduced by carefully studying the different plants and species in a particular community.

Like *Orchis*, *Ophrys* has an underground stock of two, sometimes three rounded fleshy tubers. The leaves are mostly in a basal cluster but there are usually one or two above which partly unsheath the stem below the flowers. The flowers are in short or long, rather lax spikes, or occasionally solitary. The sepals are fairly large, oblong or oval, often spreading, green or variously coloured,

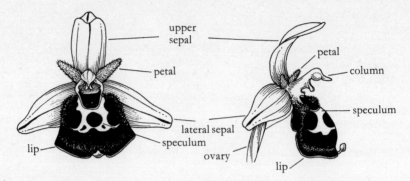

Front and side views of a typical *Ophrys* flower to illustrate the botanical details

whilst the two petals are smaller, sometimes thread-like and often hairy. The lip petal is generally large in comparison to the other flower parts, often with a thick felt of tiny hairs, giving it its insect body-like quality with the sepals and petals variously mimicking the 'insects' wings and antennae. The lip colour, shape and patterning varies from species to species, often within a species, but is generally entire or 3-lobed and in the centre there is usually a smooth shiny area or 'speculum' whose shape and size is characteristic of a particular species; there is no spur. The flowers are not brightly coloured but are most remarkable for their subtle shades and patterning, difficult often to describe but beautiful to observe, draw or photograph.

1. Mirror Orchid or **Mirror of Venus** *Ophrys speculum* [37]   Short perennial to 25cm tall, though generally less. Basal leaves oblong, rather blunt, the stem leaves narrower, pointed. Spike with 2–10 flowers; sepals green or yellowish, often purplish-brown streaked, oblong–oval; petals dark purple, hairy, lanceolate, about a third of the length of the sepals; lip 10–13mm long, broad, 3-lobed, fringed by black or brownish hairs, with a large *shiny, metallic-blue, speculum* surrounded by yellow. Grassy places, maquis and open woodland on calcareous soils, in Mediterranean areas. March–May. BAL, CO, CR, E, ſF, GR, I, P, SA, SC, TR.●

A beautiful Mediterranean region orchid often found growing in large colonies and readily identified by its large shiny metallic-blue speculum. The distribution extends to North Africa and eastwards into Asia Minor as far as Palestine.

1a. *O.s.* subsp. *lusitanica* is taller with spikes of up to 15 flowers, the *petals green* and the lip fringed by yellowish or rusty coloured hairs. P.

2. Fly Orchid *Ophrys insectifera* (=*O. muscifera*) [37]   Short slender perennial to 60cm tall. Basal leaves, lanceolate, pointed, the stem leaves smaller. Spikes with up to 14 flowers; sepals green, oblong-oval; petals blackish-violet, *thread-like*, shorter than the sepals; lip 8–10mm, oblong, 3-lobed, purplish-black or

Mirror Orchid, p.206, × 1

subsp. *lusitanica*, × 1

Fly Orchid, × 1

purplish-brown, rarely pale, with a *central, square or kidney-shaped, shiny violet-blue speculum*, the central lobe of the lip much larger than the lateral ones and notched. Woods (pine and beech in particular), thickets, banks and grassy places, usually on calcareous soils, to 1400m. May–June (July at higher altitudes in mountainous regions). T – except AL, AZ, BAL, BG, CO, CR, FA, GR, IS, K, NL, P, *e*RS, SA, SC, TR.●

The Fly Orchid is the most widespread *Ophrys* in Europe but it is often rather difficult to spot with its dark flowers and slender stems, as it usually grows in shaded places amongst tall grasses or herbs. Pale flowered forms can sometimes be seen and are sometimes distinguished as var. *ochroleuca*. In Britain it is mainly a plant of the southern counties.

3. Dull Ophrys or **Sombre Bee Orchid** *Ophrys fusca* [37]   Short to medium perennial to 40cm tall. Basal leaves oblong-lanceolate, blunt, the stem leaves narrow, pointed. Spike usually with 3–8 flowers; sepals green, rarely pinkish, oblong or oval; petals green, linear, half as long as the sepals; *lip horizontal* 13–15mm long, wedge-shaped, 3-lobed, purplish or yellowish-brown, *often yellow edged*, with a bluish, greyish or violet-blue w-shaped speculum towards the top and appearing like two 'eyes', the lateral lobes short and rounded, whilst the central one is notched in the middle. Grassy places, usually sunny meadows on calcareous soils, in Mediterranean areas, rarely above 600m. February–May. AL, BAL, CO, CR, E, ſF, GR, I, P, R, SA, SC, TR, YU.●

This is one of the earliest orchids to flower and it is certainly one of the commonest Mediterranean species. The flowers are rather duller than most other species of *Ophrys*. Besides Europe its distribution extends into North Africa, and eastwards to Turkey, Lebanon and Israel.

Dull Ophrys, × 1¼

O. fusca subsp. *omegaifera*, × 1¼

3a. *O.f.* subsp. *omegaifera* has spikes with 2–6 flowers and *a rather smaller deflexed lip* with a pale brown speculum or zone bounded by a white or yellowish N or W-shaped band. AL, CR, GR, I, SC, TR, YU.

3b. *O.f.* subsp. *iricolor* like (**3**) but spikes with 1–4 flowers; lip to 25mm long, *without a yellowish margin* but with a shiny blue speculum. AL, CR, GR, I, SC, TR, YU.

3c. *O.f.* subsp. *durieui* (=subsp. *atlantica*) like (**3b**) but spikes generally only with 1–2 flowers; lip larger, to 30mm long, purplish-violet with a shiny blue speculum *and long lateral lobes* – almost equalling the middle lobe. ʃE – also found in N. Africa.

4. *Ophrys pallida* [37]   Like (**3**) but with white or pale greenish petals and the lips only 7–9mm long. SC*.
   This pale-flowered orchid also grows in North Africa.

O. *fusca* subsp. *iricolor*, × 1   O. *pallida*, × 1   Yellow Ophrys, × 1

5. Yellow Ophrys *Ophrys lutea* [37]   Low to short perennial to 30cm tall. Basal leaves oval, pointed. Spikes with 2–7 flowers; sepals green, oblong-oval, blunt; petals greenish or yellowish, linear-oblong, usually about half as long as the sepals; lip 12–18mm long, rounded to oblong, 3-lobed, with a *broad flat yellow margin* surrounding a central reddish-brown zone which has a narrow shiny bluish-grey, 2-lobed, speculum, the central lobe of the lip usually rather larger than the lateral and notched at the end. Grassy and stony places, especially sunny meadows and maquis in Mediterranean areas, often rare but locally common. March–April. AEG, ʃF, I, SA, SC.
   The Yellow Ophrys is another typical Mediterranean species, the distribution extending into North Africa. It is a smallish plant generally and is readily distinguished by its flower colour.

5a. *O.l.* subsp. *galilaea* (=O. *lutea* var. *minor*) has a *smaller lip*, 9–12mm long, with a narrow yellow margin and a broad, often 2-lobed, speculum; central lobe of the lip generally smaller than the lateral ones. BG, CO, CR, ʃF, E, GR, I, c&ʃP, SA, SC, TR, YU.

5b. *O.l.* subsp. *melena*   Like (**5a**) but the *lip blackish-purple*, with the narrow yellowish margin covered with blackish-purple hairs. GR.

O. lutea subsp. *melena*, × 1

O. l. subsp. *galilaea*, × 1

Early Spider Orchid, × 1

6. Early Spider Orchid *Ophrys sphegodes* (=*O. aranifera*) [37]   Variable short/ medium perennial, to 45cm tall. Basal leaves oval-lanceolate, blunt, the stem leaves narrower, pointed. Spikes with 2–10 flowers; sepals green, oblong to lanceolate, blunt; petals green to greenish-purple or brownish, triangular or lanceolate, at least half the length of the sepals; lip 10–12mm long, oval, generally unlobed and with two hairy bosses near the base, velvety-brown or dark brown with an *H-shaped* violet-blue or purplish speculum, sometimes with the crossbar of the H missing. Grassy and rocky places, hillslopes or maquis, on calcareous soils. March–June. AL, A, B, BAL, BG, CH, CO, CR, CS, E, F, sGB, GR, I, K, P, R, SA, SC, TR, YU. ●

A widespread and very variable species which is locally common, particularly in Mediterranean Europe. Hybrids with *O. apifera*, *O. fuciflora* and *O. insectifera* can sometimes be observed. A number of subspecies are recognised.

6a. *O.s.* subsp. *litigiosa* (=*O. litigiosa*) [37] is more slender, the spikes with 6–10 small flowers; petals l-veined; *lip smaller*, 5–8mm long, pale-brown or blackish-brown generally *without* basal bosses. March–April. CR, E, sF, GR – including Corfu.

6b. *O.s.* subsp. *tommasinii* (=*O. tommasinii*) [37]   Like (**6a**) but with fewer flowers, 3–5 to each spike; *petals 3-veined*; lip pale brown with basal bosses and an H-shaped speculum with the crossbar towards the base. Coastal areas. nwGR, wYU.

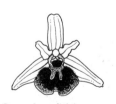

O. s. subsp. *litigiosa*, × 1

O. s. subsp. *mammosa*, × 1

O. s. subsp. *atrata*, × 1

6c. *O.s.* subsp. *atrata*   Like (**6**) but the lip blackish-brown or purple with long *velvety hairs*, often notched at the end, the crossbar of the H in the middle or at the base. Late March–May. AL, BAL, CO, CR, GR, sI, P, YU.

6d. *O.s.* subsp. *mammosa* [37] is a taller plant like (**6**) but the *lip larger*, 10–15mm long, blackish-brown or purplish with large basal bosses and an H-shaped speculum, often with the crossbar missing. February–April. AEG, BG, GR, SYU, TR; extending into Asia Minor and Cyprus.

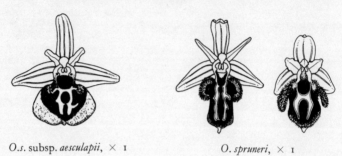

O.s. subsp. *aesculapii*, × 1   *O. spruneri*, × 1

6e. *O.s.* subsp. *aesculapii* [37]   Like (**6**) but the lip wider than long and blackish-brown with a broad *yellowish hairless margin*, the speculum H-shaped; sepals and petals pale olive-green. March-April. SGR.

6f. *O.s.* subsp. *parnassica* (=*O. sphaciotica*)   Like (**6d**) but the lip *usually 3-lobed* with small basal bosses and a yellowish hairless margin. CR, GR.

7. *Ophrys spruneri* (=*O. sphegodes* subsp. *spruneri*) [37]   Short perennial to 35cm tall. Basal leaves oblong or lanceolate, pointed. Spikes with 2–4 flowers. Sepals green or greenish-purple, oblong to lanceolate; petals usually pink, more than half as long as the sepals; lip 10–13mm, rounded or oval, *3-lobed*, blackish-brown or purple, velvety, with an H-shaped speculum *edged with white*, sometimes with the crossbar missing, the margin deflexed. Grassy and stony places, often in maquis. February–April. AEG, CR, GR.

O. s. subsp. *panormitana*, × 1   False Spider Orchid, × 1

7a. *O.s.* subsp. *panormitana* has white, pale pink or purplish sepals and petals; the lateral lobes of the lip hardly deflexed. March. SC.

Ophrys spruneri is closely related to the preceding species but distinguished from it by its distinctly 3-lobed lip and white edged speculum.

8. False Spider Orchid *Ophrys arachnitiformis* [38]   Short to medium plant to 40cm tall. Basal leaves oval-lanceolate, blunt, the stem leaves reduced, small and 'bract-like'. Spikes with 2–9 flowers; sepals *usually pink*, occasionally purplish, whitish or pale green, oblong or lanceolate, blunt; petals usually pink, slightly more than half the length of the sepals, linear-lanceolate, hairy or hairless; lip 8–10mm long, rectangular or oval, generally unlobed, the tiny tip forward-pointing, velvety-brown, tinged violet-purple, with an H or X-shaped blue or dark-purple speculum which has a whitish or yellowish margin. Grassy places, maquis, and cultivated pastures. March–May. E, *c&sF*, *n*I, SA, SC, ?YU.

This is a rather rare and very variable species which is sometime considered to be a hybrid between the Early Spider Orchid and the Late Spider Orchid. It can be readily distinguished from the former by its pink or purplish sepals and petals and from the latter by the 'bosses' at the base of the lip and by the 3-toothed upcurved tip to the lip. It is also found in North Africa (Algeria).

9. Horseshoe Orchid *Ophrys ferrum-equinum* [38]   Short plant to 35cm tall. Basal leaves lanceolate, acute, bluish-green, the stem leaves similar though smaller. Spikes with 2–5 flowers, lax; sepals purple, bright pink, rarely greenish, oblong to almost rounded; petals purple or pink, linear-lanceolate, about a half the length of the sepals, hairless; lip 10–12mm long, rounded, obscurely 3-lobed or unlobed, and *with a tiny forward-pointing tip*, velvety purple or brown with a *deep blue speculum* in the form of a horseshoe or two parallel vertical bars. Grassy slopes, often in maquis, or pine woods, generally on calcareous soils. April–May. AEG, CR, *s*GR.●

Horseshoe Orchid, × 1   subsp. *gottfriediana*, × 1

9a. *O.f.* subsp. *gottfriediana* has green, greenish-purple or almost white sepals and a *distinctly 3-lobed lip*. April. AEG.

This attractive species closely resembles *O. sphegodes* but it differs in having a small forward-pointing tooth-like appendage or tip to the lip and a horseshoe-shaped rather than H-shaped speculum, as well as having predominantly pink sepals. The Horseshoe Orchid is restricted to extreme south-eastern Europe.

10. Bertoloni's Bee Orchid or **Mirror of Venus** *Ophrys bertolonii* [38]   Short to medium plant up to 45cm tall. Basal leaves lanceolate, pointed, bluish-green, the stem leaves smaller. Spikes with 3–8 flowers; sepals pink or purplish, more rarely whitish, with 3 green veins, oval or oblong; petals pink or purple, hairy-edged, linear-lanceolate, more than half the length of the sepals; lip 10–15mm long, rounded to oblong, unlobed or faintly 3-lobed, *velvety blackish-purple* with a small greenish tip or tooth and a conspicuous bluish-violet, *shield-shaped, speculum.* Often growing in exposed places, on dry stony meadows, thickets and woodland margins and in clearings. Late March–May. AL, BAL, CO, E, sF, I, SA, SC, YU.

This species is restricted to the west and central Mediterranean region and is often considered to be rather rare. The species is named in honour of A. Bertoloni, a nineteenth century Italian Botanist, and is readily distinguished by its dark velvety, curved lip with its conspicuous shield-shaped speculum.

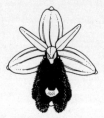

Bertoloni's Bee Orchid, p.213, × 1   Bee Orchid, × 1

11. Bee Orchid *Ophrys apifera* [38]   Short to medium plant up to 50cm tall, rarely more. Basal leaves oval to lanceolate, blunt, the stem leaves similar though smaller. Spikes with 2–9, rarely up to 15, flowers; sepals bright pink or purple, occasionally white, always with a green mid-vein, oblong-oval; petals green or purplish, linear-lanceolate to triangular, *short*, less than one third the length of the sepals; lip 10–13mm long, oval in outline, 3-lobed, the central lobe large with a tooth-like appendage *bent back underneath*, velvety brown or purplish-brown, partly velvety, with a basal shield-shaped speculum which is violet or rusty-brown with a yellow margin. Grassy meadows, usually on calcareous soils, occasionally in open woods or woodland clearings, or sometimes on dune slacks or in maquis, to 900m. May–July. T – except AEG, AZ, BG, DK, FA, IS, N, PL, RS, S, sF; rarer in the northern part of its range.●

11a. Wasp Orchid *O.a.* var. *trollii* [38] can be distinguished by its narrow, often pointed lip which is generally yellowish-green and rather mottled. It occurs throughout the range of the species.

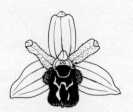

O. a. var. *trollii*, × 1   *O. a.* subsp. *jurana*, × 1

11b. *O.a.* subsp. *jurana* (=subsp. *botteronii*) has *larger petals* which are similar to the sepals but about two thirds of their length and the lip is often indistinctly 5-lobed. *w*CH, *c&sF*, *n*I. This plant is probably little more than a local variant of the Bee Orchid, like var. *trollii*.

The Bee Orchid is one of the most attractive and widespread *Ophrys* and certainly the most well known. Its flowering is spasmodic and in some years it is abundant whilst in the same localities in other years it is rare, or apparently absent altogether. In France the white-flowered form is sometimes referred to as the Cuckoo Orchid. This species is often observed to be self-pollinating in the northern part of its range. *Ophrys apifera* is frequently found in association with other species, most notably *O. fuciflora* and *O. sphegodes*, and in the south of Europe hybrids between these species can be found.

12. Bumble Bee Orchid *Ophrys bombyliflora* [38]   Low to short plant up to 25 cm tall. Basal leaves oblong-lanceolate, pointed, forming a flattish rosette, the stem leaves are erect and partly clasping the stem. Spikes with 2–5 flowers, or flowers solitary; sepals green occasionally whitish, oval, blunt; petals greenish with a purple base, triangular, about one-third the length of the sepals; *lip small*, 7–8mm long, markedly 3-lobed, with the lateral lobes deflexed and the middle one without a terminal 'tooth', *intense velvety black or deep brown* with a central bluish-violet, shield-shaped or 2-parted, speculum. Grassy places over chalk generally and maquis. March–May. BAL, CO, CR, E, *s*F, GR, I, P, SA, SC, YU.●

The Bumble Bee Orchid is a small-flowered species which is very local in the south of Europe and often considered rare, though sometimes occurring in large numbers. The distribution of this species extends into North Africa, the Canary Islands as well as Asia Minor, Lebanon and Israel.

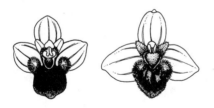

Bumble Bee Orchid, flowers, ✕ 1   Crescent Orchid, ✕ 1

13. Crescent Ophrys *Ophrys lunulata* [38]   Short plant up to 25 cm tall. Basal leaves oblong to lanceolate forming a rosette. Spikes loose, with 4–7 flowers; sepals violet-pink, occasionally whitish, oval to oblong, blunt; petals violet-pink linear-lanceolate, about two thirds the length of, or as long as, the sepals; lip 10–12mm long, oval, *markedly 3-lobed*, brown-velvety with a hairless yellowish or greenish margin and a whitish or pale violet *crescent-shaped speculum*. Grassy slopes or scrubland, in warm sunny places, generally on calcareous soils. March–May. *s*I*, M*, SA*, SC*.

This rare species is confined to southern Italy and the islands of the central

Mediterranean. It is readily recognised by the long petals, which often equal the sepals in length, and the lip which has three spreading lobes and a moon-shaped speculum.

14. *Ophrys argolica* [38]   Short plant up to 35cm tall. Basal leaves, lanceolate, pointed, the stem leaves similar though smaller. Spikes 4–6 flowered usually; sepals *purple or pinkish*, rarely whitish or green, oblong, the central one upright, often narrower; petals purple or pinkish-violet, velvety, lanceolate or triangular, more than half as long as the sepals; lip 10–12mm long, rounded to oval in outline, unlobed or 3-lobed, reddish-brown velvety, the margin generally yellow- ish and hairless, the speculum violet *with a white margin*, semicircular, H-shaped, horseshoe shaped or consisting of a single or double spot or dash. Coniferous woodland, grassy places, meadows and olive groves, on calcareous soils, at low altitudes. March–April. CR*, sGR*.

The speculum is often shaped like a pair of spectacles or consisting of two separate spots. Forms with white sepals and a yellowish lip are often assigned to var. *flavescens.*

15. Reinhold's Bee Orchid *Ophrys reinholdii* (=*O. reynholdii*) [38]   Like the previous species but the petals green, brown or pinkish-violet and the lip *more distinctly 3-lobed and blackish-purple*; speculum consisting of two white or pale violet lines, commas or spots, linked or separate from one another. Growing in short turf or sandy places, or in scrub and coniferous woods in hilly places. *n*AEG*, GR*.

A rather rare species in Europe, however, it is also found in southern Turkey and Syria.

O. argolica, × 1   Reinhold's Bee Orchid   Saw-fly Ophrys, × 1

16. Saw-fly Ophrys *Ophrys tenthredinifera* [39]   Short to medium plant up to 45cm tall. Basal leaves oval to lanceolate, blunt or pointed, the stem leaves similar though generally narrower. Spikes with 3–8 flowers; sepals pink, purplish or purplish-violet, occasionally whitish, oval; petals purplish or purplish-violet, velvety, triangular, one third the length of the sepals; lip 11–14mm long, squarish and generally unlobed, purple-brown *with a wide yellowish margin* and a small brown-spotted, generally 2-lobed, speculum. March–May. Grassy and stony places, scrub and maquis, BAL, CO, CR, E, sF*, I, GR, P, SA, SC, TR.●

This attractive large-flowered *Ophrys* is characteristic of the Mediterranean

littoral and, although widespread, it is often very localised. It is easily recognised
by its rather square lip which has a broad yellowish margin and a small rather
inconspicuous speculum.

17. Late Spider Orchid *Ophrys holoserica* (=*O. fuciflora*) [39]   Short to medium
plant up to 55cm tall, rarely more. Basal leaves oval or oblong, blunt, the stem
leaves narrower, pointed. Spikes with 2–8 flowers, occasionally more; sepals
pink, purplish or whitish, oval; petals the same colour as the sepals, velvety,
triangular or linear-lanceolate, up to one-third the length of the sepals; lip
9–13mm long, oval to rounded, generally unlobed, but with a large forward
pointing tip, velvety dark brown-purple, occasionally with a yellowish margin

Late Spider Orchid flowers, × 1

and a velvety boss on either side of the base; speculum very variable in shape but
violet or blue with a yellow or green margin. Short turf, banks, open woodland,
scrub and maquis, on calcareous soils, to 1300m. April–June. Distributed
throughout much of western and southern Europe, east to Turkey, Lebanon and
Israel. A, AL, B, BAL, CH, CO, CR, CS, D, E, F, ſBG*, GR, H, I, R, SA, SC, TR, YU.●

This attractive though variable orchid is widespread in Europe and Asia
Minor. In Britain it is now sadly reduced to a few localities in Kent. However, it
was probably never very common in this country being on the very northern
edge of its distribution. Three subspecies are currently recognised apart from the
typical plant described above.

17a. *O.h.* subsp. *candica* [39] has pink, pale purple or whitish sepals and petals
and a *brown or violet-brown shield-shaped speculum* which has a distinct whitish or
yellowish margin. April–May. CR, GR, ſeI.

This subspecies is also recorded from Rhodes.

O. h. subsp. *candica*, × 1

O. h. subsp. *oxyrrhynchos*, × 1

17b. *O.h.* subsp. *oxyrrhynchos* is like (**17**) but the *sepals and petals are green* and the
speculum is reduced or H-shaped, brown with a yellow margin; petals up to one
fifth the length of the sepals. April–May. SA, SC.

17c. *O.h.* subsp. *exaltata* (=*Ophrys exaltata*) [39] is like (**18b**) though taller and the lip has *distinct basal bosses* and the speculum is reduced, H-shaped or consisting of spots or lines; petals a third to one half the length of the sepals. Maquis turf. March–May. CO, C, ʃI, SC.

This plant is more robust than the other subspecies and is often regarded as a distinct species.

Subspecies *sundermannii* (=*Ophrys biscutella*) from Mt Gargano in south-east Italy is probably only a form of subsp. *exaltata* with red petals and a dark purplish-brown lip.

18. Woodcock Orchid *Ophrys scolopax* [39] Short to medium plant up to 45cm tall. Basal leaves lanceolate, acute, the stem leaves smaller and pointed. Spikes with 3–12 flowers; *sepals pink or purplish-violet*, occasionally green or whitish, oblong, the middle one erect; petals the same colour as the sepals usually, lanceolate-triangular, hairy, up to a half the length of the sepals; lip 8–12mm long, oval or almost rounded, 3-lobed usually, brownish or blackish-purple, velvety, except for a very narrow hairless margin, the tip often 3-toothed and the speculum large, violet or blue with a yellow or whitish margin, variable in shape from annular to shield or H-shaped – basal bosses of lip small. Wooded areas, scrub and turf. March–May. Mainly southern and south-western Europe. BAL, CO, CR, ʃE, ʃF, I, P, SA, SC, YU.●

A variable, predominantly Mediterranean species whose distribution extends into North Africa, Cyprus and Turkey.

O. *h.* subsp. *exaltata*, × 1   Woodcock Orchid, × 1   Horned Orchid, × 1

18a. *O.s.* subsp. *oestrifera* Like (**18**) but with a *wide hairless margin* to the lip. K. This subspecies is also found in the Caucasus.

18b. Horned Orchid *O.s.* subsp. *cornuta* (= *Ophrys cornuta*) [39] Like (**18**) but the lip with a wide hairless margin and a *long horn-shaped appendage* on each side of the lip near the base, these often up to 10mm long and forward projecting. April–May. Grassy, sunny hillslopes. Southern and south-eastern Europe. AL, BG, CR, GR, H, I, K, R, YU.●

This subspecies is readily recognised by the remarkable pronounced horn-like processes pointing forward from the base of the lip. It replaces the typical species in eastern Europe and occurs eastwards as far as the Caucasus.

19. Mt Carmel Ophrys *Ophrys carmelii* subsp. *attica* (=*O. attica* or *O. scolopax* subsp. *attica*) [39]   Short plant up to 35cm tall. Basal leaves linear-lanceolate, pointed, the stem leaves similar though smaller. Spikes with 3–8 flowers; sepals green, occasionally whitish, oval, the middle one *generally incurved*; petals green, rarely purplish, lanceolate-triangular, velvety, one third to a half the length of the sepals; *lip small*, 6–10mm long, oval or oblong, 3-lobed, velvety-brown with a narrow hairless margin and a blue or brown-violet shield-shaped speculum which is outlined with yellow; basal bosses of lip small, not more than 3mm long. March–April. Grassy places, olive groves, coniferous plantations and maquis, generally on calcareous soils. sGR, TR.

Rather similar to *O. scolopax* but with green rather than pink or purple sepals and a distinctly smaller lip. *Ophrys carmelii* is an early flowering species and its distribution extends eastwards into Asia Minor, Cyprus, Lebanon, Syria and Israel.

Mt Carmel Ophrys, × 1

Cretan Ophrys, × 1

20. Cretan Ophrys *Ophrys cretica* [39]   Short plant up to 30cm tall. Basal leaves oblong-lanceolate, pointed, the stem leaves smaller and narrower. Spike with 3–8 flowers; sepals green, brown or purplish, oblong; petals the same colour as the sepals but only half their length, linear-lanceolate, velvety; lip 11–14mm long, oval, 3-lobed, *blackish-purple* with hairy side-lobes, the *speculum white or bluish* with a white margin and H- or shield-shaped, or consisting of small spots. Grassy and stony places amongst trees and scrub. March–April. AEG, CR, sGR.●

The Aegean and Greek forms of this lovely species are often ascribed to subspecies *naxia* and subspecies *karpathensis* differing from the Cretan plant in minor details of the lip markings. These differences are not sufficient to warrant maintaining these subspecies.

Slipper Orchids   CYPRIPEDIUM

Perhaps the most enchanting of all the genera of European orchids, readily recognised by their ribbed leaves and their large, pouch-lipped flowers, each subtended by a large, leaf-like bract. The lip or slipper is in fact a clever device of nature to ensure cross-pollination, for an insect entering the slippery-sided slipper in search of nectar can only get out by passing close to the stigma and pollinia.

1. Lady's Slipper Orchid *Cypripedium calceolus* [39]   Short to medium rhizomatous perennial to 50cm tall, often forming small colonies. Stems hairy, with 3–4 elliptical or oval, *distinctly ribbed leaves*. Flowers usually solitary, occasionally 2 or 3 together; sepals reddish-brown, rarely yellowish-green, oval to lanceolate, the lateral two downward pointing and fused together for most of their length, the upper forming a hood; petals reddish-brown usually, linear-lanceolate, pointed, twisted; *lip large yellow*, 2.5–3cm long, forming an oval pouch or slipper with an inrolled margin. Woods and meadows, often on mountain slopes, on calcareous soils, to 2000m, May–July. Much of Europe but absent from the extreme north and south, but often rare and local. A, BG, CH, CZ, D, DK, E, F, *c*GB*, *n*GR, H, I, K, N, PL, R, RS, S, SF, YU.*

This is the rarest of all British orchids, now sadly reduced to a single locality in the north of England. In western Europe also it has become much scarcer in recent years due mainly to over-collecting and picking in the past. This beautiful plant deserves to be preserved in the wild. It is one of the most delightful of all plants to see in its native habitat and certainly one of the world's most exciting to photograph. In most countries it is now carefully protected by law. On the Continent, forms with pale yellow sepals and petals are sometimes seen.

Lady's Slipper Orchid, × ½

2. Rosy Lady's Slipper *Cypripedium macranthos* [39]   Short to medium rhizomatous perennial to 45cm tall, though often less. Stems hairy, with 3–4 leaves generally; leaves oval to elliptical, ribbed. Flowers solitary, occasionally 2 together; sepals lilac or purplish, oval, pointed, the lateral two downward pointing and fused together in the lower half, the upper one forming a hood; petals the same colour as the sepals, lanceolate, pointed; *lip pinkish or purplish*, *large*, 4.5–7cm long, forming a deep oval pouch. Woods, especially of birch, and clearings. June–July. *c*RS – particularly in the central and southern Urals.

Like the next species *C. macranthos* has its only European localities in Russia. It is also found throughout central Russia and Siberia eastwards through China and including Japan.

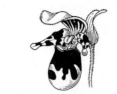

Spotted Slipper Orchid, × 1

Rosy Lady's Slipper, × ½

3. Spotted Slipper Orchid *Cypripedium guttatum* [39]   Short to medium rhizomatous perennial to 50cm tall. Stems hairy, with *only two*, rather shiny-green, elliptical leaves. Flowers solitary; sepals variable, the lateral two green, downward pointing and fused together, but the upper one oval, white, usually with purple blotches and spots; petals white, spotted and blotched purple, linear-oblong; lip white with purplish or lilac blotches and spots, smaller than (1) and (2), 2–2.5cm long, forming an oval wide-open pouch. Woods, especially of birch, scrub and clearings. May–June. *n,c&e*RS.

Serapias TONGUE ORCHIDS

Although closely related to both *Orchis* and *Ophrys*, *Serapias* species bear little initial resemblance with their strange rather sombre spikes of usually reddish or purplish flowers. The most distinctive feature is the large bracts, often coloured like the sepals. The sepals themselves form a prominent forward pointing helmet, whilst the lip (the lowermost petal) is large and downturned. The lip unlike that found in *Ophrys* is not folded or insect-like, instead it is tongue-like with two short upturned side lobes and a large projecting central lobe which is generally pointed. The petals are smaller than the sepals and are hidden within the helmet formed by the latter. The flowers are spurless and are usually bee pollinated.

Serapias is a fascinating genus and, like *Ophrys*, more typical of the Mediterranean region than any other. There they are often to be seen in large numbers, revelling in grassy and stony places, scrub or broken woodland, particularly along the seashore. Botanical authorities disagree as to the numbers of species, five are recognised here, but some would have twice as many, whilst others recognise two only. The situation is complicated by the fact that they all hybridise readily with one another where two or more species grow together. Hybrids are also produced with various other genera, especially *Anacamptis*, *Dactylorhiza*, *Ophrys*, and *Orchis*, thus producing a complicated array of hybrid offspring.

1. Long-lipped Serapias *Serapias vomeracea* (=*S. longipetala, S. pseudocordigera*) [40] Short/medium perennial to 55cm tall. Leaves linear, channelled, glaucous, the basal sheath-leaves green. *Bracts much longer than the flowers.* Spikes loose, with up to 10 flowers, each 15–30mm long; sepals pale purplish-red with darker veins; lip one and a half times as long as the sepals, with *two pale*, scarcely coloured, humps at the base, the tongue-lobe triangular, narrowed at the base, red or brownish. Meadows, heaths, scrub and damp woods, to 1100m. April–June. AL, BAL, BG, CH, CO, CR, E, *c&sF*, GR, P, SA, SC, TR, YU. ●

The distribution of this, the commonest species of Tongue Orchid, extends into N. Africa and eastwards into western Asia, as far as the Caucasus Mountains and the Lebanon.

S. *v.* subsp. *orientalis,* × ½

Long-lipped Serapias, × ½

1a. *S.v.* subsp. *orientalis* is a *shorter plant* to 30cm tall, often less. Bracts *only as long as or slightly longer than* the flowers. Spike short and dense, with up to 6 flowers; helmet often held in a horizontal position. March–May. AEG, CR, GR, *SI*, YU. Also found in N. Africa, Turkey and Rhodes.

1b. *S.v.* subsp. *laxiflora* (=*Serapias laxiflora, S. parviflora* subsp. *laxiflora*) Like (**1a**) but the *leaf-sheaths green or spotted.* Spikes lax, with 5–12 flowers; lip 18–25mm long. Late March–early May. AEG, AL, CR, GR, *SI* – Apulia and Calabria, YU. Also found in N. Africa, S. Turkey, Rhodes and Cyprus.

2. Scarce Serapias *Serapias neglecta* (=*S. cordigera* var. *neglecta*) [40] Short plant, not more than 30cm tall overall. Leaves narrow, lanceolate, pointed, channelled, the basal sheath-leaves green, *unspotted.* Bracts green, usually violet tinged, as long or slightly longer than the flowers. Spike short and dense with up to 8 flowers, each 25–40mm long; sepals and petals lilac; lip twice as long as the sepals, red or purplish, with two parallel black humps at the base, the central tongue-lobe, *broad heart-shaped*, with a yellow or orange centre. Damp meadows, maquis and sandy places near or along the coast. Late March–May. CO, *seF*, GR, *ni*, SA, YU. Rather rare.

A smaller red-flowered form found on the Ionian islands is sometimes distinguished as subsp. *ionica*.

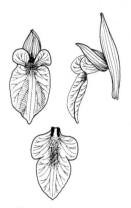

Tongue Orchid, × ½

Scarce Serapias, × ½

3. Tongue Orchid *Serapias lingua* (=*S. elongata*) [40]   Short plant rarely exceeding 25cm tall. Leaves narrow lanceolate, glaucous, the basal sheath-leaves green. Bracts *as long as the flowers*, violet-tinted. Spikes longer than 2 and 4, with up to 9 flowers, each 15–25mm long; sepals violet or purple, speckled green usually; lip oblong, narrowed at the base, twice as long as the sepals, with a *single black hump* at the base, the short side lobes purple, the long central tongue-lobe red or violet, sometimes white or yellowish. Damp meadows, olive groves, maquis, marshy areas and sandy places, often in partial shade and near or along the coast. March–May. AL, BG, CO, CR, E, ꜱF, GR, I, P, SA, SC, YU.●

S. lingua is a common species in its native home.

Small-flowered Tongue Orchid, × 1   *S. cordigera*, × ½

4. Small-flowered Tongue Orchid *Serapias parviflora* (=*S. occultata*) [40] Similar to (**3**), but a more graceful plant with the basal sheath-leaves often spotted. Flowers smaller, 15–20mm long, the lip *equal in length to the sepals*, brownish-red, rarely whitish, hairy, with two purplish-black humps near the base. Grassy places, wet and dry, coastal sands, or the fringes of olive groves. April–May. AL, BG, CO, E, ꜱF, GR, I, P, SA, SC, TR, YU.●

Serapias lingua and *S. parviflora* hybridise occasionally. In the south-east of France (Var District) this hybrid has been distinguished in the past as a distinct species under the name of *Serapias olbia* (=*S.* × *olbia*). It is rather rare and grows on lake margins and dune slacks, on acid soils, flowering from mid-April to mid-May.

5. Heart-flowered Orchid *Serapias cordigera* [40]   Short/medium plant to 50cm tall. Leaves narrow lanceolate, channelled, sharply pointed, the basal sheath-leaves *purplish and red-spotted*. Bracts shorter than the flowers. Spike short and rounded in outline with up to 10 flowers, each 20–35mm long; sepals and petals pale reddish-purple outside, deeper within; lip purplish or reddish, rarely yellowish, twice as long as the sepals, with two black humps or ridges near the base, hairy and with a broad *heart-shaped* central tongue-lobe, pointed. Damp grassy places, streamsides, scrub, maquis and open marshy woodland. Late March–June. A, AL, AZ, BG, CO, CR, E, ꟻF, GR, I, P, SA, SC, TR, YU.●

The distribution extends into N. Africa.

A small flowered form from the Azores with shorter spikes is often treated separately under the name *Serapias azorica*.

HIMANTOGLOSSUM

1. Lizard Orchid *Himantoglossum hircinum* (=*Loroglossum hircinum*) [40]   Short to tall erect perennial to 90cm. Leaves pale green, the lower oblong, blunt, the upper smaller, pointed and clasping the stem. Bracts about as long as the flowers. Spikes long, cylindrical, rather loose but many-flowered. Flowers with a strong, rather unpleasant odour; sepals and petals forming a small close hood, pale green, striped and spotted reddish-purple; lip *very long* and conspicuous, 30–50mm, with 3 long purplish limbs, outer two 'arm-like' 5–10mm long, the central one longer and notched at the tip, often curled and ribbon like, the centre of the lip whitish dotted purple; spur very short, 3–4mm, rounded. Sunny dry places, grassy meadows and banks, roadside verges, scrub and woodland clearings, on calcareous or sandy soils, to 1800m. May–July. A, B, BG, CH, CS, E, F, *c,*ꟻGB*, D, H, I, NL, R, SA, SC, TR, YU.●

1a. *H.h.* subsp. *calcaratum* (=*H. calcaratum*)   Is similar but with longer 'arms' to the hip, each 12–20mm, and a longer spur, 7–12mm. The flowers are often reddish-violet in general coloration. Mountain pastures, thickets, and scrub on calcareous soils, 400–900m usually. June–August. BG, GR, R, TR, ꟻYU.● Often treated as a distinct species.

1b. *H.h.* subsp. *caprinum*   Like (**1**) but the spikes with fewer flowers, rarely exceeding 20 in number, and the central strap-like lobe of the lip is deeply divided with two distinct 'legs' 10–15mm long. The lip is usually bright pink with red dots towards the base. May–July. K.

The distribution of this subspecies extends into Northern Turkey.

The Lizard Orchid is one of the largest European Orchids and one of the most fascinating. It is particularly delightful to watch the long lips uncurl from the buds as successive flowers open up the spike. In France it is unfortunately

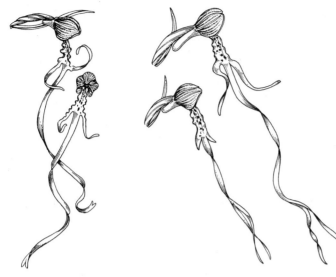

Lizard Orchid flowers, × 1   subsp. *calcaratum* upper, subsp. *caprinum* lower, × 1

known as the 'Orchis louc' or Goat Orchid because of its rather unpleasant smell. In England it is rare and at one time was almost extinct, but it appears to have made a revival in recent years. On the Continent, it is certainly rarer than it once was but it can still be found locally in large numbers. The distribution of the typical species extends eastwards into Asia Minor as well as N. Africa.

BARLIA

Giant Orchid *Barlia robertiana* (= *B. longibracteata, Himantoglossum longibracteatum, Loroglossum longibracteatum*) [40]   Stout plant up to 50cm tall. Leaves plain green, the lower large, oval or oblong, blunt, the upper smaller, bract-like. *Bracts longer than the flowers.* Spikes cylindrical, dense, the flowers with an iris-like

Giant Orchid, × 1

fragrance. Flowers rather large; sepals reddish-violet, spreading; the petals green, spotted purple, and forming a hood; lip 15–20mm, violet-pink or greenish, spotted purple in the centre, with two short 'arms', the central lobe rather longer and divided into two spreading fat 'legs'; spur short, downward pointing. Grassy places especially hillslopes, scrub and open woodland, generally along the Mediterranean coast. January–April. BG, CO, CR, E, ʃF, GR, I, P, SA, SC, YU.●

Rather like the Lizard Orchid but the lip much shorter and broader and the bracts noticeably longer than the flowers.

The Giant Orchid is one of the earliest orchids to flower and it is typical of the Mediterranean littoral. Its distribution extends south into N. Africa and the Canary Isles and eastwards into Turkey. The scent of the flowers is said to be reminiscent of irises.

ANACAMPTIS

Pyramidal Orchid *Anacamptis pyramidalis* [40]   Slender plant 20–60cm tall. Leaves pale green, linear-lanceolate, channelled, decreasing in size up the stem, the uppermost small and bract-like. *Spikes cone-shaped*, dense, with rather small bright pink flowers, rarely pale pink or white; outer two sepals spreading, the upper one and the two petals forming a small hood; lip rather short, 6–8mm, 3-lobed, the central lobe slightly smaller, not notched; *spur very long* and slender, 12–14mm, downcurved. Grassy meadows and banks, scrub, on calcareous soils, to 1900m, often in large numbers. May–July. T – except AZ, FA, IS, N, SF, *n,e*RS.●

A widespread European orchid which is very attractive with its distinct conical-shaped flower spikes which become oblong in outline as more and more flowers open. The distribution of the Pyramidal Orchid extends into N. Africa and eastwards into Asia Minor, the Caucasus, Israel and Iran.

Various varieties have been described including var. *brachystachys* from the eastern Mediterranean which has pale pink flowers. It is a smaller plant than the type and is found chiefly on mountain pastures. Another mountain variety is var. *tanayensis* described from the vicinity of Lake Tanay in the Alps up to 2000m. This has dark purple flowers with a spur shorter than the ovary.

Pyramidal Orchid, × 1

Ground Orchids ORCHIS

Among European orchids the species of the genus *Orchis* itself show the greatest variety of form and colour and are amongst the finest of all the monocots of the area to observe and photograph. Where they occur they are often to be seen in large numbers, though often locally so. However, they suffer badly from disturbance of the habitat and resent picking, herbicides, fertilizers, and in fact anything that serves to interfere with the delicate balance of their environment. Large stands of Early Purple Orchids, *Orchis mascula*, in an English beechwood, or banks of Lady Orchids, *O. purpurea*, in the French Auvergne are sights to be relished by anyone interested in plants.

The underground tubers consist of two, sometimes three, globular or egg-shaped, fleshy tubers set close together (the generic name is derived from the Greek, referring to the testicle-like character of the tubers). The leaves are mostly in a basal rosette, though there are usually several smaller leaves above, which ensheath or partly ensheath the stem. The flowers are borne in few or many-flowered spikes. The sepals are alike and generally coloured like the petals; occasionally they may be spreading, but more often they come together with the upper two petals to form a close hood or helmet, or alternatively the lateral two sepals spread outwards and upwards like a pair of wings leaving the upper sepal and two petals to form the hood. The lip petal is usually large and conspicuous, frequently 3-lobed and manikin-like, the lateral lobes forming the 'arms' whilst the lower lobe is further lobed to form the 'legs', sometimes with a short tail or 'tooth' in between. At the base of the lip there is a backward pointing spur which may be short or long. The shape of the lip and spur are the two most important characters in separating one species of *Orchis* from another.

1. Bug Orchid *Orchis coriophora* [41] Low to medium plant to 40cm tall. Leaves narrow-lanceolate, unspotted, *overlapping and sheathing the stem to the top*. Bracts lanceolate, 1-veined. Flowers small, in dense oblong spikes, supposedly smelling of bed bugs; sepals and petals violet-brown, all forming a narrow pointed helmet, 5–10mm long; lip 5–8mm long, purplish-green with 3 almost equal, blunt, lobes; spur short, downcurved, half as long as the lip. Damp poor meadows and grassy places, generally on slightly acid soils, to 1800m. April–June. T – except BAL, DK, GB, IRL, IS, N, *n*RS, S, SF.

The distribution extends into N. Africa and eastwards into south-west Asia.

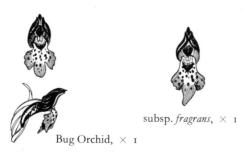

subsp. *fragrans*, × 1

Bug Orchid, × 1

1a. *O.c.* subsp. *fragrans* has darker, vanilla-fragrant flowers, the lip 8–11mm long with a *larger central lobe*; spur longer, at least as long as the lip. Mediterranean in distribution, damp pastures, hillslopes and maquis. A, AEG, AL, BG, CH, CO, CR, ꜱF, GR, I, SA, SC, TR, YU.

This subspecies is also found in N. Africa, Cyprus, Turkey and the Lebanon.

2. Holy Orchid *Orchis sancta*   Like (**1**) but with a *rosette of leaves* clasping the base of the stem; lower bracts 3–5-veined. Flowers larger, pale lilac to red, the lip 8–12mm, with strongly toothed side lobes. April. Dry grassland on calcareous soils, sandy places and maquis. AEG, GR.

The distribution of the Holy Orchid extends eastwards into Turkey, Cyprus, Syria, Lebanon and Israel.

Holy Orchid, × 1   Burnt Orchid, × 2

3. Burnt Orchid *Orchis ustulata* [41]   Variable low to short plant to 35cm tall, though generally less. Leaves oblong, pointed, channelled, unspotted; stems leafless in the upper half. Bracts oval-lanceolate, 1-veined, about as long as the ovary. Flowers tiny, in dense conical heads, elongating as the lower flowers fade; sepals and petals forming a close helmet, 3–3.5mm long, *dark brownish-purple* at first, but gradually fading; lip white or pale pink, finely spotted with purple, 3-lobed, the central lobe larger and notched in the middle; spur short, down-curved, not more than half as long as the ovary. Dry meadows, grassy places, often hillslopes or mountain-sides, on calcareous soils, to 2100m. April–July. Most of Europe except the extreme north and south and the islands. CH, D, DK, ꜯE, F, ꜰ&ꜱGB, GR, H, I, PL, R, RS – except *n,ꜱ*S, YU.●

A delicate little orchid which is quite often seen, usually growing in rather scattered colonies. It gets its common name from the brownish helmet colorating of the newly opened flowers which give the top of the spike a burnt or singed appearance. Occasionally forms can be found with very pale helmets and are sometimes referred to as var. *albiflora*.

4. Toothed Orchid *Orchis tridentata* [41]   Short to medium rather robust plant to 45cm tall. Basal leaves 3–4, oblong, pointed, unspotted; stem leaves small, sheath-like. Bracts lance-shaped, 1-veined, about as long as the ovary. Flowers in dense cone-like spikes to begin with, but eventually elongating, fragrant; sepals and petals pale violet-lilac, sharply pointed, *forming a close helmet*, 6–8mm long; lip pale violet-lilac spotted with purple, 3-lobed, the 'arms' oblong, the central one larger with two blunt 'legs' with a *small tail in between*; spur downcurved, half as long as the ovary. Wood, thickets and grassy places, sometimes in maquis, to 1500m. March–May. A, AL, BG, CH, CD, CR, CS, D, E, F, GR, H, I, K, P, PL, R, TR, YU.●

The distribution extends eastwards into S.W. Asia as far as the Caucasus and Iraq.

4a. *O.t.* subsp. *commutata* is a more slender plant with a loose spike of somewhat larger flowers, the sepals and petals ending in a *long fine point*, forming a helmet 8–10mm long. A, CH, ꜱF, I, YU.

5. Milky Orchid *Orchis lactea*   Like (3) but a shorter plant, not exceeding 20cm tall. Flowers *white or greenish-pink*, the middle lobe of the lip rounded, rarely notched, often unspotted; spur sometimes longer than the ovary. Dry grassy places and maquis, local in the Mediterranean region. February–April. AEG, BAL, CO, ꜰR, E, ꜱF, GR, I, P, SC, YU.

The distribution extends into N. Africa, Asia Minor and the Lebanon.

Toothed Orchid, × 1

Milky Orchid, × 1

Lady Orchid, × 1

6. Lady Orchid or **Dark-winged Orchid** *Orchis purpurea* [41]   Medium/tall robust plant to 80cm. Basal leaves 3–6, broad-oblong, blunt, *glossy plain green*; lower stem with 1–2 sheath leaves. Bracts oval to lanceolate, shorter than the ovary. Flowers many in dense cylindrical spikes, fragrant; sepals and petals brownish-purple, often dark purple spotted, forming a helmet 12–14mm long; lip white or pink, finely spotted with purple, 3-lobed, the 'arms' narrow oblong, the central lobe much larger with two short blunt 'legs' with a short 'tail' in between; spur downcurved, a third to half as long as the ovary. Woods, particularly of Beech, scrub, banks and grassy places, usually on calcareous soils, to 1500m. May–June. A, B, BG, CO, CH, CS, D, DK, *n*E, F, *se*GB*, *n*GR, H, I, K, NL, PL, R, *w*RS, SA, TR, YU.●

The distribution extends eastwards into S.W. Asia as far as the Caucasus and southwards into N. Africa.

The Lady Orchid is one of the most sumptuous of our native European species which can be likened to a giant Burnt Orchid but rather richer in colouring. Plants often occur in large colonies and like many other species, many more leaf rosettes can be spotted than plants actually in flower. White flowered forms with greenish sepals and petals are occasionally found. In Great Britain the species is much scarcer than a few years ago and is now almost entirely restricted to the extreme south-east of England.

7. Military or **Soldier Orchid** *Orchis militaris* [41]   Short to medium plant to 60cm tall. Basal leaves 3–5, oblong-lanceolate or oval, flat, unspotted; stems with 1–2 sheath-like leaves in the lower part. Bracts oval-lanceolate, *often violet*, and much shorter than the ovary. Flowers in dense cone-like spikes at first but soon elongating, opening from the base of the spike upwards; sepals and petals pink or pinkish-grey flushed with violet, forming a close helmet with upturned tips; lip white tipped, and spotted with violet-purple, 3-lobed, the 'arms' linear, the central lobe with oblong 'legs' with a fine 'tail' inbetween; spur down-curved, half as long as the ovary. Woodland margins, scrub and undisturbed grassy places on calcareous soils, to 1800m. April–June. A, B, BG, CH, CS, D, *n,*CE, F, *s*GB*, H, *n,*CI, P, R, RS, SC, TR, YU.●

The distribution of the species extends eastwards into central Asia and Siberia.

An attractive species which looks at first glance rather like the Monkey Orchid but it can be easily distinguished by the fact that the flowers open from the base to the top of the spike in the Military Orchid, whereas in the Monkey Orchid the situation is reversed and the uppermost flowers are the first to open. It is rare in Britain, being restricted to a few sites in southern England.

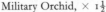

Military Orchid, × 1½   Monkey Orchid, × 1½

8. Monkey Orchid *Orchis simia* [41]   Short to medium plant to 45cm tall. Basal leaves 3–5, oblong-lanceolate or oval, flat, shiny, unspotted; stem leaves small, sheath-like. Bracts tiny oval-lanceolate, half as long as the ovary. Flowers in oblong spikes, the uppermost opening first; sepals and petals pale rose or lilac, rarely white, forming a close helmet 8–10mm long; lip whitish tipped and spotted with pinkish-purple or purple, 3-lobed, the *'arms' linear, forward curved*, the *'legs' similar*, also forward curved, with a prominent 'tail' inbetween; spur downcurved, half as long as the ovary. Open woodland, scrub, maquis and grassy places, usually on calcareous soils and in shaded or semi-shaded positions, to 1500m. April–June. B, BG, CH, CR, D, E, F, *s*GB, GR, I, K, R, TR, YU.●

The distribution extends into N. Africa and eastwards into Asia Minor, Cyprus and the Middle East (Syria, Lebanon and Israel).

9. Italian Man Orchid *Orchis italica* [41]   Short to medium rather slender plant to 40cm tall. Basal leaves 5–8, oblong-lanceolate, wavy-edged, often spotted; stem leaves sheath-like. Bracts tiny, oval, 1-veined, much shorter than the ovary. Flowers in dense cones or globular clusters, the lowermost opening first; sepals and petals pale pink or lilac, purple-veined, forming a helmet 9–11mm long; lip tipped and spotted with purple, flattish, 3-lobed, the 'arms' and 'legs' linear *with a long fine point*, 'legs' with a fine 'tail' inbetween; spur downcurved, half as long as the ovary. Scrub and evergreen forests, grassy places and maquis, on calcareous soils, in the Mediterranean region. April–June. BG, CR, E, GR, I, *c*&*s*P, SC, YU.●

Distribution extending into Asia Minor, Cyprus and the Lebanon.

Rather similar to the preceding species but the lip flattish, the 'arms' and 'legs' very finely pointed, but scarcely curved.

Italian Man Orchid, × 1½

10. Punctate Orchid *Orchis punctulata* [41]   Short to medium plant to 60cm tall. Basal leaves 4–7, oblong, unspotted; stems usually with 1–2 sheathing leaves. Bracts small, oval, much shorter than the ovary. Flowers many in cylindrical spikes; sepals and petals oblong, blunt, forming a helmet 8–15mm long; lip *yellowish-green*, usually purple spotted, 3-lobed, the 'arms' oblong, blunt, the central lobe kidney-shaped, with two very short rounded lobes (the 'legs') and a small 'tooth' in between; spur downcurved, a third as long as the ovary. March-May. Forest and woods (mixed and coniferous), thickets, sometimes in more open places. K*. Also found in Turkey, Cyprus, Syria, Palestine, Iraq, Iran and the Caucasus.●

10a. *O.p.* subsp. *sepulchralis* has larger flowers with the spur *half as long* as the ovary. GR*, TU.

Punctate Orchid, p.229, × 1   Green-winged Orchid, × 1

11. Green-winged Orchid *Orchis morio* [42]   Low to medium plant to 30cm tall. Leaves mostly in a basal rosette, broad-oval to lanceolate, unspotted; stem with sheathing leaves almost up to the flowers. Bracts lanceolate, about as long as the ovary, several-veined, green or purplish. Flowers in a rather loose oblong spike; sepals and petals forming a loose helmet 8–10mm long, purplish-violet, pink, red, greenish or white, the two lateral sepals *conspicuously green veined*; lip 8–10mm long, rather flat with 3 shallow lobes, purple, pink, red or white, often with darker spots in a central paler zone; spur upcurved, shorter than the lip, narrowed at the tip. Grassy meadows, banks, scrub and maquis, on calcareous or somewhat acid soils, to 1800m. March–June. T – except AZ, CR, FA, GR, IS, *n*N, RS, *n*S, TR, *s*YU.●

11a. *O.m.* subsp. *picta*, similar but with a laxer flower spike, the helmet smaller, 6–8mm long, and the spur *as long* as the lip. Mediterranean region. AEG, BG, *s*F, GR, I, TR, YU. Also found in Turkey, Syria, Lebanon and Israel.

11b. *O.m.* subsp. *champagneuxii* like (**11**) but the lip is *folded in the centre* and thus appearing narrower from the front, and the spur is long and thickened at the tip. E, *s*F, P. Also found in N. Africa.

An attractive and widespread plant, the Green-winged Orchid is often to be seen in large numbers, though like most other species it tends to be very local in distribution. It is sometimes confused with the Early Purple Orchid though it is very distinct usually with its green-veined lateral sepals. Furthermore, these sepals are forward directing forming part of a loose helmet, whereas in the Early Purple Orchid the lateral sepals are spreading and 'wing-like'. The distribution of the species extends into N. Africa, Asia Minor, Cyprus, Israel and the Lebanon, although in the east subsp. *picta* replaces the typical plant.

12. Long-spurred Orchid *Orchis longicornu* [42] Short plant to 25cm tall, seldom more. Leaves mostly in a basal rosette, oblong-lanceolate, unspotted; stem with sheathing leaves almost up to the flowers. Bracts lanceolate, about as long as the ovary, several-veined, often purple or reddish tinged. Flowers in loose oblong spikes; sepals and petals white or pale violet-pink, forming a small helmet 6mm long, the lateral sepals with greenish parallel veins; lip kidney-shaped, 3-lobed, folded back from the centre, purplish-violet, usually with darker spots in the paler central zone; spur upcurved, thickened at the tip, *much longer than the lip*. Dry grassy places, scrub and maquis, in the W. Mediterranean region. February–April. BAL, CO, ꜰ, I, P, SA, SC.●

A local plant with flowers resembling a small Green-winged Orchid but readily distinguished by their long spurs. It is also to be found in N. Africa.

Long-spurred Orchid, × 1

Pink Butterfly Orchid, × 1

13. Pink Butterfly Orchid *Orchis papilionacea* [42] Short to medium plant to 40cm tall. Leaves mostly in a basal rosette, lanceolate to linear-lanceolate, pointed; stem leaves sheathing the stem up to the flowers, usually tinged purple or red. Bracts lanceolate, longer than the ovary, 3–4-veined, usually tinged like the stem leaves. Flowers in a loose oblong spike; sepals and petals forming a loose or close helmet, 10–15mm long, purple or brownish or reddish-purple with darker parallel veining; lip oval or rounded, 12–16mm, *unlobed but with a finely serrated edge*, often notched at the apex, purple, reddish-pink or whitish, usually with darker spots and lines; spur slightly downturned, conical, *shorter than the ovary*. Dry grassy places, maquis and thickets, olive groves, on calcareous or somewhat acid soils. March–May. BAL, BG, CO, CR, E, ꜰ, GR, I, P, R, SA, SC, TR, YU.●

This attractive species is also found in N. Africa.

13a. *O.p.* var. *grandiflora* is often distinguished with its *larger flowers*, the lip 20–25mm long. E.

14. *Orchis boryi* [42]   Like (**13**) but the flowers violet-purple, in rounded heads, with the uppermost opening first; *lateral sepals spreading*; lip oblong or rounded, shallowly 3-lobed, smaller, 8mm long, violet-purple or whitish; spur and bracts *shorter than the ovary*. Thickets and maquis over limestone. April. CR*, *s*GR*.

    This rare orchid is sometimes likened to a large-flowered *O. quadripunctata*. Both have a lip marked with 2 or 4 reddish or purplish spots. However, its affinities are closer to *O. papilionacea*, though the flowers are only half the size. Furthermore, it differs from both these species by the upper flowers in the spike opening first rather than the lowermost.

15. Green-spotted Orchid *Orchis patens* [42]   Medium to tall plant to 70cm. Leaves mostly in a basal rosette, oblong to lanceolate, unspotted; stem with sheathing leaves in the lower part. Bracts narrow-lanceolate, pointed, half as long as the ovary, with 5−7 veins. Flowers in a *long loose cylindrical spike*; sepals and petals pink or purple with a central green zone, often spotted, the lateral sepals spreading and 'wing-like', the remainder forming a loose helmet; lip oval, 9−10mm, 3-lobed, purple or pinkish, usually dark-spotted, the middle lobe notched; *spur 'pouch-like'*, downward pointing, about half as long as the ovary. Open woodland, maquis and mountain meadows, up to 1600m, in the W. Mediterranean region. March−May. BAL, ?CR, *s*E*, *n*I*, SC*. A rare species also found in Algeria.

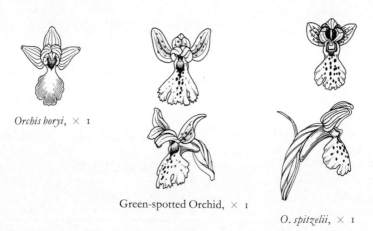

Orchis boryi, × 1

Green-spotted Orchid, × 1

O. spitzelii, × 1

16. *Orchis spitzelii* is a shorter plant than (**15**), to 40cm tall, with broader leaves and flowers in a *dense short, often rounded spike*. Bracts as long as the ovary. Sepals and petals brownish or greenish, red-spotted inside; lip pinkish or purple, spotted, with 2 ridges at the top; spur narrow, conical, one-third the length of the ovary. Mountain meadows, to 1800m. April−July. *e*A, AL, BG, CR, D, *e*E, *s*E*F, GR, I, *s*S − Gotland*, YU.

    A rare and very local species also found in Algeria, the Caucasus and Turkey.

17. Fan-lipped Orchid *Orchis collina* (=*O. saccata*) [42]   Short plant to 30cm tall. Basal rosette of 2–4 leaves, broad oblong-oval, sometimes dark-spotted; stem with sheathing leaves, sometimes purple tinged. Bracts oval-lanceolate, 5–7-veined, the lower longer than the ovary. Flowers in a loose oblong spike; sepals and petals dark olive-green or purplish, the lateral sepals spreading upwards, the upper sepal and petals forming a helmet; lip oval or oblong, 10mm long, fan-shaped, purple or pinkish, *unlobed but with a finely toothed edge*; spur 'pouch-like', blunt, half as long as the ovary. Dry grassland, open woods and maquis on calcareous soils, in the central and eastern Mediterranean region. February–April. CR, SF, GR, I, SA, SC, TR.

A local species, often very rare, but also found in N. Africa, Cyprus, Asia Minor, Iran, Syria, Iraq and the Lebanon.

Four-spotted Orchid, × 1

Fan-lipped Orchid, × 1

Anatolian Orchid, × 1

18. Four-spotted Orchid *Orchis quadripunctata* [42]   Short plant to 25cm tall, with a rather flexuous stem. Basal leaves 2–4, linear to oblong-lanceolate, unspotted; stem with sheathing leaves in the lower part. Bracts lanceolate, 1–3-veined, about as long as the ovary. Flowers rather small, in loose cylindrical or oblong spikes, purple, pinkish or sometimes whitish; *sepals spreading*, oval, blunt, the petals forming a close small helmet; lip oval or rounded, 4–5mm, with *two or more usually four prominent spots* near the top, 3-lobed, the central lobe square-ended or notched; spur slender, horizontal or downcurved, about as long as the ovary. Grassy places, hill slopes, scrub and thickets, mainly in the eastern Mediterranean region. April–May. AL, CR, GR, I, SA, SC, YU.●

An elegant small-flowered species, often very local in distribution but also found in Turkey and Cyprus. It is the commonest orchid in many parts of Crete.

19. Anatolian Orchis *Orchis anatolica* [42]   Short to medium plant to 25cm tall; stem erect or flexuous. Basal leaves 2–5, lanceolate or oblong, unspotted; stem with sheathing leaves in the lower part. Bracts narrow lanceolate, 1–3-veined, rather shorter than the ovary. Flowers few, in a loose oval spike, *purple or pinkish*; lateral sepals spreading, oblong or lanceolate, the upper sepal and petals forming a helmet; lip oval, 10–14mm, 3-lobed, with rather squarish lobes, the central one longer than the outer; spur slender, widened at the base, horizontal or slightly downcurved, *longer than the ovary*. Grassy slopes and open scrub. March–April. sAEG*●

19a. *O.a.* subsp. *sitiaca* has greenish-violet flowers, a longer lip and a prominent *upcurved* spur. CR*.

An attractive species rare in Europe but more widespread in the eastern Mediterranean, particularly Turkey, the Lebanon and Israel. It can be confused with *Orchis laxiflora* but the flowers are larger and the spur considerably longer.

20. Early Purple Orchid *Orchis mascula* [43]   Short to medium plant to 55cm tall; stem often purple tinged. Leaves 3–5, oblong, plain green or spotted with purple, the stem with sheathing leaves above the lower ones. Bracts lanceolate, 1–3-veined, often purplish, about as long as the ovary. Flowers many in a loose, blunt, oval spike, *dark purple or pink*, rarely whitish, the lip with dark spots on a pale central zone; *outer sepals spreading upwards*, the upper sepal and petals forming a hood; lip oval, 8–15mm, 3-lobed, the middle lobe half as long again as the lateral lobes, notched and slightly toothed; spur cylindrical, *upcurved*, about as long as the ovary. Meadows, grassy places, banks, deciduous woods and thickets, often on clayey soils, to 2650m. May–July. T – except AZ, CR, IS, *n*&eRS, SP.●

Early Purple Orchid, × 1   subsp. *olbiensis*, × 1

20a. *O.m.* subsp. *wanikowii* has lilac flowers, few to a spike, the outer sepals with parallel *purple-brown veins*; spur shorter than the ovary. K*. Not known elsewhere.

20b. *O.m.* subsp. *signifera*   Like (**20**) but the sepals and petals *with a pointed appendage* at the tip and the middle lobe of the lip almost twice as long as the lateral lobes. Most of *c,s*&*e* Europe.

20c. *O.m.* subsp. *olbiensis*   Like (**20**) but the lateral lobes of the lip bent backwards and the spur *noticeably longer* than the ovary. W. Mediterranean region. BAL, CO, E, sF. Also distributed in N. Africa. The leaves are generally unspotted.

The Early Purple Orchid is one of the best known and widespread European orchids, often found in scrub or rather open woodland. In Britain it is often associated with oak-hazel coppices and oak woodland, and frequently grows with bluebells in the western part of its range and flowering at about the same time. The tubers are rich in a starch-like substance, bassorine, which has a high nutritive value, though it is not a feasible economic proposition; nor is it desirable from a conservation point of view to dig up plants. In south-east Europe a drink called 'Salep' is prepared from the crushed tubers. The Early Purple Orchid has a smell reminiscent of tom cats, though subsp. *olbiensis* is said to have no scent at all. The range of the species extends eastwards into Asiatic Russia, Turkey and the Caucasus. British plants generally have more heavily blotched leaves, whereas continental forms may only be speckled towards the base, or plain green.

21. Pale-flowered Orchid *Orchis pallens* [43]   Short plant to 35cm tall; stems green. Leaves 3–6 on the lower part of the stem, oblong, narrowed at the base, plain glossy green, the stem with a few sheathing leaves above. Bracts lanceolate, 1-veined, about as long as the ovary. Flowers in dense oblong spikes, *pale yellow*, elderberry scented; outer sepals spreading upwards, the upper sepal and petals forming a hood; lip rounded, 6–8mm, 3-lobed, *unspotted*, the middle lobe squarish or slightly notched; spur upcurved, rather shorter than the ovary. Meadows and deciduous woods, to 2000m, in central and south-east Europe. April–June. A, BG, CH, CS, *C&SF*, *S*G, GR, H, *n*&*c*I, K, PO, R, YU.

A readily recognised plant with its pale yellow unspotted flowers. Some people consider the smell to be rather unpleasant. It is most typically an upland or mountain plant, though not growing at high altitudes and often very local in distribution. *O. pallens* is also found in Asia Minor and the Caucasus.

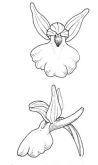

Pale-flowered Orchid, × 1½   Provence Orchid, × 1

22. Provence Orchid *Orchis provincialis* [43]   Short to medium plant to 30cm tall. Basal leaves 2–5, in a rosette, lanceolate to oblong, usually brown spotted; stem with sheathing leaves in the lower half. Bracts lanceolate, 1–3-veined, as long as, or longer than, the ovary. Flowers 5–20, in rather dense oblong spikes, pale yellow or greenish-yellow with a deeper yellow or orange, *brown-spotted, lip*, slightly scented; outer sepals spreading upwards, the upper sepal and petals forming a hood; lip 8–12mm long, 3-lobed, the cental lobe slightly longer, notched and toothed; spur upcurved, broadening towards the tip, as long as, or longer than, the ovary. Grassy and rocky places, open woodland, in southern Europe, usually on calcareous soils, to 1300m. April–June. A, BG, CH, CO, CR, E, F, GR, I, K, P, SA, SC, YU.●

22a. *O.p.* subsp. *pauciflora* has only 3–7 flowers to a spike, *larger than* (**22**), the lip 13–15mm long, and the leaves unspotted. AEG, AL, CO, GR, I, YU.●

It grows in similar habitats to the typical plant but is far less common. The range of this subspecies extends into Asia Minor.

The Provence Orchid is one of the most beautiful species with its yellow flowers. In the best forms the lip has a central orange zone speckled with reddish-purple. The leaves are usually, but not always, spotted. It is locally common in the Mediterranean borderlands.

23. Jersey, Lax or **Loose-flowered Orchid** *Orchis laxiflora* [43]   Medium to tall plant to 50cm; stem erect or flexuous, and carrying 3–8 linear or lanceolate, pointed leaves in the lower part, *no sheathing leaves above*. Bracts lanceolate 3–5-veined, often tinged with pink or purple, usually about as long as the ovary. Flowers in a long loose spike, purple, occasionally white; outer sepals spreading upwards, the upper sepal and petals forming a hood; lip almost rounded with a whitish, rarely purple spotted, zone in the centre, 7–10mm long, 3-lobed, the middle lobe shorter than the outer ones which are folded backwards; spur cylindrical, horizontal or upturned, broadened at the tip, about two-thirds the length of the ovary. March–June. Marshy meadows, boggy places and scrub in west and southern Europe, to 1150m. A, AEG, AL, B, BAL, CH, CO, CR, CS, D, E, F, *sw*GB, GR, I, SA, SC, TR, YU.

23a. Bog Orchid *O.l.* subsp. *palustris* (=*O. palustris*) middle lobe of the *lip as long as or longer* than the outer lobes and distinctly notched, the central white area flecked violet-purple; spur *not broadened* at the tip. Mainly found in Mediter-

Jersey Orchid, × 1

Bog Orchid, × 1

ranean Europe. A, AL, B, BG, CH, CR, CS, D, DK, E, ꞁF, GR, H, I, K, ꞁN, PL, R, RS, S, SC, TR, YU.

The flowers of subsp. *palustris* are often rather paler than those of the type.

23b. *O.l.* subsp. *elegans* (= *O. pseudolaxiflora*) has broader leaves than (**23**) and the lip scarcely 3-lobed. A, BG, CS, R, YU.

An attractive species locally common particularly in Mediterranean Europe but distributed in N. Africa and eastwards through Asia Minor to Syria, Iraq, Iran and Afghanistan. However, the type plant does not extend further than eastern Turkey; further east it is replaced by subsp. *palustris* which is regarded by some as a distinct species though the differences are admittedly slight.

TRAUNSTEINERA

Globular Orchid *Traunsteinera globosa* (= *Orchis globosa*) [43]   Short to medium perennial, up to 65cm tall though often less; stems slender, often curved with several brownish sheaths at the base. Leaves 5–6, bluish-green, oblong-lance-olate, the upper ones generally small, narrow, pinkish and 'bract-like'. Flowers small, many in a *tight rounded or conical-shaped head*, pinkish-lilac or violet; sepals and petals spreading, each with a *small elongated 'blob'* at the end, the petals usually purple spotted; lip 4–5mm long, purple spotted, squarish, divided into 3 short, oval lobes; spur short, up to half as long as the ovary, downward pointing. Mountain meadows and coniferous woods, on limestone, 1000–2600m. May–August. A, AL, BG, CH, CS, ꞁD, *n*E, *c*&ꞁF, H, I, K, PL, R, *w*RS, YU.

Globular Orchid, × 2

This attractive slender orchid is mainly a mountain plant, particularly in places like the Pyrenees, Alps, Carpathians and the other mountains of central Europe. The distribution of the species extends eastwards into Asia Minor as far as the Caucasus. The Globular Orchid can be easily identified by its tight heads of flowers and the curious 'spoon-like' blob on the end of the sepals and petals. The Globular Orchid is found in flower over a prolonged season due to the effect of altitude; those at higher altitudes flowering weeks later than those lower down.

COMPERIA

Komper's Orchid *Comperia comperiana* (=*Orchis comperiana*) [43]   Short to
medium perennial, to 55cm tall. Leaves mostly basal, oblong to oval; stem leaves
2–3, sheath-like. Flowers in a rather dense spike; sepal and petals brownish-
purple, forming a close hood above the lip; lip large, 3–4cm long, pale pink,
felted, 3-lobed, the central lobe itself bilobed, each lobe ending up in a *long fine
'tail-like' appendage*; spur short, downturned. Open woods, mainly coniferous, to
1200m. May–June. GR* – Lesbos and Samos, K*.●

A very rare plant in the area covered by this book. However, the species
extends southwards into Turkish Anatolia as well as the Lebanon, Iran, Iraq and
the Caucasus. This handsome plant is readily recognised by its large lip which
bears four long thread-like 'tails'.

Komper's Orchid, × ¾

Marsh and Spotted Orchids DACTYLORHIZA

A difficult group with about eighteen species in Europe which are characteristic
plants of heaths, meadows, marshy and wet places in many areas, often forming
large and spectacular colonies. The genus extends eastwards into Asia Minor and
Asia proper.

The species are readily confused with, and indeed closely resemble, a number
of *Orchis* and in fact many were once included in that genus. The truth is that the
characters of separation are neither easy to ascertain nor are they clear cut in
many instances.

There are two tubers as in *Orchis*, but they are usually lobed like the fingers of
a hand instead of being oval or rounded. There are usually quite a few leaves,
extending from ground level up the stem and decreasing in size so that the
uppermost are often small and 'bract like', and they may be spotted or unspotted

depending on the species – there are no sheathing leaves as in many species of *Orchis*. The flowers occur in dense or rather loose, often pointed, spikes, usually with the 'leaf like' flower bracts poking through below each flower. The sepals are generally spreading (except in **1**), the outer two held out like the wings of a bird, whilst the middle sepal and the two petals come close together in front to form a hood or helmet. The prominent broad lip may be 3-lobed or sometimes unlobed and is usually patterned with various dots and lines.

The species tend to hybridise readily where two or more are to be found growing together.

1. Turkish Marsh Orchid *Dactylorhiza iberica* (=*Orchis iberica*) [43]   Medium perennial to 40cm tall, forming patches by production of *basal stem stolons*. Leaves 3–5 on the lower part of the stem, linear-lanceolate, unspotted. Bracts lanceolate, as long as or longer than the ovary. Flowers in egg-shaped or cylindrical spikes, pink, the lip spotted with purple, the spur whitish towards the base; sepals and petals *all coming together to form a hood*; lip 7–10mm long, 3-lobed; spur slender, curved, half as long as the ovary. May–August. Mountain marshes and wet meadows, generally above 800m. *n*GR, K, TR.

This pale-flowered orchid is readily recognised by the sepals and petals all converging, indeed it is the only species of *Dactylorhiza* to do so. In this respect it might easily be mistaken for a species of *Orchis*. The distribution of this species extends eastwards into Asia Minor, Cyprus, the Caucasus, northern and eastern Iran and the Lebanon.

Turkish Marsh Orchid, × 1

Elder-flowered Orchid, × 1

2. Elder-flowered Orchid *Dactylorhiza sambucina* [43]   Short perennial to 30cm tall with a green or purplish stem. Leaves 4–5, clustered towards the base of the plant, unspotted, oblong-lanceolate, the upper narrower and *reaching* the lowest flowers. Bracts lanceolate, longer than the ovary, green or purplish. Flowers in dense oval spikes, pale yellow with a finely purple-spotted lip or reddish-purple with a purple lip, more rarely pinkish-yellow; outer sepals spreading upwards, the central sepal and petals forming a hood; lip 7–8mm long, rounded, shallowly 3-lobed; spur 12–15mm, *downward pointing*, about as long as the ovary. Mountain meadows, grassy places, woodland clearings and scrub, 500–2100m, mainly in central and southern Europe. April–July. T – except AL, BAL, CO, CR, FA, GB, IRL, IS, NL, *n,e*&*c*RS, SA, SF, TR.●

2a. *D.s.* subsp. *insularis* has laxer flower spikes, the flowers with a shorter, 8–10mm long, spur, *shorter than the ovary.* CO, SA.

The Elder-flowered Orchid is a beautiful plant often seen in large numbers in the mountain pastures of the Alps and Pyrenees, but widely distributed. Occasionally all yellow or all red colonies can be seen, though generally both forms and intermediates are found intermixed. *Dactylorhiza romana* has similar colour forms but the flowers are unspotted; it is generally a plant of lower altitudes. The Elder-flowered Orchid is also found in N. Africa and the Near East and much of Russia.

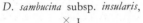

D. *sambucina* subsp. *insularis*,
× 1

Roman Orchid, × 1

Early Marsh Orchid, × 1

3. Roman Orchid *Dactylorhiza romana* (=*D. pseudosambucina*, *D. sulphurea* subsp. *pseudosambucina*)   Rather like (**2**) but leaves in a basal rosette of up to 10, narrow-oblong, also unspotted. Flowers pale yellow or purplish with a yellowish centre to the lip, *the lip unspotted*; spur 12–25mm long, *upcurved*, distinctly longer than the ovary. Rocky and sandy places, scrub and maquis, at low altitudes – to 800m, in the Mediterranean region but extending westwards to Portugal. March–May. AL, BAL, BG, CH, CR, E, G, I, K, P, R, SA, SC, TR, YU.●

3a. *D.r.* subsp. *siciliensis* (=*D. sulphurea* subsp. *siciliensis*) has *a conical spur* shorter than, or as long as, the ovary. I, SA, SC.

A form from Portugal with an orange zone at the base of the lip is sometimes referred to as subsp. *bartonii* but is doubtfully distinct from the type.

Dactylorhiza romana is also found in N. Africa and eastwards through Cyprus and Turkey as far as the Caucasus and Iran.

4. Early Marsh Orchid *Dactylorhiza incarnata* [44]   Short to medium plant to 80cm tall. Leaves 4–5 erect, on the lower half of the stem, narrow lanceolate, *hooded at the tip*, pale greenish-yellow, usually unspotted. Bracts lanceolate, the lowermost often longer than the flowers. Flowers in cylindrical spikes, pale purple, pinkish or white; outer sepals spreading upwards, the central one and the petals forming a hood; lip 5–6mm long, purple-spotted, rarely yellowish, unlobed or slightly 3-lobed, the *sides folded backwards*; spur slender, horizontal or downward pointing, half as long as the ovary. April–July. Marshes, fens and damp grassy places, sometimes on dune slacks, to 2100m. May–July. T – except the Mediterranean evergreen belt.●

4a. *D.i.* subsp. *coccinea* has *deep reddish* flowers. Damp dune slacks usually. GB, IRL.

4b. *D.i.* subsp. *pulchella* has *purple or magenta*, often carmine streaked, flowers. GB, IRL.

4c. *D.i.* subsp. *haematodes* has leaves with *brownish-purple spotting*. T – wherever the species occurs, though spasmodically.

4d. *D.i.* subsp.˙*ochroleuca* has *straw or whitish-yellow* flowers. T – as (**4c**).

A variable and often rather pale-flowered marsh orchid, widespread throughout most of Europe and extending eastwards into Asia Minor and the Middle East and southwards into N. Africa. Generally easy to identify by its narrow pale upright leaves and the flowers with a scarcely lobed lip in which the sides are characteristically folded backwards.

Dactylorhiza incarnata frequently hybridises with other closely related species and many such hybrids may be extremely difficult to identify.

5. Flecked Marsh Orchid *Dactylorhiza cruenta* [44] is a shorter plant than (**4**), to 30cm tall, the leaves *streaked and spotted dark purple* on both surfaces and not hooded at the tip. Flowers blood-red or purple, lip unlobed. April–July. Damp meadows and marshes in N. and E. Europe. A, CH, D, DK, F, H, N, RS – except *s*S, SF.

Often treated as a subspecies of the preceding species.

Flecked Marsh Orchid, × 1

Broad-leaved Marsh Orchid, × 1

6. Scandinavian Marsh Orchid *Dactylorhiza pseudocordigera*   Like (**4**) but the plants seldom more than 20cm tall, the leaves broader and *dark-purple spotted*. Flowers purplish-red, the lip 6–7mm long. July–August. Damp pastures and marshy areas. IS, N, S.

A slender and rather scarce northern species.

7. Broad-leaved Marsh Orchid *Dactylorhiza majalis* [44]   Medium to tall plant to 80cm tall. Leaves 4–6 spaced along the stem, *broad, oval to oblong or elliptical*, bluish-green, usually with large dark brownish spots, the uppermost narrower and reaching the lower flowers. Bracts lanceolate, the lower ones generally longer than the flowers. Flowers in dense oval spikes, purplish-lilac; outer sepals spreading upwards, the central one and the petals forming a loose hood; lip 9–10mm long, with darker spots and lines, 3-lobed; *spur short*, downward pointing, about half as long as the ovary. April–July. Damp meadows and marshes on calcareous soils, in west and central Europe, to 2500m. A, B, CH, CS, D, DK, E, F, H, I, N, NL, PL, RS – except *s&e*, S, YU.●

7a. *D.m.* subsp. *kerryensis* (= *D. kerryensis*, *D. majalis* subsp. *occidentalis*) is shorter than (7), rarely more than 25 cm tall; flowers dull purple or magenta, the lip with *looped-line markings*. April–May. GB, IRL.

7b. *D.m.* subsp. *brevifolia*   Like (**7a**) but leaves narrow-lanceolate, *folded along the centre*; flowers purplish-lilac, but without looped-line markings. June–July. D, S – Gotland.

7c. *D.m.* subsp. *alpestris*   Like (**7**) but shorter, rarely more than 30 cm tall, the *leaves broadest near the top*; lip of flower without loop-line markings. Mountain meadows and marshes, open woods, to 2500 m. May–August. A, D, CH, E, F, I. Known mainly in the Alps and Pyrenees.

The type species is probably the commonest Marsh Orchid in central Europe. It is confined to Europe and Russia.

8. Baltic Marsh Orchid *Dactylorhiza baltica*   Rather like (**7**) but the leaves linear-lanceolate. Flowers smaller, in loose spikes, the lip 5–8 mm long; spur three-quarters as long as the ovary. June–July. Damp pastures and marshes in E. Europe. D, DK, PL, *c,n*&*e*RS, S, SF.

Baltic Marsh Orchid, × 1   Northern Marsh Orchid, × 1

9. Northern Marsh Orchid *Dactylorhiza purpurella* [44]   Short to medium plant to 45 cm tall. Leaves 4–6, spaced along the stem, erect lanceolate or oblong, unspotted or with small O-shaped marks towards the top. Bracts lanceolate, the lowermost usually longer than the flowers. Flowers small, in dense oblong spikes, pale or deep wine-purple; outer sepals spreading upwards, the central one and the petals forming a hood; lip 5–7 mm long, shallowly 3-lobed or almost unlobed, with *looped or dashed* markings; spur narrow, tapered to the tip, downward pointing, *much shorter than the ovary*. June–July. Damp pastures and marshes. N.W. Europe. DK, FA, *n*GB, IRL, N.

A species restricted to north-western Europe and differing in only one or two characters from both *D. baltica* and *D. praetermissa*, though the former has a more easterly distribution.

10. Southern Marsh Orchid *Dactylorhiza praetermissa*   Like (**9**) but usually taller, to 75 cm, the *leaves unmarked*. Flowers larger, rose-purple, the lip 10–12 mm long with a *central cluster* of small dark dots. June–July. Damp grassy meadows, marshes, fens and dune slacks, in N.W. Europe. B, D, DK, *c*&*n*F, GB, NL. ●

10a. *D.p.* subsp. *junialis* has leaves with O-shaped markings; lip with pronounced *dashed and looped markings*. GB, NL.

Southern Marsh Orchid, × 1

Heart-shaped Marsh Orchid, × 1

11. Heart-shaped Marsh Orchid *Dactylorhiza cordigera* [44] Short plant to 30cm tall with a straight or flexuous stem. Leaves 2–5, spaced, oval to lanceolate, *usually with dark spots on both surfaces*. Bracts lanceolate, as long as the flowers. Flowers purple, in oval or oblong spikes; outer sepals spreading upwards, the central one and the petals forming a hood; lip 7–11mm long, darker in colour, *heart-shaped*, unlobed or slightly 3-lobed; spur pouch-like, 6–8mm long, downward pointing, about half as long as the ovary. July–August. Damp mountain meadows and marshes, 1000–2400m, in S.E. Europe. AL, BG, ?GR, R, *sw*RS, YU.

11a. *D.c.* subsp. *bosniaca* has a square lip *narrowed abruptly* at the base. AL, BG, YU.

11b. *D.c.* subsp. *siculorum* has a *narrower spur* than (**11**), 8–11mm long, three-quarters as long as the ovary. R, *sw*RS.

  D. cordigera is generally recognised by the broad heart-shaped lip to the flower which is scarcely lobed.

12. Lapland Marsh Orchid *Dactylorhiza lapponica* [44] Short slender plant to 20cm tall. *Leaves 2–3 only*, spaced, oblong or lanceolate, with dark purplish spots, the *lowermost leaf clasping the stem*. Bracts lanceolate. Flowers small, in loose conical spikes, purple to reddish-violet; outer sepals spreading upwards; lip 5–7mm long, rounded, slightly 3-lobed, the central lobe small and tooth-like; spur slender, 5–8mm long, downward pointing, about half as long as the ovary. July–August. Sphagnum bogs and marshes, in northern Europe. N, *n*RS, S, SF.

  A slender rather scarce northern species not unlike the Scandinavian Marsh Orchid, p.241.

Lapland Marsh Orchid, × 1

Pugsley's Marsh Orchid

13. Pugsley's Marsh Orchid *Dactylorhiza traunsteineri* [44] Short to medium plant to 45cm tall with a flexuous stem. Leaves 3–4, spaced along the stem, *narrow-lanceolate to linear, unspotted*. Bracts narrow-lanceolate, the lower generally longer than the flowers. Flowers in cylindrical spikes, purple or rose-purple;

outer sepal spreading upwards; lip 7–9mm long, 3-lobed, strongly marked with dark purple, slightly folded, the middle lobe blunt, longer than the lateral ones; spur narrow, cone-shaped, *downward pointing, half as long as the ovary*. June–August. Sphagnum bogs and marshes on acid soils, throughout Europe except the south and south-east. A, CH, CS, D, DK, GB, H, I, IRL, N, P, R, RS, S, SF, *n*YU.

13a. *D.t.* subsp. *curvifolia* has 2–3 *prominently curved leaves*, ridged above. *n*&*w*RS, S, SF.

13b. *D.t.* subsp. *pycnantha* has 3–4 erect or spreading leaves, oblong-lanceolate; lip shallowly 3-lobed, the central lobe or 'tooth' *minute*. S, SF.

13c. *D.t.* subsp. *traunsteinerioides* like (**13a**) but the leaves *usually spotted*. GB, IRL.

14. Russian Marsh Orchid *Dactylorhiza russowii*   Rather like (**13**) but taller, to 110cm, with 4–5 *dark spotted leaves*. Flowers in dense spikes, pink; lip flat, 3-lobed, the middle lobe sharply triangular; *spur almost as long as the ovary*. June–August. Marshes and boggy places. *n*&*e*D, P, R, *n*&*w*RS, S, SF.

   Very similar to the preceding species and perhaps only a form of it. However, the flowers are borne in denser spikes and the spur is rather longer.

Russian Marsh Orchid, × 1   Spotted Orchid, × 1

15. Spotted Orchid *Dactylorhiza maculata* [44]   Variable short to medium plant to 60cm tall, with an erect or flexuous stem. Leaves 6–10, spaced along the stem, erect, oval to oblong, usually purple-black spotted, the uppermost bract-like. Bracts narrow-lanceolate, the *lower shorter than, the upper longer* than, the flowers. Flowers in dense conical or oblong spikes, pink, lilac, reddish or purple; outer sepals spreading outwards; lip 7–11mm long, flat, shallowly 3-lobed, *wavy-edged*, lined or dotted purple, the middle lobe short and 'tooth-like'; spur slender, downward pointing, about three-quarters the length of the ovary. Meadows, woods, scrub, heaths and moorland, often on acid soils, through much of Europe except the south. May–August. A, CH, CS, D, DK, E, F, FA, GB, IRL, IS, N, NL, P, PL, R, RS, S, SF, *n*YU.●

15a. Heath Spotted Orchid *D.m.* subsp. *ericetorum* has 5–12 leaves, narrow oblong or linear, spotted or unspotted; *lip pale pink or whitish* with a very short central 'tooth'. Heaths and peat moors. GB, IRL, NL, S.

15b. *D.m.* subsp. *elodes*   Like (**15a**) but with *only 4–6 narrow-lanceolate leaves*, spotted; lip pink to reddish; spur half as long as the ovary. Peat moors. T – range of species except GB, R, *w*RS, YU.

15c. *D.m.* subsp. *schurii*   Like (**15b**) but with 5–8 sparsely-spotted leaves, the lowermost narrow oblong; middle lobe of lip *as long, or longer than*, the lateral lobes. Carpathian Mountains. CS, R, *w*RS.

15d. *D.m.* subsp. *islandica*   Like (**15**) but short, *never more* than 20cm tall, the lower leaves oval; lip pink to reddish or lilac. IS.

15e. *D.m.* subsp. *transsilvanica* has oblong or lanceolate, *unspotted*, leaves; *lip yellowish-white*, the middle lobe longer than the lateral lobes. CS, D, R, *w*RS, YU.

16. Common Spotted Orchid *Dactylorhiza fuchsii* [44]   Rather like (**15**) but stems with 7–12 *rounded to elliptical leaves*, erect or spreading, dark-spotted, the uppermost smaller, bract-like. Flowers pink, pale lilac or reddish-purple; lip *deeply 3-lobed*, the central lobe *longer than* the lateral lobes. June–August. Grassy places and open scrub and woodland margins, on calcareous soils, over much of Europe except the Mediterranean evergreen area, to 2200m. T – except AL, BAL, BG, CR, GR, *r*I, K, P, TR.●

Common Spotted Orchid, × 1

16a. *D.f.* subsp. *psychrophila* is a shorter plant, not more than 25cm tall, with *only 1–2 leaves*. A, CH, F, D, N, S, SF.

16b. *D.f.* subsp. *hebridensis*   Like (**16a**) but the *leaves spreading to downcurved* and the flowers dark reddish-purple. *n*GB, IRL.

16c. *D.f.* subsp. *okellyi*   Like (**16a**) but the flowers white or pale reddish-purple, the lip scarcely or only faintly marked. GB, IRL.

16d. *D.f.* subsp. *soviana*   Like (**16c**) but the *flowers white, the lip strongly lined and spotted purple*. H.
    A variable species in which many forms have been observed and described. It is a similar looking species to the Heath Spotted Orchid but apart from the differences in habitat (*D. fuchsii* prefers calcareous soils, whilst *D. maculata* is generally found on acid soils), differences can be seen in the shape of the lip. In *D. fuchsii* the central lobe of the lip is elongated and pointed whilst in *D. maculata* the central lobe is small, triangular, and tooth-like.

17. *Dactylorhiza saccifera*   Rather like (**16**) but leaves *always unspotted* and the lower bracts *conspicuously longer than the flowers*; spur conical or pouch-like. May–July. Alpine and subalpine mountain meadows and pastures in wet places, to 2500m. South and south-east Europe. AL, BG, E, GR, I, P, R, SA, SI, TR, YU.

D. *saccifera*, × 1

Robust Marsh Orchid, × 1

18. Robust Marsh Orchid *Dactylorhiza elata* [44]   Medium to tall plant to 80cm, though often less, stem erect, rather stout. Leaves 6–10, well spaced, erect, broadly elliptical to lanceolate, widest at the base, *unspotted*, the uppermost bract-like. Bracts at least as long as the flowers. Flowers in loose cylindrical spikes, violet-purple; outer *sepals erect spreading*; lip 9–16mm long, lined and spotted dark purple, 3-lobed with the lateral lobes folded back usually; spur slender to conical, *as long as the ovary*. April–June. Wet meadows and bogs. SI*. *

18a. *D.e.* subsp. *durandii* is taller, 80–110cm, with narrow lanceolate leaves widest at the base. E, P.

18b. *D.e.* subsp. *sesquipedalis* is a shorter plant than (**18**) with elliptical or oval leaves *widest in the middle*; flowers in a dense spike, the lip scarcely 3-lobed. S.W. Europe. CO, E, SF, P.*

PSEUDORCHIS

Like *Gymnadenia*, but with smaller flowers and with all 3 sepals forming a hood with the 2 sepals and not spreading.

1. Small White Orchid *Pseudorchis albida* (= *Gymnadenia albida*, *Leucorchis albida*) [45]   Slender erect, hairless, plant to 30cm tall, but generally less. Stems with *several sheathing leaves at the base* and with 4–6 oblong or lanceolate leaves above, the uppermost small and 'bract-like'. Bracts green, 3-veined, longer than the ovary. Flowers tiny, 3–5mm, whitish or pale greenish-yellow, in a dense spike 3–7cm long; sepals and petals *all forming a close hood* 2–3mm long; lip 3-lobed, the central lobe rather longer than the lateral ones; spur short, blunt, 2mm long. Rough pastures and meadows, grassy heaths with heathers and rhododendron

Small White Orchid, × 1½

Frivald's Frog Orchid, × 1½

scrub, on calcareous or non-calcareous soils, to 2500m, but only in the mountains in the southern part of its range. June–September. A, B, BG, CH, CS, D, DK, nE, F, FA, GB*, H, n&cI, IRL, IS, N, NL, PL, R, n&wS, RS, SF, nYU. Rather rare in Britain.

2. Frivald's Frog Orchid *Pseudorchis frivaldii* (= *Leucorchis frivaldii*)   Like the previous but leaves narrower, 3–4 in all; *bracts 1-veined*. Flowers rather larger, white or occasionally pale pink, in dense 3–4cm long spikes. Damp mountain meadows, 1600–2250m. June–August. w&sBG, nGR, cR*, sYU.

Fragrant Orchids GYMNADENIA

A genus with only two species in Europe, both sweetly scented with small flowers and a 3-lobed lip.

1. Fragrant Orchid *Gymnadenia conopsea* [45]   Short to medium hairless plant to 65cm tall. Stems with up to 8 narrow-lanceolate, pointed, plain green leaves in the lower part, decreasing in size upwards. Bracts green, 3-veined, longer than the ovary. Flowers small, in dense cylindrical spikes 6–16cm long, bright pink or magenta, sometimes white, *sweetly scented; lateral sepals spreading*, the upper sepal and petals forming a hood; lip 3.5–5mm long, 3-lobed; spur long and slender, 11–18mm, downcurved. Grassy meadows and slopes, often on dry calcareous soils, marshy places and open woods, scrubland, to 2500m. May–August. T – except IS, TR.●
   A widespread species whose distribution extends across Siberia to Asia and Japan. It is often rather local but then frequently occurring in large numbers over a wide range of habitats. A distinctive plant with its generally bright pink, fragrant flowers, which have a very long downcurved spur. This species occasionally hybridises with the Lesser Butterfly Orchid, *Platanthera bifolia*.

Fragrant Orchid, × 1   Short-spurred Fragrant Orchid, × 1

2. Short-spurred Fragrant Orchid *Gymnadenia odoratissima*   A shorter plant than the previous species but with all the leaves linear. Flower spike shorter, rarely more than 10cm long, the flowers rather pale pink, vanilla-scented; lip 2.5–3mm long; *spur short*, 4–5mm long, downcurved, about as long as the ovary. Grassy places and open coniferous woodland on calcareous soils, to

2700m. Mainly in central Europe. May–August. A, CH, CS, *s*D, *n*E, F, H, *n*I, R, *w,c*&*sw*RS, *s*S, *n*&*c*YU.

Readily distinguished from the Fragrant Orchid by its smaller flowers and short spur. It occurred in Britain at one time, but is in all probability now extinct.

NEOTTIANTHE

Pink Frog Orchid *Neottianthe cucullata* (=*Gymnadenia cucullata*) [45]   Short plant up to 30cm tall. Basal leaves elliptical; stem leaves 1–2, small and bract-like. Flowers in a loose one-sided spike, lilac or purplish-pink; sepals and petals almost equal, pointed, *forming a close hood above the lip*; lip 7–9mm long, almost

Pink Frog Orchid, × 1

horizontal, 3-lobed, the lobes linear, with the central one longer than the adjacent lobes; spur 5mm long, thickened and curved. Damp woods, coniferous and mixed, and mountain meadows. June–August. *n*eD*, PL*, RS*.

This interesting and uncommon species only occurs in eastern Europe, although its distribution extends eastwards through Siberia to China and Japan.

Vanilla Orchids NIGRITELLA

Small orchids with narrow spreading sepals and petals, the lip and spur uppermost.

1. Black Vanilla Orchid *Nigritella nigra* (=*N. miniata*) [45]   Low to short hairless plant to 30cm tall, though often less. Leaves linear to linear-lanceolate, spaced along the stem, the upper leaves shorter. Bracts longer than the flowers, tipped purplish-black. Flowers small, in tight conical spikes, *purple-black or reddish-black*, rarely white, yellowish or coppery, vanilla-scented; sepals and petals linear, pointed, *all spreading*; lip uppermost, 4mm long, narrow triangular, equal to the sepals; spur short, 'pouch-like'. Ovary not twisted. Alpine meadows, damp mountain woods, 1000–2800m, mainly in central and southern Europe. May–September. A, AL, BG, CH, *s*D, *n*E, F, GR, I, N, R, S, YU.●

A characteristic plant of alpine meadows with its small, almost rounded spikes of generally dark, almost black, flowers which have a distinct vanilla-fragrance. The lip, sepals and petals are more or less equal, spreading outwards to form a six-pointed star.

Black Vanilla Orchid, × 1½

Red Vanilla Orchid, × 1½

2. Red Vanilla Orchid *Nigritella rubra* (=N. *nigra* subsp. *rubra*) [45] Rather like the previous species but the spikes more cylindrical, the *flowers red* with oblong sepals and petals and with a *much broader lip*. Alpine pastures, 1600–2300m. May–July. A*, CH*, I*, R*, YU*.●

A much rarer plant than the Black Vanilla Orchid and usually found in flower rather earlier. The flower spikes are noticeably longer with red flowers which have a lip about twice as broad as the sepals. It is often considered to be only a subspecies of N. *nigra*. N. *rubra* is found only in the Alps and the mountains of Roumania.

STEVENIELLA

Hooded Orchid *Steveniella satyrioides* (=*Orchis steveniella*) [45] Short to medium, erect perennial to 40cm tall. *Basal leaf solitary, oblong to elliptical*, the stem above with two pointed sheathing leaves. Flowers in a cylindrical spike, greenish flushed with purple or brown and with a brownish lip; sepals and petals forming a close hood, the sepals oblong, fused together, the petals half as long and linear; lip 6–7mm long, 3-lobed, downturned, the central lobe long and blunt, longer than the lateral lobes; spur short, conical, downturned. Open woodland and mountain meadows, to 1600m. April–June. K*.●

A very rare orchid known only from the Crimea on the north shore of the Black Sea and also from the southern side of the same sea in the Pontus Mountains of northern Turkey.

Hooded Orchid, × 1½

Butterfly Orchids PLATANTHERA

A genus of about 70 species confined mainly to the cold temperate regions of N. America and Asia. They are related to the Fragrant Orchids *Gymnadenia*, but are readily distinguished by their unlobed rather than 3-lobed lips.

1. Lesser Butterfly Orchid *Platanthera bifolia* [45]   Short to medium erect plant to 50cm tall. *Leaves two, basal*, oblong-oval to elliptical, shiny-green, the stem with several small, spaced, 'bract-like' leaves. Flowers in a lax spike up to 20cm long, *white tinged green*, with a sweet vanilla fragrance; lateral sepals spreading, the upper sepal and petals forming a hood; lip 8–12mm long, *narrow-oblong, downturned, unlobed*; spur very long, 25–30mm, slender, horizontal or downcurved; anther cells close and parallel. Meadows, moors and open woodland, tolerant of a wide range of conditions, up to 2300m. May–August. T – except AZ, CR, IS, K, *n*N – Spitzbergen.●

The Lesser Butterfly Orchid has a wide range outside Europe, extending south into N. Africa and eastwards into Asia Minor, the Caucasus, parts of Asia and Siberia. In Britain it is one of the most frequently seen orchids.

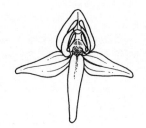

Lesser Butterfly Orchid, × 1½

Greater Butterfly Orchid, × 1½

2. Greater Butterfly Orchid *Platanthera chlorantha*   Similar to but larger than the previous species; flowers greener, scarcely scented and the spur 18–27mm long, distinctly swollen towards the tip; anther cells *diverging towards the base from one another*. Meadows, damp heaths and woods, tolerating drier and more shaded positions than the Lesser Butterfly Orchid, to 1800m. May–July. T – except AZ, CR, E, IS, P, *n*&*se*RS.●

The Greater Butterfly Orchid generally flowers a couple of weeks ahead of its cousin, the Lesser Butterfly Orchid, generally preferring habitats on calcareous soils.

3. Azores Butterfly Orchid *Platanthera azorica*   Short plant to 35cm tall. Leaves 2, close together near the base of stem, oblong, broadest above the middle. Flowers in lax spikes up to 10cm long, pale green; lip 3–4mm long, *horizontal*, narrow-oblong; *spur short*, 7–8mm long, slender, shorter than the ovary. Grassy meadows in the mountains, to 1000m. June–July. AZ*.

4. *Platanthera micrantha*   Similar to 3 but *smaller in all its parts*, the lip broader, but only 2mm long; *spur very short*, 2–2.5mm long, less than half the length of the ovary. Grassy mountain meadows and sphagnum bogs on acid soils, to 900m. May–July. AZ*.

Platanthera azorica is sometimes considered little more than a form of this species.

5. Arctic or **Icelandic Butterfly Orchid** *Platanthera hyperborea*   Low to short plant to 35cm tall, though often less. Leaves 3–4, borne towards the base of the stem, oblong; stem often with 1–2 sheath-like leaves above. *Flowers in rather dense spikes*, 3–6cm long, greenish or yellowish-green, fragrant; lip 3–3.5mm long, horizontal; spur 3.5mm long, curved, shorter than the ovary. Tundra, meadows and moors. July–August. IS.
   The distribution of this species extends into arctic and subarctic N. America.

One-leaved Butterfly Orchid, × 1½

P. *micrantha*, × 1½

6. One-leaved Butterfly Orchid *Platanthera obtusata* subsp. *oligantha*   Low to short slender plant to 20cm tall, often less. *Leaf solitary, basal*, elliptical, the upper stem with a single 'bract-like' leaf. Flowers few, rarely more than 6, in a short spike, white tinged green; lip 3–3.5mm long, lanceolate, more or less horizontal; spur 2.5–3mm long, curved, half as long as the ovary. Heaths, birch and pine woods, in the mountains, usually on calcareous soils. June–August. N*, S*, *n*RS, ?SF.
   The distribution of *P. obtusata* subsp. *oligantha* extends into east and central Asia and N. America.

GENNARIA

Gennaria diphylla (= *Coeloglossum diphyllum*) [45]   Short plant up to 30cm tall. Leaves 2, spaced along the stem, *heart-shaped*, the uppermost much smaller than

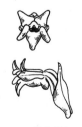

Gennaria diphylla, × 1½

the lower. Flowers many in long spikes up to 10cm long, yellowish-green; sepals and petals almost equal, oblong, *all forming a loose hood*; lip oval, 3-lobed, the side lobes narrow-lanceolate, the central lobe larger; spur short, rounded. Shaded grassy places and evergreen woods and scrub, rock crevices. February–May. *SW*E, *s*&*c*P, SA.●

An insignificant orchid readily identified by its two heart-shaped leaves. The distribution of this species extends into N. Africa and the Canary Isles.

COELOGLOSSUM

Frog Orchid *Coeloglossum viride* [45]   Short to medium plant to 35cm tall, though often less. Leaves few, the basal ones oval, the stem leaves small, lanceolate. Bracts narrow-lanceolate, exceeding the flowers. Flowers in a loose narrow spike, rather inconspicuous, green or yellowish, tinged with brown or purplish-brown; sepals and petals forming a close hood; lip 3-lobed, the *central lobe smaller than the lateral lobes*; spur 'pouch-like', not more than 2mm long. Meadows, damp woods and scrub, often on calcareous soils, to 2500m, throughout much of Europe but only on the mountains in the south. May–August. T – except CO, CR, GR, TR.

A rather common European orchid, but one that is often difficult to spot with its small greenish and brown flowers. Its distribution extends as far as central Asia (Turkestan and Kashmir) and into east N. America.

Frog Orchid, × 1½

False Orchid, × 1½

CHAMORCHIS

False Orchid *Chamorchis alpina* (=*Herminium alpinum*) [45]   Short hairless rather insignificant plant, not exceeding 10cm tall. *Leaves basal, linear and grasslike*, erect and equalling the stem. Bracts green, linear, longer than the flowers. Flowers few, in a loose spike, *spurless*; sepals and petals forming a hood, green, sometimes tinged purplish-brown or violet; lip oblong, vaguely 3-lobed, greenish-yellow. Mountain pastures, often rather wet, on calcareous soils, 1600–2700m. July–August. A, CH, CS, D, F, I, N, P, R, *n*RS, S, SF, YU.

A tiny mountain orchid which is often difficult to spot amongst the grasses and other pasture plants where it grows. The False Orchid is most common in the Alps and Carpathians, but is sometimes locally common in the Scandinavian mountains.

HERMINIUM

Musk Orchid *Herminium monorchis* [46]   Short slender plant to 25cm tall, though often less. Leaves mostly towards the base of the stem, elliptical to narrow-lanceolate, the upper, if present, small and 'bract-like'. Bracts green, about as long as the ovary. Flowers tiny, in dense narrow spikes, yellowish-green, honey-scented; *sepals narrow-oval, blunt, spreading*, the petals rather longer and *often lobed* in the middle; lip 3–4mm long, 3-lobed, the central lobes much longer than the outer ones which are at right angles to it; spur absent. Grassy slopes, damp meadows on calcareous soils, mainly in mountainous regions, to 1800m. May–August. A, B, BG, CH, CS, D, DK, F, *s*GB, H, *n*&*c*I, N, NL, PL, R, RS, S, SF, YU.

Another small and rather insignificant orchid with small greenish flowers which have a honey or musk-like fragrance. A rather uncommon plant but occasionally locally abundant. It is easy to recognise by its spurless flowers, the spreading sepals and the often slightly lobed petals.

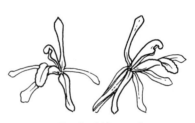

Musk Orchid, × 3   Fen Orchid, × 1½

LIPARIS

Fen Orchid *Liparis loeselii* (= *Malaxis loeselii*) [46]   Short to medium, hairless, rather insignificant plant up to 20cm tall, though often less. *Stems 3-angled in the upper half, leafless.* Leaves 2, basal, directly from the pseudo-bulb, oblong to lanceolate, pointed, erect, about half as long as the stem. *Flowers small, spurless, few*, rarely more than 8 in a loose spike, yellowish-green; sepals and petals linear, spreading; lip 5mm long, oblong, unlobed. Bogs, fens, marshes and damp dunes, in alkaline conditions and preferring cooler regions. June–August. A, B, CH, CS, D, DK, F, *w*&*e*GB, H, *n*I, N, NL, PL, R, RS, S, SF, YU.

The Fen Orchid is often a rather rare plant despite its wide distribution. It is a difficult plant to observe, both due to its colour and because it remains in flower for a very short period only. In Britain it is found only in south Wales and eastern England.

CALYPSO

Calypso *Calypso bulbosa* (*=C. borealis*) [46]   Short tuberous rooted plant, stems erect, 10–20cm tall. *Leaves solitary basal*, elliptical, short-stalked, prominently ribbed. Bract linear, pinkish, just below the flower. *Flower solitary, rather large*; sepals and petals purplish-pink, narrow-lanceolate, erect and spreading; lip large 10–20mm long, 'pouch-like' with a narrow opening, pale pink or whitish with pink or pale yellowish spots and blotches. Damp coniferous forests and marshes in the extreme north of Europe. May–June. *n&c*RS, *n&c*S, SF.●

A beautiful and rather rare northern orchid which has a pouched lip like the Lady Slipper Orchid, however, the whole appearance of the plant is very different.

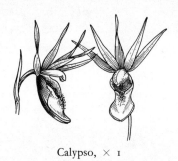

Bog Orchid, × 5

Calypso, × 1

HAMMARBYA

Bog Orchid *Hammarbya paludosa* (*=Malaxis paludosa*) [46]   Low to short plant, rarely more than 12cm tall, often less, with a slender stem, hairless. Leaves 2–5, oval, enclosing the base of the stem, often with buds at the tips which will form new plants. Flowers tiny, numerous in a rather dense spike; sepals and petals greenish-yellow, oval-lanceolate, the petals narrower than the sepals and curved backwards; *lip uppermost in the flower*, 2–2.5mm long, shorter than the sepals, lanceolate. Acid sphagnum bogs. July–September. A, B, CH, CS, D, F, GB, N, PL, RS, S, SF, YU.

The Bog Orchid is mainly a lowland plant of north and central Europe, occasionally reaching an altitude of around 800m. Its distribution extends eastwards into Siberia and as far as Japan, often growing close to the Arctic Circle. In Britain it may be locally common though it occurs far more frequently in the north than it does in the south. This small greenish orchid appears to be rather spasmodic in flowering and several years may pass before flowers are produced at a particular locality and it is often difficult to locate. Although the lip is uppermost in the flower it is due to overtwisting rather than no twisting (resupination) at all; the flowers in fact twist through 360°.

MICROSTYLIS

One-leaved Malaxis *Microstylis monophyllos* (=*Malaxis monophyllos*) [46]   Short plant to 30cm tall, generally less; stem leafless. *Leaf solitary*, oval or elliptical, arising directly from the pseudobulb. Flowers tiny, spurless, in spikes of 20 or more, greenish; sepals lanceolate, long-pointed, petals slender spreading, *lip lanceolate, uppermost in the flower*. Damp meadows, woods and bogs, usually among sphagnum mosses, mostly in north and central Europe. July–August. A*, CS*, D*, H*, I*, N*, PL*, R*, RS*, S, SF.

A rare plant which is often difficult to find because of its thin spikes of tiny green flowers. Superficially like the Bog Orchid it is readily distinguished on account of having a solitary leaf. The flowers are curious in that they twist through 360° (instead of the usual 180°), so that the lip is uppermost. The distribution of the One-leaved Malaxis extends into Asia and N. America.

Coralroot Orchid, × 1½

One-leaved Malaxis, × 4

CORALLORHIZA

Coralroot Orchid *Corallorhiza trifida* [46]   Low to short, hairless, yellowish-green, saprophytic plant, to 25cm tall. Stems leafless *but with 2–4 scaly sheaths in the lower half*. Flowers few, up to 12, in a loose spike; sepals greenish, lance-shaped, spreading, the petals narrower, yellowish with reddish spots; lip 5mm long, equalling the sepals and petals, oblong, distinctly grooved, white with red lines and blotches. Damp woods, especially beech, or in mossy areas of pine forests, or on damp dune slacks, to 2700m. May–August. A, AL, B, BG, CS, D, DK, E, F, *n*GB, H, I, IS, N, P, R, RS, S, SF, YU.

Though fairly frequent in some areas the Coralroot Orchid is generally a difficult plant to spot because it remains above ground for very short periods, though often making small colonies. It gets its name from the branched 'coral-like' rootstock. The distribution of the species extends across Asia to N. China and N. America, though it is mainly a mountain plant in the southern parts of its range. In Britain it is found only in northern England and Scotland.

Twayblades LISTERA

Easily recognised by their two, more or less opposite oval leaves situated below the middle of the stem. Flowers small, in slender spike-like racemes, each with a long forked lip; no spur.

1. Greater or **Common Twayblade** *Listera ovata* [46]   Short to medium perennial, to 60cm tall, sometimes more; stems slender, hairy in the upper part and with several brownish sheaths at the base. *Leaves two broad-oval*, deep rather shiny-green, ribbed. Spikes with numerous well spaced flowers, each with a tiny bract at the base of the flower stalk; sepals and petals green or yellowish-green, oval to oblong; lip 7−15mm long, yellowish-green, vertical, *forked from the middle into two narrow lobes*. Woods, coniferous and deciduous, scrub, grassy places and marshy ground, to 2100m. May−July. T − except AZ, BAL, TR.

The Greater Twayblade is the most widespread, and certainly the commonest European orchid, though with its small greenish flowers it is often overlooked. In bud the young spikes look like Plantains (*Plantago* spp.) though the plants are unmistakable with their two opposite and oval leaves held just above the soil surface. The species is found east as far as the Himalaya, even north of the Arctic Circle, though it is rare in the Mediterranean region.

Greater Twayblade, × 1½

Lesser Twayblade, × 2

2. Lesser Twayblade *Listera cordata* [46]   Low to short perennial, creeping, up to 20cm tall; stems slightly hairy in the upper part, with one or two brownish sheaths at the base. Leaves usually 2, oval with a slight point, shiny-green. Spikes with 4−12 tiny flowers only, each with a minute bract at its base, musky smelling; sepals tiny, green, the middle one curved forward; petals green outside, reddish inside, elliptical; lip 3.5−4.5mm long, *purplish, forked from the middle into two linear lobes*. Moorland and damp woods, particularly coniferous, mainly in mountainous regions, to 2300m. May−August. A, BG, CH, CS, D, E, F, GB, *n*GR, I, IRL, IS, N, PL, R, RS, S, SF, TR, YU.

This tiny orchid is found in many parts of Europe and although primarily a mountain plant, it is found at sea level in the north of Britain and Scandinavia. It is also found across most of temperate Asia, Japan and N. America. The Lesser Twayblade is often overlooked amongst the other plants, particularly heather, with which it commonly grows.

NEOTTIA

Bird's Nest Orchid *Neottia nidus-avis* [46]   Short to medium, yellowish-brown or greyish saprophytic plant, *no green leaves*; stems up to 45cm tall, the lower stem covered in brown membranous scales. Flowers numerous in a rather broad spike-like raceme, fragrant; *sepals and petals yellowish-green or whitish*, oval to elliptical, converging to form a loose hood; lip 8–12mm long, greyish-brown, forked towards the tip into two broad lobes, the base of the lip with 2 small teeth, one on each side. Shady woodland, particularly beech, oak, pine and birch, on rich humus calcareous soils, to 1700m. May–July. T – except AZ, BAL.

The widespread Bird's Nest Orchid gets its name from the dense tuft of intertwined fleshy roots and fibres which make up the rootstock. It often grows in deeply shaded habitats and plants are sometimes monocarpic, dying after flowering. The fragrance of the flowers may be disagreeable to some people. The biology of this interesting species is still incompletely understood. Plants can reproduce by means of buds formed at the root tips and in some instances the plants can flower and seed entirely below ground. The distribution of this species extends eastwards to Japan through much of temperate Asia, as well as southwards into N. Africa.

Bird's Nest Orchid, × 1½

Man Orchid, × 1

ACERAS

Man Orchid *Aceras anthropophorum* [47]   Short to medium, slender, perennial, to 40cm tall, though generally less. Basal leaves oval, blunt, pale shiny-green, upright at first; upper leaves smaller and clasping the stem. Bracts membranous, shorter than the flowers. Spikes long and slender *with many small, greenish-yellow flowers* which are often streaked and edged with red; sepals and petals forming a small close hood above the lip; lip 12–15mm long, pendent, oblong with 2 slender 'arms' and 2 shorter, spreading 'legs', *resembling a tiny man*; no spur. Grassy places, especially hill slopes, and pastures, occasionally woodland margin, on calcareous soils, to 1500m. April–June. A, B, BG, CH, CS, D, DK, F, GB*, H, I, K, N, R, RS, S, SF, YU.●

A quaint slender orchid which is often difficult to spot amongst grasses because of its coloration, though it is locally quite often common. In France this plant is referred to as l'homme pendu – the hanged man, because of the resemblance of the flower shape to a tiny manikin.

Where they are found growing in the same vicinity, the Man Orchid may hybridise with both the Military or Monkey Orchid.

The Man Orchid is found also in N. Africa as well as Rhodes and Cyprus and parts of the eastern Mediterranean.

NEOTINEA

Dense-flowered Orchid *Neotinea intacta* (*=Orchis intacta*) [47]   Short plant to 25cm tall, rarely more. Leaves mostly basal, oblong, ending in a small point; stem leaves smaller and erect, usually purple-spotted. Flowers small, *numerous in a dense often rather one-sided spike*, greenish-white or pinkish, scented faintly of vanilla; sepals and petals equal, oval, pointed, *forming a hood*; lip 6–7mm long, flat, pointing forward, 3-lobed, the central lobe larger than the lateral ones; spur short, conical. Woods, scrub, grassy and stony slopes, maquis, often over limestone. April–May. BAL, CO, CR, E, F, GB, GR, I, IRL, P, SA, SC, YU.

A small-flowered, rather insignificant, orchid confined mainly to the Mediterranean and Atlantic seaboard regions, including the Canary Isles and N. Africa. The flowers never really seem to open fully and are self-pollinated. Some botanists treat this as the same species as *Neotinea maculata*, a more easterly species found in Turkey, Cyprus and the Lebanon.

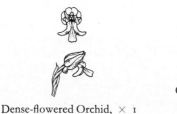

Creeping Lady's Tresses, × 2

Dense-flowered Orchid, × 1

GOODYERA

Creeping Lady's Tresses or **Adder's Tongue** *Goodyera repens* [47]   Short, slender, slightly hairy perennial up to 25cm tall, with *thin creeping and rooting stolons*. Leaves mostly in a loose basal rosette, oval, stalked, the blade net veined and often reddish; upper leaves sheath-like. Flowers white, small, 3–4mm, in a slender loose spike which is often slightly spiralled; sepals and petals oval or lanceolate, the upper sepal and two petals forming a hood; lip concave, not lobed, the tip downcurved; no spur. Creeping in leaf-litter and moss in coniferous or mixed woods, mainly in mountain areas, to 2250m, but occasionally at sea level, often local. July–August. A, BG, CH, CS, DK, E, F, G, *c&n*GB, H, I, K, N, NL, PL, R, RS, S, SF, YU.●

This interesting little plant is similar to the true Lady's Tresses (*Spiranthes*) but is easily distinguished by its creeping stolons which each bear a cluster of leaves at the end. After flowering the central stem dies away leaving the stolons to form the new plants. The distribution of the Creeping Lady's Tresses extends across much of the temperate Northern Hemisphere to include Siberia, the Himalayas, parts of China, as well as N. America.

The genus is named in honour of John Goodyer, a seventeenth-century English botanist, and contains about 80 species which are confined mainly to the warm subtropical regions of the world.

Lady's Tresses SPIRANTHES

Small, slender, perennials with basal rosettes of leaves and scale- or bract-like stem leaves. Flowers tiny, white or greenish, rarely pink, fragrant, in thin spiralled spikes; each flower like a small downturned, curved bell with the lip about as long as the sepals – spur absent.

1. Autumn or **Common Lady's Tresses** *Spiranthes spiralis* [47]   Low to short perennial to 35cm tall, though generally less, with stickily-hairy stems. Rosette leaves oval-elliptical, spreading, hairless, *to one side of the flower spike and often withered at flowering time*; stem with 3–7 scale-like leaves; bracts shorter than the flowers. Spike with up to 20 white flowers, each 6–7mm long; the outer two sepals spreading, the upper one and the petals fused and forming a tube with the lip; *lip with upcurved edges, yellowish-green.* Dry grassy places, meadows and heaths, generally on calcareous soils, occasionally on sand dunes, often in large numbers but irregular in flowering from one year to another; mainly lowland but occurring up to 850m in central Europe. August–October. T – except AZ, FA, IS, N, *n,c&e*RS, S, SF.

This charming little orchid is the most common and widespread of the European Lady's Tresses. The distribution of the species extends into N. Africa and eastwards as far as the Caucasus, but including Cyprus, Syria, Lebanon and N. Iran. In Britain it occurs only in the central and southern parts of the country.

Autumn Lady's Tresses, × 2

2. Summer Lady's Tresses *Spiranthes aestivalis* [47]   Short, slender, perennial to 40cm tall; stems stickily-hairy in the upper part. Leaves greenish-yellow, mostly in a basal rosette and *present at flowering time*, linear-lanceolate, more or less erect; upper leaves small and scale-like. Bracts shorter than the flowers. Spike with up to 20 white flowers in a single spiral. Flowers 6–7mm long, the sepals and petals all free from one another; *lip with upcurved edges, white*. Wet meadows and marshes, to 1250m. June–August. A, B, CH, CO, CS, *s*GB*, H, I, P, SA, YU.

This uncommon species is now almost extinct in Britain. In Europe it is found mainly in mountainous regions, the distribution extending into N. Africa and eastwards into Asia Minor.

Summer Lady's Tresses, p.259, × 2

Irish Lady's Tresses, × 2

3. Irish Lady's Tresses *Spiranthes ramanzoffiana* [47]   Short plant to 30cm tall, though generally less. All the leaves linear-lanceolate, erect, none scale-like. Spikes with up to 35 *flowers in more than one spiral*. Bracts *longer than* the flowers. Flowers larger than the other two species, 10–12mm long, white tinged green or creamish, fragrant; sepals, petals and the lip all joined together in the lower half. Damp peaty ground, bogs and lake margins. July–August. *w*&*nw*GB*, IRL*.

This interesting species is rare; occurring only in a few localities in Ireland, Devonshire, the Hebrides and the adjacent mainland of Scotland. However, it is found over a wide area of N. America where it is generally a more vigorous plant.

Spiranthes sinensis (=*S. amoena*) with bright pink flowers, which is similar to the Summer Lady's Tresses, possibly grows in the Central Urals – it is a native of much of temperate and south-east Asia from Japan to New Guinea and Australia.

EPIPOGIUM

Ghost Orchid or **Spurred Coralroot** *Epipogium aphyllum* [47]   Low to short saprophytic perennial to 20cm tall. Stem pink or yellowish with reddish streaks, *leafless, but with a few short brownish scale-sheaths towards the base*. Flowers few, large,

Ghost Orchid, × $\frac{3}{4}$

rarely more than 5 per stem, often solitary, drooping on slender stalks; sepals and petals whitish, yellowish or reddish, spreading, narrow-lanceolate; lip white or pinkish with purple ridges, *uppermost in the flower*, 3-lobed, wavy-edged; spur 8mm long, swollen, upward pointing. Woods, mainly beech, oak or pine, growing in decaying vegetable matter, usually in mountain areas, between 300–1900m. May–September. A, B, BG, CH, CS, D, DK, F, GB*, H, I, K, N, R, RS, S, SF, YU.

A beautiful and delicate plant which is rare and often very difficult to observe as it remains above ground for a very short period each season. The rootstock is like the true Coralroot, *Corallorhiza trifida*, being branched and coral-like; in the Coralroot the flowers are much smaller and spurless with the lip petal lowermost. In Britain the Spurred Coralroot is extremely rare and is seldom seen. The distribution of the species extends eastwards across Asia to Japan, including the Himalaya, and southwards to N. Africa.

CEPHALANTHERA

Attractive perennials with leafy stems, creeping by means of short underground rhizomes; stems with basal sheath-like leaves. Leaves generally rather narrow, alternate, with conspicuous parallel veins. Flowers few, upward pointing, in lax spikes, white or pink with a stalkless ovary, unscented; sepals and petals all similar, often rather close together – the flowers not opening much; lip similar to the petals, usually rather obscured by the sepals, the tip downcurved, with several ridges running along the upper surface; spur absent or very short.

1. White Helleborine *Cephalanthera damasonium* [47]   Short to medium plant up to 60cm tall, with angled, hairless stems; base of stems with 2–3 brownish sheaths. Leaves oval to oblong, or lanceolate, the lower shorter and broader than the upper. *Bracts longer than the flowers.* Flowers 3–16 generally, white or creamy-white, 15–20mm long, spurless; sepals and petals lanceolate, blunt-tipped; lip shorter than the sepals, yellowish inside and with an orange-yellow mark and 3–5 ridges. Ovary hairless. Woods, especially of beech, scrub and shady places, generally on calcareous soils, to 1300m. May–July. T – except IRL, IS, N, SF, P, PL.

The distribution of the White Helleborine extends into N. Africa and eastwards into Asia Minor and the Caucasus. In Britain it is found in England and Wales. It is readily identified by the long bracts and broad blunt leaves.

2. Long-leaved Helleborine *Cephalanthera longifolia* [47]   Short to medium perennial to 60cm tall, often forming groups; stems usually narrowly-ridged in the upper part, hairless, with 2–4 whitish basal sheaths. *Leaves narrow, lanceolate to linear*, long-pointed. Bracts, except lowermost, *much shorter* than the flowers. Flowers 5–16, pure white, 10–16mm long, smaller than (**1**) but more open, spurless; sepals and petals pointed; lip shorter than the sepals, with yellowish-

Long-leaved Helleborine, × 1

orange markings inside and 3–5 ridges. Ovary hairless. Woods, scrub and shady places, particularly in mountainous areas, often on calcareous soils, to 1800m. May–July. T – except AZ, BAL, CR, IS, N, SF, *n&e*RS.●

This species occurs throughout much of N. Africa and north temperate Asia eastwards as far as Japan. An attractive narrow-leaved plant which often forms clusters with several to many flower stems.

3. Cretan or **Hooded Helleborine** *Cephalanthera cucullata* is a shorter plant than (**2**), not exceeding 30cm tall, the leaves short and broad, oblong-lanceolate, *ensheathing the stem*. Flowers up to 24 in a spike, white or pinkish, 14–20mm long; lip almost as long as the sepals and *with a short spur at the base*. Forests and scrub in the mountains. March–June. CR*.

A species endemic to Crete and readily recognised by its leaves which are short and ensheath the stem.

4. Eastern Hooded Helleborine *Cephalanthera epipactoides*   A taller plant than (**2**), up to 100cm. Lower leaves ensheathing the stem, but the uppermost leaf or two oval and spreading. Spikes with 10–20 *large white flowers*, each 25–36mm long; lip with 7–9 ridges on the upper surface and a short spur at the base. Scrub and coniferous woodland over limestone. March–June, *n*AEG, GR, TR.

The distribution of this species is rather limited although it occurs also in western Turkey. Further east this form is replaced by pink or red flowered subspecies (subsp. *floribunda* and subsp. *kurdica*).

5. Red Helleborine *Cephalanthera rubra* [47]   Short to medium plant up to 60cm tall; stem lined, *stickily-hairy in the upper part* and with several brown, basal, sheaths. Leaves dark green, oblong to lanceolate, pointed, the upper ones narrower. Bracts usually shorter than the flowers. Spikes with 3–15 *bright pink* flowers, rarely white, rather open, each 17–22mm long, spurless; lip whitish, as long as the sepals, with 7–9 narrow, pale yellow ridges. Ovary stickily-hairy. Open woods, scrub and bushy places, forest clearings, usually on calcareous soils, to 1800m. May–July. T, *s*GB* – except AZ, C, IRL, IS, P.

Red Helleborine, × 1

This beautiful plant often grows in small colonies and is readily identified by its bright pink flowers which occur in rather slender, loose, spikes.

In Britain the Red Helleborine is rare, being confined to one or two localities only in the south of England. The distribution of the species however, extends eastwards into Siberia and Asia Minor, as far as the Caucasus Mountains and also into N. Africa.

LIMODORUM

Limodore or **Violet Birdsnest Orchid** *Limodorum abortioum* [48] Stout, medium to tall saprophytic perennial to 80cm tall, *no leaves*; stem violet-flushed or bluish, *with many sheathing scales*. Bracts violet-flushed, shorter than the flowers. Spikes with up to 25 large violet-coloured flowers, 30–40mm across; outer sepals and the two petals spreading, the upper sepal pointing forward and hood-like; lip 16–17mm long, triangular with a wavy edge, shorter than the sepals and pointing forwards, violet with yellowish shading; spur long, downward directed, about as long as the ovary. Woods, coppices (especially pine), scrub and grassy places, usually in hilly regions and on calcareous soils, to 1500m. May–July. A, AL, BG, BAL, CH, CO CR, CS, D, E, F, GR, H, I, K, P, PL, R, SA, SC, YU.

Limodore, × 1

L.a. var. *trabutianum* has a very *short spur* and a narrow linear lip. sE, sP – but extending into N. Africa and often growing with the more typical, long-spurred, form.

This robust orchid is readily identified by its absence of green leaves, the overall violet coloration of the plant and the rather large flowers. It is considered by some to be a parasitic plant though most botanists now consider it to be a saprophytic species thriving on decaying vegetation rather than living plants. During favourable years many plants may be seen in flower, however, on other occasions, especially after a dry spring, there may be few or else the plants may be stunted with the flowers failing to open properly. In full flower this is one of Europe's most splendid orchids to observe and photograph.

The distribution of the Limodore extends into N. Africa and eastwards into Asia Minor, the Caucasus, Palestine, Iraq and Iran.

The generic name is derived from Haemodorum, a name applied by the Greeks to a red-flowered parasitic plant.

Helleborines EPIPACTIS

Rhizomatous perennials, often forming groups; stems leafy, the leaves distinctly pleated. Flowers horizontal or nodding, stalked, in loose spike-like racemes, often one-sided; sepals and petals separate from one another, often spreading; lip concave, jointed in the middle with the end half pointing downwards; no spur. Closely allied to *Cephalanthera* but the individual flowers are clearly stalked and drooping.

1. Marsh Helleborine *Epipactis palustris* [48]   Short to medium perennial with hairy stems up to 60cm tall, rarely more. Leaves oblong to lanceolate, pointed, erect, spirally arranged, the lowermost sheath-like and purplish. Spikes with 4–20 flowers; sepals greenish with faint purple stripes, lanceolate, spreading; petals pinkish-white; lip 10–12mm long, *pinkish-white* with orange yellow ridges and red-purple lines inside, the basal half *with a triangular lobe on each side*. Damp places, particularly marshes, moorland and wet dune patches, often amongst sphagnum moss and on alkaline soils, to 1600m. June–September. T – except AZ, CR, FA, IS.*

This attractive rather elegant plant often forms large colonies and is easily recognised by its habitat and white-lipped flowers.

Marsh Helleborine, × 1   Dark Red Helleborine, × 1

2. Dark Red Helleborine *Epipactis atrorubens* (=*E. atropurpurea*) [48]   Short to tall plant up to 80cm, stems hairy or slightly hairy, red tinged. Leaves dark green, oval to oval-lanceolate, strictly alternate (in 2 rows only), the upper leaves smaller and narrower than the lower. Spikes one-sided, with up to 24 flowers; sepals *greenish tinged with deep purple*, oval; *petals blackish-purple*; lip heart-shaped, 5.5–6.5mm long, reddish-purple, the basal half greenish tinged and spotted with red. Dry pastures and woods, rocky slopes and stony places, on calcareous soils, to 2750m. June–August. T – except most of the Mediterranean region, AEG, AL, AZ, BAL, CO, CR, IS, M, SA.●

This is the darkest flowered Helleborine. The distribution of the species extends eastwards into Siberia and the Caucasus. In Britain it is rather local, a rare plant in the south of the country.

3. Broad-leaved Helleborine *Epipactis helleborine* [48]   Medium to tall plant up to 120cm, though often less; stems usually purplish in the lower part. Leaves green, *oval, elliptical or rounded, broad*, spirally arranged, *longer than the internodes*.

Spikes with up to 50 flowers, sometimes more; sepals greenish, elliptical; petals pinkish-violet with a green mid-vein; lip 9–11mm long, pink with a reddish-brown base, *much recurved*. Woods, both coniferous and mixed, and scrub, often on acid soils, occasionally on sand dunes or in more exposed places, to 1800m. July–August. T – except IS.●

The most widespread species of Helleborine, occurring east through much of Asia and the Himalayas, but also found in parts of N. Africa. It grows in a variety of different habitats, often making large colonies, and is readily identified by its broad leaves which are noticeably longer than the internodes. In N. America where it has been introduced it has become a weed in some places.

4. Violet or **Clustered Helleborine** *Epipactis purpurata* [48]   Short to tall plant up to 90cm; stems *in clusters usually*, purplish below, hairy above. *Leaves greyish or purplish*, oval or lanceolate, spirally arranged, longer than the internodes. Spikes compact, with many flowers; sepals green outside, whitish inside, lanceolate; petals whitish, sometimes with a pink tinge; lip 7–8mm long, triangular-oval, greenish or whitish tinged violet inside, purple at the base. Dry woodland, particularly beech, on deep calcareous soils, up to 1100m. June–September. Most of west and central Europe, A, B, BG, CH, CS, D, DK, F, *c&s*GB, H, PL, R, YU.

Readily identified by its grey or purplish leaves. The distribution of the species extends east into W. Siberia. In Britain it is found only in central and southern England.

| Broad-leaved Helleborine, × 1 | Violet Helleborine, 1 | Green-flowered Helleborine, × 1 |

5. Green-leaved or **Narrow-lipped Helleborine** *Epipactis leptochila*   Short to tall plant up to 70cm; stems hairy, often purplish in the lower part and with sheathing scales at the base. Leaves dull yellowish-green or dark green, oval to lanceolate, strictly alternate (in 2 rows), the margins wavy. Spikes with up to 25 *horizontal flowers*, the bracts linear; sepals and petals pale green, lanceolate, pointed; lip short, 4–9mm long, yellowish-green with a white margin and 2 basal white or pink bosses, *tip of lip flat and long-pointed*. Ovary with blackish hairs. Woods, particularly of beech or conifers, and scrub, in dense shade and usually on calcareous soils, sometimes on dune slacks, to 1000m. July–August. A, *w*CH, *w*D, DK, F, *s*GB.

6. Dune Helleborine *Epipactis dunensis* [48]   Like (**5**) but leaves always yellowish-green, oval, *blunt-ended*. Lip 6mm long, white with a greenish or pink tinge, rather blunt with a broad recurved end. Ovary *more or less hairless*. Sand

Dune Helleborine, × 1

Mueller's Helleborine, × 1

dunes, coastal pine plantations. June–July. nGB – northern England and north Wales.

The flowers of the Dune Helleborine are generally a rather dingy yellowish- or pinkish-green and often do not open widely.

7. Mueller's Helleborine *Epipactis muelleri*   Like (**6**) but the end half of the lip wider than long. Open woods and grassy clearings on calcareous soils. July–August. B, wCH, wD, seF, N. An uncommon species which can be considered the continental form of the preceding species.

8. Green-flowered or **Pendulous-flowered Helleborine** *Epipactis phyllanthes* (= *E. confusa*) [48]   Short to medium plant up to 85cm tall, though generally less; stems green, *hairless*. Leaves thin, rounded to lanceolate with wavy margins often, strictly alternate (in 2 rows). Spikes with up to 35 *nodding flowers*, often not opening properly; sepals and petals pale yellowish-green, lanceolate, the petals sometimes tinged violet or pink; lip 6–8mm long, whitish or greenish, slightly pink or reddish inside, the end half lanceolate, pointed. Ovary hairless. Open woods and scrub in light shade on calcareous soils, or on coastal dune slacks. July–August. A, D, DK, wF, c&sGB, IRL, S.

This species is generally recognised by its pale-green flowers which are often more pendulous than other species, and by the short broad leaves.

Green-flowered Helleborine, × 1

Small-flowered Helleborine, × 1

9. Small-leaved Helleborine *Epipactis microphylla* [48]   Short to medium plant up to 50cm; stems with basal sheathing-scales, hairy in the upper part. *Leaves lanceolate to linear-lanceolate, short* (not more than 3cm long), spirally arranged. Spike one-sided with up to 15, widely spaced, horizontal flowers; sepals green tinged red outside, whitish-green with a purplish edge inside, elliptical-oval; petals whitish-green; lip 6.5–7mm long, whitish or pale pink with a greenish-brown base. Dry woods, often of beech, on calcareous soils, from sea level to 1350m. June–August. A, AL, B, BAL, BG, CO, CH, CS, D, E, F, GR, H, I, K, P, R, SA, SC, YU.

Though fairly widespread in central and southern Europe, the Small-leaved Helleborine is often considered to be one of the rarest species. Its distribution extends east into Cyprus, Asia Minor, the Caucasus and N. Iran. This plant is easily recognised by its small leaves which are mostly very short and scale-like.

Hybrid orchids

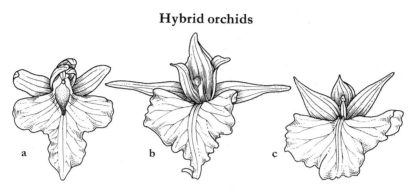

a. *Orchis morio* × *Serapias neglecta*
b. *Orchis papilionacea* × *Serapias neglecta*   All × 2
c. *Orchis laxiflora* × *Serapias neglecta*

Many species of orchid hybridise where two or more species are found growing side by side, especially in S. Europe and the Mediterranean region. Identifying hybrids can often be easy because of the unusual colouring of the flowers or their bizarre shape. Determining the parentage can be more of a problem, though one should look around the area to see which species are present.

Glossary

alternate: leaves placed alternately along the stem, not opposite or whorled.

amphibious: capable of living in water or on land at the edge of water.

appendages: an extra attachment to an organ, often of no apparent use.

appendix: the pencil-like organ in arums (Cuckoo-pint, Lords and Ladies) carrying the flowers at its base – see also spadix.

aquatic: living in water.

axil: the junction between leaf and stem.

axillary: produced from the axil (usually said of a flower).

basal: leaves arising at or below ground level, not from an aerial stem.

beak: a pointed extension to seeds, ovaries or capsules (e.g. some Iris).

berry: a fleshy fruit, often rounded and colourful, containing several seeds.

blade: the expanded part of a leaf, excluding the stalk. Same as the lamina.

bract: small leaf-like or scale-like organs that subtend the flowers, usually at the base of the flower stalk. Not always present.

bracteole: as above, but is an extra, smaller, bract often enclosed within the main bract. Not always present.

bulb: underground storage organs consisting of one to many fleshy scales attached to a basal 'plate' of solid tissue and enclosing a growing point. Bulbs in fact consist of fleshy leaf bases wrapped around one another.

bulbil: a little bulb usually produced above ground in the axils of leaves, or in the flowering head, (as in some onion relatives); bulbils eventually grow into ordinary bulbs, once established in the soil.

bulblet: a little bulb produced around the parent bulb.

capsule: a dry fruit which splits (usually into 3 in bulbous plants) to shed its seeds.

chequered: a regular mottling, usually rather geometrical as in many fritillaries and Colchicums.

cladode: modified stems, appearing leaf-like as in Asparagus and Butcher's Broom.

corm: underground storage organ consisting of solid tissue, not scaly like a bulb; the whole corm is replaced each year by a new one and represent the swollen base of a stem. Crocus, Gladiolus and Colchicum have corms.

corona: an extra organ produced between the tepals and the stamens, as in the cup or trumpet of a Narcissus or Daffodil, or alternatively as part of the stamens themselves, as in the Sea Daffodil.

elliptical: more or less oblong with pointed ends.

endemic: confined to definitive areas such as one mountain, an island, or country.

epiphyte: growing up in the air, not touching the ground as in many orchids which live on the branches of trees.

evergreen: leaves which are not shed or do not die away in winter or summer, unlike those of herbaceous plants and many bulbous plants.

falls: the three outer, drooping, tepals of an Iris flower.

family: a large unit of classification made up of genera e.g. *Crocus* (genus) belongs to Iridaceae family. All members of a particular family share a number of characters in common.

fan: applied to a cluster of basal leaves which are produced in a flattened plane like an old-fashioned fan.

fibrous: slender roots, not swollen at all, *or* referring to a bulb or corm coat which is made up of a mat of fibres.

filament: the stalk of the stamen.

flexuous: wavy, as in some flower stalks or leaves.

free: not joined to each other, referring usually to tepals.

fruit: the seed bearing organ of a plant, whatever its form, whether dry or fleshy.

genus: a natural group of plants all bearing the same first (generic) name e.g. *Narcissus, Crocus* etc. This is divided into species (the second name or epiphet) e.g. *Narcissus bulbocodium*.

head: refers to closely, often tightly grouped, flower clusters, usually terminating the stem(s).

herbaceous: usually applied to plants which are non-woody, dying down in winter to a perennial stock.

inferior: an ovary is said to be inferior when it is carried below all the rest of the flower parts, as in an *Iris*, or an orchid.

inflorescence: the whole of the flowering portion of the plant, with its flowers.

irregular: a flower which is not regular and cannot be split into 2 equal portions in all direction e.g. *Gladiolus*, the flower of which can only be split equally straight down the middle but not in any other plane.

keel: referring to the underside of a leaf or tepal which has an angular shape, like the keel of a boat.

labellum: lip, usually referring to the enlarged lower petal of an orchid flower.

lanceolate: lance-shaped, tapering at both ends but broadest just below the middle.

lax: loose, usually referring to flowers which are loosely spaced out on a stem.

linear: rather narrow with the edges more or less parallel, like grass leaves.

lip: see labellum.

monocotyledon: plants with a single seed leaf or cotyledon; see introduction 'What is a Monocotyledon'.

native: occurring naturally in an area.

naturalised: of foreign origin but reproducing and establishing as if a native.

nectary: an organ in which nectar is produced, usually at or near the base of tepals, as in the flowers of *Fritillaria* which have glistening sunken areas on the inside of each tepal, or alternatively in a nectar producing organ or spur as in many orchids.

netted: usually referring to the coat of a bulb or corm in which the fibres are arranged in a net-like manner.

node: the point on a stem where leaves and/or branches arise.

nutlet: a loose term applied to a small dry fruit, usually part of a fruit cluster.

oblanceolate: as in lance-shaped, but wider above the middle.

obovate: reversed egg-shaped, wider above the middle, applied to flat objects such as leaves.

obovoid: as obovate, but applied to 3-dimensional objects such as fruits, flowers.

offset: a small vegetatively produced bulbet at the base of a parent bulb.

opposite: usually referring to leaves when two arise at the same node, one on each side of the stem; paired.

ovary: the female portion of the flower containing the ovules; after fertilization this becomes the fruit containing the seeds.

ovoid: egg-shaped.

panicle: a loose flower cluster, usually a branched raceme.

perennial: normally living for more than two years and not dying after flowering. Nearly all members of Lily, Iris and Amaryllis families are perennials.

petal: the inner set of floral leaves of a flower usually showy and brightly coloured. In Monocotyledons the flowers are usually not clearly separated into sepals and petals but have six tepals or perianth segments.

petaloid: usually referring to the branches of the style which are expanded, flattened and often colourful as in an *Iris*, or alternatively sepals that look like petals.

pleated: leaves which have folds or pleats, along their length, e.g. *Veratrum*.

pollinia: a pollen mass, made up of all the pollen grains stuck together and typical of orchids.

pseudobulb: the thickened bulb-like storage organ found in orchids.

raceme: an elongate flower spike in which the individual flowers are stalked.

regular: a flower which can be divided into equal parts in any vertical direction.

resupinate: twisting, referring to flowers which twist through 180° or perhaps more, a common feature of the Orchid family.

rhizome: a swollen rootstock capable of producing both roots and shoots, with dormant lateral buds at the nodes; rhizomes can be above or below ground.

rosette: a cluster of leaves densely arranged in circular form, usually at ground level.

saprophyte: a plant which lives on dead organic matter, and generally devoid of any green pigment or chlorophyll.

scale: one of the fleshy 'leaves' forming a bulb, or alternatively it may refer to a reduced leaf ('scale-like').

scape: an inflorescence which carries no leaves, these all being produced basally and separately, direct from the bulb.

sepal: the outer (lower) ring of floral-leaves which form the calyx; not present in many monocotyledons.

sheath: usually applied to the base of leaves, when they are widened and enclose the stem, or alternatively a leaf which is modified into a sheath.

spadix: the thick fleshy pencil-like organ in an *Arum* flower.

spathe: the expanded colourful portion of an *Arum* (Cuckoo Pint) flower, or the leaf-like organ which encloses buds before they expand. There may be one or more of these 'spathe valves' which are often called bracts and bracteoles.

species: the basic unit of classification; species consist of a group of individuals, distinct from one another but interbreeding freely.

spike: an elongated inflorescence in which the individual flowers are stalkless; when the flowers are stalked it is called a raceme.

spur: a hollow tubular or sac-like extension to a petal, sepal or tepal, often containing nectar.

stamen: the male part of a flower, consisting of anther (producing pollen) and the filament (stalk).

standard: In *Iris* the inner three tepals, usually erect or 'standing-up'.

stigma: the tip(s) of a style which receives the pollen.

stolon: an underground or overground stem giving rise to a new individual at its apex; some corms send out stolons which form new corms at the tips.

style: the elongated organ linking the ovary to the stigma, sometimes expanded and petal-like (e.g. *Iris*); the style may be simple or branched, the branches being known as style arms, style branches or lobes.

subspecies: the unit of classification immediately below that of species. Subspecies are generally geographical variants differing from the type by two or perhaps more characters.

subtend: arising below; a bract or spathe may be said to subtend a flower or flower stalk.

superior: an ovary is said to be superior when it is carried above the rest of the parts of the flower, as in Lilies.

teeth: any tooth-like organ, often referring to the jagged margins of leaves etc; in *Muscari* (Grape Hyacinth), the very tiny tepal lobes are often called 'teeth'.

tepal: the floral-leaves of a monocot flower, equivalent to sepals and petals of a dicot; often called perianth segments, and usually six in number – they may be separate or fused together.

tepal-tube: the tube formed when tepals fuse or join together at their bases.

tepal-lobe: the free parts of the tepals, usually six; some flowers have tepals free to the base, others have them fused with only short free lobes.

tesselated: chequered; a regular mottling as in the flowers of many Fritillaries and Colchicums.

throat: the inner, upper part of a tepal tube where it opens out into tepal lobes.

tuber: a swollen underground organ of solid tissue, not scaly as in most bulbs; usually capable of producing shoots from dormant buds.

tubular: tube-like as in the fused part of the tepals of *Crocus* and *Colchicum*, but sometimes referring to hollow, cylindrical leaves or stems.

tunics: the coats covering bulbs or corms.

umbel: an inflorescence or flower-head in which the flower stalks arise as in the spokes of an umbrella; as in most *Allium* (onion) species and the cluster headed *Narcissus*.

unisexual: one sex only, either male or female.

valve: referring to the chambers of a fruit, as in 3-valved capsules; 'spathe-valves' – see under spathe.

variety: a subordinate rank to species and subspecies; varieties are generally local variants differing from the type in one or perhaps two characters.

whorl: a group of flowers or leaves arising from a central point on a stem.

Further Reading

Beck, C. (1953), *Fritillaries*. Faber.

Bowles, E. A. (1924, Rev. Ed. 1952), *Handbook of Crocus & Colchicum*. Bodley-Head.

Danesch, E. (1962), *Orchideen Europas Mitteleuropa*. Hallwag.

Danesch, E. (1969), *Orchideen Europas Südeuropa*. Hallwag.

Dykes, W. R. (1924), *Handbook of Garden Irises*. Hopkinson.

Flora Europaea, Volume 5 (1980). Cambridge University Press.

Grey, C. H. (1938), *Hardy Bulbs* (3 Vols.). Dutton.

Hall, A. D. (1940), *The Genus Tulipa*. Royal Horticultural Society.

Mathew, B. (1973), *Dwarf Bulbs*. Batsford.

Mathew, B. (1978), *The Larger Bulbs*. Batsford.

Schauenberg, P. (1965), *The Bulb Book* (Engl. Ed.). Warne.

Stern, F. C. (1956), *Snowdrops & Snowflakes*. Royal Horticultural Society.

Sundermann, H. (1975), *Europäische und Mediterrane Orchideen*. Brücke-Verlag. Kurt Schmersow.

Synge, P. M. (1961), *Collins Guide to Bulbs*. Collins.

Synge, P. M. (1980), *Lilies*. Batsford.

Woodcock, H. B. D. & Stearn, W. T. (1949), *Lilies of the World*. Country Life.

Index to Scientific Names

(Synonyms are in *italics*)

Index to English Names